Excel® Formulas & Functions

FOR DUMMIES®

A Wiley Brand

4th Edition

Excel® Formulas & Functions

FOR DUMMIES®
A Wiley Brand

4th Edition

by Ken Bluttman

Excel® Formulas & Functions For Dummies®, 4th Edition

Published by: **John Wiley & Sons, Inc.,** 111 River Street, Hoboken, NJ 07030-5774, `www.wiley.com`

Copyright © 2016 by John Wiley & Sons, Inc., Hoboken, New Jersey

Published simultaneously in Canada

For general information on our other products and services, please contact our Customer Care Department within the U.S. at 877-762-2974, outside the U.S. at 317-572-3993, or fax 317-572-4002. For technical support, please visit `www.wiley.com/techsupport`.

Wiley publishes in a variety of print and electronic formats and by print-on-demand. Some material included with standard print versions of this book may not be included in e-books or in print-on-demand. If this book refers to media such as a CD or DVD that is not included in the version you purchased, you may download this material at `http://booksupport.wiley.com`. For more information about Wiley products, visit `www.wiley.com`.

Library of Congress Control Number: 2015955844

ISBN: 978-1-119-07678-0 (pbk); 978-1-119-07680-3 (ebk); 978-1-119-07679-7 (ebk)

Manufactured in the United States of America

10 9 8 7 6 5 4 3 2 1

Contents at a Glance

Table of Contents

Introduction

· ·

*E*xcel worksheets are used in many walks of life: business, education, home finances, and even hobbies (keeping track of your baseball-card collection). In my house, we use Excel for a lot, from our taxes (boring!) to our ever-growing recipe collection (yummy!). Often, I use Excel in place of a calculator. After all, Excel is like a calculator on steroids!

In the workplace, Excel is one of the most commonly used analysis and reporting tools. Financial statements, sales reports, inventory, project scheduling, customer activity — so much of this stuff is kept in Excel. The program's capability to manipulate and give feedback about the data makes it attractive. Excel's flexibility in storing and presenting data is like magic.

About This Book

This book is about the number-crunching side of Excel. Formulas are the keystone to analyzing data — that is, digging out nuggets of important information. What is the average sale? How many times did we do better than average? How many days are left on the project? How much progress have we made? That sort of thing.

Formulas calculate answers, straight and to the point. But that's not all. Excel has dozens of built-in functions that calculate everything from a simple average to a useful analysis of your investments to complex inferential statistics. But you don't have to know it all or use it all; just use the parts that are relevant to your work.

This book discusses more than 150 of these functions. But rather than just show their syntax and list them alphabetically, I assemble them by category and provide real examples of how to use them alone, and in formulas, along with step-by-step instructions and illustrations of the results.

Foolish Assumptions

I assume that you have a PC with Excel 2016 loaded. That's a no-brainer! Nearly all the material is relevant for use with earlier versions of Excel as well. I also assume that you know how to navigate with a keyboard and mouse. Last, I assume that you have used Excel before, even just once. I do discuss basics in Chapter 1, but not all of them. If you really need to start from scratch, I suggest that you read the excellent *Excel 2016 For Dummies,* by Greg Harvey (John Wiley & Sons, Inc.).

Other than that, this book is written for Excel 2016, but just between you and me, it works fine with older versions of Excel. There could be a function or two that isn't in an older version or works slightly differently. But Microsoft has done an excellent job of maintaining compatibility between versions of Excel, so when it comes to formulas and functions, you can be confident that what works in one version works in another.

How to Use This Book

You do not have to read the book sequentially from start to finish, although you certainly can. Each chapter deals with a specific category of functions — financial in one chapter, statistical in another, and so on. Some categories are split over two or more chapters. I suggest two ways for you to use this book:

- Use the table of contents to find the chapters that are of interest to you.
- Use the index to look up specific functions you are interested in.

Icons Used in This Book

A Tip gives you a little extra piece of info on the subject at hand. It may offer an alternative method. It may lead you to a conclusion. It may, well, give you a tip (just no stock tips — sorry).

The Remember icon holds some basic concept that is good to keep tucked somewhere in your brain.

As it implies, a Warning is serious stuff. This icon tells you to be careful —
usually because you can accidentally erase your data or some such
horrible event.

Once in a while, some tidbit is interesting to the tech-head types, but not to
anyone else. You can read these items or ignore them as you see fit.

Beyond the Book

This section describes where readers can find book content that exists outside the book itself. A *For Dummies* technical book may include the following, although only rarely does a book include all these items:

- **Cheat Sheet:** In a rush? The Excel Formulas and Functions Cheat Sheet
  at www.dummies.com/cheatsheet/excelformulasfunctions
  is the super-duper fast way to the basics. On the Cheat Sheet you will
  find the top functions, the ever-important order of operations, and
  what those non-friendly Excel errors mean!

- **Dummies.com online articles:** Did you think I would leave you
  hanging without some extra material? Fear not! I have provided a
  few online articles to give your formulas and functions knowledge
  an extra lift! Find the articles at www.dummies.com/extras/
  excelformulasfunctions.

- **Updates:** I pour my heart and soul into my books — and so do the
  slew of editors working with me — yet still things can go awry. If there
  are updates or important changes, find them at www.dummies.com/
  extras/excelformulasfunctions.

Where to Go from Here

Roll up your sleeves, take a deep breath, and then forget all that preparing-
for-a-hard-task stuff. Using Excel is easy. You can hardly make a mistake
without Excel's catching it. If you need to brush up on the basics, go to
Chapter 1. This chapter is also the best place to get your first taste of
formulas and functions. After that, it's up to you. The book is organized
more by area of focus than anything else. If finance is what you do, go to
Part II. If working with dates is what you do, go to Part IV. Seek, and you
will find.

Part I

Getting Started with Formulas and Functions

getting started

with

Formulas and Functions

Read more about Excel at www.dummies.com/extras/excelformulasfunctions.

In this part . . .

- ✔ Get to know formula and function fundamentals.
- ✔ Discover the different ways to enter functions.
- ✔ Understand array-based formulas and functions.
- ✔ Find out about formula errors and how to fix them.

Chapter 1

Tapping Into Formula and Function Fundamentals

In This Chapter

▶ Getting the skinny on the Excel basics

▶ Writing formulas

▶ Working with functions in formulas

Excel is to computer programs what a Ferrari is to cars: sleek on the outside and a lot of power under the hood. Excel is also like a truck. It can handle all your data — lots of it. In fact, in Excel 2016, a single worksheet has 17,179,869,184 places to hold data. Yes, that's what I said — more than 17 *billion* data placeholders. And that's on just *one* worksheet!

Opening files created in earlier versions of Excel may show just the number of worksheet rows and columns available in the version the workbook was created with.

Excel is used in all types of businesses. And you know how that's possible? By being able to store and work with any kind of data. It doesn't matter whether you're in finance or sales, whether you run an online video store or organize wilderness trips, or whether you're charting party RSVPs or tracking the scores of your favorite sports teams — Excel can handle all of it. Its number-crunching ability is just awesome! And so easy to use!

Just putting a bunch of information on worksheets doesn't crunch the data or give you sums, results, or analyses. If you want to just store your data somewhere, you can use Excel or get a database program instead. In this book, I show you how to build formulas and how to use the dozens of built-in functions that Excel provides. That's where the real power of Excel is — making sense of your data.

Don't fret that this is a challenge and that you may make mistakes. I did when I was ramping up. Besides, Excel is very forgiving. It won't crash on you. Excel usually tells you when you made a mistake, and sometimes it even helps you correct it. How many programs do that? But first, the basics. This first chapter gives you the springboard you need to use the rest of the book. I wish books like this were around when I was introduced to computers. I had to stumble through a lot of this.

Working with Excel Fundamentals

Before you can write any formulas or crunch any numbers, you have to know where the data goes and how to find it again. I wouldn't want your data to get lost! Knowing how worksheets store your data and present it is critical to your analysis efforts.

Understanding workbooks and worksheets

A *workbook* is the same as a file. Excel opens and closes workbooks, just as a word processor program opens and closes documents. When you start up Excel you are presented with a selection of templates to use, the first one being the standard blank workbook. Also there is a selection of recent files to select from. After you open a new or already created workbook, click the File tab to view basic functions such as opening, saving, printing, and closing your Excel files (not to mention a number of other nifty functions to boot!). Figure 1-1 shows the contents presented on the Info tab.

Figure 1-1: Seeing how to use basic Excel program functions.

Excel 2016 (also Excel 2013, Excel 2010, and Excel 2007) files have the .xlsx extension. Older version Excel files have the .xls extension.

Start Excel and select to open a blank workbook. Double-click the Blank Workbook icon and you're ready to go. When you have more than one workbook open, you pick the one you want to work on by selecting it on the Windows Taskbar.

A worksheet is where your data actually goes. A workbook contains at least one worksheet. If you didn't have at least one, where would you put the data? Figure 1-2 shows an open workbook that has two sheets, aptly named Sheet1 and Sheet2. To the right of these worksheet tabs is the New Sheet button (looks like a plus sign), used to add worksheets to the workbook.

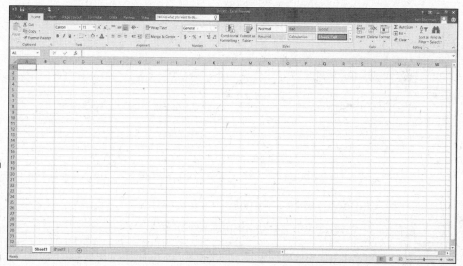

Figure 1-2:
Looking at a workbook and worksheets.

At any given moment, one worksheet is always on top. In Figure 1-2, Sheet1 is on top. Another way of saying this is that Sheet1 is the *active* worksheet. There is always one and only one active worksheet. To make another worksheet active, just click its tab.

Worksheet, spreadsheet, and just plain old *sheet* are used interchangeably to mean the worksheet.

Guess what's really cool? You can change the name of the worksheets. Names like Sheet1 and Sheet2 are just not exciting. How about Baseball Card Collection or Last Year's Taxes? Well, actually Last Year's Taxes isn't too exciting either.

The point is, you can give your worksheets meaningful names. You have two ways to do this:

- Double-click the worksheet tab and then type a new name.
- Right-click the worksheet tab, select Rename from the menu, and then type a new name.

Figure 1-3 shows one worksheet name already changed and another about to be changed by right-clicking its tab.

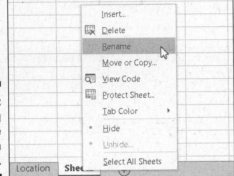

Figure 1-3: Changing the name of a worksheet.

You can try changing a worksheet name on your own. Do it the easy way:

1. **Double-click a worksheet's tab.**

2. **Type a new name and press Enter.**

You can change the color of worksheet tabs. Right-click the tab and select Tab Color from the menu.

To insert a new worksheet into a workbook, click the New Sheet button, which is located after the last worksheet tab. Figure 1-4 shows how. To delete a worksheet, just right-click the worksheet's tab and select Delete from the menu.

Don't delete a worksheet unless you really mean to. You cannot get it back after it is gone. It does not go into the Windows Recycle Bin.

Figure 1-4: Inserting a new worksheet.

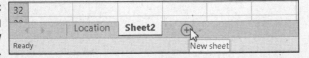

You can insert many new worksheets. The limit of how many is based on your computer's memory, but you should have no problem inserting 200 or more. Of course, I hope you have a good reason for having so many, which brings me to the next point.

Worksheets organize your data. Use them wisely, and you will find it easy to manage your data. For example, say that you are the boss (I thought you'd like that!), and over the course of a year you track information about 30 employees. You may have 30 worksheets — one for each employee. Or you may have 12 worksheets — one for each month. Or you may just keep it all on one worksheet. How you use Excel is up to you, but Excel is ready to handle whatever you throw at it.

You can set how many worksheets a new workbook has as the default. To do this, click the File tab, click Options, and then click the General tab. Under the section "When creating new workbooks," use the spinner control to select a number.

Introducing the Formulas Ribbon

Without further ado, I present the Formulas Ribbon. The Ribbon sits at the top of Excel. Items on the Ribbon appear as menu headers along the top of the Excel screen, but they actually work more like tabs. Click them, and no menus appear. Instead, the Ribbon presents the items that are related to the clicked Ribbon tab.

Figure 1-5 shows the top part of the screen, in which the Ribbon displays the items that appear when you click the Formulas header. In the figure, the Ribbon is set to show formula-based methods. At the left end of the Formula Ribbon, functions are categorized. One of the categories is opened to show how you can access a particular function.

Quick Access Toolbar

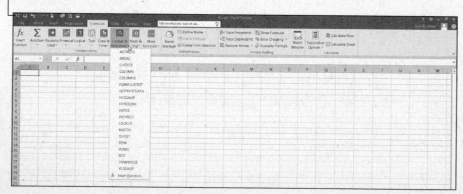

Figure 1-5:
Getting to
know the
Ribbon.

These categories are along the bottom of the Formulas Ribbon:

- **Function Library:** This includes the Function Wizard, the AutoSum feature, and the categorized functions.
- **Defined Names:** These features manage named areas.
- **Formula Auditing:** These features have been through many Excel incarnations, but never before have the features been so prominent. Also here is the Watch Window, which lets you keep an eye on the values in designated cells, but within one window. In Figure 1-6 you can see that a few cells have been assigned to the Watch Window. If any values change, you can see this in the Watch Window. Note how the watched cells are on sheets that are not the current active sheet. Neat! By the way, you can move the Watch Window around the screen by clicking the title area of the window and dragging it with the mouse.
- **Calculation:** This is where you manage calculation settings, such as whether calculation is automatic or manual.

Book	Sheet	Name	Cell	Value	Formula
Book2	Location		C3		
Book2	Inventory		B5	87	=SUM(B3:B4)
Book2	Inventory		C5	105	=SUM(C3:C4)

Figure 1-6: Eyeing the Watch Window.

Another great feature that goes hand in hand with the Ribbon is the Quick Access Toolbar. (So there is a toolbar after all!) In Figure 1-5 the Quick Access Toolbar sits just above the left side of the Ribbon. On it are icons that perform actions with a single click. The icons are ones you select by using the Quick Access Toolbar tab in the Excel Options dialog box. You can put the toolbar above or below the Ribbon by clicking the small drop-down arrow on the Quick Access Toolbar and choosing an option. In this area too are the other options for the Quick Access Toolbar.

Working with rows, column, cells, ranges, and tables

A *worksheet* contains cells. Lots of them. Billions of them. This might seem unmanageable, but actually it's pretty straightforward. Figure 1-7 shows a worksheet filled with data. Use this to look at a worksheet's components. Each *cell* can contain data or a formula. In Figure 1-7, the cells contain data. Some, or even all, cells could contain formulas, but that's not the case here.

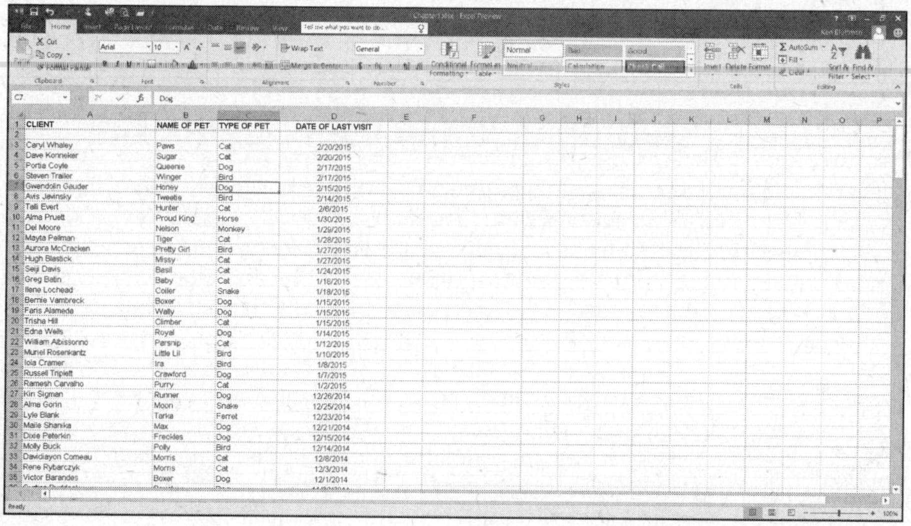

Figure 1-7:
Looking at
what goes
into a
worksheet.

Columns have letter headers — A, B, C, and so on. You can see these listed horizontally just above the area where the cells are. After you get past the 26th column, a double lettering system is used — AA, AB, and so on. After all the two-letter combinations are used up, a triple-letter scheme is used. Rows are listed vertically down the left side of the screen and use a numbering system.

You find cells at the intersection of rows and columns. Cell A1 is the cell at the intersection of column A and row 1. A1 is the cell's *address*. There is always an *active* cell — that is, a cell in which any entry would go into should you start typing. The active cell has a border around it. Also, the contents of the active cell appear in the *Formula Box*.

When I speak of, or reference, *cell,* I am referring to its address. The address is the intersection of a column and row. To talk about cell D20 means to talk about the cell that you find at the intersection of column D and row 20.

In Figure 1-7, the active cell is C7. You have a couple of ways to see this. For starters, cell C7 has a border around it. Also notice that the column head C is shaded, as well as row number 7. Just above the column headers are the Name Box and the Formula Box. The Name Box is all the way to the left and shows the active cell's address of C7. To the right of the Name Box, the Formula Box shows the contents of cell C7.

If the Formula Bar is not visible, choose File ⇨ Options, and click the Advanced tab. Then, in the Display section in the Excel Options dialog box, choose to make it visible.

Getting to know the Formula Bar

Taken together, the Formula Box and the Name Box make up the Formula Bar. You use the Formula Bar quite a bit as you work with formulas and functions. The Formula Box is used to enter and edit formulas. The Formula Box is the long entry box that starts in the middle of the bar. When you enter a formula into this box, you can click the little checkmark button to finish the entry. The check-mark button is visible only when you are entering a formula. Pressing the Enter key also completes your entry; clicking the X cancels the entry.

An alternative is to enter a formula directly into a cell. The Formula Box displays the formula as it is being entered into the cell. When you want to see just the contents of a cell that has a formula, make that cell active and look at its contents in the Formula Box. Cells that have formulas do not normally display the formula, but instead display the result of the formula. When you want to see the actual formula, the Formula Box is the place to do it. The Name Box, on the left side of the Formula Bar, is used to select named areas in the workbook.

A *range* is usually a group of adjacent cells, although noncontiguous cells can be included in the same range (but that's mostly for rocket scientists and those obsessed with calculus). For your purposes, assume a range is a group of continuous cells. Make a range right now! Here's how:

1. **Position the mouse pointer over the first cell where you want to define a range.**

2. **Press and hold the left mouse button.**

3. **Move the pointer to the last cell of your desired area.**

4. **Release the mouse button.**

Figure 1-8 shows what happened when I did this. I selected a *range* of cells. The address of this range is A3:D21.

REMEMBER

A range address looks like two cell addresses put together, with a colon (:) in the middle. And that's what it is! A range address starts with the address of the cell in the upper left of the range, then has a colon, and ends with the address of the cell in the lower right.

One more detail about ranges: You can give them a name. This is a great feature because you can think about a range in terms of what it is used for, instead of what its address is. Also, if I did not take the extra step to assign a name, the range would be gone as soon as I clicked anywhere on the worksheet. When a range is given a name, you can repeatedly use the range by using its name.

	A	B	C	D	E	F
1	CLIENT	NAME OF PET	TYPE OF PET	DATE OF LAST VISIT		
2						
3	Caryl Whaley		Cat	2/20/2015		
4	Dave Konneker	Sugar	Cat	2/20/2015		
5	Portia Coyle	Queenie	Dog	2/17/2015		
6	Steven Trailer	Winger	Bird	2/17/2015		
7	Gwendolin Gauder	Honey	Dog	2/15/2015		
8	Avis Javinsky	Tweetie	Bird	2/14/2015		
9	Talli Evert	Hunter	Cat	2/6/2015		
10	Alma Pruett	Proud King	Horse	1/30/2015		
11	Del Moore	Nelson	Monkey	1/29/2015		
12	Mayta Pelman	Tiger	Cat	1/28/2015		
13	Aurora McCracken	Pretty Girl	Bird	1/27/2015		
14	Hugh Blastick	Missy	Cat	1/27/2015		
15	Seiji Davis	Basil	Cat	1/24/2015		
16	Greg Batin	Baby	Cat	1/18/2015		
17	Ilene Lochead	Coller	Snake	1/18/2015		
18	Bernie Vambreck	Boxer	Dog	1/15/2015		
19	Faris Alameda	Wally	Dog	1/15/2015		
20	Trisha Hill	Climber	Cat	1/15/2015		
21	Edna Wells	Royal	Dog	1/14/2015		
22	William Albissonno	Parsnip	Cat	1/12/2015		
23	Muriel Rosenkantz	Little Lil	Bird	1/10/2015		
24	Iola Cramer	Ira	Bird	1/8/2015		
25	Russell Triplett	Crawford	Dog	1/7/2015		
26	Ramesh Carvalho	Purry	Cat	1/2/2015		
27	Kin Sigman	Runner	Dog	12/26/2014		

Figure 1-8:
Selecting a
range of
cells.

Say you have a list of clients on a worksheet. What's easier — thinking of exactly which cells are occupied, or thinking that there is your list of clients?

Throughout this book, I use areas made of cell addresses and ranges, which have been given names. It's time to get your feet wet creating a *named area*. Here's what you do:

1. **Position the mouse pointer over a cell, click and hold the left mouse button, and drag the pointer around.**

2. **Release the mouse button when you're done.**

   You've selected an area of the worksheet.

3. **Click Define Name in the Defined Names category on the Formulas Ribbon.**

   The New Name dialog box appears. Figure 1-9 shows you how it looks so far.

4. **Name the area, if need be.**

   Excel guesses that you want to name the area with the value it finds in the top cell of the range. That may or may not be what you want. Change the name if you need to. In Figure 1-9, I changed the name to Clients.

   An alternative method of naming an area is to select it, type the name in the Name Box (left of the Formula Bar), and press the Enter key.

5. **Click the OK button.**

That's it. Hey, you're already on your way to being an Excel pro! Now that you have a named area, you can easily select your data at any time. Just go to the Name Box and select it from the list. Figure 1-10 shows how to select the Clients area.

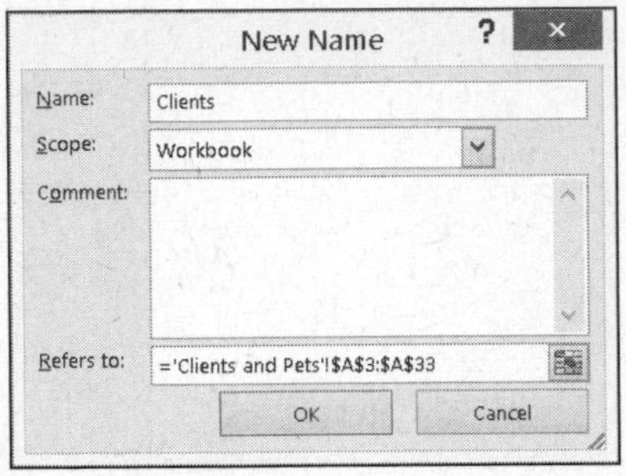

Figure 1-9:
Adding a name to the workbook.

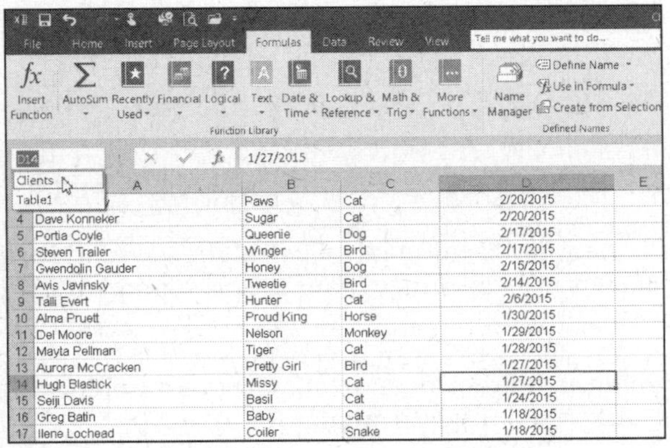

New Name	? ✕
Name:	Clients
Scope:	Workbook
Comment:	
Refers to:	='Clients and Pets'!$A$3:$A$33

OK   Cancel

Figure 1-10:
Using the Name Box to find the named area.

	A	B	C	D	E
		Paws	Cat	2/20/2015	
4	Dave Konneker	Sugar	Cat	2/20/2015	
5	Portia Coyle	Queenie	Dog	2/17/2015	
6	Steven Trailer	Winger	Bird	2/17/2015	
7	Gwendolin Gauder	Honey	Dog	2/15/2015	
8	Avis Javinsky	Tweetie	Bird	2/14/2015	
9	Talli Evert	Hunter	Cat	2/6/2015	
10	Alma Pruett	Proud King	Horse	1/30/2015	
11	Del Moore	Nelson	Monkey	1/29/2015	
12	Mayla Pellman	Tiger	Cat	1/28/2015	
13	Aurora McCracken	Pretty Girl	Bird	1/27/2015	
14	Hugh Blastick	Missy	Cat	1/27/2015	
15	Seiji Davis	Basil	Cat	1/24/2015	
16	Greg Batin	Baby	Cat	1/18/2015	
17	Ilene Lochead	Coiler	Snake	1/18/2015	

Tables work in much the same manner as named areas. Tables have a few features that are unavailable to simple named areas. With tables you can indicate that the top row contains header labels. Further, tables default to have filtering ability. Figure 1-11 shows a table on a worksheet, with headings and filtering ability.

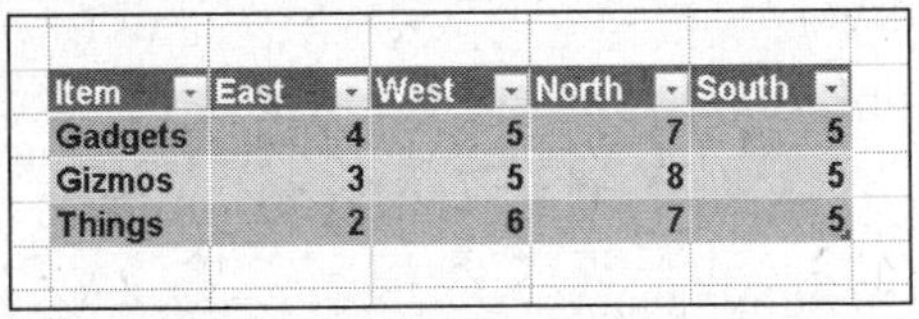

Figure 1-11:
Trying a table.

Item	East	West	North	South
Gadgets	4	5	7	5
Gizmos	3	5	8	5
Things	2	6	7	5

With filtering, you can limit which rows show, based on which values you select to display.

The Insert Ribbon contains the button to use for inserting a table.

Formatting your data

Of course you want to make your data look all spiffy and shiny. Bosses like that. Is the number 98.6 someone's temperature? Is it a score on a test? Is it 98 dollars and 60 cents? Is it a percentage? Any of these formats is correct:

- 98.6
- $98.60
- 98.6%

Excel lets you format your data in just the way you need. Formatting options are on the Home Ribbon, in the Number category.

Figure 1-12 shows how formatting helps in the readability and understanding of a worksheet. Cell B1 has a monetary amount and is formatted with the Accounting style. Cell B2 is formatted as a percentage. The actual value in cell B2 is .05. Cell B7 is formatted as currency. The currency format displays a negative value in parentheses. This is just one of the formatting options for currency. Chapter 5 explains further about formatting currency.

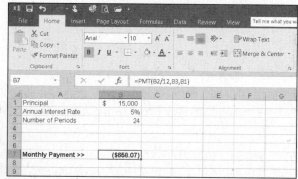

Figure 1-12:
Formatting
data.

Besides selecting formatting on the Home Ribbon, you can use the familiar (in previous versions) Format Cells dialog box. This is the place to go for all your formatting needs beyond what's available on the toolbar. You can even create custom formats. You can display the Format Cells dialog box two ways:

- On the Home Ribbon, click the drop-down list in the Number category and then click More Number Formats.
- Right-click any cell and select Format Cells from the pop-up menu.

Figure 1-13 shows the Format Cells dialog box. So many settings are there, it can make your head spin! I discuss this dialog box and formatting more extensively in Chapter 5.

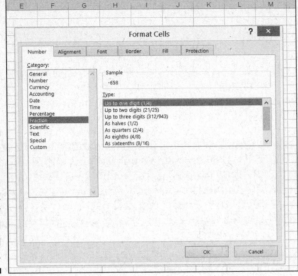

Figure 1-13:
Using the Format Cells dialog box for advanced formatting options.

Getting help

Excel is complex; you can't deny that. And lucky for all of us, help is just a key press away. Yes, literally one key press — just press the F1 key. Try it now.

This starts the Help system. From there you can search on a keyword or browse through the Help table of contents. Later on, when you are working with Excel functions, you can get help on specific functions directly by clicking the Help on This Function link in the Insert Function dialog box. Chapter 2 covers the Insert Function dialog box in detail.

Gaining the Upper Hand on Formulas

Okay, time to get to the nitty-gritty of what Excel is all about. Sure, you can just enter data and leave it as is, and even generate some pretty charts from it. But getting answers from your data, or creating a summary of your data, or applying what-if tests — all of this takes formulas.

To be specific, a formula in Excel calculates something or returns some result based on data in the worksheet. A formula is placed in cells and must start with an equal sign (=) to tell Excel that it is a formula and not data. Sounds simple, and it is.

All formulas start with an equal (=) sign.

Look at some very basic formulas. Table 1-1 shows a few formulas and tells you what they do.

I use the word *return* to refer to what displays after a formula or function does its thing. So saying "The formula returns a 7" is the same as saying "The formula calculated the answer to be 7."

Table 1-1	Basic Formulas
Formula	*What It Does*
=2 + 2	Returns the number 4.
=A1 + A2	Returns the sum of the values in cells A1 and A2, whatever those values may be. If either A1 or A2 has text in it, an error is returned.
=D5	The cell that contains this formula ends up displaying the value that is in cell D5. If you try to enter this formula into cell D5 itself, you create a circular reference. That is a no-no. See Chapter 4.
=SUM(A2:A5)	Returns the sum of the values in cells A2, A3, A4, and A5. This formula uses the SUM function to sum up all the values in the range.

Entering your first formula

Ready to enter your first formula? Make sure Excel is running and a worksheet is in front of you, and then follow these steps:

1. **Click an empty cell.**
2. **Type** = 10 + 10.
3. **Press Enter.**

That was easy, wasn't it? You should see the *result* of the formula — the number 20.

Try another. This time you create a formula that adds the value of two cells:

1. **Click any cell.**

2. **Type any number.**

3. **Click another cell.**

4. **Type another number.**

5. **Click a third cell.**

   This cell will contain the formula.

6. **Type =.**

7. **Click the first cell.**

   This is an important point in the creation of the formula. The formula is being written by both your keyboard entry and your clicks of the mouse. The formula should look about half complete, with an equal sign immediately followed by the address of the cell you just clicked. Figure 1-14 shows what this looks like. In the example, the value 15 has been entered into cell B3 and the value 35 into cell B6. The formula was started in cell E3. Cell E3 so far has =B3 in it.

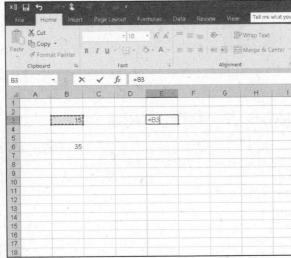

Figure 1-14:
Entering a
formula that
references
cells.

8. **Type +.**

9. **Click the cell that has the second entered value.**

   In this example, this is cell B6. The formula in cell E3 now looks like this: =B3 + B6. You can see this in Figure 1-15.

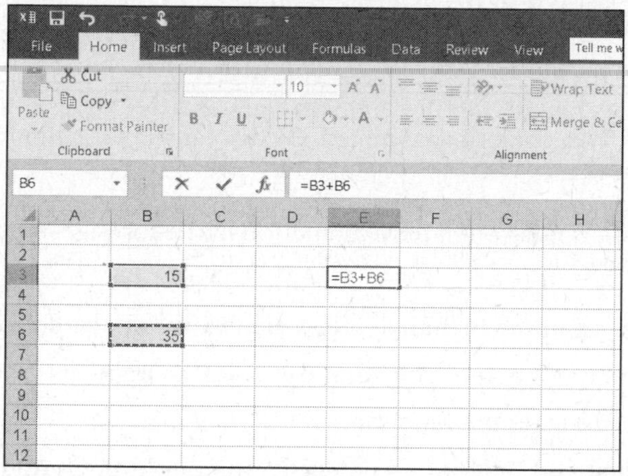

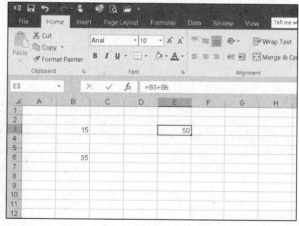

Figure 1-15:
Completing
the formula.

10. **Press Enter.**

This ends the entry of the function. All done! Congratulations!

Figure 1-16 shows how the example ended up. Cell E3 displays the result of the calculation. Also notice that the Formula Bar displays the content of cell E3, which really is the formula.

Figure 1-16:
A finished
formula.

Understanding references

References abound in Excel formulas. You can reference cells. You can reference ranges. You can reference cells and ranges on other worksheets. You can reference cells and ranges in other workbooks. Formulas and functions are at their most useful when you're using references, so you need to understand them.

And if that isn't enough to stir the pot, you can use three types of cell references: relative, absolute, and mixed. Okay, one step at a time here. Try a formula that uses a range.

Formulas that use ranges often have a function in the formula, so use the SUM function here:

1. **Enter some numbers in many cells going down one column.**

2. **Click another cell where you want the result to appear.**

3. **Type =SUM(to start the function.**

4. **Click the first cell that has an entered value, hold the left mouse button down, and drag the mouse pointer over all the cells that have values.**

5. **Release the mouse button.**

    The range address appears where the formula and function are being entered.

6. **Type).**

7. **Press Enter.**

8. **Give yourself a pat on the back.**

Wherever you drag the mouse to enter the range address into a function, you can also just type the address of the range, if you know what it is.

Excel is *dynamic* when it comes to cell addresses. If you have a cell with a formula that references a different cell's address, and you copy the formula from the first cell to another cell, the address of the reference inside the formula changes. Excel updates the reference inside the formula to match the number of rows and/or columns that separate the original cell (where the formula is being copied from) from the new cell (where the formula is being copied to). This may be confusing, so try an example so you can see this for yourself:

1. **In cell B2, type** 100.

2. **In cell C2, type** =B2 * 2.

3. **Press Enter.**

    Cell C2 now returns the value 200.

4. **If C2 is not the active cell, click it once.**

5. **Press Ctrl + C, or click the Copy button in the Clipboard category on the Home Ribbon.**

6. **Click cell C3.**

7. **Press Ctrl + V, or click the Paste button in the Clipboard category on the Home Ribbon.**

8. **If you see a strange moving line around cell C2, press the Esc key.**

   Cell C3 should be the active cell, but if it is not, just click it once. Look at the Formula Bar. The contents of cell C3 are =B3 * 2, and not the =B2 * 2 that you copied.

Did you see a moving line around a cell? That line's called a *marquee*. It's a reminder that you are in the middle of a cut or copy operation, and the marquee goes around the cut or copied data.

What happened? Excel, in its wisdom, assumed that if a formula in cell C2 references the cell B2 — one cell to the left — the same formula put into cell C3 is supposed to reference cell B3 — also one cell to the left.

When you're copying formulas in Excel, relative addressing is usually what you want. That's why it is the default behavior. Sometimes you do not want relative addressing, but *absolute* addressing. This is making a cell reference fixed to an absolute cell address so that it does not change when the formula is copied.

In an absolute cell reference, a dollar sign ($) precedes both the column letter and the row number. You can also have a mixed reference in which the column is absolute and the row is relative, or vice versa. To create a mixed reference, you use the dollar sign in front of just the column letter or row number. Here are some examples:

Reference Type	Formula	What Happens After Copying the Formula
Relative	=A1	Either, or both, the column letter A and the row number 1 can change.
Absolute	=$A$1	The column letter A and the row number 1 do not change.
Mixed	=$A1	The column letter A does not change. The row number 1 can change.
Mixed	=A$1	The column letter A can change. The row number 1 does not change.

Copying formulas with the fill handle

As long as I'm on the subject of copying formulas around, take a look at the fill handle. You're gonna love this one! The fill handle is a quick way to copy the contents of a cell to other cells with just a single click and drag.

The active cell always has a little square box in the lower-right side of its border. That is the fill handle. When you move the mouse pointer over the fill handle, the mouse pointer changes shape. If you click and hold the mouse button, you can drag up, down, or across over other cells. When you let go of the mouse button, the contents of the active cell automatically copy to the cells you dragged over.

A picture is worth a thousand words, so take a look at Figure 1-17, which shows a worksheet that adds some numbers. Cell E4 has this formula: =B4 + C4 + D4. This formula needs to be placed in cells E5 through E15. Look closely at cell E4. The mouse pointer is over the fill handle, and it has changed to what looks like a small, black plus sign. I am about to use the fill handle to drag that formula to the other cells. Clicking and holding the left mouse button down and then dragging down to E15 does the trick.

Figure 1-17: Getting ready to drag the formula down.

E4		f_x	=B4 + C4 + D4		
	A	B	C	D	E	F
1	Number of Orders					
2						
3		Retail	Mail Order	Internet	TOTAL BY MONTH	
4	January	1015	107	906	2028	
5	February	882	115	793		
6	March	960	150	907		
7	April	1020	141	1004		
8	May	1145	175	1015		
9	June	1287	199	1259		
10	July	1235	166	1181		
11	August	1044	135	1032		
12	September	994	122	851		
13	October	921	80	741		
14	November	742	55	652		
15	December	616	28	614		
16						
17						
18						

Figure 1-18 shows what the worksheet looks like after the fill handle is used to get the formula into all the cells. This is a real time saver. Also, you can see that the formula in each cell of column E correctly references the cells to its left. This is the intention of using relative referencing. For example, the formula in cell E15 ended up with this formula: =B15 + C15 + D15.

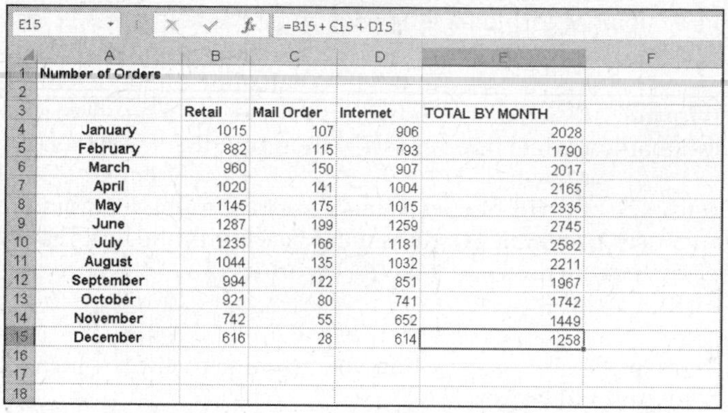

E15	▼	:	×	✓	fx	=B15 + C15 + D15

	A	B	C	D	E	F
1	Number of Orders					
2						
3		Retail	Mail Order	Internet	TOTAL BY MONTH	
4	January	1015	107	906	2028	
5	February	882	115	793	1790	
6	March	960	150	907	2017	
7	April	1020	141	1004	2165	
8	May	1145	175	1015	2335	
9	June	1287	199	1259	2745	
10	July	1235	166	1181	2582	
11	August	1044	135	1032	2211	
12	September	994	122	851	1967	
13	October	921	80	741	1742	
14	November	742	55	652	1449	
15	December	616	28	614	1258	
16						
17						
18						

Figure 1-18:
Populating
cells with a
formula by
using the fill
handle.

Assembling formulas the right way

There's a saying in the computer business: Garbage in, garbage out. And that applies to how formulas are put together. If a formula is constructed the wrong way, it returns an incorrect result or an error.

Two types of errors can occur in formulas. In one type, Excel can calculate the formula, but the result is wrong. In the other type, Excel is not able to calculate the formula. Check out both of these.

A formula can work and still produce an incorrect result. Excel does not report an error because there is no error for it to find. Often, this is the result of not using parentheses properly in the formula. Take a look at some examples:

Formula	Result
=7 + 5 * 20 + 25 / 5	112
=(7 + 5) * 20 + 25 / 5	245
=7 + 5 *(20 + 25) / 5	52
=(7 + 5 * 20 + 25) / 5	26.4

All of these are valid formulas, but the placement of parentheses makes a difference in the outcome. You must take into account the order of mathematical operators when writing formulas. Here's the order of precedence:

1. Parentheses
2. Exponents
3. Multiplication and division
4. Addition and subtraction

This is a key point of formulas. It is easy to just accept a returned answer. After all, Excel is so smart. Right? Wrong! Like all computer programs, Excel can do only what it is told. If you tell it to calculate an incorrect but structurally valid formula, it will do so. So watch your p's and q's — er, your parentheses and mathematical operators — when building formulas.

The second type of error occurs when a mistake in the formula or in the data the formula uses prevents Excel from calculating the result. Excel makes your life easier by telling you when such an error occurs. To be precise, it does one of the following:

✔ Excel displays a message when you attempt to enter a formula that is not constructed correctly.

✔ Excel returns an error message in the cell when there is something wrong with the result of the calculation.

First, look at what happened when I tried to finish entering a formula that had the wrong number of parentheses. Figure 1-19 shows this.

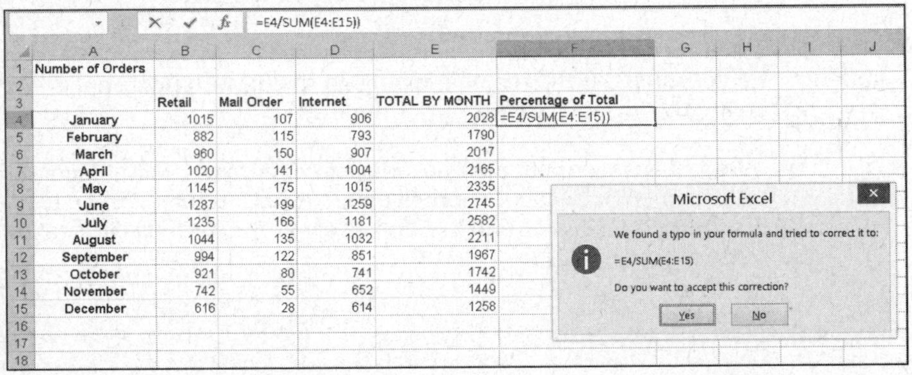

Figure 1-19:
Getting a
message
from Excel.

Excel finds an uneven number of open and closed parentheses. Therefore, the formula cannot work (it does not make sense mathematically), and Excel tells you so. Watch for these messages; they often offer solutions.

On the other side of the fence are errors in returned values. If you got this far, the formula's syntax passed muster, but something went awry nonetheless. Possible errors include

✔ Attempting to perform a mathematical operation on text

✔ Attempting to divide a number by 0 (a mathematical no-no)

✔ Trying to reference a nonexistent cell, range, worksheet, or workbook

✔ Entering the wrong type of information into an argument function

This is by no means an exhaustive list of possible error conditions, but you get the idea. So what does Excel do about it? There are a handful of errors that Excel places into the cell with the problem formula.

Error Type	When It Happens
#DIV/0!	When you're trying to divide by 0.
#N/A!	When a formula or a function inside a formula cannot find the referenced data.
#NAME?	When text in a formula is not recognized.
#NULL!	When a space was used instead of a comma in formulas that reference multiple ranges. A comma is necessary to separate range references.
#NUM!	When a formula has numeric data that is invalid for the operation type.
#REF!	When a reference is invalid.
#VALUE!	When the wrong type of operand or function argument is used.

Chapter 4 discusses catching and handling formula errors in detail.

Using Functions in Formulas

Functions are like little utility programs that do a single thing. For example, the SUM function sums numbers, the COUNT function counts, and the AVERAGE function calculates an average.

There are functions to handle many needs: working with numbers, working with text, working with dates and times, working with finance, and so on. Functions can be combined and nested (one goes inside another). Functions return a value, and this value can be combined with the results of another function or formula. The possibilities are nearly endless.

But functions do not exist on their own. They are always a part of a formula. Now, that can mean that the formula is made up completely of the function or that the formula combines the function with other functions, data, operators, or references. But functions must follow the formula golden rule: *Start with the equal sign.* Look at some examples:

Function/Formula	Result
=SUM(A1:A5)	Returns the sum of the values in the range A1:A5. This is an example of a function serving as the whole formula.
=SUM(A1:A5) /B5	Returns the sum of the values in the range A1:A5 divided by the value in cell B5. This is an example of mixing a function's result with other data.
=SUM(A1:A5) + AVERAGE(B1:B5)	Returns the sum of the range A1:A5 added with the average of the range B1:B5. This is an example of a formula that combines the result of two functions.

Ready to write your first formula with a function in it? Use the following steps to write a function that creates an average:

1. **Enter some numbers in a column's cells.**

2. **Click an empty cell where you want to see the result.**

3. **Type** =AVERAGE(**to start the function.**

   Note: Excel presents a list of functions that have the same spelling as the function name you type. The more letters you type, the shorter the list becomes. The advantage is, for example, typing the letter A, using ↓ to select the AVERAGE function and then pressing the Tab key.

4. **Click the first cell with an entered value and, while holding the mouse button, drag the mouse pointer over the other cells that have values.**

   An alternative is to enter the range of those cells.

5. **Type).**

6. **Press Enter.**

If all went well, your worksheet should look a little bit like mine, in Figure 1-20. Cell B10 has the calculated result, but look up at the Formula Bar, and you can see the actual function as it was entered.

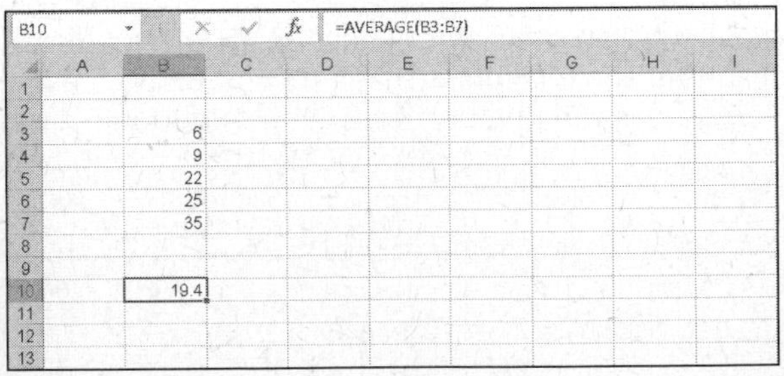

Figure 1-20: Entering the AVERAGE function.

Formulas and functions are dependent on the cells and ranges to which they refer. If you change the data in one of the cells, the result returned by the function updates. You can try this now. In the example you just did with making an average, click one of the cells with the values and enter a different number. The returned average changes.

A formula can consist of nothing but a single function — preceded by an equal sign, of course!

Looking at what goes into a function

Most functions take inputs — called *arguments* or *parameters* — that specify the data the function is to use. Some functions take no arguments, some take one, and others take many; it all depends on the function. The argument list is always enclosed in parentheses following the function name. If there's more than one argument, the arguments are separated by commas. Look at a few examples:

Function	Comment
`=NOW()`	Takes no arguments.
`=AVERAGE(A6,A11,B7)`	Can take up to 255 arguments. Here, three cell references are included as arguments. The arguments are separated by commas.
`=AVERAGE(A6:A10,A13:A19,A23:A29)`	In this example, the arguments are range references instead of cell references. The arguments are separated by commas.
`=IPMT(B5, B6, B7, B8)`	Requires four arguments. Commas separate the arguments.

Some functions have required arguments and optional arguments. You must provide the required ones. The optional ones are, well, optional. But you may want to include them if their presence helps the function return the value you need.

The IPMT function is a good example. Four arguments are required, and two more are optional. You can read more about the IPMT function in Chapter 5. You can read more about function arguments in Chapter 2.

Arguing with a function

Memorizing the arguments that every function takes would be a daunting task. I can only think that if you could pull that off, you could be on television. But back to reality. You don't have to memorize arguments because

Excel helps you select what function to use and then tells you which arguments are needed.

Figure 1-21 shows the Insert Function dialog box. You access this great helper by clicking the Insert Function button on the Formulas Ribbon. The dialog box is where you select a function to use.

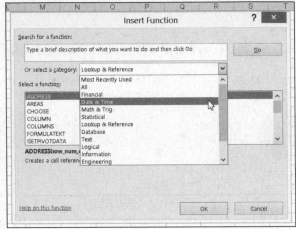

Figure 1-21:
Using the
Insert Func-
tion dialog
box.

The dialog box contains a listing of all available functions — and there are a lot of them! So to make matters easier, the dialog box gives you a way to search for a function by a keyword, or you can filter the list of functions by category.

TIP

If you know which category a function belongs in, you can click the function category button on the Formulas Ribbon and select the function from the menu.

Try it! Here's an example of how to use the Insert Function dialog box to multiply a few numbers:

1. **Enter three numbers in three different cells.**

2. **Click an empty cell where you want the result to appear.**

3. **Click the Insert Function button on the Formulas Ribbon.**

   As an alternative, you can just click the little *fx* button on the Formula Bar. The Insert Function dialog box appears.

4. **From the category drop-down list, select either All or Math & Trig.**

5. **In the list of functions, find and select the PRODUCT function.**

6. Click the OK button.

This closes the Insert Function dialog box and displays the Function Arguments dialog box (see Figure 1-22), where you can enter as many arguments as needed. Initially, the dialog box may not look like it can accommodate enough arguments. You need to enter three in this example, but it looks like there is only room for two. This is like musical chairs!

More argument entry boxes appear as you need them. First, though, how do you enter the argument? There are two ways.

Figure 1-22:
Getting ready to enter some arguments to the function.

7. Enter the argument in one of two ways:

- Type the numbers or cell references in the boxes.
- Use those funny-looking squares to the right of the entry boxes.

In Figure 1-22, two entry boxes are ready to go. To the left of them are the names Number1 and Number2. To the right of the boxes are the little squares. These squares are actually called *RefEdit controls.* They make argument entry a snap. All you do is click one, click the cell with the value, and then press Enter.

8. Click the RefEdit control to the right of the Number1 entry box.

The Function Arguments dialog box shrinks to just the size of the entry box.

9. Click the cell with the first number.

Figure 1-23 shows what the screen looks like at this point.

10. Press Enter.

The Function Arguments dialog box reappears with the argument entered in the box. The argument is not the value in the cell, but the address of the cell that contains the value — exactly what you want.

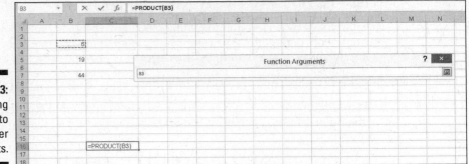

Figure 1-23:
Using
RefEdit to
enter
arguments.

11. Repeat Steps 7–9 to enter the other two cell references.

Figure 1-24 shows what the screen should now look like.

The number of entry boxes and associated RefEdit controls grow to match the number of needed entry boxes.

12. Click OK or press Enter to complete the function.

Figure 1-24:
Completing
the function
entry.

Figure 1-25 shows the result of all this hoopla. The PRODUCT function returns the result of the individual numbers being multiplied together.

You do not have to use the Insert Function dialog box to enter functions into cells. It is there for convenience. As you become familiar with certain functions that you use repeatedly, you may find it faster to just type the function directly in the cell.

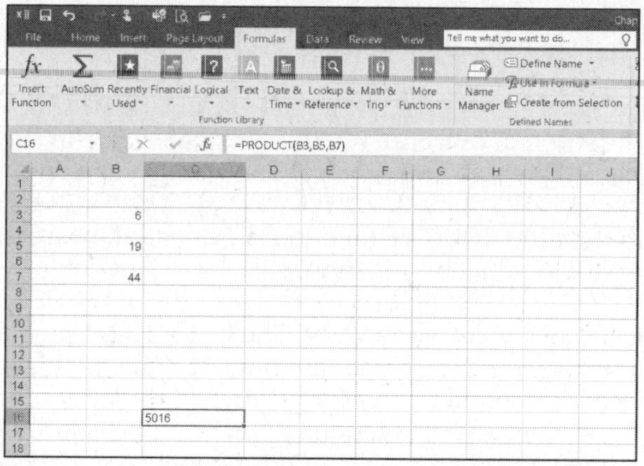

Figure 1-25:
Math was
never this
easy!

Nesting functions

Nesting is something a bird does, isn't it? Well, a bird expert would know the answer to that one; however, I do know how to nest Excel functions. A *nested function* is tucked inside another function as one of its arguments. Nesting functions let you return results you would have a hard time getting otherwise. (Nested functions are used in examples in various places in the book. The COUNTIF, AVERAGE, and MAX functions are discussed in Chapter 9.)

Figure 1-26 shows the daily closing price for the Standard & Poor's 500 for the month of September 2004. A possible analysis is to see how many times the closing price was higher than the average for the month. Therefore, you need to calculate the average before you can compare any single price. Embed the AVERAGE function inside another function to calculate the average first.

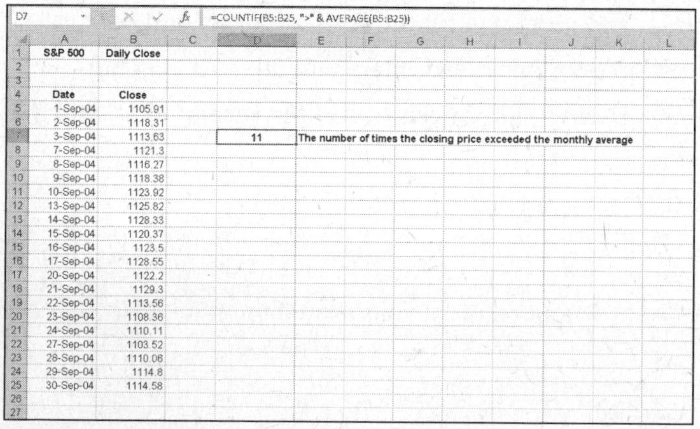

Figure 1-26:
Nesting
functions.

When a function is nested inside another, the inner function is calculated first. Then that result is used as an argument for the outer function.

The COUNTIF function counts the number of cells in a range that meet a condition. The condition in this case is that any single value in the range is greater than (>) the average of the range. The formula in cell D7 is =COUNTIF(B5:B25, ">" & AVERAGE(B5:B25)). The AVERAGE function is evaluated first; then the COUNTIF function is evaluated, using the returned value from the nested function as an argument.

Nested functions are best entered directly. The Insert Function dialog box does not make it easy to enter a nested function. Try one. In this example, you use the AVERAGE function to find the average of the largest values from two sets of numbers. The nested function in this example is MAX. You enter the MAX function twice within the AVERAGE function. Follow these steps:

1. **Enter a few different numbers in one column.**

2. **Enter a few different numbers in a different column.**

3. **Click an empty cell where you want the result to appear.**

4. **Type** =AVERAGE(**to start the function entry.**

5. **Type** MAX(.

6. **Click the first cell in the second set of numbers, press the mouse button, and drag over all the cells of the first set.**

   The address of this range enters into the MAX function.

7. **Enter a closing parenthesis to end the first MAX function.**

8. **Enter a comma (,).**

9. **Once again, type** MAX(.

10. **Click the first cell in the second set of numbers, press the mouse button, and drag over all the cells of the second set.**

    The address of this range enters into the MAX function.

11. **Enter a closing parenthesis to end the second MAX function.**

12. **Enter a**).

    This ends the AVERAGE function.

13. **Press Enter.**

Figure 1-27 shows the result of your nested function. Cell C14 has this formula: =AVERAGE(MAX(B4:B10),MAX(D4:D10)).

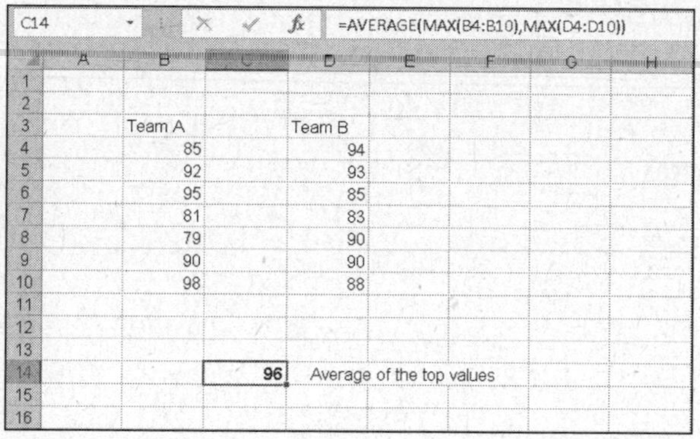

C14	▾	✕ ✓	*fx*	=AVERAGE(MAX(B4:B10),MAX(D4:D10))			
◢	A	B	C	D	E	F	G	H
1							
2							
3		Team A		Team B			
4		85		94			
5		92		93			
6		95		85			
7		81		83			
8		79		90			
9		90		90			
10		98		88			
11							
12							
13							
14			96	Average of the top values			
15							
16							

Figure 1-27: Getting a result from nested functions.

When you use nested functions, the outer function is preceded with an equal sign (=) if it is the beginning of the formula. Any nested functions are *not* preceded with an equal sign.

You can nest functions up to 64 levels.

Chapter 2

Saving Time with Function Tools

· ·

In This Chapter

▶ Displaying the Insert Function dialog box

▶ Finding the function you need

▶ Using the Function Arguments dialog box

▶ Entering formulas and functions

· ·

*E*xcel has so many functions that it's both a blessing and a curse. You can do many things with Excel functions — if you can remember them all! Even if you remember many function names, memorizing all the arguments the functions can use is a challenge.

Arguments are pieces of information that functions use to calculate and return a value.

Never fear: Microsoft hasn't left you in the dark with figuring out which arguments to use. Excel has a great utility to help you insert functions, and their arguments, into your worksheet. This makes it a snap to find and use the functions you need. You can save both time and headaches, and make fewer errors to boot — so read on!

Getting Familiar with the Insert Function Dialog Box

The Insert Function dialog box (shown in Figure 2-1) is designed to simplify the task of using functions in your worksheet. The dialog box not only helps you locate the proper function for the task at hand, but also provides information about the arguments that the function takes. If you use the Insert Function dialog box, you don't have to type functions directly in worksheet cells. Instead, the dialog box guides you through a (mostly) point-and-click procedure — a good thing, because if you're anything like me, you need all the help you can get.

Figure 2-1:
Use the
Insert
Function
dialog box
to easily
enter
functions
in a
worksheet.

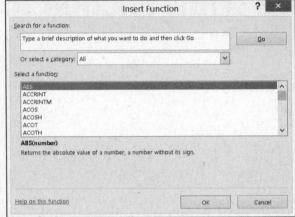

In the Insert Function dialog box, you can browse functions by category or scroll the complete alphabetical list. A search feature — you type a phrase in the Search for a Function box, click the Go button, and see what comes up — is helpful. When you highlight a function in the Select a Function box, a brief description of what the function does appears under the list. You can also click the Help on This Function link at the bottom of the dialog box to view more detailed information about the function.

You can display the Insert Function dialog box in three ways:

- Click the Insert Function button on the Formulas Ribbon.

- On the Formula Bar, click the smaller Insert Function button (which looks like f_x).

- Click the small arrow to the right of the AutoSum feature on the Formulas Ribbon, and select More Functions (see Figure 2-2). AutoSum has a list of commonly used functions that you can insert with a click. If you select More Functions, the Insert Function dialog box opens.

Figure 2-2:
The
AutoSum
button
offers quick
access to
basic
functions
and the
Insert
Function
dialog box.

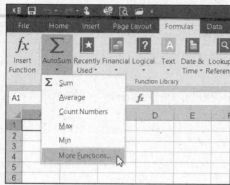

Finding the Correct Function

The first step in using a function is finding the one you need! Even when you do know the one you need, you may not remember all the arguments it takes. You can find a function in the Insert Function dialog box in two ways:

- ✔ **Search:** Type one or more keywords or a phrase in the Search for a Function box; then click the Go button.

  - If a match is made, the Or Select a Category drop-down menu displays Recommended, and the Select a Function box displays a list of the functions that match your search.

  - If no match is made, the Or Select a Category drop-down menu displays Most Recently Used functions, and the most recently used functions appear in the Select a Function dialog box. The Search for a Function box displays a message to rephrase the text entered for the search.

- ✔ **Browse:** Click the Or Select a Category down arrow, and from the drop-down menu, select All or an actual function category. When an actual category is selected, the Select a Function box updates to show just the relevant functions. You can look through the list to find the function you want. Alternatively, if you know the category, you can select it on the Formulas Ribbon.

Table 2-1 lists the categories in the Or Select a Category drop-down menu. Finding the function you need is different from knowing which function you need. Excel is great at giving you the functions, but you do need to know what to ask for.

Table 2-1	Function Categories in the Insert Function Dialog Box
Category	**Type of Functions**
Most Recently Used	The last several functions you used.
All	The entire function list, sorted alphabetically.
Financial	Functions for managing loans, analyzing investments, and so on.
Date & Time	Functions for calculating days of the week, elapsed time, and so on.
Math & Trig	A considerable number of mathematical functions.
Statistical	Functions for using descriptive and inferential statistics.
Lookup & Reference	Functions for obtaining facts about and data on worksheets.
Database	Functions for selecting data in structured rows and columns.
Text	Functions for manipulating and searching text values.
Logical	Boolean functions (AND, OR, and so on).
Information	Functions for getting facts about worksheet cells and the data therein.
Web	A few functions that are useful when sharing data with web services.
Engineering	Engineering and some conversion functions. These functions are also provided in the Analysis ToolPak.
Cube	Functions used with online analytical processing (OLAP) cubes.
Compatibility	Some functions were updated as of Excel 2010 and Excel 2013. The functions in this category are the older versions that remain compatible with Excel 2007 and earlier versions.
User Defined	Any available custom functions created in VBA code or from add-ins. This category may not be listed.

Entering Functions Using the Insert Function Dialog Box

Now that you've seen how to search for or select a function, it's time to use the Insert Function dialog box to actually insert a function. The dialog box makes it easy to enter functions that take no arguments and functions that *do* take arguments. Either way, the dialog box guides you through the process of entering the function.

Sometimes, function arguments are not values, but references to cells, ranges, named areas, or tables. That this is also handled in the Insert Function dialog box makes its use so beneficial.

Selecting a function that takes no arguments

Some functions return a value, period. No arguments are needed for these functions. This means you don't have to have some arguments ready to go. What could be easier? Here's how to enter a function that does not take any arguments. The TODAY function is used in this example:

1. **Position the cursor in the cell where you want the results to appear.**

2. **Click the Insert Function button on the Ribbon to open the Insert Function dialog box.**

3. **Select All in the Or Select a Category drop-down menu.**

4. **Scroll through the Select a Function list until you see the TODAY function, and click it.**

    Figure 2-3 shows what my screen looks like.

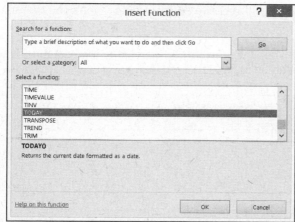

Figure 2-3:
Selecting a function.

5. Click the OK button.

The Insert Function dialog box closes, and the Function Arguments dialog box opens. The dialog box tells you that function does not take any arguments. Figure 2-4 shows how the screen looks now.

Figure 2-4:
Confirming
that no
arguments
exist with
the Function
Arguments
dialog box.

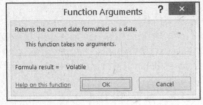

6. Click the OK button.

Doing this closes the Function Arguments dialog box, and the function entry is complete.

You may have noticed that the Function Arguments dialog box says that the Formula result will equal `Volatile`. This is nothing to be alarmed about! This just means the answer can be different each time you use the function. For example, TODAY will return a different date when used tomorrow.

Figure 2-5 shows how the function's result has been returned to the worksheet. Cell B2 displays the date when I wrote this example. The date you see on your screen is the current date.

Figure 2-5:
Populating a
worksheet
cell with
today's
date.

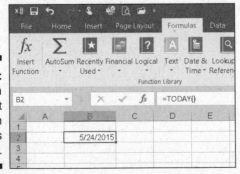

Most functions do take arguments. The few that *do not* take arguments can return a result without needing any information. For example, the TODAY function just returns the current date. It doesn't need any information to figure this out.

Selecting a function that uses arguments

Most functions take arguments to provide the information that the functions need to perform their calculations. Some functions use a single argument; others use many. *Taking arguments* and *using arguments* are interchangeable terms. Most functions take arguments, but the number of arguments depends on the actual function. Some functions take a single argument, and some can take up to 255.

The following example shows how to use the Insert Function dialog box to enter a function that *does* use arguments. The example uses the PRODUCT function. Here's how to enter the function and its arguments:

1. **Position the cursor in the cell where you want the results to appear.**

2. **Click the Insert Function button on the Ribbon.**

   Doing this opens the Insert Function dialog box.

3. **Select Math & Trig in the Or Select a Category drop-down menu.**

4. **Scroll through the Select a Function list until you see the PRODUCT function and then click it.**

   Figure 2-6 shows what the screen looks like.

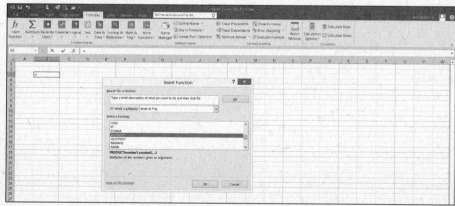

Figure 2-6: Preparing to multiply some numbers with the PRODUCT function.

5. Click the OK button.

The Insert Function dialog box closes, and the Function Arguments dialog box opens. Figure 2-7 shows what the screen looks like. The dialog box tells you that this function can take up to 255 arguments, yet there appears to be room for only 2. As you enter arguments, the dialog box provides a scroll bar to manage multiple arguments.

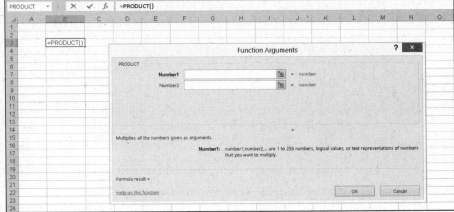

Figure 2-7:
Ready to
input
function
arguments.

6. In the Function Arguments dialog box, enter a number in the Number1 box.

7. Enter another number in the Number2 box.

You are entering actual arguments. As you enter numbers in the dialog box, a scroll bar appears, letting you add arguments. Enter as many as you like, up to 255. Figure 2-8 shows how I entered eight arguments. Also look at the bottom left of the dialog box. As you enter functions, the formula result is instantly calculated. Wouldn't it be nice to be that smart?

8. Click OK to complete the function entry.

Figure 2-9 shows the worksheet's result.

Figure 2-8:
Getting
instant
results in
the Function
Arguments
dialog box.

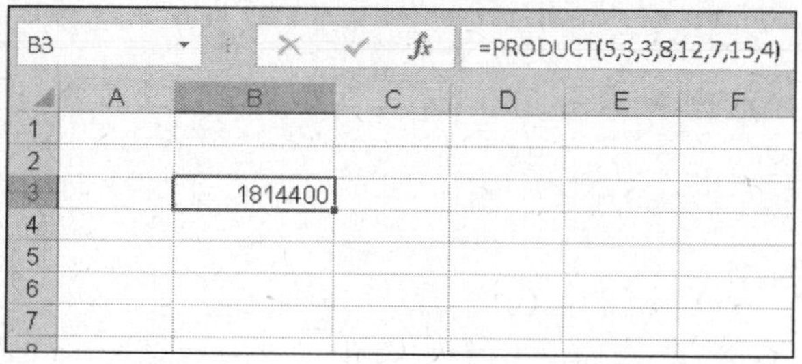

Figure 2-9:
Getting the
final answer
from the
function.

Entering cells, ranges, named areas, and tables as function arguments

Excel is so cool. You can not only provide single cell references as arguments, but also, in many cases you can enter an entire range reference, or the name of an area or table, as a single argument! What's more, you can enter these arguments by using either the keyboard or the mouse.

This example demonstrates using both single cell and range references as well as a named area and table as arguments. For this example, I use the SUM function. Here's how to use the Insert Function dialog box to enter the function and its arguments:

1. **Enter some numbers in a worksheet in contiguous cells.**

2. **Select the cells and then click the Table button on the Insert Ribbon.**

   The Create Table dialog box opens.

3. **Click the OK button to complete making the table.**

   The Ribbon should display table style and other options. (If not, look along the Excel title bar for Table Tools, and click it.) On the left end of the Ribbon is the name that Excel gave the table. You can change the name of the table, as well as the appearance. Jot down the name of the table. You need to re-enter the table name further in these steps.

4. **Somewhere else on the worksheet, enter numbers in contiguous cells.**

5. **Select the cells and then click the Define Name button on the Formulas Ribbon.**

   The New Name dialog box opens.

6. **Enter a name for the area.**

   I used the name MyArea. See Figure 2-10 to see how the worksheet is shaping up.

Figure 2-10:
Adding a
table and a
named area
to a work-
sheet.

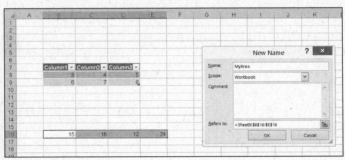

7. **Enter some more numbers in contiguous cells, either across a row or down a column.**

8. **Enter a single number in cell A1.**

9. **Click an empty cell where you want the result to appear.**

10. **Click the Insert Function button on the Formulas Ribbon.**

    The Insert Function dialog box opens.

11. **Select the SUM function.**

    SUM is in the All or Math & Trig category, and possibly in the Recently Used category.

12. **Click OK.**

    The Function Arguments dialog box opens.

To the right of each Number box is a small fancy button — a special Excel control sometimes called the *RefEdit*. It allows you to leave the dialog box, select a cell or range on the worksheet, and then go back to the dialog box. Whatever cell or range you click or drag over on the worksheet is brought into the entry box as a reference.

You can type cell and range references, named areas, and table names directly in the Number boxes as well. The RefEdit controls are there to use if you want to work with the mouse instead.

13. **Click the first RefEdit.**

The dialog box shrinks so that the only thing visible is the field where you enter data. Click cell A1, where you entered a number.

14. **Press the Enter key.**

The Function Arguments dialog box reappears.

15. **In the second entry box, type the name of your named area.**

If you don't remember the name you used, use the RefEdit control to select the area on the worksheet.

16. **In the third entry box, enter your table name, and press the Enter key.**

17. **If you don't remember the name you used, use the RefEdit control to select the table.**

18. **In the fourth entry box, enter a range from the worksheet where some values are located.**

It does not matter if this range is part of a named area or table. Use the RefEdit control if you want to just drag the mouse over a range of numbers. Your screen should look similar to Figure 2-11.

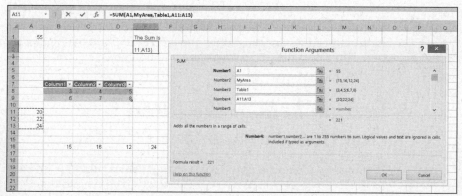

Figure 2-11: Entering arguments.

19. Click the OK button.

The final sum from the various parts of the worksheet displays in the cell where the function was entered. Figure 2-12 shows how the example worksheet turned out.

E2	▼		✕ ✓ *fx*	=SUM(A1,MyArea,Table1,A11:A13)			
◢	A	B	C	D	E	F	G
1	55				The Sum Is		
2					221		
3							
4							
5							
6							
7		Column1 ▾	Column2 ▾	Column3 ▾			
8		3	4	5			
9		6	7	8			
10							
11	20						
12	22						
13	24						
14							
15							
16		15	16	12	24		
17							
18							
19							

Figure 2-12: Calculating a sum based on cell and range references.

Congratulations! You did it. You successfully inserted a function that took a cell reference, a range reference, a named area, and a table name. You're harnessing the power of Excel. Look at the result — the sum of many numbers located in various parts of the worksheet. Just imagine how much summing you can do. You can have up to 255 inputs, and if necessary, each one can be a *range* of cells.

You can use the Insert Function dialog box at any time while entering a formula. This is helpful when the formula uses some values and references in addition to a function. Just open the Insert Function dialog box when the formula entry is at the point where the function goes.

Getting help in the Insert Function dialog box

The number of functions and their exhaustive capabilities give you the power to do great things in Excel. However, from time to time, you may need guidance on how to get functions to work. Luckily for you, help is just a click away.

Both the Insert Function and Function Arguments dialog boxes have a link to the Help system. At any time, you can click the Help on This Function link in the lower-left corner of the dialog box and get help on the function you're using. The Help system has many examples. Often, reviewing how a function works leads you to other, similar functions that may be better suited to your situation.

Using the Function Arguments dialog box to edit functions

Excel makes entering functions with the Insert Function dialog box easy. But what do you do when you need to change a function that has already been entered in a cell? What about adding arguments or taking some away? There is an easy way to do this! Follow these steps:

1. **Click the cell with the existing function.**

2. **Click the Insert Function button.**

   The Function Argument dialog box appears. This dialog box is already set to work with your function. In fact, the arguments that have already been entered in the function are displayed in the dialog box as well!

3. **Add, edit, or delete arguments, as follows:**

   - To add an argument (if the function allows), use the RefEdit control to pick up the extra values from the worksheet. Alternatively, if you click the bottom argument reference, a new box opens below it, and you can enter a value or range in that box.

   - To edit an argument, simply click it and change it.

   - To delete an argument, click it and press the Backspace key.

4. **Click OK when you're finished.**

   The function is updated with your changes.

Directly Entering Formulas and Functions

As you get sharp with functions, you will likely bypass the Insert Function dialog box altogether and enter functions directly. One place you can do this is in the Formula Bar. Another way is to just type in a cell.

Entering formulas and functions in the Formula Bar

When you place your entry in the Formula Bar, the entry is really going into the active cell. However, because the active cell can be anywhere, you may prefer entering formulas and functions directly in the Formula Bar. That way, you know that the entry will land where you need it. Before you enter a formula in the Formula Box (on the right end of the Formula Bar), the Name Box on the left lets you know where the entry will end up. The cell receiving the entry may be not be in the visible area of the worksheet. Gosh, it could be a million rows down and thousands of columns to the right! After you start entering the formula, the Name Box becomes a drop-down menu of functions. This menu is useful for nesting functions. As you enter a function in the Formula Box, you can click a function in the Name Box, and the function is inserted into the entry you started in the Formula Box. Confused? Imagine what I went through explaining that! Seriously, though, this is a helpful way to assemble nested functions. Try it, and get used to it; it will add to your Excel smarts.

When your entry is finished, press the Enter key or click the little check-mark button to the left of the Formula Box.

Figure 2-13 makes this clear. A formula is being entered in the Formula Box, and the Name Box follows along with the function(s) being entered. Note, though, that the active cell is not in the viewable area of the worksheet. It must be below and/or to the right of the viewable area because the top-left portion of the worksheet is shown in Figure 2-13.

Figure 2-13:
Entering a
formula in
the Formula
Box has its
conve-
niences.

In between the Name Box and the Formula Box are three small buttons. From left to right, they do the following:

- ✔ Cancel the entry.
- ✔ Complete the entry.
- ✔ Display the Insert Function dialog box.

The Cancel and Complete Function buttons are enabled only when you enter a formula, a function, or just plain old values on the Formula Bar or directly in a cell.

Entering formulas and functions directly in worksheet cells

Perhaps the easiest entry method is typing the formula directly in a cell. Just type formulas that contain no functions and press the Enter key to complete the entry. Try this simple example:

1. **Click a cell where the formula is to be entered.**

2. **Enter this simple math-based formula:**

   =6 + (9/5) *100

3. **Press the Enter key.**

   The answer is 186. (Don't forget the order of operators; see Chapter 18 for more information about the order of mathematical operators.)

Excel makes entering functions in your formulas as easy as a click. As you type the first letter of a function in a cell, a list of functions starting with that letter is listed immediately (see Figure 2-14.)

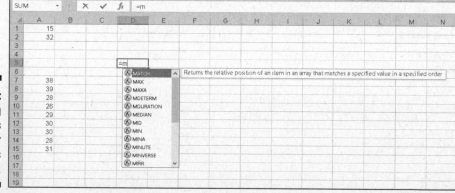

Figure 2-14:
Entering functions has never been this easy.

The desired function in this example is MIN, which returns the minimum value from a group of values. As soon as you type **M** (first enter the equal sign if this is the start of a formula entry), the list in Figure 2-14 appears, showing all the M functions. Now that an option exists, either keep typing the full function name, or scroll to MIN and press the Tab key. Figure 2-15 shows just what happens when you do the latter. MIN is completed and provides the required syntax structure — not much thinking involved! Now your brain can concentrate on more interesting things, such as poker odds. (Will Microsoft ever create a function category for calculating poker odds? Please?) In Figure 2-15, the MIN function is used to find the minimum value in the range A7:A15 (which is multiplied with the sum of the values in A1 plus A2). Entering the closing parenthesis and then pressing the Enter key completes the function. In this example, the answer is 1222.

A1: 15
A2: 32
A7: 38
A8: 39
A9: 28
A10: 26
A11: 29
A12: 30
A13: 30
A14: 28
A15: 31

The formula in D5 is =(A1+A2) * MIN(A7:A15).

Excel's capability to show a list of functions based on spelling is called *Formula AutoComplete*.

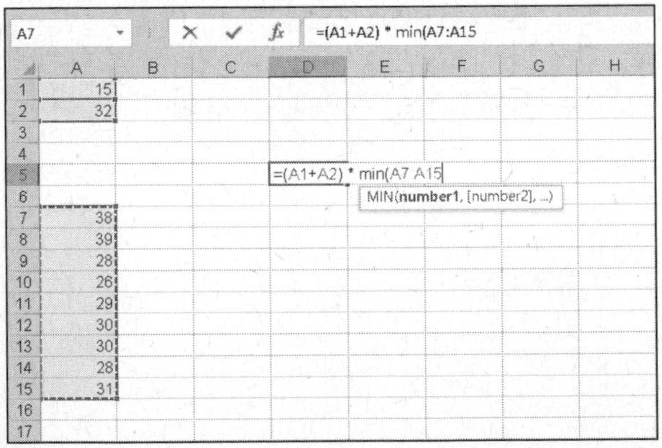

Figure 2-15: Completing the direct-in-the-cell formula entry.

You can turn Formula AutoComplete on or off in the Excel Options dialog box by following these steps:

1. **Click the File tab at the top left of the screen.**

2. **Click Options.**

3. **In the Excel Options dialog box, select the Formulas tab.**

4. **In the Working with Formulas section, check or clear the Formula AutoComplete check box.**

   See Figure 2-16 for the check box's placement.

5. **Click the OK button.**

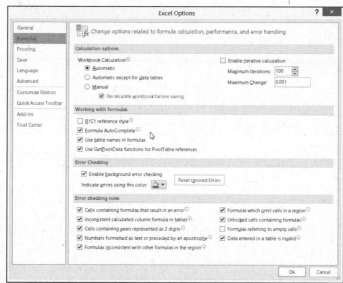

Figure 2-16:
Setting
Formula
Auto-
Complete.

Chapter 3

Saying "Array!" for Formulas and Functions

In This Chapter

▶ Understanding arrays

▶ Creating formulas that use arrays

▶ Using functions that return arrays of data

Excel is really quite sophisticated; its many built-in functions make your work easier. On top of that, Excel allows you to tell functions to work on entire sets of values, called *arrays,* which makes for even more clever analysis.

An *array* is a set of two or more values (for example, the contents of two or more worksheet cells, or even the contents of two or more worksheet ranges). Certain functions use arrays for arguments.

You may be thinking, "Hey, how is this different from just entering a bunch of arguments?" You're right in the comparison. For example, the SUM function can take up to 255 arguments. Isn't this the same as giving the function an array with 255 values? Well, yes and no. It's the same idea, but using the array approach can streamline your work, as you soon see.

There is even another side to array functions. Some of the functions *return* an array. Yes, that's right. Most of the time a function returns a single value into a single cell. In this chapter, I show you how a function returns a group of values into multiple cells.

Discovering Arrays

An array is like a box. It can hold a number of items. In Excel, an array holds a collection of values or cell references. These arrays are used exclusively in formulas and functions. That is, the association of some values as one cohesive group exists just for the purpose of calculating results. An array differs from the named areas (a range of cells) that you can create in Excel. Named areas become part of the worksheet and can be referenced at any time.

Named areas are set using the New Name dialog box, shown in Figure 3-1. By contrast, there is no such dialog box or method to create arrays that can be referenced from functions or formulas. Arrays, instead, are embedded in formulas.

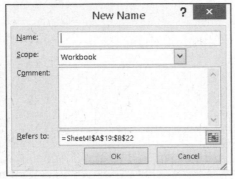

Figure 3-1:
Creating a
named area
with the
New Name
dialog box.

Named areas are easily referenced in formulas. For example, if a workbook contains a named area Sales, the values of all the cells in Sales can be summed up like this:

```
=SUM(Sales)
```

Assume that Sales contains three cells with these values: 10, 15, and 20. These values, of course, can be entered directly in the SUM function like this:

```
=SUM(10,15,20)
```

This is almost an array, but not quite. Excel recognizes a group of values to be an array when they are enclosed in braces ({ and }). Therefore, to enter the array of values into the function, you make an entry that looks like this:

```
=SUM({10,15,20})
```

Essentially the braces tell Excel to treat the group of values as an array. So far, you may be wondering about the usefulness of an array, but in the next section, I show you how using arrays with standard functions such as SUM can provide sophisticated results.

To enter values as an array within a function, enclose them in braces. Braces have a curly look and are not to be confused with brackets. On a typical keyboard, braces and brackets are on the same key. Holding the Shift key while pressing the brace/bracket key provides the brace.

However, getting the braces into the formula takes a particular keystroke. You don't type braces directly.

Using Arrays in Formulas

You can use arrays when entering formulas and functions. Typically, the arguments to a function are entered in a different manner, which I demonstrate in this section. Using arrays can save entry steps and deliver an answer in a single formula. This is useful in situations that normally require a set of intermediate calculations from which the final result is calculated. I don't know about you, but I like shortcuts, especially when I have too much to do!

Here's an example: The SUM function is normally used to add a few numbers together. Summing up a few numbers doesn't require an array formula per se, but what about summing up the results of other calculations? This next example shows how using an array simplifies getting to the final result.

Figure 3-2 shows a small portfolio of stocks. Column A has the stock symbols, Column B has the number of shares per stock, and Column C has a recent price for each stock.

	A	B	C	D	E
1					
2	**Stock**	**# of Shares**	**Price**		
3					
4	IBM	100	$120.82		
5	MSFT	200	$25.71		
6	YHOO	200	$17.21		
7	INTC	300	$19.88		
8	BA	150	$25.37		
9					
10					
11					

Figure 3-2:
A stock portfolio.

The task is to find out the *total* value of the portfolio. The typical way to do this is to

1. **Multiply the number of shares for each stock by its price.**

2. **Sum up the results from Step 1.**

Figure 3-3 shows a very common way to do this. Column D contains formulas to calculate the value of each stock in the portfolio. This is done by multiplying the number of shares for each stock by its price. For example, cell D4 contains the formula =B4*C4. Cell D10 sums up the interim results with the formula =SUM(D4:D8).

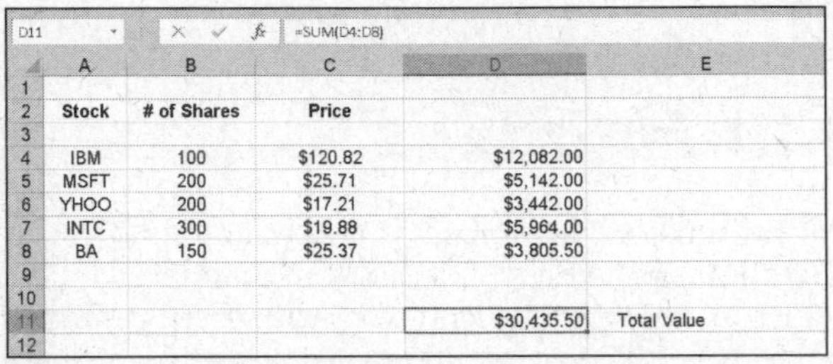

Figure 3-3:
Calculating
the value of
a stock
portfolio,
the old-
fashioned
way.

	A	B	C	D	E
1					
2	Stock	# of Shares	Price		
3					
4	IBM	100	$120.82	$12,082.00	
5	MSFT	200	$25.71	$5,142.00	
6	YHOO	200	$17.21	$3,442.00	
7	INTC	300	$19.88	$5,964.00	
8	BA	150	$25.37	$3,805.50	
9					
10					
11				$30,435.50	Total Value
12					

D11 · X ✓ *fx* =SUM(D4:D8)

The method shown in Figure 3-3 requires creating additional calculations — those in Column D. These calculations are necessary if you need to know the value of each stock, but not if all you need to know is the value of the portfolio as a whole.

Fortunately, alternatives to this standard approach exist. One is to embed the separate multiplicative steps directly in the SUM function, like this:

```
=SUM(B4*C4,B5*C5,B6*C6,B7*C7,B8*C8)
```

That works, but it's bloated, to say the least. What if you had 20 stocks in the portfolio? Forget it!

Another alternative is the SUMPRODUCT function. This function sums the products, just as the other methods shown here do. The limitation, however, is that SUMPRODUCT can be used only for summing. It cannot, for example, give you an average.

In many situations such as this one, your best bet is to use an array function. Figure 3-4 shows the correct result from using the SUM function entered as an array function. Notice that the formula in the Formula Bar begins and ends with a brace.

The syntax is important. Two ranges are entered in the function: One contains the cells that hold the number of shares, and the other contains the cells that have the stock prices. These are multiplied in the function by entering the multiplication operator (*):

```
{=SUM(B4:B8*C4:C8)}
```

Figure 3-4:
Calculating
the value of
a stock port-
folio using
an array
function.

	A	B	C	D	E
1					
2	Stock	# of Shares	Price		
3					
4	IBM	100	$120.82		
5	MSFT	200	$25.71		
6	YHOO	200	$17.21		
7	INTC	300	$19.88		
8	BA	150	$25.37		
9					
10					
11				$30,435.50	Total Value
12					
13					
14					

D11   fx   {=SUM(B4:B8*C4:C8)}

Ctrl+Shift+Enter had been pressed to turn the whole thing into an array
function. You use that special keystroke combination when you finish the
formula, not before. Note the lack of subtotals (per stock) in cells D4:D8.
Compare Figure 3-4 with Figure 3-3, and you can see the difference.

TIP

Use Ctrl+Shift+Enter to turn a formula into an array formula. You must use
the key combination after entering the formula instead of pressing the Enter
key. The key combination takes the place of pressing the Enter key.

Here's how you use an array with the SUM function:

1. **Enter two columns of values.**

   The two lists must be the same size.

2. **Position the cursor in the cell where you want the result to appear.**

3. **Type =SUM(to start the function.**

   Note that a brace is *not* entered in this step.

4. **Click the first cell in the first list, hold the left mouse button down,
   drag the pointer over the first list, and then release the mouse button.**

5. **Type the multiplication sign (*).**

6. **Click the first cell of the second list, hold down the left mouse button,
   and drag the pointer over the second list.**

7. **Release the mouse button.**

8. **Type).**

REMEMBER

9. **Press Ctrl+Shift+Enter to end the function.**

   Do not just press the Enter key by itself when using an array with the
   SUM function.

Array functions are useful for saving steps in mathematical operations. Therefore, you can apply these examples to a number of functions, such as AVERAGE, MAX, MIN, and so on.

As another example, suppose that you run a fleet of taxis, and you need to calculate the average cost of gasoline per mile driven. This is easy to calculate for a single vehicle. You just divide the total spent on gasoline by the total miles driven for a given period of time. The calculation looks like this:

```
cost of gasoline per mile = total spent on gasoline ÷ total miles driven
```

How can you easily calculate this for a fleet of vehicles? Figure 3-5 shows how this is done. The vehicles are listed in Column A, the total miles driven for the month appear in Column B, and the total amounts spent on gasoline appear in Column C.

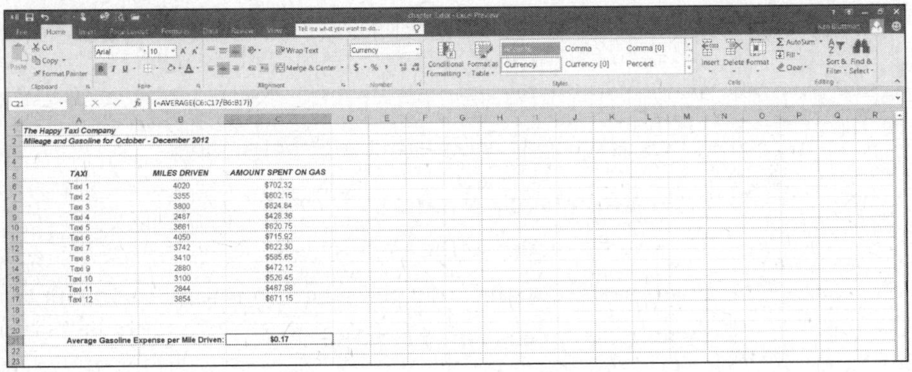

Figure 3-5:
Making an
easy
calculation
using an
array
formula.

One single formula in cell C21 answers the question. When you use the AVERAGE function in an array formula, the result is returned without the need for any intermediate calculations. The formula looks like this:

```
{=AVERAGE(C6:C17/B6:B17)}
```

Working with Functions That Return Arrays

A few functions actually return arrays of data. Instead of providing a single result, as most functions do, these functions return several values. The number of actual returned values is directly related to the function's arguments. The returned values go into a range of cells.

REMEMBER

Excel array functions accept arrays as arguments and possibly return arrays of data.

A good example of this is the TRANSPOSE function. This interesting function is used to reorient data. Data situated a given way in columns and rows is transposed (changed to be presented instead in rows and columns). Figure 3-6 shows how this works.

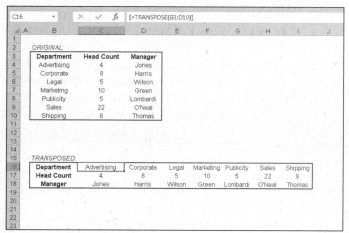

Figure 3-6: Transposing data.

Cells B3 through D10 contain information about departments in a company. Departments are listed going down Column B. Note that the area of B3 through D10 specifically occupies three columns and eight rows. The header row is included in the area.

Cells B16 through I18 contain the transposed data. It is the same data, but now it occupies eight columns and three rows. In total number of cells, this is the same size as the original area. Just as important is that the area is made up of the same dimensions, just reversed. That is, a 3-by-8 area became an 8-by-3 area. The number of cells remains 24. However, the transposed area has not been altered to be 6 by 4, 2 by 12, or any other two dimensions that cover 24 cells.

Every single cell in the B16:I18 range contains the same formula: {=TRANSPOSE(B3:D10)}. However, the function was entered only once.

In detail, here is how you can use the TRANSPOSE function:

1. **Enter some data that occupies at least two adjacent cells.**

   Creating an area of data that spans multiple rows and columns is best for seeing how useful the function is.

2. **Elsewhere on the worksheet, select an area that covers the same number of cells but has the length of the sides of the original area reversed.**

   For example:

   - If the original area is two columns and six rows, select an area that is six columns and two rows.

   - If the original area is one column and two rows, select an area that is two columns and one row.

   - If the original area is 200 columns and 201 rows, select an area that is 201 columns and 200 rows.

   - If the original area is five columns and five rows, select an area that is five columns and five rows. (A square area is transposed into a square area.)

   Figure 3-7 shows an area of data and a selected area ready to receive the transposed data. The original data area occupies 11 columns and 3 rows. The selected area is 3 columns by 11 rows.

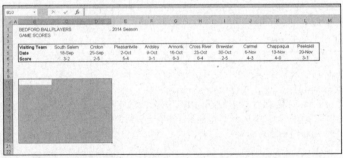

Figure 3-7: Preparing an area to receive transposed data.

3. **Type** =TRANSPOSE(**to start the function.**

   Because the receiving area is already selected, the entry goes into the first cell of the area.

4. **Click the first cell in the original data, drag the pointer over the entire original data area while keeping the mouse button down, and release the mouse button when the area is selected.**

   The function now shows the range of the original area. Figure 3-8 shows how the entry should appear at this step.

5. **Type**).

6. **Press Ctrl+Shift+Enter to end the function.**

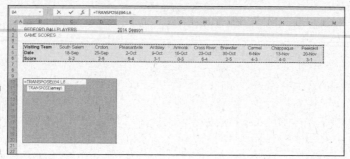

Figure 3-8:
Completing
the function.

Note: The transposed data does not necessarily take on the formatting of the
original area. You may need to format the area. Figure 3-9 shows the result of
using TRANSPOSE *and* then formatting the transposed data.

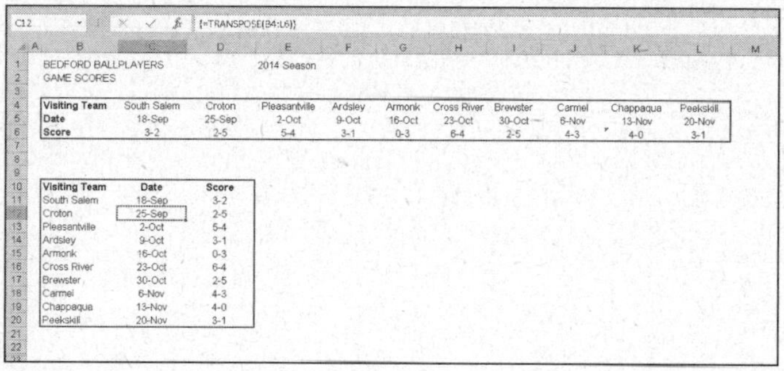

Figure 3-9:
Transposed
data after
formatting.

Wait! Isn't this a waste of time? Excel can easily transpose data when you use
the Paste Special dialog box. Simply copying a range of data and using this
dialog box to paste the data gives the same result as the TRANSPOSE function. Or does it?

Figure 3-10 shows the Paste Special dialog box with the Transpose check box
checked. This option transposes the data. You don't even have to select the
correct number of rows and columns where the transposed data will land. It
just appears transposed, with the active cell as the corner of the area.

However, when data is transposed with the Paste Special dialog box, the
actual data is *copied* to the new area. By contrast, the TRANSPOSE function
pastes a formula that references the original data — and that is the key point.
When data is changed in the original area, the change is reflected in the new,
transposed area if the TRANSPOSE function was used.

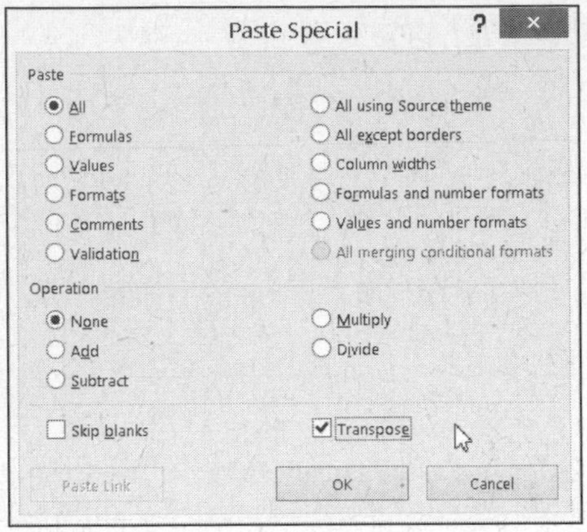

Paste Special ? ×

Paste
- ◉ All
- ○ Formulas
- ○ Values
- ○ Formats
- ○ Comments
- ○ Validation

- ○ All using Source theme
- ○ All except borders
- ○ Column widths
- ○ Formulas and number formats
- ○ Values and number formats
- ○ All merging conditional formats

Operation
- ◉ None
- ○ Add
- ○ Subtract

- ○ Multiply
- ○ Divide

- ☐ Skip blanks
- ☑ Transpose

Paste Link   OK   Cancel

Figure 3-10:
Using the
Paste Spe-
cial dialog
box to trans-
pose data.

REMEMBER

You can transpose data in two ways. The area filled with the TRANSPOSE function references the original data and will update as original data is changed. Using the Paste Special dialog box to transpose data creates values that do not update when the original data changes.

Chapter 4

Fixing Formula Boo-Boos

*E*xcel would be nothing if it didn't enable you to create formulas. Creating formulas is, after all, the real purpose of a worksheet: to allow you to build a solution that pertains to your specific needs. Without formulas, Excel would be no more than a place to store information. Boring!

Excel allows formulas to have up to 8,192 characters. This means you can create some monster formulas! Formulas can reference cells that have formulas that reference other cells that have formulas that reference . . . well, you get the idea!

Ah, but this comes at a price. How can you track down errors in long formulas? How can you avoid them in the first place? In this chapter, I explain how Excel steers you away from entering problematic formulas, and discuss how to correct completed formulas that are not working the way you intended.

Catching Errors As You Enter Them

Excel is keeping an eye on you when you enter formulas. Don't be worried! This is a good thing. You aren't being graded. Excel is helping you, not testing you.

All formulas start with an equal sign. When you complete an entry by pressing Enter or Tab (or clicking another cell), Excel scans the entry. If the entry did indeed start with an equal sign, Excel immediately looks for three major problems:

- ✔ Do the numbers of open and closed parentheses match?

- ✔ Does the formula reference the same cell it is entered in? Suppose that cell A1 has this formula: =A1*5. This is called a *circular reference*. This is a bit like a dog chasing its tail.

- ✔ Does the formula refer to a nonexistent reference?

Each of the problems is handled differently. Excel offers a fix for mismatched parentheses but only *warns* you about formulas that reference the cell they are entered in. For nonexistent references, Excel asks you where to find them. Excel displays an Open File dialog box that you use to browse to the reference, assuming that the reference is meant to come from an external workbook. If a reference to an external workbook was not the intention, the dialog box won't make sense. In this case, dismiss the dialog box and edit the formula.

Getting parentheses to match

In a mathematical formula, each open parenthesis must have a matching closing parenthesis. Excel checks your formulas to make sure they comply. Figure 4-1 shows a simple business calculation that requires parentheses to make sense. The result is based on multiplying units by price per unit, adding an additional purchase amount to that, applying a discount, and finally applying tax.

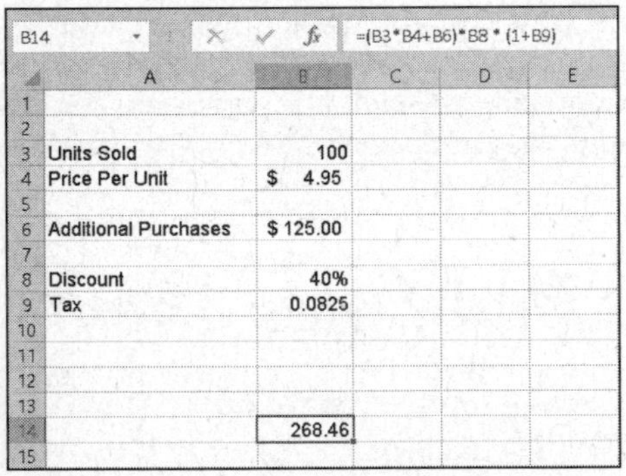

B14		✕ ✓	f_x	=(B3*B4+B6)*B8 * (1+B9)	
	A	B	C	D	E
1					
2					
3	Units Sold	100			
4	Price Per Unit	$ 4.95			
5					
6	Additional Purchases	$ 125.00			
7					
8	Discount	40%			
9	Tax	0.0825			
10					
11					
12					
13					
14		268.46			
15					

Figure 4-1:
Using parentheses in a formula.

In math terms, here is how the formula works:

(units sold × price per unit + additional purchases) × discount × (1 + tax rate)

The placement of the parentheses is critical to making the formula work. Excel won't sense a problem if any particular parenthesis is in the wrong place as long as there are matching numbers of open and closed parentheses. For example, using the cells and values from Figure 4-1, here are some possibilities of valid formulas that return incorrect answers:

Formula	*Result*
=B3*(B4+B6) * B8 * (1 + B9)	5626.84
=B3*B4+(B6 * B8) * (1 + B9)	549.13
=(B3*B4+B6 * B8) * (1 + B9)	589.96
=(B3*B4+B6) * (B8 * 1 + B9)	299.15

Correct parentheses placement and a firm understanding of mathematical-operator precedence are critical to calculating correct answers. I suggest a brush-up on these basic math concepts if you aren't sure how to construct your formulas. See Chapter 18 for more.

There is a great mnemonic for orders of operation: *P*lease *e*xcuse *m*y *d*ear *A*unt *S*ally. That is meant to help you remember parentheses, exponents, multiplication, division, addition, and subtraction. By the way, I had to excuse my dear Aunt Honey for undercooking the stuffing one year at Thanksgiving. Great meal, and then we all got sick!

What if, during entry, a parenthesis is left out? When you try to complete the entry, Excel pops up a warning and a suggestion. In this example, the first closed parenthesis is purposely left out. Here is the *incorrect* formula: =(B3*B4+B6*B8*(1+B9).

Figure 4-2 shows how Excel catches the error and offers a solution.

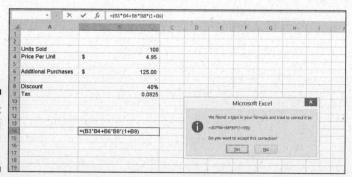

Figure 4-2:
Fixing
mismatched
parentheses.

Don't be hasty! The correction proposed by Excel corrects the mismatched parentheses but does not create the correct formula. Look closely at the following example of a proposed correction by Excel: =(B3*B4+B6*B8*(1+B9)).

But what you really need is this: =(B3*B4+B6)*B8*(1+B9).

Excel simply added the missing parenthesis to the end of the formula. A good idea, but not good enough. If the proposed correction were accepted, a result of $549.13 would be returned in this example. The correct answer is $268.46. In this case, you should reject the proposal and fix the formula yourself.

Do not assume Excel's proposed formula corrections are right for you. Carefully review the proposed correction, and accept or reject it accordingly.

Avoiding circular references

A *circular reference* occurs when a cell refers to itself, whether directly or indirectly. For example, if =100 + A2 is entered in cell A2, a direct circular reference has been created. An indirect circular reference is when the formula in a given cell refers to one or more other cells that in return refer to the original cell. For example, a formula in A1 refers to cell A2, A2 refers to A3, and A3 refers back to A1.

Figure 4-3 shows a worksheet that has a direct circular reference. Cell D10 is meant to sum the values above it but mistakenly includes itself in the sum: =SUM(D4:D10). Excel reports the problem in the message box shown in Figure 4-3.

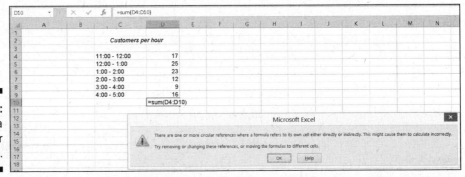

Figure 4-3:
Correcting a
circular
reference.

If Automatic Calculation is turned off, the circular reference is unnoticed until you do a manual calc (by pressing F9) or change the setting to Automatic Calculation.

When the dialog box in Figure 4-3 appears, you have a few choices:

- Clicking OK lets the formula entry complete, but the result is not correct. In fact, you may just end up with a zero.
- Clicking Help takes you to the Help system's Circular Reference topic.

Figure 4-4 shows the Formulas tab of the Excel Options dialog box. Here is where calculation — automatic or manual — is set. Note that the iteration check box is here as well. When this option is set, circular references are allowed. How they calculate values in this case is dependent on the Maximum Iterations and Maximum Change settings.

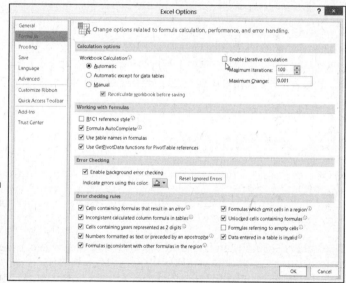

Figure 4-4: Setting calculation and iteration settings.

Checking and applying iterations on the Calculation tab of the Options dialog box enables you to use circular references in your formulas. These references are useful for certain advanced calculations that are beyond the scope of this book. (See Excel Help for more information.)

Excel 2016 has an approach to hunting down circular references. The Formulas tab on the Ribbon has a section named Formula Auditing. In this section is an Error Checking drop-down menu that shows any circular references (see Figure 4-5).

The drop-down menu lists circular references, and clicking one takes you to the listed cell with the circular reference. This enables you to get to circular references easily instead of having to review all your formulas. Hey, that's a time saver!

You may notice that the circular reference error message appears only the first time you enter a circular reference formula. Excel's behavior after that is to place a zero in the cell with the problematic formula. However, you are still notified of the issue by viewing the status bar or by seeing it in the Error Checking drop-down menu, as shown in Figure 4-5.

Figure 4-5: Hunting down circular references.

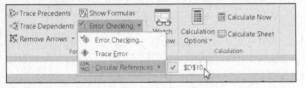

Mending broken links

Formulas can reference external workbooks. As an example, a formula could be written like this: `='C:\Inventory\[Inventory.xlsx]Engine Parts'!$D$8`. The formula uses the value in the external workbook `Inventory.xlsx`. What if the workbook is not found?

When a formula references an unfound workbook, a dialog box opens to let you navigate to an appropriate workbook elsewhere. Figure 4-6 shows that the dialog box has opened after the `Inventory.xslx` file is referenced. This file could not be found, and Excel is prompting you to find it. Excel is so helpful!

The Edit Links dialog box gives you other options for handling broken links. Click the Data tab on the Ribbon, and click Edit Links in the Connections section. Doing this opens the Edit Links dialog box, shown in Figure 4-7.

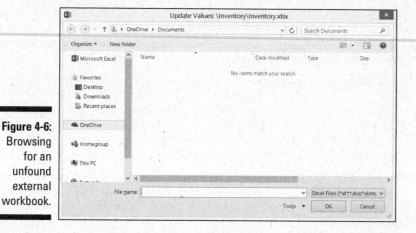

Figure 4-6:
Browsing
for an
unfound
external
workbook.

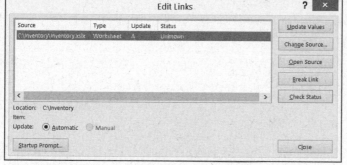

Figure 4-7:
Using the
Edit Links
dialog box
to correct
external
reference
problems.

The buttons along the right side of the dialog box work like this:

- **Update Values:** When external workbooks are where they should be, this action gets the values from the external workbooks, and the cells with those formulas are recalculated. When there are broken links, an Open File dialog box appears, letting you browse to a file from which to get the values. This file does not necessarily have to be the missing workbook; it could be another workbook. A point to be aware of is that using Update Values in this manner does not fix the link. It helps you get values but does not change the way formulas are written. Instead, use the Change Source option, listed next.

- **Change Source:** This option displays an Open File dialog box that lets you select an external workbook to use. Selecting a workbook in this dialog box actually alters the formula that references the external workbook. So this is the best course to take to permanently fix a broken link.

✔ **Open Source:** In the case of broken links, this action does nothing because the source (the external workbook) cannot be found. An error message confirms this. In the case of working links, this action opens the workbook referenced in the link.

✔ **Break Link:** This action converts formulas that contain external links to the calculated values. In other words, the cells that contain formulas with external links are replaced with a value; the formulas are removed. Make sure this is what you want to do. You cannot undo this action, and it can be a serious mistake if you do it unintentionally. Excel displays a warning dialog box, shown in Figure 4-8.

✔ **Check Status:** This action provides the status of links. A number of values are possible (OK, Unknown, Error: Source not found, Error: Worksheet not found, and so on). In the Edit Links dialog box (refer to Figure 4-7), Status is a column in the middle of the dialog box. Each link receives its own status.

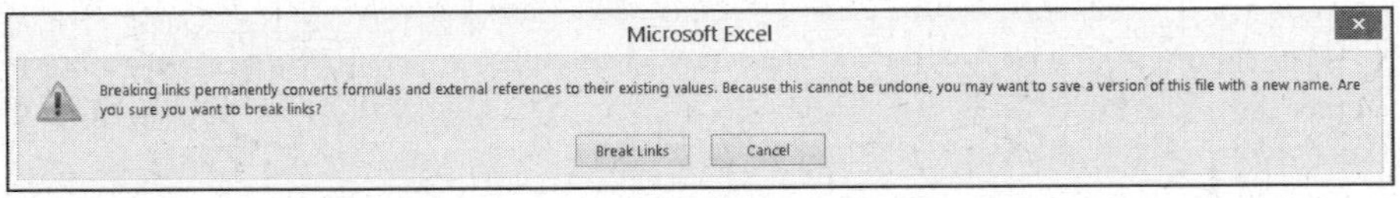

Figure 4-8: Confirming that you mean to break links.

The Edit Links dialog box, shown in Figure 4-7, also has a Startup Prompt button in the bottom-left corner. Clicking this button lets you choose what the workbook should do when it's opened and there are missing external links. The choices are

✔ Let users choose whether to display the alert.

✔ Don't display the alert, and don't update automatic links.

✔ Don't display the alert, and update links.

Using the Formula Error Checker

Some errors are immediately apparent, such as mismatched parentheses explained earlier. Other types of entries are not blatant errors, but *resemble* errors. In this case, Excel alerts you to the possible problem and lets you choose how to handle it.

Figure 4-9 shows a few numbers and a sum at the bottom. The formula in cell B10 is =SUM(B4:B9). There is nothing wrong here — no possible error yet.

B10	▾	× ✓ fx	=SUM(B4:B9)

	A	B	C
1	Employee	Units Sold	
2			
3			
4	Cindy	2200	
5	Juan	2300	
6	Tara	2450	
7	Bill	2400	
8	Gary	2300	
9	Sally	2500	
10	TOTAL SALES	14150	
11			

Figure 4-9: Calculating a sum with no possible error.

Note that in Figure 4-9, the headings row is not adjacent to the rows of information. Rows 2 and 3 are between the headings and the data. This is not unusual, because it leads to a clean-looking report.

However, watch what happens if a value is accidentally entered in the area between the headings and the data. The formula in cell B10 calculates values starting in Row 4. When a value is entered in cell B3, Excel alerts you that there *may* be an error. You can see this in Figure 4-10. A small triangle is now visible in the upper-left corner of cell B10 — the cell with the formula.

B3	▾	× ✓ fx	2450

	A	B	C
1	Employee	Units Sold	
2			
3		2450	
4	Cindy	2200	
5	Juan	2300	
6	Tara	2450	
7	Bill	2400	
8	Gary	2300	
9	Sally	2500	
10	TOTAL SALES	14150	
11			

Figure 4-10: Excel senses a possible error.

Clicking cell B10 and moving the pointer over the triangle causes a small symbol with an exclamation point to appear. Clicking the symbol displays a list of choices, shown in Figure 4-11.

An error is represented by a triangle in the upper-left corner of a cell. This is different from a smart tag, which appears as a triangle in the lower-right corner of a cell. Smart tags lead to helpful options based on the contents of the cell. See the Excel Help system for more information on smart tags.

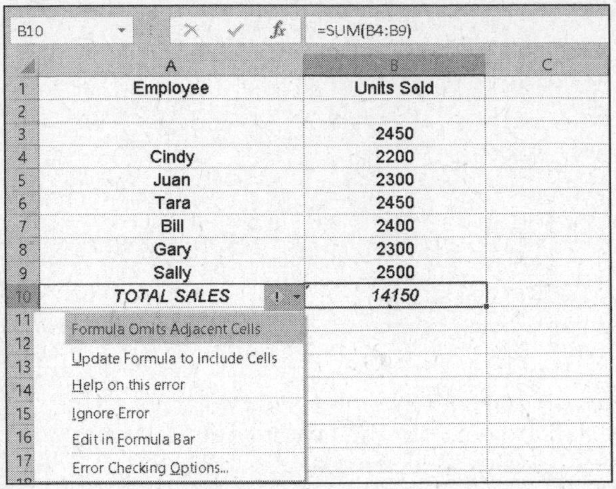

Figure 4-11:
Deciding
what to do
with the
possible
error.

The first item in the list is just a statement of the problem. In this example, the statement is Formula Omits Adjacent Cells. Sure enough, it does just that! But is it an error? Did you mean to enter the extra value in cell B3? Perhaps it has some other meaning or use.

The other items in the list give you options:

- **Update Formula to Include Cells:** Automatically changes the formula to include the extra cell in this example. So the formula in cell B10 changes from =SUM(B4:B9) to =SUM(B3:B9). Of course, the calculated sum changes as well.

- **Help on This Error:** Steers you to Excel's Help system.

- **Ignore Error:** Closes the list and returns you to the worksheet. The triangle is removed from the cell in question. You've told Excel that you know what you're doing, and you want Excel to butt out. Good job!

- **Edit in Formula Bar:** Places the cursor in the Formula Bar so you can easily edit the formula.

- **Error Checking Options:** Displays the Formulas tab of the Excel Options dialog box (shown in Figure 4-12). On this tab, you set options for how Excel handles errors.

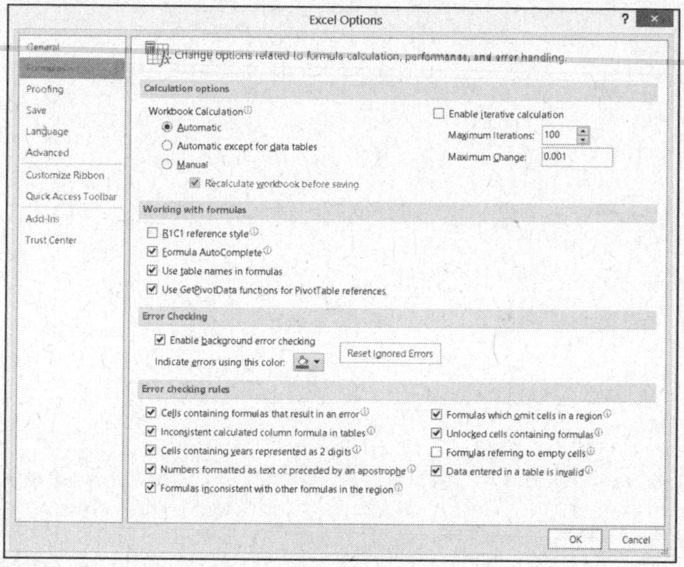

Figure 4-12:
Setting
error-
handling
options.

Auditing Formulas

With Excel, you can create some fairly complex solutions. A cell can contain a formula that uses values from multitudes of other cells and ranges. Working through long, complex formulas to track down problems can be quite tedious. The good news is that Excel has a way to help!

Formulas may contain precedents and may serve as dependents to other formulas:

- *Precedents* are cells or ranges that affect the active cell's value.
- *Dependents* are cells or ranges affected by the active cell.

It's all relative! A cell often serves as both a precedent and a dependent. Figure 4-13 shows a simple worksheet with some values and some calculations. Cell B9 contains the formula =SUM(B3:B8). Cell F9 contains the formula =SUM(F3:F8). Cell B18 contains the formula =B9-F9.

- Cells B3:B8 are precedents of B9, but at the same time, cell B9 is dependent on all the cells in B3:B8.
- Cells F3:F8 are precedents of F9, but at the same time, cell F9 is dependent on all the cells in F3:F8.
- Cells B9 and F9 are precedents of B18, but at the same time, cell B18 is dependent on cells B9 and F9.

B18	▼	×	✓	*fx*	=B9-F9		
▲	A		B	C	D	E	F
1	Employee		Units Sold			Employee	Units Returned
2							
3	Cindy		2200			Cindy	0
4	Juan		2300			Juan	100
5	Tara		2450			Tara	350
6	Bill		2400			Bill	50
7	Gary		2300			Gary	0
8	Sally		2500			Sally	0
9	TOTAL SALES		14150			TOTAL RETURNS	500
10							
11							
12							
13							
14							
15							
16							
17							
18	TOTAL NET UNITS		13650				

Figure 4-13:
Under-
standing
precedents
and
dependents.

To help you follow and fix formulas, Excel provides formula auditing tools.
The Formula Auditing section of the Formulas tab on the Ribbon has three
buttons that let you use formula auditing. Figure 4-14 shows the worksheet
from Figure 4-13 with visible precedent and dependent lines. The methods for
displaying these lines are shown on the Ribbon.

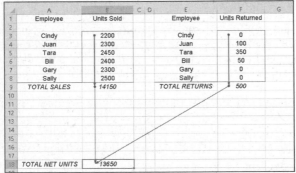

▲	A	B	C	D	E	F	G
1	Employee	Units Sold			Employee	Units Returned	
2							
3	Cindy	2200			Cindy	0	
4	Juan	2300			Juan	100	
5	Tara	2450			Tara	350	
6	Bill	2400			Bill	50	
7	Gary	2300			Gary	0	
8	Sally	2500			Sally	0	
9	TOTAL SALES	14150			TOTAL RETURNS	500	
10							
11							
12							
13							
14							
15							
16							
17							
18	TOTAL NET UNITS	13650					

Figure 4-14:
Tracing
formulas.

Precedent and dependent lines are always inserted from or to the active cell.
From the active cell:

   ✔ To see what other cells are referenced in the active cell's formula, click
     the Trace Precedents button.

   ✔ To see which other cells contain a reference to the active cell, click the
     Trace Dependents button.

The Remove Arrows drop-down menu has three choices:

- ✔ Remove Arrows
- ✔ Remove Precedent Arrows
- ✔ Remove Dependent Arrows

In Figure 4-14, cells B9 and F9 have arrows that originate in the cells above. This shows the flow of precedents into the given cells. The arrow head rests in the cell that has the formula that contains the references of the precedents.

On the other hand, cells B9 and F9 themselves then have lines coming from them and ending as arrow heads in cell B18. Therefore, B9 and F9 serve as precedents to cell B18. Put another way, cell B18 is dependent on cells B9 and F9.

Double-clicking a tracer arrow activates the cell on one end of the line. Double-clicking again activates the cell on the other end.

Tracing precedents and dependents can lead to some interesting conclusions about a worksheet. Complex formulas can be difficult to follow, but by displaying tracer arrows, you can better see what is going on. Figure 4-15 shows a piece of a worksheet used in a comprehensive financial solution. The active cell, H2, has a complex formula in it, as you can see by looking at the Formula Bar. The tracer arrows show that numerous precedents are feeding the formula in the active cell.

Figure 4-15: Examining the components of a complex formula.

H2			f_x	=E3+E4+E14 + F18				
	A	B	C	D	E	F	G	H	I
1								Summary by Season	
2		sales	commision	vendor fees	total paid out			$ 52,661.12	Winter
3	Jan	$ 14,050.00	$ 210.75	$ 449.60	$ 14,710.35			$ 66,329.50	Spring
4	Feb	$ 16,252.00	$ 243.78	$ 520.06	$ 17,015.84			$ 66,901.13	Summer
5	Mar	$ 18,667.00	$ 280.01	$ 597.34	$ 19,544.35			$ 66,169.07	Autumn
6	Apr	$ 22,615.00	$ 339.23	$ 723.68	$ 23,677.91				
7	May	$ 20,303.00	$ 304.55	$ 649.70	$ 21,257.24				
8	Jun	$ 18,563.00	$ 278.45	$ 594.02	$ 19,435.46				
9	Jul	$ 19,259.00	$ 288.89	$ 616.29	$ 20,164.17				
10	Aug	$ 24,500.00	$ 367.50	$ 784.00	$ 25,651.50				
11	Sep	$ 21,684.00	$ 325.26	$ 693.89	$ 22,703.15				
12	Oct	$ 19,981.00	$ 299.72	$ 639.39	$ 20,920.11				
13	Nov	$ 19,528.00	$ 292.92	$ 624.90	$ 20,445.82				
14	Dec	$ 18,658.00	$ 279.87	$ 597.06	$ 19,534.93				
15	TOTALS	$ 234,060.00	$ 3,510.90	$ 7,489.92					
16									
17									
18				Donations:	Winter	$	1,400.00		
19					Spring	$	1,850.00		
20					Summer	$	1,650.00		
21					Autumn	$	2,100.00		

When a cell references a cell on a different worksheet, an icon that looks like a worksheet appears at the end of the precedent line. This serves as a visual clue that the formula is composed of values from more than the current worksheet.

The tracer arrows make it easy to see the values that are feeding the formula and, therefore, make it easier to look for the source of a problem. For example, cell H2 may be returning a negative number as an answer. The formula adds certain values. Positive numbers added with a negative number may return a negative number as the result of the calculation. Therefore, just looking for a negative number among the values at the end of the tracer arrows may help identify the problem, perhaps within just a few seconds!

Watching the Watch Window

The Watch Window lets you watch the calculated results of a formula but without the limitation of having the cell be in the viewing area of Excel. This feature is helpful when you're working on correcting formulas that use precedents that are scattered about the worksheet or workbook.

First, to set up a watch, follow these steps:

1. **Click the Watch Window button on the Formulas tab of the Ribbon.**
2. **In the Watch Window, click the Add Watch button.**

   The Add Watch dialog box opens.
3. **Use the RefEdit control (the square button to the right of the entry box) to specify the cell(s), or type in the cell address or range.**
4. **Click the Add button in the Add Watch dialog box to complete setting up the watch.**

Figure 4-16 shows the Watch Window with a watch already in place. Cell C6 of the Costs worksheet is being watched. The formula uses precedents from both the Orders and Shipping worksheets. The Watch Window sits on top of the workbook and stays visible regardless of which worksheet is active. This means, for example, that you could try different values on the Orders worksheet and see the result in the calculation in Costs!C6, but without having to bounce around the worksheets to see how new values alter the calculated result.

Figure 4-16:
Using the
Watch
Window to
keep an eye
on a
formula's
result.

The Watch Window also lets you delete a watch. That's a good thing; otherwise, you would end up with a bunch of watches you no longer need! To delete a watch, perform these steps:

1. **Select a watch from the list of watches in the Watch Window.**
2. **Click the Delete Watch button.**

Evaluating and Checking Errors

The Evaluate Formula dialog box walks you through the sequential steps used in calculating a result from a formula. These steps are useful for tracking down errors in formulas that are long or have precedents. For example, the formula `=IF(MAX(Orders!B2:B29)>200,MAX(Orders!B2:B29)*Shipping!C22,Shipping!C24)` refers to different worksheets. Using the Evaluate Formula dialog box makes it easy to see how Excel works out this formula. The step-by-step approach lets you see what is done at each step.

Figure 4-17 shows the Evaluate Formula dialog box at the start of evaluating the formula. To display the Evaluate Formula dialog box, simply click the Evaluate Formula button in the Formula Auditing section of the Formulas tab of the Ribbon. With each successive click of the Evaluate button, the Evaluation box displays the interim results. The Step In and Step Out buttons are enabled during the steps that work on the precedents.

The Evaluate Formula dialog box is great for really seeing how each little step feeds into the final calculated result. Using this dialog box lets you pinpoint exactly where a complex formula has gone sour.

A similar error-hunting tool is the Error Checking dialog box. (Excel really wants to help you!) Figure 4-18 shows the dialog box.

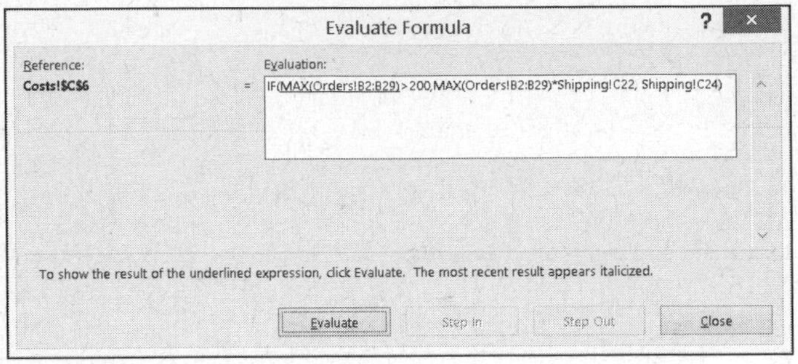

Evaluate Formula

Reference:
Costs!$C$6

Evaluation:
= IF(MAX(Orders!B2:B29)>200,MAX(Orders!B2:B29)*Shipping!C22, Shipping!C24)

To show the result of the underlined expression, click Evaluate. The most recent result appears italicized.

Evaluate | Step In | Step Out | Close

Figure 4-17:
Evaluating a
formula.

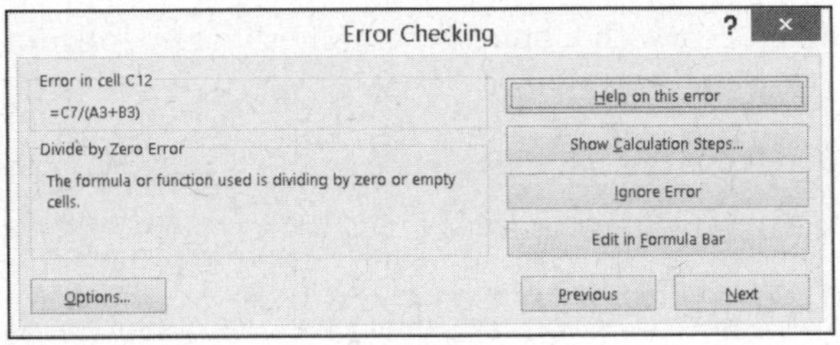

Error Checking

Error in cell C12

=C7/(A3+B3)

Divide by Zero Error

The formula or function used is dividing by zero or empty cells.

Help on this error

Show Calculation Steps...

Ignore Error

Edit in Formula Bar

Options... | Previous | Next

Figure 4-18:
Checking
the cause of
an error.

Display the Error Checking dialog box by choosing Error Checking from the Error Checking drop-down menu on the Ribbon (on the Formulas tab, of course).

The dialog box has a handful of buttons that let you analyze the error and make decisions about it:

✔ **Help on This Error** starts the Excel Help system.

✔ **Show Calculation Steps** opens the Evaluate Formula dialog box.

✔ **Ignore Error** ensures that Excel no longer cares about the error. The cell may still display an error symbol, but Excel does not give a hoot, and you probably won't either, because you clicked the button.

✔ **Edit in Formula Bar** places the cursor in the Formula Bar, making it easy for you to edit the formula.

✔ **Options** opens the Excel Options dialog box.

✔ **Previous and Next** cycle through the multiple errors on the worksheet, assuming that there is more than one error.

The Error Checking drop-down menu hosts the Trace Error command. Only precedents are pointed out by the tracer lines. This makes it easy to see the cells that feed into a cell that has an error.

Making an Error Behave the Way You Want

Excel has a neat function: IfError. Don't confuse it with IsError, which is similar but not as slick. Figure 4-19 shows how IfError one-ups IsError. In the figure, F7 has the dreaded Divide by Zero error. It's not a pretty thing to see, and I am sure the boss would appreciate a cleaner visual to work with.

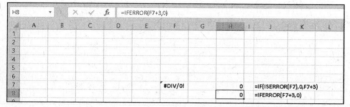

Figure 4-19: Two ways to prevent an error from being seen.

Cell H7 has the tried-and-true way to make the error *not* look like an error. Using the IsError function nested inside an If function takes care of the error's appearance, as shown in cell H7 (which refers to cell F7). Cell H8 achieves the same result with the IfError function. Cells J7 and J8, respectively, show the formulas that are in cells H7 and H8.

- In cell H7 is `=IF(ISERROR(F7),0,F7+3)`.
- In cell H8 is `=IFERROR(F7+3,0)`.

The main distinction is that IfError, as a single function, does what used to take two functions. I don't know how many times the "keep it simple" approach has been bantered around, but what the heck — aren't we all for making our work easier? With IfError, the first argument is being tested. If the test makes sense, Excel goes with it. Otherwise, the second argument is used.

IfError can return a message. For example, consider this: `=IFERROR(F7+3, "Somebody Goofed!")`.

Part II
Doing the Math

F16		▼	:	✕	✓	*fx*	=SUM(C6:C12,F6:F12,I6:I12)		

◢ A	B	C	D	E	F	G	H	I
1	**Trip Expenses**							
2								
3	Expenses for John			Expenses for Mary			Expenses for Bob	
4	Item	Amount		Item	Amount		Item	Amount
5								
6	Tickets	$ 255.50		Tickets	$ 176.88		Tickets	$ 255.50
7	Hotel	$ 315.80		Hotel	$ 315.80		Hotel	$ 315.80
8	Meals	$ 115.42		Meals	$ 122.65		Meals	$ 101.45
9	Phone Calls	$ 18.35		Phone Calls	$ 16.70		Phone Calls	$ 17.35
10	Cab Fare	$ 27.00		Cab Fare	$ 26.50		Cab Fare	$ 28.25
11	Entertainment	$ 62.00		Entertainment	$ 80.00		Entertainment	$ 94.00
12	Gifts	$ 24.45		Gifts	$ 20.95		Gifts	$ -
13								
14								
15								
16				TOTAL TRIP EXPENSES:	$ 2,390.35			
17								
18								

Get the skinny on an important business need in the article "Using Excel to Calculate Percent Change" at www.dummies.com/extras/excelformulasfunctions.

In this part . . .

- ✔ Get a handle on your loans.
- ✔ Find out how to appreciate depreciation.
- ✔ Review math basics.
- ✔ Get math-savvy with some really cool functions.

Chapter 5

Calculating Loan Payments and Interest Rates

- -

In This Chapter

▶ Formatting monetary values

▶ Working with loan calculations

- -

A penny saved is a penny earned. A penny by itself is not much. But add a little savings here and there over the life of a loan, and the sum could be significant! Just think of what you can do with the extra money — extend a vacation, give it to charity, or save it for a rainy day.

Taking out a car loan, a mortgage, or another type of loan involves planning how you want to manage the loan payments. In the simplest terms, all you may need to know is the amount of your monthly payment. But knowing the components of a loan and being able to compare one loan with another can help you manage your financial resources in your own best interest.

Consider an auto loan, one of the most common loan types. The factors involved include the cost of the vehicle, the down payment, the length of the loan, and the interest rate. Excel can help you see how all these factors affect your bottom line, letting you make the best decision (I would love to get a Ferrari, but a Hyundai will have to do).

You can use the financial functions in Excel to crunch the numbers for your loans. You supply these functions the relevant numbers: the principal amount, the interest rate, the *period* (how often you make a payment), and the length of the loan. Then the functions return an answer, such as your payment amount. In this chapter, I show you how to use these functions to turn your finance figures into meaningful results.

The *principal* is the amount being borrowed. The *interest rate* is the annual percentage that the lender charges for lending the money. Your total payments equal the principal plus the sum of all interest charges.

Understanding How Excel Handles Money

Excel is a lot more than a simple adding machine. It has great tools for working with money values and a number of ways of presenting the amounts. For example, Excel makes it easy for you to make sure that your financial amounts are displayed with two decimal points. You can even work with different currencies from around the world.

Going with the cash flow

Excel works with money on a cash-flow basis. In other words, money amounts are treated either as a cash flow *in* (money you receive) or a cash flow *out* (money you pay out). Yes, there always seem to be too many of the latter and not enough of the former — but hey, you can't blame Excel for that!

Excel represents cash flows *in* as positive numbers and cash flows *out* as negative numbers. For example, when you calculate the payments on a loan, the situation is as follows:

- The amount of the loan is entered as a positive value, because this is the money you'll receive from the bank or whoever is giving you the loan.

- The monthly payment that Excel calculates is a negative value, because this is money that you'll be paying out.

Formatting for currency

One of Excel's shining strengths is accepting, manipulating, and reporting on monetary data. As such, Excel provides robust formatting for numeric data, including the ability to control the placement of commas and decimals, and even how to format negative values.

People are used to seeing money amounts formatted with a currency symbol and a certain number of decimal places. In the United States and Canada, that is the dollar sign and two decimal places. Let's face it — $199.95 looks like money, but 199.950 does not. Excel makes formatting cells to display money amounts as easy as clicking a button. To format amounts as dollars, follow these steps:

1. **Select the cell or cells you want to format.**

2. **Click the Dollar ($) button on the Ribbon's Home tab, in the Number group.**

This technique assigns Excel's default Accounting format to the selected cells. In the United States, the default currency format follows:

✔ A dollar sign, aligned to the left of the cell

✔ Two decimal places

✔ Negative numbers enclosed in parentheses

The default format depends on your locale, which is a setting of the operating system. If you're in Italy, for example, the locale should be set so that the default currency format is the euro (€).

But suppose that you don't want the default currency formatting. Perhaps you're in the United States and are working on a spreadsheet for the London office. You can specify the currency symbol, the number of decimal places, and how negative values are shown by following these steps:

1. **Select the cell or cells you want to format.**

2. **Right-click the cell(s) and choose Format Cells from the drop-down menu.**

3. **In the Format Cells dialog box, select the Number tab, shown in Figure 5-1.**

4. **Click Currency in the Category list.**

5. **Select the desired number of decimal places with the Decimal Places spinner control.**

6. **Select the desired currency symbol from the Symbol drop-down menu.**

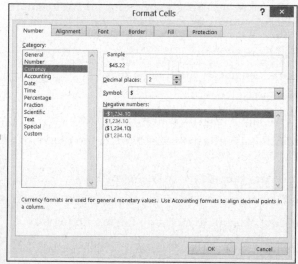

Figure 5-1: Using the Format Cells dialog box to control numeric display.

7. **Select the desired format for negative numbers in the Negative Numbers list.**

8. **Click OK to apply the formatting.**

The Currency and Accounting formats are similar except for a couple of key points. Currency provides choices for displaying negative values; Accounting uses one fixed display with parentheses. Currency places the currency symbol next to the number; Accounting places the currency symbol at the left of the cell.

Choosing separators

When numbers are formatted as currency, two separator symbols are typically used — one to separate thousands and the other to separate the decimal part of the value. In the United States, commas are used for thousands and the period for the decimal, as follows:

$12,345.67

Other countries have different ways of doing this. In many European countries, for example, the period is used to separate thousands, and the comma is used for the decimal. In addition, the currency symbol is often at the end of the number. An amount in euros, for example, may be formatted as follows:

12.345,67€

In almost all situations, the operating system's locale settings result in the automatic use of the proper separators. If you need to change the separators from the defaults, do so in the Regional and Language Options section of the Windows Control Panel. ***Note:*** These instructions are for computers running the Windows operating system.

1. **Choose Start ⇨ Control Panel.**

2. **Click the Clock, Language, and Region link.**

3. **Click the Region link.**

   The Region dialog box opens, as shown in Figure 5-2.

4. **Click the Additional Settings button to open the Customize Format dialog box.**

5. **Click the Currency tab, as shown in Figure 5-3.**

6. **Click OK or Cancel to close the Customize Format dialog box.**

7. **Click OK or Cancel again to close the Region dialog box.**

You can change settings for numbers, currency, dates, and time in the Customize Format dialog box.

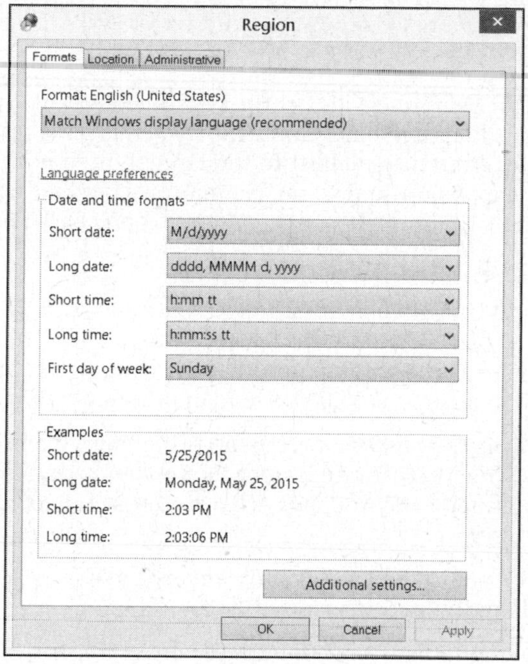

Figure 5-2:
Viewing
regional
settings.

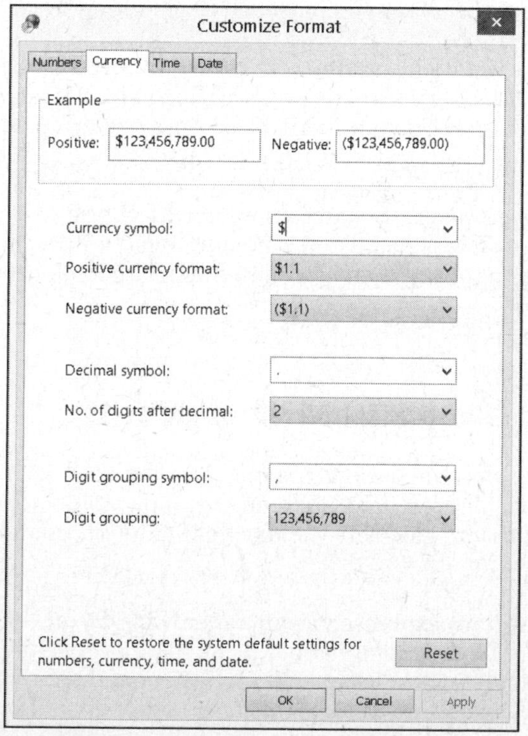

Figure 5-3:
Customizing
how
numeric
values are
handled.

Figuring Loan Calculations

Loans are part of almost everyone's life. At the personal level, you may need to deal with car loans, education loans, and a mortgage. From a business perspective, companies from the smallest to the largest often use loans to fund new equipment, expansion, and so on. No matter what kind of loan you need, Excel has the tools that permit you to evaluate loans and calculate specific details.

Most loans have the following five factors:

- **Loan principal:** This is the amount you're borrowing. For example, if you're interested in a loan for $5,000, the loan principal *is* $5,000.
- **Interest rate:** This is the cost to borrow the principal. This is how lenders make money. The interest rate is a fee, so to speak, that a borrower pays to a lender. Usually, but not always, the interest rate is expressed as a percent per year.
- **Payment period:** Loans are usually paid back by paying a periodic amount. Most often, the period is monthly.
- **Duration of the loan:** This is the count of payment periods. For example, a loan may have 36 monthly payments.
- **Payment:** This is the amount you pay each payment period.

Each of these factors is related to all the others. If you borrow more, your monthly payments will be higher; that's no surprise. If you get a low interest rate, you may be able to pay off your loan in less time; that may be something to consider!

The functions used to calculate loan factors work with the same group of inputs, namely the five factors just listed. The functions typically accept three or four inputs as data and then calculate the desired value, kind of like the way algebra works.

Calculating the payment amount

The PMT function tells you the periodic payment amount for your loan. If you know the principal, interest rate, and number of payments for a loan, you can use the PMT function to calculate the payment amount. But first, a word about interest rates.

Most loan interest rates are expressed as an annual rate. However, Excel needs the interest rate per payment *period* to calculate properly. For example, if you're calculating for a loan with monthly payments, you need the monthly interest rate. You can easily get this number by dividing the annual interest rate by 12, the number of months in a year. To calculate a loan payment, follow these steps:

1. **Enter the loan principal, annual interest rate, and number of payment periods in separate cells of the worksheet.**

   You can add labels to adjacent cells to identify the values, if desired.

2. **Position the cursor in the cell where you want the results to display.**

3. **Type =PMT(to begin the function entry.**

   A small pop-up menu shows the arguments used in the function.

4. **Click the cell where you entered the interest rate, or just enter the cell address.**

5. **Type /12 to divide the annual interest rate to get the monthly interest rate.**

6. **Type a comma (,).**

7. **Click the cell where you entered the number of payments, or enter the cell address.**

8. **Type a comma (,).**

9. **Click the cell where you entered the principal amount, or enter the cell address.**

10. **Type a), and press Enter.**

Watch those percentages! Remember that a percent is really one one-hundredth, so 5 percent is the numerical value 0.05. You can format values to display as percentages in Excel, but you must enter the proper value.

Figure 5-4 shows how I set up a worksheet with values and returned the periodic payment amount for a loan. The amount is expressed as a negative number because payments are cash flow out. For example, you may be considering taking out a loan from the bank for some house additions. Using real numbers, the loan may be structured like this:

- A loan amount of $15,000 (the principal)
- An annual interest rate of 5 percent
- A monthly payment period
- A payment period of 24 payments

This summarizes four of the key parameters. The PMT function figures out the fifth: the periodic payment, which is the amount you have to shell out each month.

Figure 5-4:
The PMT
function
calculates
the loan
payment
amount.

B7		✕ ✓ fx	=PMT(B2/12,B3,B1)		
	A	B	C	D
1	Principal	15000		
2	Annual Interest Rate	0.05		
3	Number of Periods	24		
4				
5				
6				
7	Monthly Payment	($658.07)		

Although the PMT function returns the constant periodic payback amount for a loan, note that each payment actually consists of two portions. One portion goes toward reducing the principal, and the other portion is the interest payment. As if this weren't already confusing enough!

You may notice some new terms when using this function: Pv, Fv, and Nper. In financial terminology, *present value* (Pv) refers to the value of a transaction at the present moment. When you're dealing with a loan, for example, the present value is the amount you receive from the loan — in other words, the principal. The term *future value* (Fv) refers to the value of a transaction at some point in the future, such as the amount you'll accumulate by saving $50 a month for five years. *Nper* stands for the number of payment periods in the loan.

Calculating interest payments

The IPMT function tells you the interest payment for a given period. In each payment period during a typical loan, the payment consists of a portion set to reduce the principal of the loan, with the other portion of the payment being the interest on the principal. The amount of interest varies payment by payment. In a typical loan, the portion of the payment that is interest is highest in the first period and is reduced in each successive period.

The IPMT function takes four inputs: the principal, the interest rate, the number of payments for the loan, and the number of the payment you're interested in. For example, a loan may have 24 payments, and you're interested in how much interest is included in the 12th payment. For some types of loans, the interest is tax deductible, so this information may literally be worth something! Here are the steps to use the IMPT function:

1. **Enter the following information in separate cells in a column of the worksheet:**

   • Loan principal

   • Annual interest rate

- Number of payment periods
- Number of the actual period for which you want to calculate the interest

You can add labels to adjacent cells to identify the values, if desired.

2. **Position the cursor in the cell where you want the results to appear.**

3. **Type =IPMT(to begin the function entry.**

4. **Click the cell where you entered the interest rate, or just enter the cell address.**

5. **Type /12.**

This divides the annual interest rate to get the monthly interest rate.

6. **Type a comma (,).**

7. **Click the cell where you entered the number of the payment to analyze, or just enter the cell address.**

8. **Type a comma (,).**

9. **Click the cell where you entered the number of payments, or just enter the cell address.**

10. **Type a comma (,).**

11. **Click the cell where you entered the principal amount, or just enter the cell address.**

12. **Type a), and press Enter.**

The IPMT function returns the interest portion of the amount of the specified payment. This amount is smaller than the full periodic payment amount. How much smaller depends on which sequential payment is being examined. The remainder of the payment — the part that is not interest — goes to reduce the principal.

You can use two optional arguments with IPMT:

✔ **Future Value:** This is the amount you want the loan to be worth at the end of its life. The default is 0.

✔ **Type:** This tells the function whether payments are applied at the end of the period or the beginning of the period. A value of 0 indicates the end of the period. A value of 1 indicates the beginning of the period. The default is 0.

These optional arguments, when used, become the fifth and sixth arguments, respectively.

Calculating payments toward principal

The PPMT function tells you the payment on principal for a given period. In each payment period during a typical loan, the payment consists of a portion that goes toward reducing the principal of the loan and another portion that is interest. With the PPMT function, you can find out the amount that reduces the principal.

The ratio of the interest portion to the payment on principal portion varies payment by payment. In a typical loan, the portion of the payment that is interest is highest in the first period and is reduced in each successive period. Turning that around, the last payment is almost all toward paying down the principal.

The PPMT function takes four inputs: the principal, the interest rate, the number of payments for the loan, and the number of the payment in question. For example, a loan may have 36 payments, and you're interested in how much principal is included in just the last payment. Here are the steps to use this function:

1. **Enter the loan principal, the annual interest rate, the number of payment periods, and the number of the actual period for which the interest is to be calculated in separate cells within the worksheet.**

   You can add labels to adjacent cells to identify the values, if you want.

2. **Position the cursor in the cell where you want the results to appear.**

3. **Type =PPMT(to begin the function entry.**

4. **Click the cell where you entered the interest rate, or just enter the cell address.**

5. **Type /12 to divide the annual interest rate to get the monthly interest rate.**

6. **Type a comma (,).**

7. **Click the cell where you entered the number of the payment to analyze, or just enter the cell address.**

8. **Type a comma (,).**

9. **Click the cell where you entered the number of payments, or just enter the cell address.**

10. **Type a comma (,).**

11. **Click the cell where you entered the principal amount, or just enter the cell address.**

12. **Type a), and press Enter.**

The PPMT function returns the amount of the payment that reduces the principal. This amount is smaller than the full periodic payment amount. How much smaller depends on which sequential payment is being examined. The remainder of the payment, of course, is the interest charge.

The PMT function tells how much each payment is. The IPMT function tells you the interest portion. The PPMT tells you the principal function. For any given payment period, the amounts returned by IPMT and PPMT should equal the amount returned by PMT.

You can use two optional arguments with PPMT:

- **Future Value:** This is the amount you want the loan to be worth at the end of its life. The default is 0.

- **Type:** This tells the function whether payments are applied at the end of the period or the beginning of the period. A value of 0 indicates the end of the period. A value of 1 indicates the beginning of the period. The default is 0.

These optional arguments, when used, become the fifth and sixth arguments, respectively.

Calculating the number of payments

The NPER function tells you how many payments are necessary to pay off a loan. This is useful when you know how much you can afford to pay per month and need to know how long it will take to pay off the loan. The inputs for this function are the principal, the interest rate, and the periodic payment amount.

Here's how to use the NPER function:

1. **Enter the following in separate cells on your worksheet:**
   - Loan principal
   - Annual interest rate
   - Periodic payment amount (the amount you can afford to pay)

   Enter the periodic payment amount as a negative number because payments are cash flow out. You can add labels to adjacent cells to identify the values, if you want.

2. **Position the cursor in the cell where you want the results to display.**

3. **Type =NPER(to begin the function entry.**

4. **Click the cell where you entered the interest rate, or just enter the cell address.**

5. Type **/12 to divide the annual interest rate to get the monthly interest rate.**

6. Type **a comma (,).**

7. Click **the cell where you entered the periodic payment amount, or just enter the cell address.**

8. Type **a comma (,).**

9. Click **the cell where you entered the principal amount, or just enter the cell address.**

10. Type **a), and press Enter.**

Figure 5-5 shows how I set up a worksheet with values and used the NPER function to find out how many payments are necessary to pay off a loan. In this example, I assume you can afford to pay $200 per month for a loan. The amount you need is $4,000, and you're able to get a 6 percent interest rate.

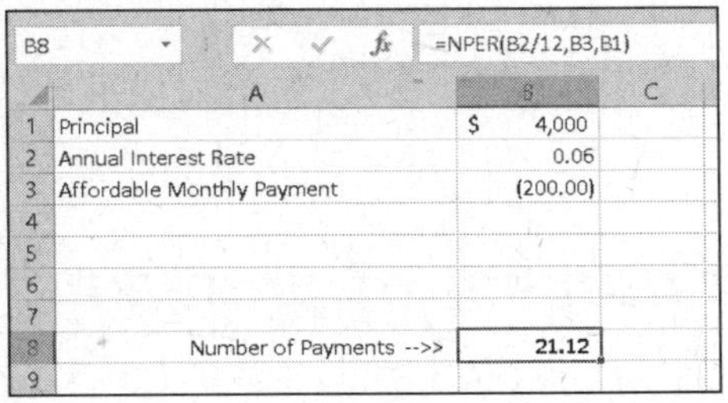

Figure 5-5:
The NPER function calculates the number of payments for a loan.

With this set of assumptions, the NPER function returns a value of 21.12 months to pay off the loan. I don't think anyone will mind if you round that off to 21 months. Knowing you'll pay off the loan in less than two years may very well allow you to plan ahead for some other activity at that time. Did someone say "Las Vegas"?

You can use two optional arguments with NPER:

- **Future Value:** This is the amount you want the loan to be worth at the end of its life. The default is 0.

- **Type:** This tells the function whether payments are applied at the end of the period or the beginning of the period. A value of 0 indicates the end of the period. A value of 1 indicates the beginning of the period. The default is 0.

These optional arguments, when used, become the fifth and sixth arguments, respectively.

Calculating the number of payments with PDURATION

This function is a twist on determining the number of payments. Instead of using a periodic payment amount in the calculation, PDURATION uses the present value of the loan (the borrowed amount) and the future value of the loan (what you will have paid in total when the loan is paid off). This calculation is useful if and when you know just three pieces of information:

- ✔ The loan principal
- ✔ Annual interest rate
- ✔ The amount paid back (the combined principal and interest)

The result PDURATION gives you is the number of periods based on the previously listed factors.

Here's how to use the PDURATION function:

1. **Enter the following in separate cells of your worksheet:**
    - Loan principal
    - Annual interest rate
    - The expected total amount you will have paid back at the end of the loan

2. **Position the cursor in the cell where you want the results to display.**

3. **Type =PDURATION(to begin the function entry.**

4. **Click the cell where you entered the interest rate, or just enter the cell address.**

5. **Type /12 to divide the annual interest rate to get the monthly interest rate.**

6. **Type a comma (,).**

7. **Click the cell where you entered the principal, or just enter the cell address.**

8. **Type a comma (,).**

9. **Click the cell where you entered the payback amount, or just enter the cell address.**

10. **Type a), and press Enter.**

Figure 5-6 shows how I set up a worksheet with values and used the PDURATION function to find out how many payments are necessary to pay off a loan. In this example, I assume that the amount paid off is $4,400 (includes principal and interest). The amount borrowed is $4,000, and the annual interest rate is 6 percent.

The number of payments is 22.92, so I'll call that 23 payments — just under 2 years.

Figure 5-6:
The PDURATION function calculates the number of payments for a loan.

B8		$\times$ $\checkmark$ fx	=PDURATION(B2/12,B1,B3)	
	A		B	C
1	Principal (Present Value)		$ 4,000	
2	Annual Interest Rate		0.05	
3	Amount Paid by Loan's End Future Value		$ 4,400	
4				
5				
6				
7				
8	Number of Payments -->>		**22.92**	

Calculating the interest rate

The RATE function tells you what the interest rate is on a loan. This function is great for comparing loan offers. Although a loan offer always includes an interest rate, you may want to use Excel to double-check to ensure that some other fees are not included in the payments. Then you can compare different loan scenarios to see which one offers the true lowest interest rate. I don't think anyone wants to pay more than necessary!

Some lenders charge fees as well as an annual interest rate. When these fees are figured in, the *effective interest rate* will be higher than the stated interest rate. You can use the RATE function to determine the effective interest rate for a loan. If it's the same as the stated interest rate, you know no fees are being added.

The inputs for this function are the principal, the number of payments, and the fixed amount of the periodic payment. Here's how to use the RATE function:

1. Enter the following in separate cells of the worksheet:

- Loan principal
- Number of payment periods
- Amount you will pay each month

Enter the monthly payment amount as a negative number because it is cash flow out. You can add labels to adjacent cells to identify the values, if you want.

2. **Position the cursor in the cell where you want the results to appear.**

3. **Type =RATE(to begin the function entry.**

4. **Click the cell where you entered the number of periods, or just enter the cell address.**

5. **Type a comma (,).**

6. **Click the cell where you entered the monthly payment amount, or just enter the cell address.**

7. **Type a comma (,).**

8. **Click the cell where you entered the principal amount, or just enter the cell address.**

9. **Type a), and press Enter.**

The RATE function returns the interest rate *per period*. This number can be misleading. The periodic interest amount may be small enough that it is displayed as 0 percent if the formatting in the cell isn't set to display enough decimal points.

To find out the annual rate, you simply need to take the number returned by RATE and multiply it by 12. To do this, follow these steps:

1. **Position the cursor in the cell where you want the annual interest rate to appear.**

2. **Type a =.**

3. **Click the cell where the RATE function returned the periodic interest rate.**

4. **Type a ×.**

5. **Type 12.**

6. **Press Enter.**

As an example, assume a loan principal of $15,000 with a monthly payment of $650. The loan is to be paid off in 24 months. Figure 5-7 shows a worksheet with these figures. The periodic interest rate is calculated with the RATE function, and the annual rate is calculated by multiplying the periodic interest rate by 12.

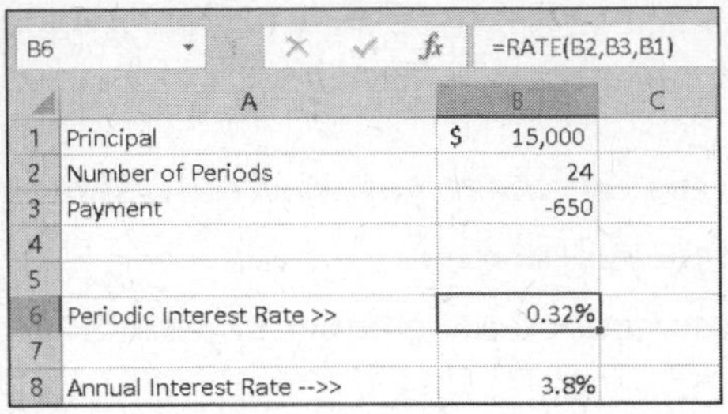
B6 =RATE(B2,B3,B1)

	A	B	C
1	Principal	$ 15,000	
2	Number of Periods	24	
3	Payment	-650	
4			
5			
6	Periodic Interest Rate >>	0.32%	
7			
8	Annual Interest Rate -->>	3.8%	

Figure 5-7: The RATE function calculates the periodic interest rate.

You can use three optional arguments with RATE:

- **Future Value:** This is the amount you want the loan to be worth at the end of its life. The default is 0.
- **Type:** This tells the function whether payments are applied at the end of the period or the beginning of the period. A value of 0 indicates the end of the period. A value of 1 indicates the beginning of the period. The default is 0.
- **Guess:** This estimates what the interest rate should be. It is possible that the function will need this value to determine a result. (See Excel's Help system for further information.) The default value is 0.1 (for 10 percent).

These optional arguments, when used, become the fourth, fifth, and sixth arguments, respectively.

Calculating the principal

The PV function tells you what the principal amount of a loan is when you know the other loan factors, such as the interest rate and the number of payment periods. You can use PV to determine how much you can borrow when you already know how much you can pay each month and how long you can make payments.

The inputs for this function are the interest rate, the number of payment periods, and the monthly payment amount. The interest rate used in the function is the periodic rate, not the annual rate. Here's how to use the PV function:

1. **Enter the following in separate cells of your worksheet:**
   - Annual interest rate
   - Number of payment periods
   - Periodic payment amount

Enter the periodic payment amount as a negative number because payments are cash flow out. You can add labels to adjacent cells to identify the values, if desired.

2. **Position the cursor in the cell where you want the results to appear.**

3. **Type =PV(to begin the function entry.**

4. **Click the cell where you entered the interest rate, or just enter the cell address.**

5. **Type /12 to divide the annual interest rate to get the monthly interest rate.**

6. **Type a comma (,).**

7. **Click the cell where you entered the number of payments, or just enter the cell address.**

8. **Type a comma (,).**

9. **Click the cell where you entered the periodic payment amount, or just enter the cell address.**

10. **Type a), and press Enter.**

As an example, assume a monthly payment amount of $600. The annual interest rate is 5 percent. There are 24 monthly payments. Figure 5-8 shows a worksheet with these figures.

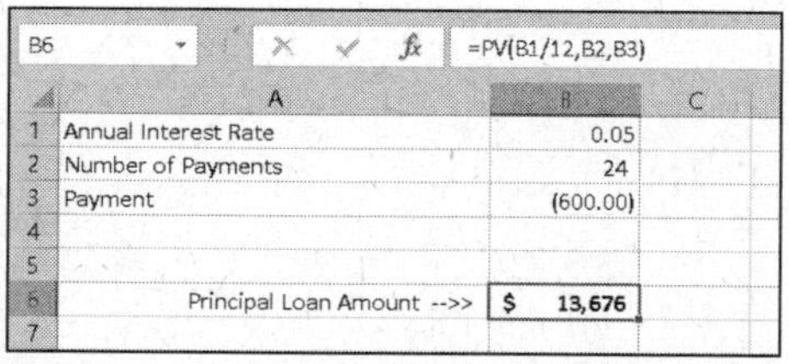

Figure 5-8: The PV function calculates the principal amount of a loan.

With these assumptions, the loan principal is $13,676. Altering any of the parameters causes PV to return a different amount of principal. For example, raising the interest rate to 7.5 percent tells you that you can borrow only

$13,333. Although you may often think of how much you're borrowing, having interest in the interest is just as important!

You can use two optional arguments with PV:

✔ **Future Value:** This is the amount you want the loan to be worth at the end of its life. The default is 0.

✔ **Type:** This value tells the function whether payments are applied at the end of the period or the beginning of the period. A value of 0 indicates the end of the period. A value of 1 indicates the beginning of the period. The default is 0.

These optional arguments, when used, become the fifth and sixth arguments, respectively.

Chapter 6

Appreciating What You'll Get, Depreciating What You've Got

....

In This Chapter

▶ Determining what an investment is worth

▶ Using different depreciation methods

▶ Evaluating business opportunities

....

*M*oney makes the world go 'round, so the saying goes. I have a new one: Excel functions make the money go 'round. Excel has functions that let you figure out what an investment will be worth at a future date. We all know it's a good thing to look for a good interest rate on an investment. With the FV (Future Value) function, you can take this a step further and know how much the investment will be worth down the road.

Have you ever wondered what to do with some extra money? You can put it in the bank, you can pay off a debt, or you can purchase something. Excel helps you figure out the best course of action by using the IRR (Internal Rate of Return) function. The IRR function lets you boil down each option to a single value that you can then use to compare opportunities and select the best one.

For the business set, Excel has a number of functions to help create depreciation schedules. Look no further than the SLN, SYD, DB, and DDB functions for help in this area. Brush up on these, and you can talk shop with your accountant!

SLN is a function used to calculate straight-line deprecation. SYD is a function to calculate sum-of-years'-digits depreciation. DB and DDB are variations of the declining-balance method of depreciation.

Looking into the Future

The FV function tells you what an investment will be worth in the future. The function takes an initial amount of money and also takes into account additional periodic fixed payments. You also specify a rate of return — the interest rate — and the returned value tells you what the investment will be worth after a specified period of time.

For example, you start a savings account with a certain amount, say $1,000. Every month you add $50 to the account. The bank pays an annual interest rate of 5 percent. At the end of two years, what is value of the account?

This is the type of question the FV function answers. The function takes five arguments:

- ✔ **Interest rate:** This argument is the annual interest rate. When entered in the function, it needs to be divided by the number of payments per year — presumably 12, if the payments are monthly.

- ✔ **Number of payments:** This argument is the total number of payments in the investment. These payments are the ones beyond the initial investment; don't include the initial investment in this figure. If payments occur monthly and the investment is for three years, there are 36 payments.

- ✔ **Payment amount:** This argument is the fixed amount contributed to the investment each payment period.

- ✔ **Initial investment (also called PV or present value):** This argument is the amount the investment starts with. A possible value is 0, which means no initial amount is used to start the investment. This is an optional argument. If left out, 0 is assumed.

- ✔ **How payments are applied:** The periodic payments may be applied at either the beginning of each period or the end of each period. This argument affects the result to a small but noticeable degree. Either a 0 or a 1 can be entered. A 0 tells the function that payments occur at the end of the period. A 1 tells the function that payments occur at the start of the period. This is an optional argument. If it's left out, 0 is assumed.

When using the FV function, be sure to enter the initial investment amount and the periodic payment amount as negative numbers. Although you're investing these monies, you're essentially paying out (even if it's into your own account). Therefore, these are cash flows out.

Here's how to use the FV function:

1. **Enter the following data in separate cells of the worksheet:**

   - Annual interest rate
   - Number of payment periods
   - Periodic payment amount
   - Initial investment amount

   You can add labels to adjacent cells to identify the values, if desired.

2. **Position the cursor in the cell where you want the results to appear.**

3. **Type =FV(to begin the function entry.**

4. **Click the cell where you entered the annual interest rate, or enter the cell address.**

5. **Type /12 to divide the annual interest rate to get the monthly interest rate.**

6. **Type a comma (,).**

7. **Click the cell where you entered the total number of payments, or enter the cell address.**

8. **Type a comma (,).**

9. **Click the cell where you entered the periodic payment amount, or enter the cell address.**

10. **Type a comma (,).**

11. **Click the cell where you entered the initial investment amount, or enter the cell address.**

12. **(Optional) Type a comma (,) and then type either 0 or 1 to identify whether payments are made at the beginning of the period (0) or at the end of the period (1).**

13. **Type a), and press the Enter key.**

Figure 6-1 shows how much an investment is worth after two years. The investment is begun with $1,000, and $50 is added each month. The interest rate is 5 percent. The value of the investment at the end is $2,364.24. The actual layout was $2,200 ($1,000 + [$50 × 24]). The account has earned $164.24.

B12		× ✓ fx	=FV(B1/12,B2,B3,B4)	
	A		B	C
1	Annual Interest Rate		0.05	
2	Number of Periods		24	
3	Payment per Period	$	(50.00)	
4	Initial Investment	$	(1,000.00)	
5				
6				
7				
8				
9	A $1000 initial investment			
10	with monthly $50 payments			
11	and a 5% annual interest rate,			
12	at the end of two years is worth:		$2,364.24	
13				

Figure 6-1: Earning extra money in an investment.

Depreciating the Finer Things in Life

Depreciation is the technique of allocating the cost of an asset over the useful period that the asset is used. Depreciation is applied to *capital assets,* which are tangible goods that provide usefulness for a year or more.

Vehicles, buildings, and equipment are the types of assets that depreciation can be applied to. A tuna sandwich is not a capital asset because its usefulness is going to last for just the few minutes it takes someone to eat it — although the person eating it may expect to capitalize on it!

Take the example of a business purchasing a delivery truck. The truck costs $35,000. It's expected to be used for 12 years; this is known as the *life* of the asset. At the end of 12 years, the vehicle's estimated worth will be $8,000. These figures follow certain terminology used in the depreciation formulas:

- **Cost:** This is the initial cost of the item ($35,000). This could include not just the price of the item, but also, costs associated with getting and installing the item, such as delivery costs.

- **Salvage:** This is the value of the item at the end of the useful life of the item ($8,000).

- **Life:** This is the number of periods that the depreciation is applied to. This is usually expressed in years (in this case, 12 years).

Depreciation is calculated in different ways. Some techniques assume that an asset provides the majority of its usefulness during the early periods of its life. Depreciation in this case is applied on a sliding scale from the first period to the last. The bulk of the depreciation gets applied in the first few periods. This is known as an *accelerated depreciation schedule.* Sometimes, the depreciation amount runs out sooner than the asset's life. Alternatively, depreciation can be applied evenly over all the periods. In this case, each period of the asset's life has an equal amount of depreciation to apply. The different depreciation methods are summarized in Table 6-1.

The *depreciable cost* is the original cost minus the salvage value.

Table 6-1	Depreciation Methods	
Method	**Comments**	**Excel Function That Uses the Method**
Straight Line	Evenly applies the depreciable cost (Cost – Salvage) among the periods. Uses the formula (Cost – Salvage) ÷ Number of Periods.	SLN
Sum of Years' Digits	First sums up the periods, literally. For example, if there are five periods, the method first calculates the sum of the years' digits as 1 + 2 + 3 + 4 + 5 = 15. This method creates an accelerated depreciation schedule. See Excel Help for more information.	SYD
Double Declining Balance	Creates an accelerated depreciation schedule by doubling the straight-line depreciation rate but then applies it to the running declining balance of the asset cost, instead of to the fixed depreciable cost.	DDB, DB

Figure 6-2 shows a worksheet with a few different methods. The methods use the example of a delivery truck that costs $35,000, is used for 12 years, and has an ending value of $8,000. An important calculation in all these methods is the depreciable cost, which is the original cost minus the salvage value. In this example, the depreciable cost is $27,000, calculated as $35,000 – $8,000.

In the three depreciation methods shown in Figure 6-2 — Straight Line, Sum of Years' Digits, and Double Declining Balance — all end with the accumulated depreciation at the end of life equal to the depreciable cost, or the cost minus the salvage.

However, each method arrives at the total in a different way. The Straight Line method simply applies an even amount among the periods. The Sum of Years' Digits and Double Declining Balance methods accelerate the depreciation. In fact the Double Declining Balance method does it to such a degree that all the depreciation is accounted for before the asset's life is over.

			D9				f_x	=SLN($B$2,$B$3,$B$4)		

Depreciation Methods

	A	B	C D E	F	G H
1					
2	Cost of Asset	$ 35,000			
3	Salvage Cost	$ 8,000			
4	Life (in years)	12			
5					
6			Straight Line	Sum of Years' Digits	Double Declining Balance
7					
8		Year			
9		1	$2,250.00	$4,153.85	$5,833.33
10		2	$2,250.00	$3,807.69	$4,861.11
11		3	$2,250.00	$3,461.54	$4,050.93
12		4	$2,250.00	$3,115.38	$3,375.77
13		5	$2,250.00	$2,769.23	$2,813.14
14		6	$2,250.00	$2,423.08	$2,344.29
15		7	$2,250.00	$2,076.92	$1,953.57
16		8	$2,250.00	$1,730.77	$1,627.98
17		9	$2,250.00	$1,384.62	$139.88
18		10	$2,250.00	$1,038.46	$0.00
19		11	$2,250.00	$692.31	$0.00
20		12	$2,250.00	$346.15	$0.00
21					
22		Total Depreciation	$27,000.00	$27,000.00	$27,000.00
23					

Figure 6-2:
Depreciat-
ing an asset.

Calculating straight-line depreciation

The SLN function calculates the depreciation amount for each period of the life of the asset. The arguments are simple: just the cost, salvage, and the number of periods. In Figure 6-2, each cell in the range D9:D20 has the same formula: =SLN($B$2,$B$3,$B$4). Because straight-line depreciation provides an equal amount of depreciation to each period, it makes sense that each cell uses the formula verbatim. The answer is the same regardless of the period. (This approach differs from the accelerated depreciation methods that follow.)

Using dollar signs ($) in front of column and row indicators fixes the cell address so it won't change.

Here's how to use the SLN function:

1. **Enter three values in a worksheet:**
   - Cost of an asset
   - Salvage value (always less than the original cost)
   - Number of periods in the life of the asset (usually, years)

2. **Type =SLN(to begin the function entry.**

3. **Click the cell that has the original cost, or enter its address.**

4. **Type a comma (,).**

5. **Click the cell that has the salvage amount, or enter its address.**

6. **Type a comma (,).**

7. **Click the cell that has the number of periods, or enter its address.**

8. **Type a), and press the Enter key.**

The returned value is the amount of depreciation per period. Each period has the same depreciation amount. The same formula, referencing the same cells (using $ for absolute referencing), is in each cell in the D9:D20 range.

Creating an accelerated depreciation schedule

The SYD function creates an accelerated depreciation schedule (that is, more depreciation is applied in the early periods of the asset's life). The method uses an interesting technique of first summing up the years' digits. So for a depreciation schedule that covers five years, a value of 15 is first calculated as $1 + 2 + 3 + 4 + 5 = 15$. If the schedule is for ten years, the first step of the method is to calculate the sum of the digits 1 through 10, like this: $1 + 2 + 3 + 4 + 5 + 6 + 7 + 8 + 9 + 10 = 55$.

Then the years'-digit sum is used as the denominator in calculations with the actual digits themselves to determine a percentage per period. The digits in the calculations are the reverse of the actual periods. In other words, in a five-year depreciation schedule, the depreciation for the first period is calculated as $(5 \div 15) \times$ Depreciable Cost. The second-period depreciation is calculated as $(4 \div 15) \times$ Depreciable Cost. The following table makes it clear, with an assumed five-year depreciation on a depreciable cost of $6,000, and a salvage value of $0:

Period	Calculation	Result
1	$(5/15) \times 6,000$	$2,000
2	$(4/15) \times 6,000$	$1,600
3	$(3/15) \times 6,000$	$1,200
4	$(2/15) \times 6,000$	$800
5	$(1/15) \times 6,000$	$400

Guess what? You don't even need to know how this works! Excel does all the figuring for you. The SYD function takes four arguments: the cost, the salvage, the life (the number of periods), and the period to be calculated.

SYD returns the depreciation for a single period. Earlier in this chapter, I show you that the SLN function also returns the depreciation per period, but because all periods are the same, the SLN function doesn't need to have an actual period entered as an argument.

The SYD function returns a different depreciation amount for each period, so the period must be entered as an argument. In Figure 6-2, each formula in the range F9:F20 uses the SYD function but has a different period as the fourth argument. For example, cell F9 has the formula =SYD($B$2,$B$3,$B$4,B9), and cell F10 has the formula =SYD($B$2,$B$3,$B$4,B10). The last argument provides a different value.

Here's how to use the SYD function to calculate the depreciation for one period:

1. **Enter three values in a worksheet:**

    • Cost of an asset

    • Salvage value (always less than the original cost)

    • Number of periods in the life of the asset (usually, years)

2. **Type =SYD(to begin the function entry.**

3. **Click the cell that has the original cost, or enter its address.**

4. **Type a comma (,).**

5. **Click the cell that has the salvage amount, or enter its address.**

6. **Type a comma (,).**

7. **Click the cell that has the number of periods, or enter its address.**

8. **Type a comma (,).**

9. **Enter a number for the period for which to calculate the depreciation.**

10. **Type a), and press the Enter key.**

The *returned value* is the amount of depreciation for the entered period. To calculate the depreciation for the entire set of periods, enter a formula with the SYD function in the same number of cells as there are periods. In this case, each cell has a different period entered for the fourth argument. To make this type of entry easy to do, enter the first three arguments as absolute cell addresses. In other words, use the dollar sign ($) in front of the row and column indicators. Leave the fourth argument in the relative address format.

In cell F9 in Figure 6-2, the formula is =SYD($B$2,$B$3,$B$4,B9). Note that the first three arguments are fixed to the cells B2, B3, and B4. With this formula entered in cell F9, simply dragging the formula (using the fill handle in the lower-right corner of the cell) down to F20 fills the range of cells that need the calculation. The fourth argument changes in each row. For example, cell F20 has this formula: =SYD($B$2,$B$3,$B$4,B20).

Creating an even faster accelerated depreciation schedule

The Double Declining Balance method provides an accelerated depreciation schedule but calculates the amounts differently from the Sum of Years' Digits method.

Although rooted in the doubling of the Straight Line method (which is not an accelerated method), the calculation for each successive period is based on the remaining value of the asset after each period instead of to the depreciable cost. Because the remaining value is reduced each period, the schedule for each period is different.

The DDB function takes five arguments. The first four are required:

- ✔ Cost

- ✔ Salvage

- ✔ Life (the number of periods)

- ✔ Period for which the depreciation is to be calculated

The fifth argument is the factor. A factor of 2 tells the function to use the Double Declining Balance method. Other values can be used, such as 1.5. The factor is the rate at which the balance declines. A smaller value (than the default of 2) results in a longer time for the balance to decline. When the fifth argument is omitted, the value of 2 is the default.

The DDB function returns a different depreciation amount for each period, so the period must be entered as an argument. In Figure 6-2, each formula in the range H9:H20 uses the DDB function but has a different period as the fourth argument. For example, cell H9 has the formula =DDB($B$2,$B$3,$B$4,B9), and cell H10 has the formula =DDB($B$2,$B$3,$B$4,B10). The last argument provides a different value.

As shown in Figure 6-2 earlier in this chapter, the Double Declining Balance method provides an even more accelerated depreciation schedule than the Sum of Years' Digits method does. In fact, the depreciation is fully accounted for before the asset has reached the end of its life.

Here's how to use the DDB function to calculate the depreciation for one period:

1. **Enter three values in a worksheet:**

   - Cost of an asset

   - Salvage value (always less than the original cost)

   - Number of periods in the life of the asset (usually, years)

2. **Type =DDB(to begin the function entry.**

3. **Click the cell that has the original cost, or enter its address.**

4. **Type a comma (,).**

5. **Click the cell that has the salvage amount, or enter its address.**

6. **Type a comma (,).**

7. **Click the cell that has the number of periods.**

8. **Type a comma (,).**

9. **Enter a number for the period for which to calculate the depreciation.**

10. **If a variation on the Double Declining Balance method is desired, enter a comma (,) and a value other than 2.**

11. **Type a), and press the Enter key.**

The returned value is the amount of depreciation for the entered period. To calculate the depreciation for the entire set of periods, you need to enter a formula with the DDB function in the same number of cells as there are periods. In this case, each cell would have a different period entered for the fourth argument. One of the best approaches is to use absolute addressing for the first three function arguments. Then, when you fill the rest of the cells by dragging or copying, the references to original cost, salvage amount, and number of periods stay constant. You can see an example of absolute addressing in the Formula Bar in Figure 6-2.

There is no hard-and-fast rule for selecting the best depreciation method. However, it makes sense to use one that matches the depreciating value of the asset. For example, cars lose a good deal of their value in the first few years, so applying an accelerated depreciation schedule makes sense.

Calculating a midyear depreciation schedule

Most assets are not purchased, delivered, and put into service on January 1. Excel provides a depreciation formula, DB, that accounts for the periods being offset from the calendar year. The DB function takes five arguments. The first four are the typical ones: the cost, the salvage, the life (the number of periods), and the period for which the depreciation is to be calculated. The fifth argument is the number of months in the first year. The fifth argument is optional; when it's left out, the function uses 12 as a default.

For the fifth argument, a value of 3 means the depreciation starts in October (October through December is 3 months), so the amount of depreciation charged in the first calendar year is small. A value of 11 means that the depreciation starts in February (February through December is 11 months).

Figure 6-3 shows a depreciation schedule created with the DB function. Note that the life of the asset is 12 years (in cell B4) but that the formula is applied to 13 different periods. Including an extra year is necessary because the first year is partial. The remaining months must spill into an extra calendar year. The depreciation periods and the calendar years are offset.

D9			fx	=DB($B$2,$B$3,$B$4,B9,5)

	A	B	D	E
1				
2	Cost of Asset	$ 35,000		
3	Salvage Cost	$ 8,000		
4	Life (in years)	12		
5				
6			Fixed Depreciation	
7				
8		Year		
9		1	$1,691.67	
10		2	$3,863.77	
11		3	$3,415.57	
12		4	$3,019.36	
13		5	$2,669.12	
14		6	$2,359.50	
15		7	$2,085.80	
16		8	$1,843.85	
17		9	$1,629.96	
18		10	$1,440.88	
19		11	$1,273.74	
20		12	$1,125.99	
21		13	$580.63	
22				
23				
24	Total Depreciation		$26,999.83	
25				

Figure 6-3:
Offsetting depreciation periods from the calendar.

The example in Figure 6-3 is for an asset put into service in August. Cell D9 has the formula =DB($B$2,$B$3,$B$4,B9,5). The fifth argument is 5, which indicates that the first-year depreciation covers 5 months: August, September, October, November, and December.

Here's how to use the DB function to calculate the depreciation for one period:

1. **Enter three values in a worksheet:**

    - Cost of an asset

    - Salvage value (always less than the original cost)

    - Number of periods in the life of the asset (usually, years)

2. **Type =DB(to begin the function entry.**

3. **Click the cell that has the original cost, or enter its address.**

4. **Type a comma (,).**

5. **Click the cell that has the salvage amount, or enter its address.**

6. **Type a comma (,).**

7. **Click the cell that has the number of periods.**

8. **Type a comma (,).**

9. **Enter a number for the period for which to calculate the depreciation.**

10. **Type a comma (,).**

11. **Enter the number of months within the first year that the depreciation is applied to.**

12. **Type a), and press the Enter key.**

The returned value is the amount of depreciation for the entered period. To calculate the depreciation for the entire set of periods, you need to enter a formula with the DB function in the same number of cells as there are periods. However, you should make space for an additional period (refer to Figure 6-3).

Enter the constant arguments of the function with absolute addressing (the dollar signs used in front of row numbers or column letters). This makes the function easy to apply across multiple cells by copying the formula. The references to the pertinent function arguments stay constant.

Measuring Your Internals

Which is better to do: pay off your credit card or invest in Uncle Ralph's new business venture? You're about to finance a car. Should you put down a large down payment? Or should you put down a small amount and invest the rest? How can you make decisions about alternative financial opportunities like these?

The Internal Rate of Return (IRR) method helps answer these types of questions. The IRR function analyzes the cash flows in and out of an investment and calculates an interest rate that is the effective result of the cash flows. In other words, all the various cash flows are accounted for, and one interest rate is returned. Then you can compare this figure with other financial opportunities.

Perhaps Uncle Ralph's business venture will provide a 10 percent return on your investment. On the other hand, the credit card company charges you 12 percent on your balance. In this case, paying off the credit card is wiser. Why? Because earning 10 percent is pointless when you're just losing 12 percent elsewhere. Uncle Ralph will understand, won't he?

The IRR function takes two arguments. The first is required; the second is optional in some situations and required in others.

The first argument is an array of cash flows. Following the cash-flows standard, money coming in is entered as a positive value, and money going out is entered as a negative value. Assuming that the particular cash flows in and out are entered on a worksheet, the first argument to the function is the range of cells.

The second argument is a guess at what the result should be. I know this sounds crazy, but Excel may need your help here (though most times, it won't). The IRR function works by starting by guessing the result and calculating how closely the guess matches the data. Then it adjusts the guess up or down and repeats the process (a technique called *iteration*) until it arrives at the correct answer. If Excel doesn't figure it out in 20 tries, the #NUM! error is returned. In this case, you could enter a guess in the function to help it along. For example, 0.05 indicates a guess of 5 percent, 0.15 indicates a guess of 15 percent, and so on. You can enter a negative number, too. For example, entering –0.05 tells the function that you expect a 5 percent loss. If you don't enter a guess, Excel assumes 0.1 (10 percent).

Figure 6-4 shows a business venture that has been evaluated with IRR. The project is to create and market t-shirts. Assorted costs such as paying artists are cash flows out, entered as negative numbers. The one positive value in cell B7 is the expected revenue.

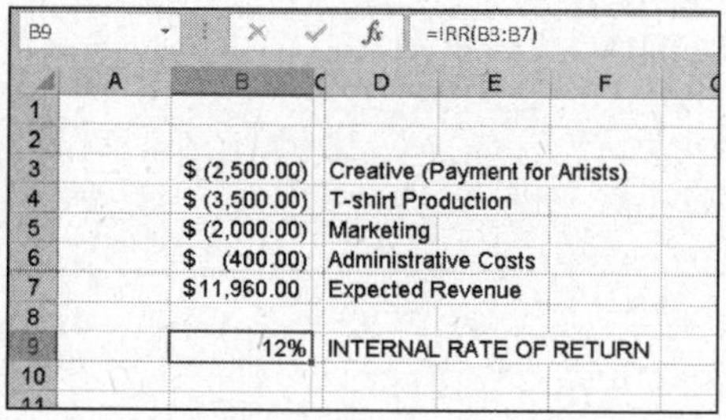

Figure 6-4:
Calculating the return on a business venture.

The IRR function has been used to calculate an expected rate of return. The formula in cell B10 is =IRR(B3:B7). The entered range includes all the cash flows, in and out.

This project has an internal rate of return of 12 percent. By the way, the investment amount in this case is the sum of all the cash flows out: $8,400. Earning back $11,960 makes this a good investment. The revenue is significantly higher than the outlay.

Even though a business opportunity seems worthy after IRR has been applied, you must consider other factors. For example, you may have to *borrow* the money to invest in the business venture. The real number to look at is the IRR of the business venture less the cost of borrowing the money to invest.

However, the project can now be compared with other investments. Another project may calculate to a higher internal rate of return. Then the second project would make sense to pursue. Of course, don't forget the fun factor. Making t-shirts may be worth giving up a few extra points!

When you're comparing opportunities with the IRR function, a higher returned value is a better result than a lower IRR.

Figure 6-5 compares the business venture in Figure 6-4 with another investment opportunity. The second business venture is a startup videography business for weddings and other affairs. There is a significant outlay for equipment and marketing. An internal rate of return is calculated for the first year, and then for the first and second year together. Cell H10 has the formula =IRR(H3:H5), and cell H11 has the formula =IRR(H3:H6). It's clear that even within the first year, the second business venture surpasses the first.

Figure 6-5: Comparing business opportunities.

	Business Venture 1		Business Venture 2	
	$ (2,500.00)	Creative (Payment for Artists)	$ (9,000.00)	Purchase of Video Equipment
	$ (3,500.00)	T-shirt Production	$ (6,500.00)	Marketing
	$ (2,000.00)	Marketing	$26,000.00	First Year Expected Revenue
	$ (400.00)	Administrative Costs	$54,000.00	Second Year Expected Revenue
	$11,960.00	Expected Revenue		
	12%	INTERNAL RATE OF RETURN	38%	INTERNAL RATE OF RETURN AFTER 1 YEAR
			107%	INTERNAL RATE OF RETURN AFTER 2 YEARS

This is how to use the IRR function:

1. **Enter a series of cash-flow values:**
   - Money paid out, such as the initial investment, as a negative value
   - Money coming in, such as revenue, as a positive value

2. **Type =IRR(to begin the function entry.**

3. **Drag the cursor over the range of cells containing the cash flows, or enter the range address.**

4. **Optionally, enter a guess to help the function.**

To do this, type a comma (,) and then enter a decimal value to be used as a percentage (such as 0.2 for 20 percent). You can enter a positive or negative value.

5. Type a), and press Enter.

Considering that IRR is based on cash flows, in and out, it's prudent to include paying yourself, as well as accounting for investments back in the business. Salary is cash flow out; investment is cash flow in.

Figure 6-6 expands on the videography business with a detailed example. As a business, it has various cash flows in and out — investment, utility payments, professional fees (to the accountant and lawyer), advertising, salary, and so on.

	A	B	C	D	E	F
	E1		f_x	=IRR(B4:B25,-0.2)		
1	Internal Rate of Return for (March - May, 2015) -->>				-5%	
2						
3	Date	Amount		Item		
4	03/02/15	$ 13,000.00		Initial Cash Investment		
5	03/05/15	$ (9,000.00)		Purchase of Video Equipment		
6	03/18/15	$ (325.00)		Office Supplies		
7	03/20/15	$ (700.00)		Advertising		
8	03/20/15	$ (1,450.00)		Professional Fees		
9	03/24/15	$ 1,800.00		Payment for Job		
10	03/28/15	$ 2,400.00		Payment for Job		
11	03/31/15	$ (3,000.00)		Salary		
12	04/04/15	$ 500.00		Additional Cash Invesment		
13	04/12/15	$ 1,295.00		Payment for Job		
14	04/19/15	$ 1,600.00		Payment for Job		
15	04/20/15	$ (350.00)		Additional Video Equipment		
16	04/21/15	$ (225.00)		Insurance		
17	04/21/15	$ (140.00)		Phone/Utilities		
18	04/24/15	$ 2,650.00		Payment for Job		
19	04/27/15	$ 1,725.00		Payment for Job		
20	04/28/15	$ (1,000.00)		Advertising		
21	04/30/15	$ (4,500.00)		Salary		
22	05/12/15	$ 2,000.00		Payment for Job		
23	05/20/15	$ (140.00)		Phone/Utilities		
24	05/20/15	$ 1,700.00		Payment for Job		
25	05/31/15	$ (4,000.00)		Salary		

Figure 6-6: Calculating IRR with several cash flows.

The internal rate of return for the first three months of the business is displayed in cell E1. The formula is =IRR(B4:B25,-0.2). By the way, this one needed a guess to return the answer. The guess is –0.2. The internal rate or return is –5 percent. The videography business is not a moneymaker after a few months, but this is true of many startups.

Note that this example includes dates. The IRR function works with an assumption that cash flows are periodic, which they aren't in this example. Another function, XIRR, handles dates in its calculation of the internal rate of return.

Chapter 7

Using Basic Math Functions

- -

In This Chapter

▶ Summing, rounding, and truncating values

▶ Using a value's sign in a calculation

▶ Removing the sign from a number

- -

*E*xcel is excellent for working with advanced math and complex calcula- tions. You can do so many complex things with Excel that it's easy to forget that Excel is great at basic math, too.

Need the sum of a batch of numbers? No problem. Need to round a number? Read on! In this chapter, I show you not just how to sum and round num- bers, but also how to use these methods in ways that give you just the answers you need.

Adding It All Together with the SUM Function

Just adding numbers together is something Excel is great at. Oh, you can use your calculator to add numbers as well, but think about it: On a calculator you enter a number, then press the + button, then enter another number, then press the + button, and so on. Eventually you press the = button, and you get your answer. But if you made an entry mistake in the middle, you have to start all over!

The SUM function in Excel adds numbers together in a more efficient way. First, you list all your numbers on the worksheet. You can see them all and verify that they're correct. Then you use the SUM function to add them all together. Here's how:

1. **Enter some numbers in a worksheet.**

   These numbers can be both integer and *real* (decimal) values. You can add labels to adjacent cells to identify the values, if you want.

2. **Position the cursor in the cell where you want the results to appear.**

3. **Type =SUM (to begin the function entry.**

4. **Click a cell where you entered a number.**

5. **Type a comma (,).**

6. **Click a cell where you entered another number.**

7. **Repeat Steps 5 and 6 until all the numbers have been entered into the function.**

8. **Type a), and press the Enter key.**

Figure 7-1 shows an example of how these steps help sum up amounts that are not situated next to one another on a worksheet. Cell F6 contains the sum of values in cells C2, E2, G2, and I2.

Figure 7-1:
Using
the SUM
function to
add non-
contiguous
numbers.

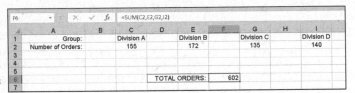

Using SUM is even easier when the numbers you're adding are next to one another in a column or row. The SUM function lets you enter a range of cells in place of single cells in the arguments of the function. So adding a list of contiguous numbers is as easy as giving SUM a single argument. Here's how you enter a range as a single argument:

1. **Enter some numbers in a worksheet.**

   Be sure the numbers are continuous in a row or column. You can add labels to adjacent cells to identify the values, if desired, but this doesn't affect the SUM function.

2. **Position the cursor in the cell where you want the results to appear.**

3. **Type =SUM(to begin the function entry.**

4. **Enter the range address that contains the numbers.**

   Alternatively, you can click the first cell with a number, hold down the left mouse button, and drag the mouse over the range of cells.

5. **Type a), and press the Enter key.**

Using a range address in the function is a real time saver — and is easier on the fingers, too. Figure 7-2 shows how a single range is used with the SUM function. Look at the Formula Bar, and you'll see that the entire function's syntax is =SUM(B6:B12). A single range takes the place of multiple individual cell addresses.

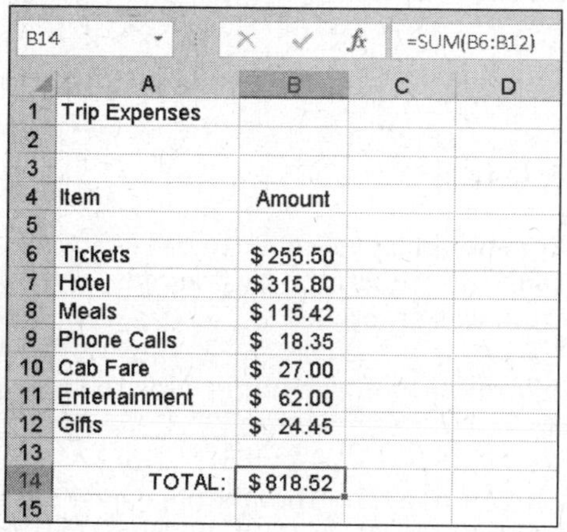

Figure 7-2:
Calculating a sum from a range of cells.

You can sum multiple ranges in a single formula, which is great when multiple distinct contiguous cell ranges all must feed a grand total. Figure 7-3 shows just such a situation.

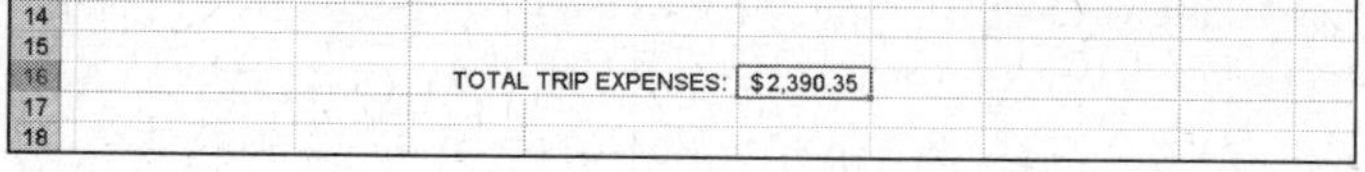

Figure 7-3:
Calculating a sum of multiple ranges.

Here's how you use SUM to add the values in multiple ranges:

1. **Enter some lists of numbers in a worksheet.**

   You can add labels to adjacent cells to identify the values, if desired.

2. **Position the cursor in the cell where you want the results to appear.**

3. **Type** =SUM(**to begin the function entry.**

4. **Click the first cell in a range, hold down the left mouse button, drag the mouse over all the cells in the range, and then release the mouse button.**

5. **Type a comma (,).**

6. **Click the first cell in another range, hold down the left mouse button, drag the mouse over all the cells in this range, and then release the mouse button.**

7. **Repeat Steps 5 and 6 until all the ranges have been entered into the function.**

8. **Type a), and press the Enter key.**

The completed function entry should look similar to the entry shown in the Formula Bar in Figure 7-3. Range are separated by commas, and a grand sum is in the cell where the function was entered.

When entering ranges into a formula, you can either type them or use the mouse to drag over the range.

Excel has a special button, the AutoSum button, that makes it easier to use the SUM function. The AutoSum button is on both the Home tab and the Formulas tab of the Ribbon. The AutoSum feature works best with numbers that are in a vertical or horizontal list. In a nutshell, AutoSum creates a range reference for the SUM function to use. AutoSum makes its best guess about what the range should be. Often, it gets it right — but sometimes, you have to help it along.

Using AutoSum is as easy as clicking and then pressing the Enter key. Figure 7-4 shows that the AutoSum button on the Ribbon has been clicked, and Excel, in its infinite wisdom, guessed correctly that the operation is to sum cells B6:B13. At this point, the operation is incomplete. Pressing the Enter key finishes the formula.

Figure 7-4:
Using Auto-
Sum to
guess a
range for
the SUM
function.

SUM	▾	X ✓ fx	=SUM(B6:B13)	
	A	B	C	D
1	Trip Expenses			
2				
3				
4	Item	Amount		
5				
6	Tickets	$ 255.50		
7	Hotel	$ 315.80		
8	Meals	$ 115.42		
9	Phone Calls	$ 18.35		
10	Cab Fare	$ 27.00		
11	Entertainment	$ 62.00		
12	Gifts	$ 24.45		
13				
14	TOTAL:	=SUM(B6:B13)		
15		SUM(**number1**, [number2], ...)		
16				

You can click the check mark to the left of the formula to complete the operation.

Follow these steps to use AutoSum:

1. **Enter some lists of numbers in a worksheet.**

   You can add labels to adjacent cells to identify the values, if desired.

2. **Position the cursor in the cell where you want the results to appear.**

3. **Click the AutoSum button.**

   AutoSum has entered a suggested range in the SUM function.

4. **Change the suggested range, if necessary, by entering it with the keyboard or using the mouse to drag over a range of cells.**

5. **Press the Enter key or click the check mark on the Formula Bar to complete the function.**

It's easy to use AutoSum to tally multiple ranges, such as those shown in Figure 7-3. Before ending the function with the Enter key or the check mark, instead enter a comma and then drag the mouse over another range. Do this for as many ranges as you need to sum. Finally, finish the function by pressing Enter or clicking the check mark.

By the way, the AutoSum button can do more than addition. If you click the down arrow on the button, you have a choice of a few other key functions, such as Average (see Figure 7-5).

Figure 7-5:
Using Auto-
Sum to work
with other
popular
functions.

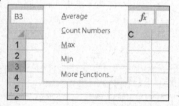

Rounding Out Your Knowledge

Excel calculates answers to many decimal places. Unless you're doing rocket science, you probably don't need such precise answers. Excel has a great set of functions for rounding numbers so they're usable for the rest of us.

Excel's rounding functions are really helpful. The other day, my son had a couple of his friends over. I ordered a large pizza for their lunch. That's eight slices for three hungry boys. How many slices does each boy get? Presto magic, I went over to the computer where Excel was already running (okay, I am an Excel nut, after all), and I entered this simple formula: =8/3.

Of course, Excel gave me the perfect answer. Each boy gets 2.66667 slices. Have you ever tried to cut 66,667/100,000ths of a slice of pizza? Not easy! This is the type of answer that rounding is used for. To tell you the truth, I did solve the pizza problem a different way. I gave each boy two slices, and I ate the last two (pretty good with mushrooms!).

Just plain old rounding

Easy to use, the ROUND function is the old tried-and-true method for rounding off a number. It takes two arguments. One argument is the number to round (typically, this is a cell reference), and the other argument indicates how many decimal places to round to.

The ROUND function rounds up or down, depending on the number being rounded. When the value is less than the halfway point of the next significant digit, the number is rounded down. When the value is at or greater than the halfway point, the number is rounded up, as follows:

✔ 10.4 rounds down to 10.

✔ 10.6 rounds up to 11.

✔ 10.5 also rounds up to 11.

Table 7-1 shows some examples of the ROUND function.

Table 7-1		Using the ROUND Function
Example of Function	**Result**	**Comment**
=ROUND(12.3456,1)	12.3	The second argument is 1. The result is rounded to a single decimal place.
=ROUND(12.3456,2)	12.35	The second argument is 2. The result is rounded to two decimal places. Note that the full decimal of .3456 becomes .35 because the .0456 portion of the decimal value rounds to the closest second-place decimal, which is .05.

Example of Function	Result	Comment
=ROUND(12.3456,3)	12.346	The second argument is 3. The result is rounded to three decimal places. Note that the full decimal or .3456 becomes .346 because the .0056 portion of the decimal value rounds to the closest third-place decimal, which is .006.
=ROUND(12.3456,4)	12.3456	The second argument is 4. There are four decimal places. No rounding takes place.
=ROUND(12.3456,0)	12	When the second argument is 0, the number is rounded to the nearest integer. Because 12.3456 is closer to 12 than to 13, the number rounds to 12.
=ROUND(12.3456,-1)	10	When negative values are used in the second argument, the rounding occurs on the left side of the decimal (the integer portion). A second argument value of −1 tells the function to round to the closest value of 10. In this example, that value is 10 because 12 is closer to 10 than to 20.

Here's how to use the ROUND function:

1. **In a cell of your choice, enter a number that has a decimal portion.**

2. **Position the cursor in the cell where you want the results to appear.**

3. **Type =ROUND(to begin the function entry.**

4. **Click the cell where you entered the number.**

5. **Type a comma (,).**

6. **Enter a number to indicate how many decimal places to round to.**

7. **Type a), and press the Enter key.**

Rounding functions make the most sense when the first argument is a cell reference, not an actual number. Think about it: If you know what a number should appear as, you would just enter the number. You would not need a function to round it.

Rounding in one direction

Excel has a handful of functions that always round numbers either up or always down. That is, when Excel is rounding a number, the functions that round down always give a result that is lower than the number itself.

Functions that round up, of course, always give a higher number. These functions are useful when letting the good ol' ROUND function determine which way to round just isn't going to do.

A few of these rounding functions not only round in the desired direction, but also allow you to specify some additional ways of rounding. The EVEN and ODD functions, for example, round to the closest even or odd number, respectively. The CEILING and FLOOR functions let you round to a multiple. EVEN, ODD, CEILING, and FLOOR are discussed later in this section.

Directional rounding, pure and simple

ROUNDUP and ROUNDDOWN are similar to the ROUND function. The first argument to the function is the cell reference of the number to be rounded. The second argument indicates the number of decimal places to round to. But unlike with plain old ROUND, the rounding direction is not based on the halfway point of the next significant digit, but on which function you use.

For example, =ROUND(4.22,1) returns 4.2, but =ROUNDUP(4.22,1) returns 4.3. ROUNDDOWN, however, returns 4.2 because 4.2 is less than 4.22. Table 7-2 shows some examples of ROUNDUP and ROUNDDOWN.

Table 7-2   Using the ROUNDUP and ROUNDDOWN Functions

Example of Function	Result	Comment
=ROUNDUP(150.255,0)	151	The second argument is 0. The result is rounded up to the next higher integer, regardless of the fact that the decimal portion would normally indicate the rounding would go to the next lower integer.
=ROUNDUP(150.255,1)	150.3	The second argument is 1. The result is rounded to a single decimal point. Note that the full decimal of .255 rounds up to .3. This would also happen with the standard ROUND function.
=ROUNDUP(150.255,2)	150.26	The second argument is 2. The result is rounded to two decimal places. Note that the full decimal of .255 becomes .26. This would also happen with the standard ROUND function.

Example of Function	Result	Comment
=ROUNDUP(150.255,3)	150.255	The second argument is 3, and there are three decimal places. No rounding takes place.
=ROUNDDOWN(155.798,0)	155	The second argument is 0. The result is rounded down to the integer portion of the number, regardless of the fact that the decimal portion would normally indicate that the rounding would go to the next higher integer.
=ROUNDDOWN(155.798,1)	155.7	The second argument is 1. The result is rounded to a single decimal place. Note that the full decimal of .798 rounds down to .7. The standard ROUND function would round the decimal up to .8.
=ROUNDDOWN(155.798,2)	155.79	The second argument is 2. The result is rounded to two decimal places. Note that the full decimal of .798 becomes .79. The standard ROUND function would round the decimal up to .8.
=ROUNDDOWN(155.798,3)	155.798	The second argument is 3, and there are three decimal places. No rounding takes place.

Here's how to use the ROUNDUP and ROUNDDOWN functions:

1. **In a cell of your choice, enter a number with a decimal portion.**

2. **Position the cursor in the cell where you want the results to appear.**

3. **Type** =ROUNDUP(**or** =ROUNDDOWN(**to begin the function entry.**

4. **Click the cell where you entered the number.**

5. **Type a comma (,).**

6. **Enter a number to indicate how many decimal places to round to.**

7. **Type a), and press the Enter key.**

Rounding to the multiple of choice

The FLOOR and CEILING functions take directional rounding to a new level. With these functions, the second argument is a multiple to which to round to. What does that mean?

Well, imagine this: You're a human-resources manager, and you need to prepare a summary report of employee salaries. You don't need the figures to be reported down to the last penny — just rounded to the closest $250 multiple. Either FLOOR or CEILING can do this. For this example, FLOOR can be used to round down to the closest multiple of $250 that is less than the salary, or CEILING can be used to round up to the next $250 multiple greater than the salary. Figure 7-6 shows how FLOOR and CEILING return rounded values.

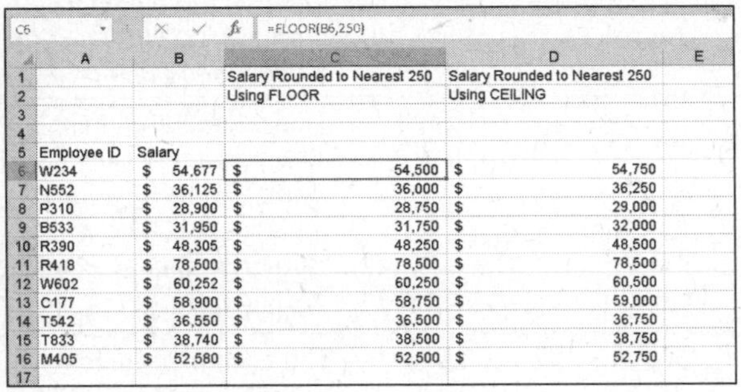

C6 =FLOOR(B6,250)

	A	B	C	D	E
1			Salary Rounded to Nearest 250	Salary Rounded to Nearest 250	
2			Using FLOOR	Using CEILING	
3					
4					
5	Employee ID	Salary			
6	W234	$ 54,677	$ 54,500	$ 54,750	
7	N552	$ 36,125	$ 36,000	$ 36,250	
8	P310	$ 28,900	$ 28,750	$ 29,000	
9	B533	$ 31,950	$ 31,750	$ 32,000	
10	R390	$ 48,305	$ 48,250	$ 48,500	
11	R418	$ 78,500	$ 78,500	$ 78,500	
12	W602	$ 60,252	$ 60,250	$ 60,500	
13	C177	$ 58,900	$ 58,750	$ 59,000	
14	T542	$ 36,550	$ 36,500	$ 36,750	
15	T833	$ 38,740	$ 38,500	$ 38,750	
16	M405	$ 52,580	$ 52,500	$ 52,750	
17					

Figure 7-6: Using FLOOR or CEILING to round to a desired multiple.

FLOOR and CEILING exceed the rounding ability of ROUND, ROUNDUP, and ROUNDDOWN. These three functions can use the positioning of digit placeholders in how they work. For example, `=ROUND(B4,-3)` tells the ROUND function to round on the thousandth position. On the other hand, FLOOR and CEILING can round to whatever specific multiple you set.

The FLOOR function rounds toward 0, returning the closest multiple of the second argument that is lower than the number itself.

The CEILING function works in the opposite direction. CEILING will round its first argument, the number to be rounded, to the next multiple of the second number that is in the direction away from 0.

Certainly, a few examples will make this clear! Table 7-3 shows ways that FLOOR and CEILING can be used.

Table 7-3 Using FLOOR and CEILING for Sophisticated Rounding

Example of Function	*Result*	*Comment*
`=FLOOR(30.17,0.05)`	30.15	The second argument says to round to the next 0.05 multiple, in the direction of 0.
`=FLOOR(30.17,0.1)`	30.1	The second argument says to round to the next 0.1 multiple, in the direction of 0.

Example of Function	Result	Comment
=FLOOR(-30.17,-0.1)	−30.1	The second argument says to round to the next 0.1 multiple, in the direction of 0.
=CEILING(30.17,0.05)	30.2	The second argument says to round to the next 0.05 multiple, away from 0.
=CEILING(30.17,0.1)	30.2	The second argument says to round to the next 0.1 multiple, away from 0.
=CEILING(-30.17,-0.1)	−30.2	The second argument says to round to the next 0.1 multiple, away from 0.

FLOOR and CEILING can be used to round negative numbers. FLOOR rounds toward 0, and CEILING rounds away from 0. FLOOR decreases a positive number as it rounds it toward 0 and also decreases a negative number toward 0, although in absolute terms, FLOOR actually increases the value of a negative number. Weird, huh?

CEILING does the opposite. It increases a positive number away from 0 and also increases a negative number away from 0, which in absolute terms means the number is getting smaller.

For both the FLOOR and CEILING functions, the first and second arguments must match signs. Trying to apply a positive number with a negative multiple, or vice versa, results in an error.

Here's how to use the FLOOR and CEILING functions:

1. **Enter a number in any cell.**

2. **Position the cursor in the cell where you want the results to appear.**

3. **Type =FLOOR(or =CEILING(to begin the function entry.**

4. **Click the cell where you entered the number.**

5. **Type a comma (,).**

6. **Enter a number that is the next multiple you want to round the number to.**

   For example, to get the floor value, at the ones place, make sure 1 is the second argument. The first argument should, of course, be a number larger than 1 and should be a decimal value, like this: =Floor(19.77, 1). This returns 19 as the floor, but hey — don't hit the ceiling about it!

7. **Type a), and press the Enter key.**

Rounding to the next even or odd number

The EVEN and ODD functions round numbers away from 0. The EVEN function rounds a number to the next highest even integer. ODD rounds a number to the next highest odd integer. Table 7-4 has examples of how these functions work.

Table 7-4		Rounding to Even or Odd Integers
Example of Function	*Result*	*Comment*
=EVEN(3)	4	Rounds to the next even integer, moving away from 0.
=EVEN(4)	4	Because 4 is an even number, no rounding takes place. The number 4 itself is returned.
=EVEN(4.01)	6	Rounds to the next even integer, moving away from 0.
=EVEN(-3.5)	−4	Rounds to the next even integer, moving away from 0.
=ODD(3)	3	Because 3 is an odd number, no rounding takes place. The number 3 itself is returned.
=ODD(4)	5	Rounds to the next odd integer, moving away from 0.
=ODD(5.01)	7	Rounds to the next odd integer, moving away from 0.
=ODD(-3.5)	−5	Rounds to the next odd integer, moving away from 0.

The EVEN function is helpful in calculations that depend on multiples of two. Say you're in charge of planning a school trip. You need to figure out how many bus seats are needed for each class. A seat can fit two children. When a class has an odd number of children, you still have to count that last seat as taken, even though only one child will sit there.

Say the class has 17 children. This formula tells you how many seats are needed: =EVEN(17)/2. The EVEN function returns the number 18 (the next higher integer), and that result is divided by 2 because 2 children fit on each seat. The answer is 9 seats are needed for a class of 17.

Here's how to use the EVEN and ODD functions:

1. Position the cursor in the cell where you want the results to appear.

2. Type =EVEN(or =ODD(to begin the function entry.

3. **Click a cell where you entered a number, or enter a number.**

4. **Type a), and press the Enter key.**

Leaving All Decimals Behind with INT

The INT function rounds a number down to the next lowest integer. The effect is as if the decimal portion is just dropped, and often, INT is used to facilitate just that: dropping the decimal.

INT comes in handy when all you need to know is the integer part of a number or the integer part of a calculation's result. For example, you may be estimating what it will cost to build a piece of furniture. You have the prices for each type of raw material, and you just want a ballpark total.

Figure 7-7 shows a worksheet in which a project has been set up. Column A contains item descriptions, and Column B has the price for each item. Columns C and D contain the parameters for the project. That is, Column C contains the count of each item needed, and Column D has the amount to be spent for each item — that is, the price per item multiplied by the number of items needed.

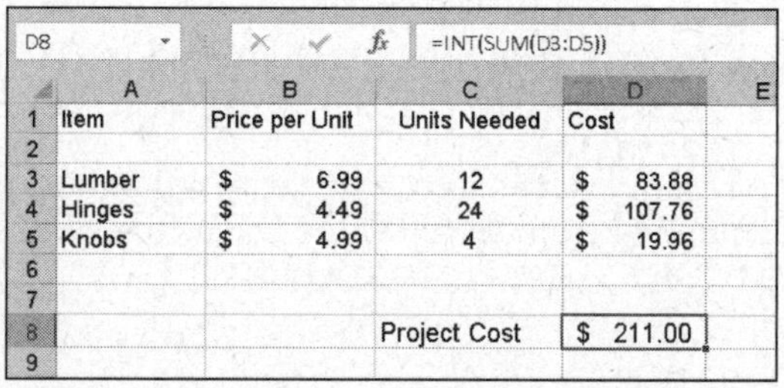

Figure 7-7:
Using INT to drop unnec-
essary
decimals.

	A	B	C	D	E
				=INT(SUM(D3:D5))	
1	Item	Price per Unit	Units Needed	Cost	
2					
3	Lumber	$ 6.99	12	$ 83.88	
4	Hinges	$ 4.49	24	$ 107.76	
5	Knobs	$ 4.99	4	$ 19.96	
6					
7					
8			Project Cost	$ 211.00	
9					

The sums to be spent are then summed into a project total. If you added the item sums as they are — 83.88, 107.76, and 19.96 — you get a total of $211.60. Instead, the INT function is used to round the total to a ballpark figure of $211.

In cell D8, INT is applied to the total sum, like this:

```
=INT(SUM(D3:D5))
```

The INT function effectively drops the decimal portion, .60, and returns the integer part, 211. The project estimate is $211.

INT takes only the number as an argument. INT can work on positive or negative values but works a little differently with negative numbers. INT actually rounds down a number to the next lower integer. When INT is working with positive numbers, the effect appears the same as just dropping the decimal. With negative numbers, the function drops the decimal portion and subtracts 1.

With negative numbers, the function produces an integer that is farther away from 0. Therefore, a number such as –25.25 becomes –26. Here are some examples:

- ✔ INT(25.25) returns 25.
- ✔ INT(25.75) returns 25.
- ✔ INT(-25.25) returns –26.
- ✔ INT(-25.75) returns –26.

Here's how to use the INT function:

1. **In a cell of your choice, enter a number that has a decimal portion.**

2. **Position the cursor in the cell where you want the results to appear.**

3. **Type =INT(to begin the function entry.**

4. **Click the cell where you entered the number.**

5. **Enter a closing parenthesis to end the function, and press the Enter key.**

INT can also be used to return just the decimal part of a number. Subtracting the integer portion of a number from its full value leaves just the decimal as the answer. For example, 10.95-INT(10.95) equals 0.95.

Leaving Some Decimals Behind with TRUNC

The TRUNC function drops a part of a number. The function takes two arguments. The first argument is the number to be changed. The second argument indicates how much of the number is to be dropped. A value of 2 for the second argument says to leave 2 decimal places remaining. A value of 1 for the second argument says to leave 1 decimal place remaining.

TRUNC does no rounding as it truncates numbers. Here are some examples:

✔ =TRUNC(212.65, 2) returns 212.65.

✔ =TRUNC(212.65, 1) returns 212.6.

✔ =TRUNC(212.65, 0) returns 212.

You can even use TRUNC to drop a portion of the number from the integer side. To do this, you enter negative values for the second argument, like this:

✔ =TRUNC(212.65, -1) returns 210.

✔ =TRUNC(212.65, -2) returns 200.

The INT and TRUNC functions work exactly the same way for positive numbers. The only difference is when negative numbers are being changed. Then INT's rounding produces a different result than TRUNC's truncation.

Looking for a Sign

Excel's SIGN function tells you whether a number is positive or negative. The SIGN function does not alter the number in any way but is used to find out information about the number.

SIGN does actually return a number, but it isn't a variation of the number being tested in the function. SIGN returns only three numbers:

✔ 1 if the number being tested is positive

✔ –1 if the number being tested is negative

✔ 0 if the number being tested is 0

Consider these examples:

✔ =SIGN(5) returns 1.

✔ =SIGN(-5) returns –1.

✔ =SIGN(0) returns 0.

Using SIGN in combination with other functions presents sophisticated ways of working with your information. As an example, you may be tallying up a day's receipts from your store. You want to know the total value of sold merchandise and the total value of returned merchandise. Sales are recorded as positive amounts, and returns are recorded as negative amounts.

Figure 7-8 shows a worksheet with these facts. Column A shows individual transaction amounts. Most amounts are sales and are positive. A few returns occurred during the day, entered as negative amounts.

B18		×	✓	f_x	=SUMIF(B3:B15,1,A3:A15)		
	A		**B**		**C**	**D**	
1	Daily Reciepts						
2							
3	$	34.95	1				
4	$	24.82	1				
5	$	90.63	1				
6	$	44.50	1				
7	$	(17.24)	-1				
8	$	12.00	1				
9	$	25.90	1				
10	$	28.99	1				
11	$	(30.15)	-1				
12	$	115.99	1				
13	$	104.10	1				
14	$	(16.79)	-1				
15	$	32.35	1				
16							
17							
18		Sales:	$	514.23			
19		Returns:	$	64.18			
20							

Figure 7-8: Using SIGN to sum amounts correctly.

Just summing the whole transaction list would calculate the net revenue of the day, but often, a business needs better information. Instead, two sums are calculated: the sum of sales and the sum of returns.

For each value in Column A, there is a value in Column B. The Column B values are the result of using the SIGN function. For example, cell B3 has this formula: =SIGN(A3).

As shown in Figure 7-8, values in Column B equal 1 when the associated value in Column A is positive. Column B displays –1 when the associated value is negative. This information is then used in a SUMIF function, which selectively sums information from Column A.

In cell B18 is this formula: =SUMIF(B3:B15,1,A3:A15).

In cell B19 is this formula: =ABS(SUMIF(B3:B15,-1,A3:A15)).

The SUMIF function is used to indicate a criterion to use in determining which values to sum. For the sum of sales in cell B18, the presence of the value 1 in Column B determines which values to sum in Column A. For the sum of returns in cell B19, the presence of the value –1 in Column B determines which values to sum in Column A.

Also, the ABSOLUTE function (ABS) is used to present the number in cell B19 as a positive number. The answer in cell B19 is the sum of merchandise returns. You would say there was $64.18 (not –$64.18) in returned merchandise, if you were asked.

The SUMIF function is covered in Chapter 8. The ABS function is covered next in this chapter.

Here's how to use the SIGN function:

1. **Position the cursor in the cell where you want the results to appear.**
2. **Type** =SIGN(**to begin the function entry.**
3. **Click a cell where you entered a number, or enter a number.**
4. **Type a), and press Enter.**

Ignoring Signs

The ABS function returns the absolute value of a number. The absolute number is always a positive. The absolute of a positive number is the number itself. The absolute of a negative number is the number but with the sign changed to positive. For example, =ABS(100) returns 100, as does =ABS(-100).

The ABS function is handy in a number of situations. For example, sometimes imported data comes in as negative values, which need to be converted to their positive equivalents. Or, when you're working with cash flows as discussed in Chapter 3, you can use the ABS function to present cash flows as positive numbers.

A common use of the ABS function is to calculate the difference between two numbers when you don't know which number has the greater value to begin with. Say you need to calculate the difference between scores for two contestants. Score 1 is in cell A5, and score 2 is in cell B5. The result goes in cell C5. The formula in cell C5 would be =A5-B5.

Plugging in some numbers, assume that score 1 is 90 and score 2 is 75. The difference is 15. Okay, that's a good answer. What happens when score 1 is 75 and score 2 is 90? The answer is –15. This answer is mathematically correct but not presented in a useful way. The difference is still 15, not –15. When you use the ABS function, the result is always returned as positive. Therefore, for this example, the best formula coding is this: =ABS(A5-A6).

Now, whether score 1 is greater than score 2 or score 2 is greater than score 1, the correct difference is returned.

Here's how to use the ABS function:

1. **Position the cursor in the cell where you want the results to appear.**

2. **Type** =ABS(**to begin the function entry.**

3. **Click a cell where you entered a number, or enter a number.**

4. **Type a), and press the Enter key.**

Chapter 8

Advancing Your Math

● ●

In This Chapter

▶ Calculating the diameter, circumference, and area of a circle

▶ Returning random numbers

▶ Working with combinations and permutations

▶ Performing sophisticated multiplication

▶ Using the MOD function to test other numerical values

▶ Using the SUBTOTAL function for a variety of arithmetic and statistical totals

▶ Using the SUMIF and SUMIFS functions for selective summation

▶ Getting an angle on trigonometry functions

● ●

*I*n this chapter, I show you some of the more advanced math functions. You won't use these functions every day, but they're just the right thing when you need them. Some of this will come back to you because you probably learned most of this in school.

Using PI to Calculate Circumference and Diameter

Pi is the ratio of a circle's circumference to its diameter. A circle's *circumference* is its outer edge and is equal to the complete distance around the circle. A circle's *diameter* is the length of a straight line running from one side of the circle, through the middle, and reaching the other side.

Dividing a circle's circumference by its diameter returns a value of approximately 3.14159, known as *pi*. Pi is represented with the Greek letter pi and the symbol π.

Mathematicians have proved that pi is an *irrational number* — in other words, that it has an infinite number of decimal places. They have calculated the value of pi to many thousands of decimal places, but you don't need that level of precision in most calculations. Many people use the value 3.14159 for pi, but the PI function in Excel does a bit better than that. Excel returns a value of pi accurate to 15 digits — that is 14 decimal places in addition to the integer 3. This function has no input arguments. The function uses this syntax:

```
=PI()
```

 In Excel, the PI function always returns 3.14159265358979, but initially, it may look like some of the digits after the decimal point are missing. Change the formatting of the cell to display numbers with 14 decimal places to see the entire number.

If you know the circumference of a circle, you can calculate its diameter with this formula:

diameter = circumference ÷ pi

If you know the diameter of a circle, you can calculate its circumference with this formula:

circumference = diameter × pi

If you know the diameter of a circle, you can calculate the area of the circle. A component of this calculation is the *radius,* which equals one half of the diameter. The formula is

area = (diameter × 0.5)^2 × pi

Generating and Using Random Numbers

Random numbers are, by definition, unpredictable. That is, given a series of random numbers, you can't predict the next number from what has come before. Random numbers are quite useful for trying formulas and calculations. Suppose that you're creating a worksheet to perform various kinds of data analysis. You may not have any real data yet, but you can generate random numbers to test the formulas and charts in the worksheet.

For example, an actuary may want to test some calculations based on a distribution of people's ages. Random numbers between 18 and 65 can be used for this task. You don't have to manually enter fixed values between 18 and 65, because Excel can generate them automatically via the RAND function.

The all-purpose RAND function

The RAND function is simple; it takes no arguments and returns a decimal value between 0 and 1. That is, RAND never actually returns 0 or 1; the value is always in between these two numbers. The function is entered like this:

```
=RAND()
```

The RAND function returns values such as 0.136852731, 0.856104058, or 0.009277161. "Yikes!" you may be thinking. "How do these numbers help if you need values between 18 and 65?" Actually, it's easy with a little extra math.

There is a standard calculation for generating random numbers within a determined range. The calculation follows:

```
= RAND() * (high number - low number) + low number
```

Using 18 and 65 as a desired range of numbers, the formula looks like `=RAND()*(65-18)+18`. Some sample values returned with this formula follow:

> 51.71777896
>
> 27.20727871
>
> 24.61657068
>
> 55.27298686
>
> 49.93632709
>
> 43.60069745

Almost usable! But what about the long decimal portions of these numbers? Some people lie about their ages, but I've never heard someone say he's 27.2 years old!

All that is needed now for this 18-to-65 age example is to include the INT or ROUND function. INT simply discards the decimal portion of a number. ROUND allows control of how to handle the decimal portion.

The syntax for using the INT function with the RAND function follows:

```
= INT((high number - low number + 1) * RAND() + low number)
```

The syntax for using the ROUND function with the RAND function follows:

```
=ROUND(RAND() * (high number-low number) + low number,0)
```

Try it yourself! Here's how to use RAND and INT together:

1. **Position the pointer in the cell where you want the results displayed.**

2. **Type =INT((to begin the formula.**

3. **Click the cell that has the highest number to be used, or enter such a value.**

4. **Type – (a minus sign).**

5. **Click the cell that has the lowest number to be used, or enter such a value.**

6. **Type +1) * RAND() + .**

7. **Again, click the cell that has the lowest number to be used, or enter the value again.**

8. **Type a), and press Enter.**

A random number, somewhere in the range between the low and high number, is returned.

Table 8-1 shows how returned random numbers can be altered with the INT and ROUND functions.

Table 8-1	Using INT and ROUND to Process Random Values	
Value	*Value Returned with INT*	*Value Returned with ROUND*
51.71777896	51	52
27.20727871	27	27
24.61657068	24	25
55.27298686	55	55
49.93632709	49	50
43.60069745	43	44

Table 8-1 points out how the INT and ROUND functions return different numbers. For example, 51.71777896 is more accurately rounded to 52. Bear in mind that the second argument in the ROUND function, 0 in this case, has an effect on how the rounding works. A 0 tells the ROUND function to round the number to the nearest integer, up or down to whichever integer is closest to the number.

Random values are volatile. Each time a worksheet is recalculated, the random values change. You can prevent this behavior by typing the formula directly in the Formula Bar, pressing the F9 key, and then pressing the Enter key.

A last but not insignificant note about using the RAND function: It is subject to the recalculation feature built into worksheets. In other words, each time the worksheet calculates, the RAND function is rerun and returns a new random number. The calculation setting in your worksheet is probably set to automatic. You can check this by looking at the Formulas tab of the Excel Options dialog box. Figure 8-1 shows the calculation setting. On a setting of Automatic, the worksheet recalculates with every action. The random generated numbers keep changing, which can become quite annoying if this is not what you intended to have happen. However, I bet you did want the number to change; otherwise, why use something "random" in the first place?

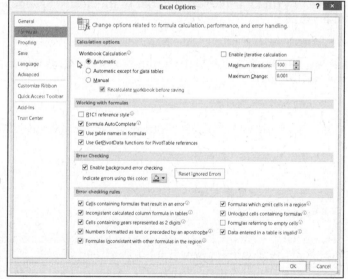

Figure 8-1:
Setting
worksheet
calculation
options.

Luckily, you can generate a random number but have it remain fixed regardless of the calculation setting. The method is to type the RAND function, along with any other parts of a larger formula, directly in the Formula Bar. After you type your formula, press the F9 key and then press the Enter key. This tells Excel to calculate the formula and enter the returned random number as a fixed number instead of a formula. If you press the Enter key or finish the entry in some way without pressing the F9 key, you have to enter it again.

Precise randomness with RANDBETWEEN

Using the RAND function returns a value between 0 and 1, and when you use it with other functions, such as ROUND, you can get a random number within a range that you specify. If you just need a quick way to get an integer (no decimal portion!) within a given range, use RANDBETWEEN.

The RANDBETWEEN function takes two arguments: the low and high numbers of the desired range. It works only with integers. You can put real numbers in the range, but the result will still be an integer.

To use RANDBETWEEN, follow these steps:

1. **Position the pointer in the cell where you want the results displayed.**

2. **Type** =RANDBETWEEN(**to begin the formula.**

3. **Click the cell that has the low number of the desired range, or enter such a value.**

4. **Type a comma (,).**

5. **Click the cell that has the highest number of the desired range, or enter such a value.**

6. **Type a), and press Enter.**

For example, =RANDBETWEEN(10,20) returns a random integer between 10 and 20.

Ordering Items

Remember the Beatles? John, Paul, George, and Ringo? If you're a drummer, you may think of the Beatles as Ringo, John, Paul, and George. The order of items in a list is known as a *permutation*. The more items in a list, the more possible permutations exist.

Excel provides the PERMUT function. It takes two arguments: the total number of items to choose among and the number of items to be used in determining the permutations. The function returns a single whole number. The syntax of the function follows:

```
=PERMUT(total number of items, number of items to use)
```

Use permutations when the order of items is important.

The total number of items must be the same as or greater than the number of items to use; otherwise, an error is generated.

You may be confused about why the function takes two arguments. On the surface, it seems that the first argument is sufficient. Well, not quite. Getting back to the Beatles, anyone have a copy of *Abbey Road* I can borrow? If we plug in 4 as the number for both arguments

```
=PERMUT(4,4)
```

Twenty-four permutations are returned:

- John Paul George Ringo
- John Paul Ringo George
- John George Paul Ringo
- John George Ringo Paul
- John Ringo Paul George
- John Ringo George Paul
- Paul John George Ringo
- Paul John Ringo George
- Paul George John Ringo
- Paul George Ringo John
- Paul Ringo John George
- Paul Ringo George John

- George John Paul Ringo
- George John Ringo Paul
- George Paul John Ringo
- George Paul Ringo John
- George Ringo John Paul
- George Ringo Paul John
- Ringo John Paul George
- Ringo John George Paul
- Ringo Paul John George
- Ringo Paul George John
- Ringo George John Paul
- Ringo George Paul John

Altering the function to use 2 items at a time from the total of 4 items — PERMUT(4,2) — returns just 12 permutations. They are

- John Paul
- John George
- John Ringo
- Paul John
- Paul George
- Paul Ringo

- George John
- George Paul
- George Ringo
- Ringo John
- Ringo Paul
- Ringo George

Just for contrast, using the number 2 for both arguments — PERMUT(2,2) — returns just two items! When using PERMUT, make sure you've selected the correct numbers for the two arguments; otherwise, you'll end up with an incorrect result and may not be aware of the mistake. The PERMUT function simply returns a number. The validity of the number is in your hands.

Combining

Combinations are similar to permutations but with a distinct difference. The order of items is intrinsic to permutations. Combinations, however, are groupings of items in which the order doesn't matter. For example, "John Paul George Ringo" and "Ringo George Paul John" are two distinct permutations but identical combinations.

Combinations are groupings of items, regardless of the order of the items.

The syntax of the function follows:

```
=COMBIN(total number of items, number of items to use)
```

The first argument is the total number of items to choose among, and the second argument is the number of items to be used in determining the combinations. The function returns a single whole number. The arguments for the COMBIN function are the same as those for the PERMUT function. The first argument must be equal to or greater than the second argument.

Plugging in the number 4 for both arguments — COMBIN(4,4) — returns 1. Yes, there is just one combination of four items selected from a total of four items! Using the Beatles once again, just one combination of the four musicians exists, because the order of names doesn't matter.

Selecting to use two items from a total of four — COMBIN(4,2) — returns 6. Selecting two items out of two — COMBIN(2,2) — returns 1. In fact, whenever the two arguments to the COMBIN function are the same, the result is always 1.

Raising Numbers to New Heights

There is an old tale about a king who loved chess so much, he decided to reward the inventor of chess by granting any request he had. The inventor asked for a grain of wheat for the first square of the chessboard on Monday, two grains for the second square on Tuesday, four for the third square on Wednesday, eight for the fourth square on Thursday, and so on, each day doubling the amount until the 64th square was filled with wheat. The king thought this was a silly request. The inventor could have asked for riches!

What happened was that the kingdom quickly ran out of wheat. By the 15th day, the number equaled 16,384. By the 20th day, the number was 524,288. On the 64th day, the number would have been an astonishing 9,223,372,036,854,780,000, but the kingdom had run out of wheat at least a couple of weeks earlier!

This "powerful" math is literally known as raising a number to a power. The *power,* in this case, means how many times a number is to be multiplied by itself. The notation is typically a superscript (2^3 for example). Another common way of noting the use of a power is with the caret symbol: 2^3. The verbiage for this is *two to the third power.*

In the chess example, 2 is raised to a higher power each day. Table 8-2 shows the first ten days.

Day	Power That 2 Is Raised To	Power Notation	Basic Math Notation	Result
			The Power of Raising Numbers to a Power	
1	0	2^0	1	1
2	1	2^1	2	2
3	2	2^2	2×2	4
4	3	2^3	$2 \times 2 \times 2$	8
5	4	2^4	$2 \times 2 \times 2 \times 2$	16
6	5	2^5	$2 \times 2 \times 2 \times 2 \times 2$	32
7	6	2^6	$2 \times 2 \times 2 \times 2 \times 2 \times 2$	64
8	7	2^7	$2 \times 2 \times 2 \times 2 \times 2 \times 2 \times 2$	128
9	8	2^8	$2 \times 2 \times 2 \times 2 \times 2 \times 2 \times 2 \times 2$	256
10	9	2^9	$2 \times 2 \times 2 \times 2 \times 2 \times 2 \times 2 \times 2 \times 2$	512

Table 8-2

The concept is easy enough. Each time the power is incremented by 1, the result doubles. Note that the first entry raises 2 to the 0 power. Isn't that strange? Well, not really. Any number raised to the 0 power = 1. Also note that any number raised to the power of 1 equals the number itself.

Excel provides the POWER function, whose syntax follows:

```
=POWER(number, power)
```

Both the number and power arguments can be integer or real numbers, and negative numbers are allowed.

In a worksheet, either the POWER function or the caret can be used. For example, in a cell you can enter =POWER(4,3), or =4^3. The result is the same either way. You insert the caret by holding Shift and pressing the number 6 key on the keyboard.

Multiplying Multiple Numbers

The PRODUCT function is useful for multiplying up to 255 numbers at a time. The syntax follows:

```
=PRODUCT (number1, number2,...)
```

Cell references can be included in the argument list, as well as actual numbers, and of course, they can be mixed. Therefore, all these variations work:

```
=PRODUCT(A2, B15, C20)
=PRODUCT(5, 8, 22)
=PRODUCT(A10, 5, B9)
```

In fact, you can use arrays of numbers as the arguments. In this case, the notation looks like this:

```
=PRODUCT(B85:B88,C85:C88, D86:D88)
```

Here's how to use the PRODUCT function:

1. **Enter some values in a worksheet.**

   You can include many values, going down columns or across in rows.

2. **Position the pointer in the cell where you want the results displayed.**

3. **Type =PRODUCT(to begin the function.**

4. **Click a cell that has a number.**

   Alternatively, you can hold down the left mouse button and drag the pointer over a range of cells with numbers.

5. Type a comma (,).

6. Repeat Steps 4 and 5 up to 255 times.

7. Type a), and press Enter.

The result you see is calculated by multiplying all the numbers you selected. Your fingers would probably hurt if you had done this on a calculator.

Figure 8-2 shows this on a worksheet. Cell C10 shows the result of multiplying 12 numbers, although only three arguments, as ranges, have been used in the function.

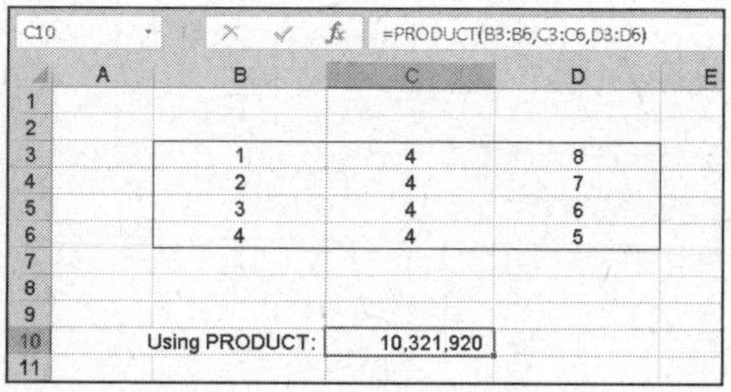

Figure 8-2:
Putting the
PRODUCT
function to
work.

Using What Remains with the MOD Function

The MOD function returns the remainder from an integer division operation. This is called the *modulus*, hence the function's name. The function has two arguments: the number being divided and the number being used to divide the first argument. The second argument is the divisor. The syntax follows:

```
=MOD(number, divisor)
```

These are examples of the MOD function:

=MOD(12,6) returns 0.

=MOD(14,5) returns 4.

=MOD(27,7) returns 6.

=MOD(25,10) returns 5.

=MOD(25,10) returns –5.

=MOD(15.675,8.25) returns 7.425.

The returned value is always the same sign as the divisor.

You can use MOD to tell whether a number is odd or even. If you simply use a number 2 as the second argument, the returned value will be 0 if the first argument is an even number and 1 if it is not.

But what's so great about that? You can just look at a number and tell whether it's odd or even. The power of the MOD function is apparent when you're testing a reference or formula, such as =MOD(D12 - G15,2). In a complex worksheet with many formulas, you may not be able to tell when a cell will contain an odd or even number.

Taking this a step further, the MOD function can be used to identify cells in a worksheet that are multiples of the divisor. Figure 8-3 shows how this works.

	A	B	C
	Data	Uses =MOD(VALUE,4)	Uses =MOD(VALUE,10)
2	39	3	9
3	16	0	6
4	10	2	0
5	14	2	4
6	55	3	5
7	93	1	3
8	68	0	8
9	70	2	0
10	44	0	4
11	40	0	0
12	32	0	2
13	38	2	8
14	77	1	7
15	90	2	0
16	45	1	5

C4 f_x =MOD(A4,10)

Figure 8-3:
Using MOD
to find
specific
values.

Row 1 of the worksheet in Figure 8-3 shows examples of the formulas that are entered in the successive rows of Columns B and C, starting from the second row. Column A contains numbers that will be tested with the MOD function. If you're looking for multiples of 4, the MOD function has 4 as the divisor, and when a value is a multiple of 4, MOD returns 0. This is evident when you compare the numbers in Column A with the returned values in Column B.

The same approach is used in Column C, only here the divisor is 10, so multiples of 10 are being tested for in Column A. Where a 0 appears in Column C, the associated number in Column A is a multiple of 10.

In this way, you can use the MOD function to find meaningful values in a worksheet.

Summing Things Up

Ah ha! Just when you think you know how to sum up numbers (really, haven't you been doing this since your early school years?), I present a fancy-footwork summing that makes you think twice before going for that quick total.

The functions here are very cool — very "in" with the math crowd. To be a true Excel guru, try the SUBTOTAL, SUMPRODUCT, SUMIF, and SUMIFS functions shown here and then strut your stuff around the office!

Using SUBTOTAL

The SUBTOTAL function is very flexible. It doesn't perform just one calculation; it can do any of 11 calculations depending on what you need. What's more, SUBTOTAL can perform these calculations on up to 255 ranges of numbers. This gives you the ability to get exactly the type of summary you need without creating a complex set of formulas. The syntax of the function follows:

```
=SUBTOTAL(function number, range1, range2,...)
```

The first argument determines which calculation is performed. It can be any of the values shown in Table 8-3. The remaining arguments identify the ranges containing the numbers to be used in the calculation.

Figure 8-4 exemplifies a few uses of the SUBTOTAL function. Raw data values are listed in Column A. The results of using the function in a few variations are listed in Column C. Column E displays the actual function entries that returned the respective results in Column C.

Using named ranges with the SUBTOTAL function is useful. For example, `=SUBTOTAL(1, October_Sales, November_Sales, December_sales)` makes for an easy way to calculate the average sale of the fourth quarter.

A second set of numbers can be used for the Function Number (the first argument in the SUBTOTAL function). These numbers start with 101 and are the same functions as shown in Table 8-3. For example, 101 is AVERAGE, 102 is COUNT, and so on.

Table 8-3	Argument Values for the SUBTOTAL Function	
Function Number for First Argument	**Function**	**Description**
1	AVERAGE	Returns the average value of a group of numbers
2	COUNT	Returns the count of cells that contain numbers and also numbers within the list of arguments
3	COUNTA	Returns the count of cells that are not empty and only nonempty values within the list of arguments
4	MAX	Returns the maximum value in a group of numbers
5	MIN	Returns the minimum value in a group of numbers
6	PRODUCT	Returns the product of a group of numbers
7	STDEV.S	Returns the standard deviation from a sample of values
8	STDEV.P	Returns the standard deviation from an entire population, including text and logical values
9	SUM	Returns the sum of a group of numbers
10	VAR.S	Returns variance based on a sample
11	VAR.P	Returns variance based on an entire population

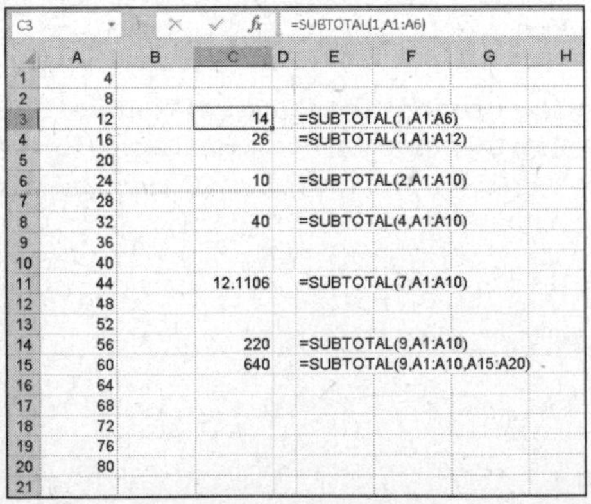

Figure 8-4:
Working
with the
SUBTOTAL
function.

The 1 through 11 Function Numbers consider all values in a range. The 101 through 111 Function Numbers tell the function to ignore values that are in hidden rows or columns. Figure 8-5 shows SUBTOTAL in use with both Function Number systems. Comparing Figure 8-5 to Figure 8-4, you can see that Row 2 has been set to hidden. In Figure 8-5, the values in Column B are calculated using the same Function Numbers as in Figure 8-4; Column G shows SUBTOTAL using the Function Numbers that start with 101. For example, cell B3 still shows the average of the numbers in the range A1:A6 as equal to 14. The result in cell G3 shows the average of A1:A6 equal to 15.2. The value of 8 in cell A2 is not used because it is hidden.

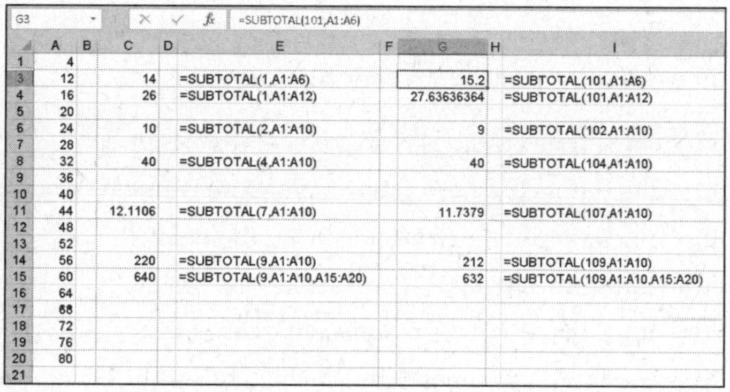

Figure 8-5:
Getting
SUBTOTAL
to ignore
hidden
values.

	A	B	C	D	E	F	G	H	I
					=SUBTOTAL(101,A1:A6)				
1	4								
3	12		14		=SUBTOTAL(1,A1:A6)		15.2		=SUBTOTAL(101,A1:A6)
4	16		26		=SUBTOTAL(1,A1:A12)	27.63636364			=SUBTOTAL(101,A1:A12)
5	20								
6	24		10		=SUBTOTAL(2,A1:A10)		9		=SUBTOTAL(102,A1:A10)
7	28								
8	32		40		=SUBTOTAL(4,A1:A10)		40		=SUBTOTAL(104,A1:A10)
9	36								
10	40								
11	44		12.1106		=SUBTOTAL(7,A1:A10)		11.7379		=SUBTOTAL(107,A1:A10)
12	48								
13	52								
14	56		220		=SUBTOTAL(9,A1:A10)		212		=SUBTOTAL(109,A1:A10)
15	60		640		=SUBTOTAL(9,A1:A10,A15:A20)		632		=SUBTOTAL(109,A1:A10,A15:A20)
16	64								
17	68								
18	72								
19	76								
20	80								
21									

Using SUMPRODUCT

The SUMPRODUCT function provides a sophisticated way to add various products — across ranges of values. It doesn't just add the products of separate ranges; it produces products of the values positioned in the same place in each range and then sums up those products. The syntax of the function follows:

```
=SUMPRODUCT(Range1, Range2, ...)
```

The arguments to SUMPRODUCT must be ranges, although a range can be a single value. What is required is that all the ranges be the same size, both rows and columns. Up to 255 ranges are allowed, and at least 2 are required.

SUMPRODUCT works by first multiplying elements, by position, across the ranges and then adding all the results. To see how this works, take a look at the three ranges of values in Figure 8-6. I put letters in the ranges instead of numbers to make this easier to explain.

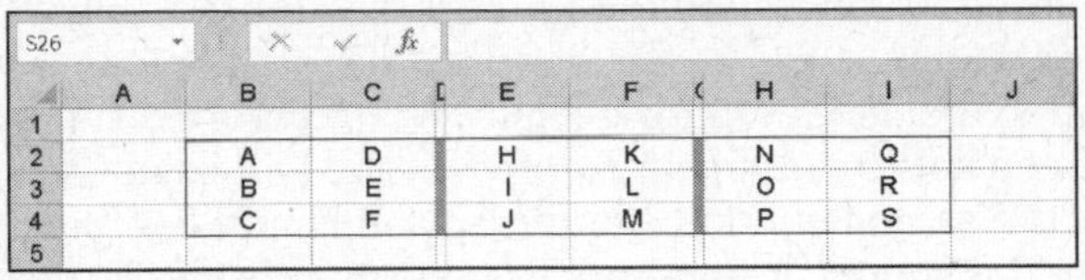

Figure 8-6:
Following
the steps
used by
SUMPROD-
UCT.

Suppose that you entered the following formula in the worksheet:

```
=SUMPRODUCT(B2:C4, E2:F4, H2:I4)
```

The result would be calculated by the following steps:

1. Multiplying A times H times N and saving the result

2. Multiplying D times K times Q and saving the result

3. Multiplying B times I times O and saving the result

4. Multiplying E times L times R and saving the result

5. Multiplying C times J times P and saving the result

6. Multiplying F times M times S and saving the result

7. Adding all six results to get the final answer

Be careful when you're using the SUMPRODUCT function. It's easy to mistakenly assume that the function adds products of individual ranges. It doesn't. SUMPRODUCT returns the sums of products across positional elements.

As confusing as SUMPRODUCT seems, it actually has a sophisticated use. Imagine that you have a list of units sold by product and another list of the products' prices. You need to know total sales (that is, the sum of the amounts), in which an amount is units sold times the unit price.

In the old days of spreadsheets, you would use an additional column to first multiply each unit sold figure by its price. Then you would sum those intermediate values. Now, with SUMPRODUCT, the drudgery is over. The single use of SUMPRODUCT gets the final answer in one step. Figure 8-7 shows how one cell contains the needed grand total. No intermediate steps are necessary.

D11		f_x	=SUMPRODUCT(C3:C7,D3:D7)	
	A	B	C	D	E
1					
2		Item	Units Sold	Price per Unit	
3		Desks	15	$60	
4		Tables	10	$85	
5		Chairs	22	$25	
6		Sofas	6	$450	
7		Bookcases	24	$30	
8					
9					
10					
11				$ 5,720	
12					

Figure 8-7: Being productive with SUM-PRODUCT.

Using SUMIF and SUMIFS

SUMIF is one of the real gemstones of Excel functions. It calculates the sum of a range of values, including only those values that meet a specified criterion. The criterion can be based on the same column that is being summed, or it can be based on an adjacent column.

Suppose that you use a worksheet to keep track of all your food-store purchases. For each shopping trip, you put the date in Column A, the amount in Column B, and the name of the store in Column C. You can use the SUMIF function to tell Excel to add all the values in Column B only where Column C contains "Great Grocery". That's it. SUMIF gives you the answer. Neat!

Figure 8-8 shows this example. The date of purchase, place of purchase, and amount spent are listed in three columns. SUMIF calculates the sum of purchases at Great Grocery. Here is how the function is written for the example:

```
=SUMIF(C3:C15,"Great Grocery",B3:B15)
```

Here are a couple of important points about the SUMIF function:

✔ The second argument can accommodate several variations of expressions, such as including greater than (>) or less than (<) signs or other operators. For example, if a column has regions such as North, South, East, and West, the criteria could be <>North, which would return the sum of rows that are *not* for the North region.

✔ Unpredictable results occur if the ranges in the first and third arguments do not match in size.

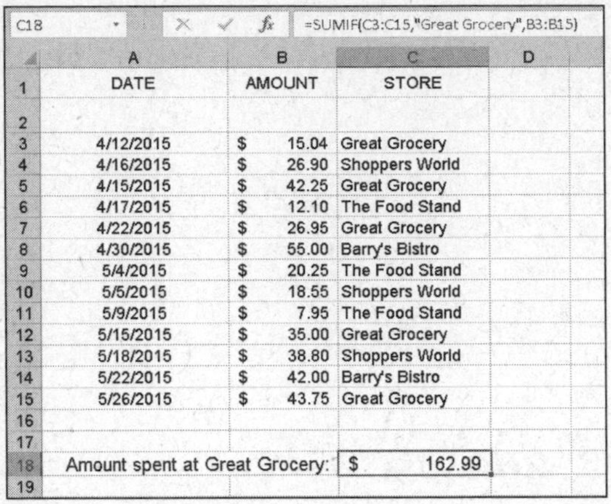

C18 =SUMIF(C3:C15,"Great Grocery",B3:B15)

	A	B	C	D
1	DATE	AMOUNT	STORE	
2				
3	4/12/2015	$ 15.04	Great Grocery	
4	4/16/2015	$ 26.90	Shoppers World	
5	4/15/2015	$ 42.25	Great Grocery	
6	4/17/2015	$ 12.10	The Food Stand	
7	4/22/2015	$ 26.95	Great Grocery	
8	4/30/2015	$ 55.00	Barry's Bistro	
9	5/4/2015	$ 20.25	The Food Stand	
10	5/5/2015	$ 18.55	Shoppers World	
11	5/9/2015	$ 7.95	The Food Stand	
12	5/15/2015	$ 35.00	Great Grocery	
13	5/18/2015	$ 38.80	Shoppers World	
14	5/22/2015	$ 42.00	Barry's Bistro	
15	5/26/2015	$ 43.75	Great Grocery	
16				
17				
18	Amount spent at Great Grocery:		$ 162.99	
19				

Figure 8-8: Using SUMIF for targeted tallying.

Try it yourself! Here's how to use the SUMIF function:

1. **Enter two ranges of data in a worksheet.**

   At least one should contain numerical data. Make sure both ranges are the same size.

2. **Position the pointer in the cell where you want the results displayed.**
3. **Type** =SUMIF(**to begin the function.**
4. **Hold down the left mouse button and drag the pointer over one of the ranges.**

   This is the range that can be other than numerical data.

5. **Type a comma (,).**
6. **Click one of the cells in the first range.**

   This is the criterion.

7. **Type a comma (,).**
8. **Hold down the left mouse button and drag the pointer over the second range.**

   This is the range that must contain numerical data.

9. **Type a), and press Enter.**

The result you see is a sum of the numeric values where the items in the first range matched the selected criteria.

The example in Figure 8-8 sums values when the store is Great Grocery but does not use the date in the calculation. What if you need to know how much was spent at Great Grocery in April only? Excel provides a function for this, of course: SUMIFS.

SUMIFS lets you apply multiple "if" conditions to a sum. The format of SUMIFS is a bit different from SUMIF. SUMIFS uses this structure:

```
=SUMIFS(range to be summed, criteria range 1, criteria 1, criteria range 2,
          criteria 2)
```

The structure requires the range of numerical values to be entered first, followed by pairs of criteria ranges and the criteria itself. In Figure 8-9, the formula is

```
=SUMIFS(B3:B15,A3:A15,"<5/1/2015",C3:C15,"Great Grocery")
```

The Function uses B3:B15 as the source of values to sum. A1:A15 is the first criteria range, and "<5/1/2015" is the criteria. This tells the function to look for any date that is earlier than May 1, 2015 (which filters the dates to just April). This is followed by a second criteria range and value: In C3:C15, look just for Great Grocery. The final sum of $84.24 adds just three numbers — 15.04, 42.25, and 26.95 — because these are the only values in April for Great Grocery.

C18 =SUMIFS(B3:B15,A3:A15,"<5/1/2015",C3:C15,"Great Grocery")

	A	B	C	D	E
1	DATE	AMOUNT	STORE		
2					
3	4/12/2015	$ 15.04	Great Grocery		
4	4/16/2015	$ 26.90	Shoppers World		
5	4/15/2015	$ 42.25	Great Grocery		
6	4/17/2015	$ 12.10	The Food Stand		
7	4/22/2015	$ 26.95	Great Grocery		
8	4/30/2015	$ 55.00	Barry's Bistro		
9	5/4/2015	$ 20.25	The Food Stand		
10	5/5/2015	$ 18.55	Shoppers World		
11	5/9/2015	$ 7.95	The Food Stand		
12	5/15/2015	$ 35.00	Great Grocery		
13	5/18/2015	$ 38.80	Shoppers World		
14	5/22/2015	$ 42.00	Barry's Bistro		
15	5/26/2015	$ 43.75	Great Grocery		
16					
17					
18	Amount spent at Great Grocery:		$ 84.24		
19					

Figure 8-9: Using SUMIFS to get a multiple filtered sum.

Getting an Angle on Trigonometry

Did you think Excel was not up to snuff to provide some tricks for trigonometry? Then think again. Who can resist playing around with such exciting things like cosines and tangents? All right, I admit this is not for everyone, but here are the trig functions nonetheless. Besides, even if the concepts are difficult, you can always throw around the terms at a party and be recognized as the brainiest person there.

Three basic trigonometry functions

The sine, cosine, and tangent of an angle are likely the most used values in trigonometry calculations. They provide answers about the relationships of a triangle's angles to the sides of the triangle. (See how I boiled down the bulk of trigonometry into a single sentence!)

Figure 8-10 shows a handful of angles in Column A and their corresponding sine, cosine, and tangent values in Columns B, C, and D, respectively.

Figure 8-10: Using SIN, COS, and TAN functions.

B3		✕ ✓ *fx*	=SIN(RADIANS(A3))	
	A	B	C	D
1	Angle (in degrees)	Sine	Cosine	Tangent
2				
3	23	0.390731128	0.920504853	0.424474816
4	45	0.707106781	0.707106781	1
5	60	0.866025404	0.5	1.732050808
6	90	1	6.12574E-17	1.63246E+16
7	129	0.777145961	-0.629320391	-1.234897157
8	180	1.22515E-16	-1	-1.22515E-16
9	200	-0.342020143	-0.939692621	0.363970234
10	360	-2.4503E-16	1	-2.4503E-16
11				

The SIN, COS, and TAN functions take just the single argument of a number (the angle) and return the converted values. The functions look like this if the angles are in radians:

```
=SIN(angle)
=COS(angle)
=TAN(angle)
```

If the angles are in degrees, they need to be converted to radians by the RADIANS function. In this case, you would use these:

```
=SIN(RADIANS(angle))
=COS(RADIANS(angle))
=TAN(RADIANS(angle))
```

Which leads you to. . .

Degrees and radians

An angle can be expressed in degrees or radians. A degree is more common to us non–rocket scientists. Most everyone know that there are 360 degrees in a circle, that a right angle is 90 degrees, and even that "doing a 180" means turning completely around and going the other way.

One radian = 180/pi degrees, and one degree = pi/180 radians. All this talk about pi is making me hungry! For lowdown and quick conversion: 1 radian = 57.3 degrees.

Pi is approximately equal to 3.14159. See the beginning of this chapter for a forkful of pi.

Excel provides the RADIANS and DEGREES functions to convert a number from radians to degrees or vice versa. I think the real reason Excel did this was to keep pi out of the picture so you would concentrate on work and not dessert.

The functions are the single argument type:

```
=RADIANS(angle in degrees)
=DEGREES(angle in radians)
```

Using some numbers, you can see that 90 degrees = 1.5707963267949 radians and so 1.5707963267949 radians must equal 90 degrees. And it does.

Part III
Solving with Statistics

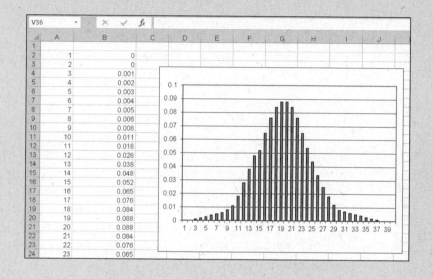

Find out how to calculate an average by using a subset of values in "Calculating an Average based on Criteria" online at www.dummies.com/extras/excel formulasfunctions.

In this part . . .

✔ Get familiar with basic statistics.

✔ See how estimating works.

✔ Make predictions and find out what is probable.

Chapter 9

Throwing Statistics a Curve

*J*ust pick up the newspaper, or turn on the television or the radio. We're bombarded with interesting facts and figures that are the result of statistical work: There is a 60 percent chance of rain, the Dow Jones Industrial Average gained 2.8 percent, the Yankees are favored over the Red Sox 4-3, and so on.

Statistics are used to tell us facts about the world around us. Statistics are also used to tell us lies about our world. Statistics can be used to confuse or obscure information. Imagine that you try a new candy bar, and you like it. Well, then you can boast that 100 percent of the people who tried it liked it!

Sometimes, statistics produce odd conclusions — to say the least! Imagine this: Bill Gates helps at a homeless shelter. The average wealth of the 40 or so people in the room is $1 billion. Why? Because Bill's worth is counted in the average, thereby skewing the average past the point of making sense. How about this? You hear on the news that the price of gasoline dropped 6 percent. Hurray! Let's go on a trip. But what is that 6 percent decrease based on? Is it a comparison with last week's price, last month's price, or last year's price? Perhaps the price of gasoline dropped 6 percent compared with last month. But prices are still 20 percent higher than last year. Is this good news?

Statistics are traditionally divided into two types. *Descriptive statistics,* covered in this chapter, help you summarize and understand data. *Inferential statistics,* covered in Chapter 10, are used to draw conclusions about data comparisons.

Getting Stuck in the Middle with AVERAGE, MEDIAN, and MODE

Are you of average height? Do you earn an average income? Are your children getting above-average grades? There is more than a single way to determine the middle value from a group of values. There are three common statistical functions that describe the center value from a population of values. These are the mean, the median, and the mode.

The term *population* refers to all possible measurements or data points, whereas the term *sample* refers to the measurements or data points that you actually have. For example, if you are conducting a survey of registered voters in New Jersey, the population is all registered voters in the state, and the sample is those voters who actually took the survey.

Technically, the term *average* refers to the mean value, but in common language, *average* can also be used to mean the median or the mode instead of the mean. This leads to all sorts of wonderful claims by advertisers and anyone else who wants to make a point.

It's important to understand the difference between these terms:

- **Mean:** The mean is a calculated value. It's the result of summing the values in a list or set of values and then dividing the sum by the number of values. For example, the average of the numbers 1, 2, and 3 equals 2. This is calculated as $(1 + 2 + 3) \div 3$ or $6 \div 3$.

- **Median:** The median is the middle value in a sorted list of values. If there are an odd number of items in the list, the median is the actual middle value. In lists with an even number of items, there is no actual middle value. In this case, the median is the mean of the two values in the middle. For example, the median of 1, 2, 3, 4, 5 is 3 because the middle value is 3. The median of 1, 2, 3, 4, 5, 6 is 3.5 because the mean of the two middle values, 3 and 4, is 3.5.

- **Mode:** The mode is the value that has the highest occurrence in a list of values. It may not exist! In the list of values 1, 2, 3, 4, there is no mode because each number is present the same number of times. In the list of values 1, 2, 2, 3, 4, the mode is 2 because 2 is used twice and the other numbers are used once.

The mean, median, and mode are sometimes called *measures of central tendency* because they serve to summarize a data sample in a single statistic.

Let's get started! These steps create three results in your worksheet, using the AVERAGE, MEDIAN, and MODE functions:

1. **Enter a list of numerical values.**

   Any mix of numbers will do.

2. **Position the cursor in the cell where you want the *mean* to appear.**

3. **Type =AVERAGE(to start the function.**

4. **Drag the pointer over the list or enter the address of the range.**

5. **Type a) to end the AVERAGE function.**

6. **Position the cursor in the cell where you want the *median* to appear.**

7. **Type =MEDIAN(to start the function.**

8. **Drag the pointer over the list or enter the address of the range.**

9. **Type a) to end the MEDIAN function.**

10. **Position the cursor in the cell where you want the *mode* to appear.**

11. **Type =MODE.SNGL(to start the function.**

12. **Drag the pointer over the list or enter the address of the range.**

13. **Type a) to end the MODE function.**

Depending on the numbers you entered, the three results may be the same (very unlikely!), about the same, or quite different. The MODE function will have returned #N/A if there were no repeating values in your data.

The mean is calculated by the AVERAGE function.

Imagine this: Three people use a new toothpaste for six months, and then all go to the dentist. Two have no cavities. Hey, this toothpaste is great! The third person has three cavities. Uh-oh!

Person	*Cavities*
A	0
B	0
C	3

The average number of cavities for this group is 1 — that is, if you're using the *mean* as the average. This doesn't sound like a good toothpaste if, on average, each person who used it got a cavity! On the other hand, both the median and the mode equal 0. The median equals 0 because that's the middle value in the sorted list. The mode equals 0 because that's the highest occurring value. As you can see, statistics prove that the new toothpaste gives 0 cavities, on average — sort of.

Look at another example. Figure 9-1 shows the results of a midterm test for a hypothetical class. The mean, median, and mode are shown for the distribution of grades.

DS			× ✓ f_x	=MODE.SNGL(A3:A20)		
	A	B	C	D	E	F
1	Student Grades					
2						
3	94					
4	94		The Mean Is	86.72		
5	91					
6	77		The Median Is	89		
7	95					
8	84		The Mode Is	94		
9	93					
10	68					
11	80					
12	83					
13	92					
14	77					
15	91					
16	99					
17	80					
18	94					
19	87					
20	82					
21						

Figure 9-1: Defining central tendencies in a list of grades.

As almost always happens, the mean, the median, and the mode each return a different number. Strictly speaking, we should say that the average grade is 86.72, the mean value. But if the teacher or the school wants to make the impact on students look better, they could point out that the most frequently occurring score is 94. This is the mode, and sure enough, three students did receive a 94. But is this the best representation of the overall results? Probably not.

Working with the functions that return these measures of central tendencies — AVERAGE, MEDIAN, and MODE — can make for interesting and sometimes misleading results. Here is one more example of how these three functions can give widely different results for the same data. Here is data for six customers and what they spent with a company last year:

Customer	Total Amount Spent Last Year
A	$300
B	$90
C	$2,600
D	$850
E	$28,400
F	$300

The mean (using the AVERAGE function) is $5,423.33. The median is $575, and the mode is $300. These three amounts aren't even close! Which one best represents the typical amount that a customer spent last year?

The issue with this set of data is that one value — $28,400 — is so much larger than the other values that it skews the mean. You may be led to believe that each customer spent about $5,423. But looking at the real values, only one customer spent a lot of money, relatively speaking. Customers A, B, C, D, and F spent nowhere near $5,423.33, so how can that "average" apply to them?

Figure 9-2 shows a situation in which one value is way out of league with the rest — sometimes called an *outlier*, which makes the average not too useful. Figure 9-2 also shows how much the mean changes if the one spendthrift customer is left out, but if you leave out any other customer, there is very little change in the mean.

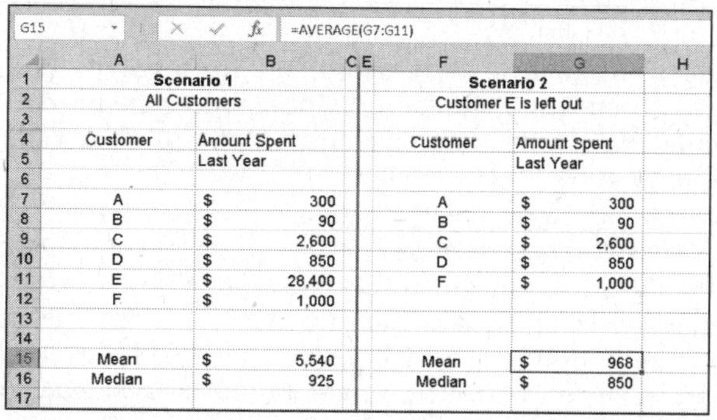

Figure 9-2:
Deciding
what to do
with an
unusual
value.

	A	B	C	E	F	G	H
1	Scenario 1				Scenario 2		
2	All Customers				Customer E is left out		
3							
4	Customer	Amount Spent			Customer	Amount Spent	
5		Last Year				Last Year	
6							
7	A	$	300		A	$	300
8	B	$	90		B	$	90
9	C	$	2,600		C	$	2,600
10	D	$	850		D	$	850
11	E	$	28,400		F	$	1,000
12	F	$	1,000				
13							
14							
15	Mean	$	5,540		Mean	$	968
16	Median	$	925		Median	$	850
17							

G15 — =AVERAGE(G7:G11)

In Scenario 2, Customer E is left out. The mean and the median are much closer together — $968 and $850, respectively. Either amount reasonably represents the mid value of what customers spent last year.

But can you just drop a customer like that (not to mention the biggest customer)? Yikes! Instead, you can consider a couple of creative averaging solutions. Either use the median or use a weighted average (a calculation of the mean in which the relevance of each value is taken into account). Figure 9-3 shows the result of each approach.

Scenario 1 shows the mean and the median for the set of customer amounts. Here, using the median is a better representation of the central tendency of the group.

| F18 | ▾ | × ✓ *fx* | =SUMPRODUCT(F9:F14,G9:G14)/SUM(G9:G14) |

	A	B	C	D	E	F	G	H	I
1									
2			Scenario 1				Scenario 2		
3			Just the Facts!			Customer E is treated with a dampening weight factor			
4									
5									
6		Customer	Amount Spent		Customer	Amount Spent	Weight		
7			Last Year			Last Year	Factor		
8									
9		A	$	300	A	$	300	18	
10		B	$	90	B	$	90	18	
11		C	$	2,600	C	$	2,600	18	
12		D	$	850	D	$	850	18	
13		E	$	28,400	E	$	28,400	10	
14		F	$	1,000	F	$	1,000	18	
15									
16		Total	$	33,240					
17									
18		Mean	$	5,540	Mean	$	3,711		
19		Median	$	925	Median	$	925		
20									

Figure 9-3:
Calculating
a creative
mean.

TIP

When reporting results based on an atypical calculation, it's good practice to add a footnote that explains how the answer was determined. If you were to report that the "average" expenditure was $925, a note should explain this is the median, not the mean.

Scenario 2 in Figure 9-3 is a little more complex. This involves making a weighted average, which is used to let individual values be more or less influential in the calculation of a mean. This is just what you need! Customer E needs to be less influential.

Weighted averages are the result of applying a weighting factor to each value that is used in calculating the mean. In this example, all the customers are given a weight factor of 18 except Customer E, who has a weight factor of 10. All customers except Customer E have been given increased weight, and Customer E has been given decreased weight because his sales value is so different from all the others. When weights are applied in an average, the sum of the weights must equal 100. If no weighting factor is applied, each customer effectively has a weight of 16.667 — the number of customers divided into 100. Applying a weight of 10 to Customer E and 18 to all the other customers keeps the sum of the weights at 100: $18 \times 5 + 10$. The values of 18 and 10 have been subjectively chosen. When you use weighting factors to calculate a weighted average, you must make that fact known when you present the results.

The mean in Scenario 2 is $3,711. This figure is still way above the median or even the mean of just the five customers without Customer E (refer to Figure 9-2 earlier in this chapter). Even so, it's less than the unweighted mean shown in Scenario 1 and is probably a more accurate reflection of the data.

By the way, the mean in Scenario 2 is not calculated with the AVERAGE function, which cannot handle weighted means. Instead, the SUMPRODUCT function is used. The actual formula in cell F18 looks like this:

```
=SUMPRODUCT(F9:F14,G9:G14)/SUM(G9:G14)
```

The amount that each customer spent last year is multiplied by that customer's weight, and a sum of those products is calculated with SUMPRODUCT. Finally, the sum of the products is divided by the sum of the weights.

Deviating from the Middle

Life is full of variety! Calculating the mean for a group will not reflect that variety. Suppose that you are doing a survey of salaries for different occupations and that occupation A has a mean salary of $75,000 a year and occupation B has the same mean of $75,000 a year. Does this mean that the two groups are the same? Not necessarily. Suppose that in group A, the salaries range from $65,000 to $85,000, but in group B, they range from $35,000 to $115,000. This difference — how much the values differ from the mean — is called *variance*. Excel provides functions that calculate and evaluate variance, and variance is an important part of many statistical presentations.

Measuring variance

Variance is a measure of how spread out a set of data is in relation to the mean. Variance is calculated by summing the squared deviations from the mean.

Mathematics that make you work

Specifically, variance is calculated as follows:

1. **Calculate the mean of the set of values.**
2. **Calculate the difference from the mean for each value.**
3. **Square each difference.**
4. **Sum up the squares.**
5. **Divide the sum of the squares by the number of items in the sample, minus 1.**

A sample is a selected set of values taken from the population. A sample is easier to work with. For example, any statistical results found on 1,000 sales transactions probably would return the same, or close to the same, results if run on the entire population of 10,000 transactions.

Note that the last step differs depending on whether the VAR.S or VAR.P function is used. VAR.S uses the number of items, minus 1, as the denominator. VAR.P uses the number of items.

Figure 9-4 shows these steps in calculating a variance without using Excel's built-in function for the task. Column B has a handful of values. Column C shows the deviation of each figure from the *mean* of the values. The mean, which equals 7.8, is never actually shown. Instead, the mean is calculated within the formula that computes the difference. For example, cell C8 has this formula:

```
=B8-AVERAGE($B$4:$B$8)
```

Column D squares the values in Column C. This is an easy calculation. Here are the contents of cell D8: `=C8^2`. Finally, the sum of the squared deviations is divided by the number of items, less one item. The formula in cell D12 is `=SUM(D4:D8)/(COUNT(B4:B8)-1)`.

Figure 9-4: Calculating variance from the mean.

	D15			✕ ✓ ƒx	=VAR.S(B4:B8)	
	A	B	C		D	E
1						
2		**Values**	**Deviation from mean**		**Deviation from mean, squared**	
3						
4		3	-4.8		23.04	
5		5	-2.8		7.84	
6		8	0.2		0.04	
7		9	1.2		1.44	
8		14	6.2		38.44	
9						
10						
11						
12			**Calculated variance:**		17.7	
13						
14						
15			**Variance from the VAR.S function:**		17.7	
16						
17						

Functions that do the work: VAR.S and VAR.P

Now that you know how to create a variance the textbook way, you can forget it all! Here, I show the mathematical steps so you can understand what happens, but Excel provides the VAR.S and VAR.P functions to do all the grunge work for you.

In Figure 9-4 earlier in this chapter, cell D15 shows the variance calculated directly with the VAR.S function: `=VAR.S(B4:B8)`.

Try it yourself. Here's how:

1. **Enter a list of numerical values.**

   Any mix of numbers will do.

2. **Position the cursor in the cell where you want the *variance* to appear.**

3. **Type =VAR.S(to start the function.**

4. Drag the pointer over the list or enter the address of the range.

5. Type a) and press the Enter key.

Variance is calculated on a population of data or a sample of the population:

✔ The VAR.S function calculates variance on a sample of a population's data.

✔ The VAR.P function calculates variance on the full population.

The calculation is slightly different in that the denominator for variance of a population is the number of items. The denominator for variance of a sample is the number of items less one. Figure 9-5 shows how VAR.S and VAR.P are used on a sample and the full population. Cells A4:A43 contain the number of hours spent on the Internet daily by 40 individuals.

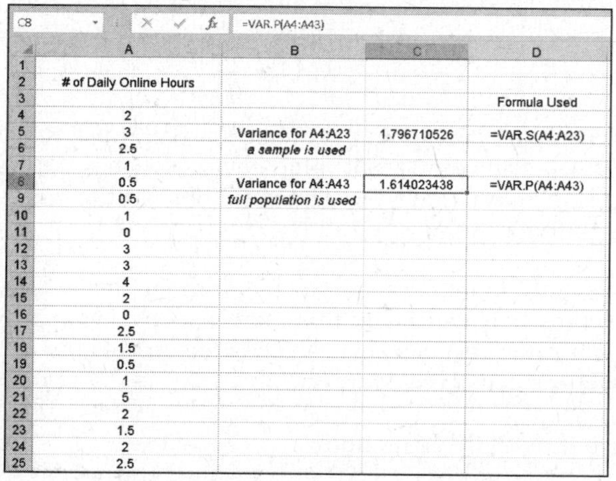

Figure 9-5:
Calculating
variance
from the
mean.

The VAR.S function calculates the variance of a sample of 20 values. The VAR.P function calculates the variance of the full population of 40 values. VAR.P is entered in the same fashion as VAR.S. Here's how:

1. Enter a list of numerical values.

Any mix of numbers will do.

2. Position the cursor in the cell where you want the *variance* to appear.

3. Type =VAR.P(to start the function.

4. Drag the pointer over the list or enter the address of the range.

5. Type a) and press the Enter key.

Analyzing deviations

Often, finding the mean is an adequate measure of a sample of data. Sometimes, the mean is not enough — you also want to know the average *deviation* from the mean. That is, you want to find the average of how far individual values differ from the mean of the sample. For example, you may need to know the average score on a test and how far the scores, on average, differ from the mean. Average deviation is another way to specify variance.

Here's an example:

Score	*Deviation from 84.83 Mean*
78	6.83
92	7.17
97	12.17
80	4.83
72	12.83
90	5.17

The mean of this sample of values is 84.83. Use the AVERAGE function, if you want to double-check. Each individual value deviates somewhat from the mean. For example, 92 has a deviation value of 7.17 from the mean. A simple equation proves this: 92 − 84.83 = 7.17.

If you use the AVERAGE function to get the mean of the deviations, you have the average deviation. It's even easier than that, though. Excel provides the AVEDEV function for this very purpose! AVEDEV calculates the mean and averages the deviations all in one step.

Here's how to use the AVEDEV function:

1. **Enter a list of numerical values.**

2. **Position the cursor in the cell where you want the *average deviation* to appear.**

3. **Type** =AVEDEV(**to start the function.**

4. **Drag the pointer over the list or enter the address of the range.**

5. **Type a**) **and press the Enter key.**

The AVEDEV function averages the *absolute* deviations. In other words, *negative deviations* (where the data point is less than the mean) are converted to positive values for the calculation. For example, a value of 10 has a deviation of −40 from a mean of 50: 10 − 50 = −40. However, AVEDEV uses the absolute value of the deviation, 40, instead of −40.

The variance, explained earlier in the chapter, serves as the basis for a common statistical value called the *standard deviation.* Technically speaking, the standard deviation is the square root of the variance. Variance is calculated by *squaring* deviations from the mean.

The variance and the standard deviation are both valid measurements of deviation. However, the variance can be a confusing number to work with. In Figure 9-4 earlier in this chapter, the variance is calculated to be 17.7 for a group of values whose range is just 11 (14 − 3). How can a range that is only a size of 11 show a variance of 17.7? Well, it does, as shown in Figure 9-4.

This oddity is removed when you use the standard deviation. The reversing of the squaring brings the result back to the range of the data. The standard deviation value fits inside the range of the sample values. In addition, you'll find the standard deviation is more commonly used than the variance in statistical analyses. Excel has a standard deviation formula: STDEV.P. This is how you use it:

1. **Enter a list of numerical values.**

2. **Position the cursor in the cell where you want the *standard deviation* to appear.**

3. **Type =STDEV.P(to start the function.**

4. **Drag the pointer over the list or enter the address of the range.**

5. **Type a) and press the Enter key.**

Figure 9-6 takes the data and variance shown in Figure 9-4 and adds the standard deviation to the picture. The standard deviation is 3.762977544. This number fits inside the range of the sample data.

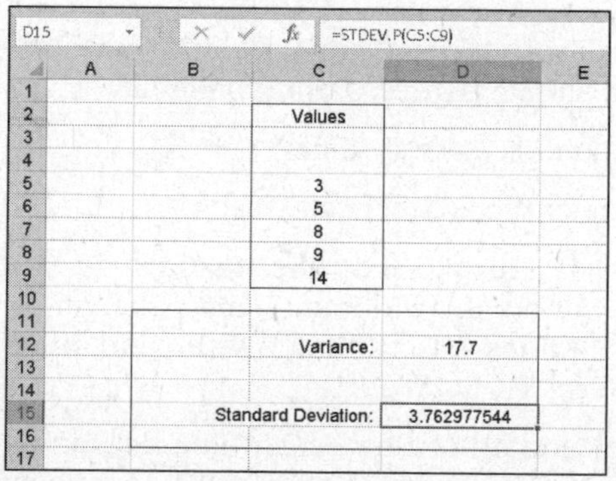

Figure 9-6: Calculating the standard deviation.

Looking for normal distribution

The standard deviation is one of the most widely used measures in statistical work. It's often used to analyze deviation in a normal distribution. A distribution is the frequency of occurrences of values in a population or sample. A *normal* distribution often occurs in large data sets that have a *natural,* or random, attribute. For example, taking a measurement of the height of 1,000 10-year-old children will produce a normal distribution. Most of the measured heights center on and deviate somewhat from the mean. A few measured heights will be extreme — both considerably larger than the mean and considerably smaller than the mean.

Ringing the bell curve

A normal distribution is often visually represented as a graph in the shape of a bell — hence, the popular term *bell curve.* Figure 9-7 shows a normal distribution.

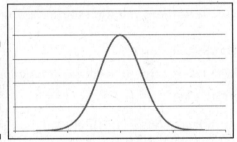

Figure 9-7:
Displaying a normal distribution in a graph.

A normal distribution has a few key characteristics:

✔ The curve is symmetrical around the mean. Half the measurements are greater than the mean, and half are less than the mean.

✔ The mean, median, and mode are the same.

✔ The highest point of the curve is the mean.

✔ The width and height are determined by the standard deviation. The larger the standard deviation, the wider and flatter the curve. You can have two normal distributions with the same mean and different standard deviations.

✔ 68.2 percent of the area under the curve is within one standard deviation of the mean (both to the left and the right), 95.44 percent of the area under the curve is within two standard deviations, and 99.72 percent of the area under the curve is within three standard deviations.

✔ The extreme left and right ends of the curve are called the *tails*. Extreme values are found in the tails. For example, in a distribution of height, very short heights are in the left tail, and very large heights are in the right tail.

Different sets of data almost always produce different means and standard deviations and, therefore, different-shaped bell curves. Figure 9-8 shows two superimposed normal distributions. Each is a perfectly valid normal distribution; however, each has its own mean and standard deviation, with the narrower curve having a smaller standard deviation.

Figure 9-8:
Normal distributions come in different heights and widths.

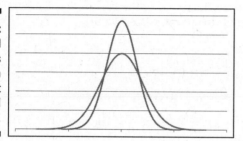

Analysis is often done with normal distributions to determine probabilities. For example, what is the probability that a 10-year-old child's height is 54 inches? Somewhere along the curve is a discrete point that represents this height. Further computation (outside the scope of this discussion) returns the probability. What about finding the probability that a 10-year-old is 54 inches high *or greater*? Then the *area* under the curve is considered. These are the type of questions and answers determined with normal distributions.

A good amount of analysis of normal distributions involves the values in the *tails:* the areas to the extreme left and right of the normal distribution curve.

All normal distributions have a mean and a standard deviation. However, the *standard normal distribution* is characterized by having the mean equal 0 and the standard deviation equal 1.

A table of values serves as a lookup in determining probabilities for areas under the standard normal curve. This table is useful for working with data that has been modified to fit the standard normal distribution. This table is often found in the appendix section of statistics books and on the Internet as well. A search on the Internet for "*areas under the normal standard curve*" returns many useful results.

Using STANDARDIZE

To use this table of standard normal curve probabilities, you must standardize the data being analyzed. Excel provides the STANDARDIZE function for just this purpose. STANDARDIZE takes three arguments: the data point, the mean, and the standard deviation. The returned value is what the data point value is when the mean is 0 and the standard deviation is 1.

An individual value from a nonstandard normal distribution is referred to as x. An individual value from a standard normal distribution is referred to as z.

Figure 9-9 shows how the STANDARDIZE function changes raw values to standard values. The standard deviation of the raw data is 7.438637452, but the standard deviation of the standardized values is 1. The mean of the standardized values is 0.

	A	B	C	D	E	F	G	H	I
					=STDEV.P(E7:E1207)				
1									
2		Mean:	17.23473829						
3		Standard Deviation:	7.438637452						
4									
5		Raw Values			Standardized Values				
6									
7		4.806195244			-1.67080909			Min Value:	-1.76934598
8		6.764168773			-1.4075924			Max Value:	1.712956472
9		19.70832122			0.332531723			Standard Deviation:	1
10		13.39483084			-0.51621113			Mean:	0
11		21.96972861			0.636540005				
12		27.46533867			1.375332572				
13		6.432661234			-1.45215802				
14		22.57557011			0.71798523				
15		4.358859408			-1.73094588				
16		8.806730797			-1.1330042				
17		23.94519864			0.902108806				
18		20.27440868			0.408632684				
19		26.30413196			1.219227813				
20		8.023703889			-1.23826903				
21		10.35655964			-0.92465572				
22		28.68766541			1.539653894				
23		23.41416556			0.830720317				

Figure 9-9: Standardizing a distribution of data.

Column B in Figure 9-9 has a long list of 1,200 random values. The mean is 17.23473829, as shown in cell C2. The standard deviation is 7.438637452, as shown in cell C3. For each data point in Column B, the standardized value is displayed in Column E. The list of values in Column E are those returned with the STANDARDIZE function.

The STANDARDIZE function takes three arguments:

✔ Data point

✔ Mean of the distribution

✔ Standard deviation of the distribution

For example, this is the formula in cell E7:

```
=STANDARDIZE(B7,C$2,C$3)
```

Note that a few key properties of the distribution have changed after the values are standardized:

- ✔ The standard deviation is 1.
- ✔ The mean is 0.
- ✔ The standardized values fall within the range –1.77 to 1.72.

This third point is determined by using the MIN and MAX functions, respectively, in cells I7 and I8. Having values fall in the range –1.7 to 1.7 allows the values to be analyzed with the Areas Under the Standard Normal Curve table mentioned earlier. That is, it's a property of standard normal curves to have all values fit into this range.

Here's how to use the STANDARDIZE function:

1. **Enter a list of numerical values in a column.**

   It makes sense if this list is a set of random observable data, such as heights, weights, or amounts of monthly rainfall.

2. **Calculate the mean and standard deviation.**

   See "Getting Stuck in the Middle with AVERAGE, MEDIAN, and MODE" earlier in this chapter for more about the mean.

   The STANDARDIZE function references these values. The mean is calculated with the AVERAGE function, and the standard deviation is calculated with the STDEV.P function. STDEV.P is used instead of STDEV.S because the whole data population is used.

3. **Place the cursor in the cell adjacent to the first data point entered in Step 1.**

4. **Type =STANDARDIZE(to start the function.**

5. **Click the cell that has the first data point.**

6. **Type a comma (,).**

7. **Click the cell that has the mean.**

8. **Type a comma (,).**

9. **Click the cell that has the standard deviation.**

10. **Type a) to end the function.**

    The formula with the STANDARDIZE function is now complete. However, you must edit it to fix the references to the mean and standard deviation.

The references need to be made absolute so they won't change when the formula is dragged down to other cells.

11. **Double-click the cell with the formula to enter the edit mode.**

12. **Precede the column and row parts of the reference to the cell that contains the mean with a dollar sign ($).**

13. **Precede the column and row parts of the reference to the cell that contains the standard deviation with a dollar sign ($).**

14. **Press the Enter key or the Tab key to end the editing.**

15. **Use the fill handle to drag the formula down to the rest of the cells that are adjacent to the source data points.**

It's important that the references to the mean and standard deviation are treated as absolute references so they won't change when the formula is dragged to the other cells. Therefore, the formula should end up looking like this: =STANDARDIZE(B7,$C$2,$C$3). Note the $ signs.

Skewing from the norm

There is deviation in a distribution, but who says the deviation has to be uniform with deviation the same on both sides of the mean? Not all distributions are normal. Some are *skewed,* with more values clustered either below the mean or above it:

- When more values fall below the mean, the distribution is *positively* skewed.

- When more values fall above the mean, the distribution is *negatively* skewed.

The following minitable has a few examples:

Values	Mean	Comment
1, 2, 3, 4, 5	3	There is no skew. An even number of values fall above and below the mean.
1, 2, 3, 6, 8	4	The distribution is positively skewed. More values fall below the mean.
1, 2, 8, 9, 10	6	The distribution is negatively skewed. More values fall above the mean.

Figure 9-10 shows a distribution plot, where 1,000 values are in the distribution, ranging between 1 and 100. The values are summarized in a table of frequencies (discussed later in this chapter). The table of frequencies is the source of the chart.

	A	B	C	D	E ... L
A24			*fx*	67.0114748443296	
1	62.22717				
2	50.62773				
3	62.55201		Bin	Frequency	
4	88.03311		10	26	
5	59.39882		20	69	
6	72.79763		30	89	
7	53.46602		40	105	
8	71.04916		50	114	
9	55.31592		60	173	
10	56.35039		70	155	
11	99.64792		80	144	
12	55.05815		90	95	
13	57.98499		100	30	
14	63.76048				
15	62.81488				
16	20.50704				
17	21.04579		Mean:	53.6697083	
18	1.823257				
19	51.85294		# of points<=50:	403	
20	77.75417		# of points >50:	597	
21	9.792653				
22	67.28764		Skew:	-0.27323459	
23	68.64623				
24	67.01147				
25	58.99782				

Figure 9-10: Working with skewed data.

The mean of the distribution is 53.669, shown in cell D17. Cells D19 and D20 show the number of values that fall above and below the mean. There are more values above the mean than below. The distribution, therefore, is negatively skewed.

The actual skew factor is –0.27323459. The formula in cell D22 is =SKEW(A1: A1000). The chart makes it easy to see the amount of skew. The plot is leaning to the right.

Finding out the amount of skew in a distribution can help identify bias in the data. If, for example, the data is expected to fall into a normal (unskewed) distribution (such as a random sampling of height for 10-year-old children) and the data is skewed, you have to wonder whether some bias got into the data. Perhaps some 14-year-old children were measured by mistake and those heights were mixed in with the data. Of course, being skewed is not itself an indication of bias. Some distributions are skewed by their very nature.

SKEW

Here's how to use the SKEW function to determine the skewness of a distribution:

1. **Enter a list of numerical values.**
2. **Position the cursor in the cell where you want the amount of skew to appear.**
3. **Type =SKEW(to start the function.**
4. **Drag the pointer over the list or enter the address of the range.**
5. **Type a) and press the Enter key.**

KURT

Another way that a distribution can differ from the normal distribution is *kurtosis*. This is a measure of the peakedness or flatness of a distribution compared with the normal distribution. It is also a measure of the size of the curves' tails. You determine kurtosis with the KURT function, which returns a positive value if the distribution is relatively peaked with small tails compared with the normal distribution. A negative result means that the distribution is relatively flat with large tails.

Figure 9-11 shows the curves of two distributions. The one on the left has a negative kurtosis of –0.82096, indicating a somewhat flat distribution. The distribution on the right is above 1, which means that the distribution has a pronounced peak and relatively shorter tails.

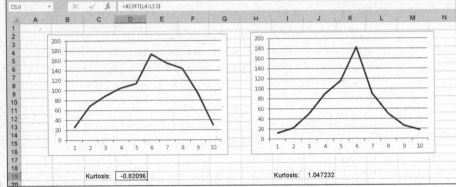

Figure 9-11: Measuring the kurtosis of two distributions.

This is how to use the KURT function:

1. **Enter a list of numerical values.**

2. **Position the cursor in the cell where you want kurtosis to appear.**

3. **Type** =KURT(**to start the function.**

4. **Drag the pointer over the list or enter the address of the range.**

5. **Type a) and press the Enter key.**

Comparing data sets

At times, you need to compare two sets of data to see how they relate to each other. For example, how does the amount of snowfall affect the number of customers entering a store? Does the money spent on advertising increase the number of new customers? You answer these questions by determining whether the two data sets are correlated.

Excel provides two functions for this task: COVARIANCE.S (or COVARIANCE.P) and CORREL. These functions return the *covariance* and *correlation* coefficient results from comparing two sets of data.

COVARIANCE.S and COVARIANCE.P

Either COVARIANCE function takes two arrays as its arguments and returns a single value. The value can be positive or negative. A positive value means that the two arrays of data tend to move in the same direction: If data set A increases (or decreases), data set B also increases (or decreases). A negative value means that the two data sets tend to move in opposite directions: When A increases, B decreases, and vice versa. The covariance's absolute value reflects the strength of the relationship.

When COVARIANCE.S or COVARIANCE.P returns 0, there is no relationship between the two sets of data.

Sales of bread will likely create sales of butter; they're somewhat related. In other words, the amount of butter a store sells is likely to follow the amount of bread it sells: more bread, more butter.

Day	Loaves of Bread Sold	Tubs of Butter Sold
Monday	62	12
Tuesday	77	15
Wednesday	95	26

As bread sales increase, so do sales of butter. Therefore, sales of butter are expected to have a positive relation to sales of bread. These items complement each other. By contrast, bread and muffins compete against each other. As bread is purchased, the sales of muffins likely suffer because people will eat one or the other. Without even using any function, you can conclude that bread sales and butter sales move in the same direction and that bread sales and muffin sales move in differing directions. But by how much?

Figure 9-12 shows an example that measures snowfall and the number of customers coming into a store. Two covariance calculations are given: one for snowfall between 0 and 3 inches, and one for snowfall between 0 and 8 inches.

In Figure 9-12, the first COVARIANCE measures the similarity of the amount of snowfall with the number of customers, but just for 0 to 3 inches of snow. The formula in cell G7 is =COVARIANCE.P(B5:B8,D5:D8). The answer is –6.875. This means that as snowfall increases, the number of customers decreases. The two sets of data go in opposite directions. As one goes up, the other goes down. This is confirmed by the result's being negative.

Figure 9-12:
Using
COVARI-
ANCE to
look for a
relationship
between
two data
sets.

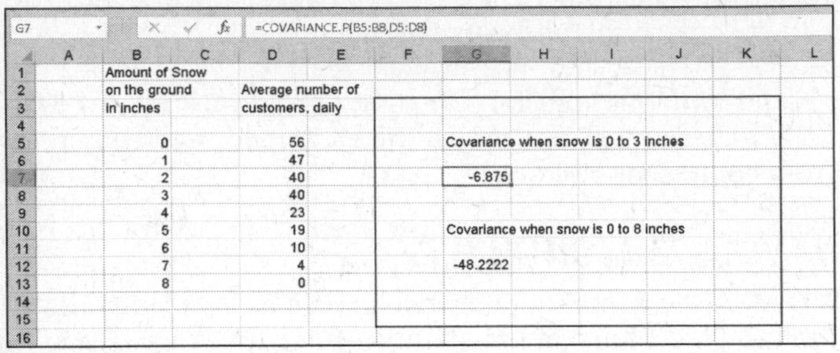

The formula in cell G12 is =COVARIANCE.P(B5:B13,D5:D13). This examines all the values of the data sets, inclusive of 0 to 8 inches of snow. The covariance is –47.7778. This, too, confirms that as snowfall increases, the number of customers decreases.

However, note that the covariance of the first calculation, for 0 to 3 inches of snow, is not as severe as the second calculation for 0 to 8 inches. When there are just up to 3 inches of snow on the ground, some customers stay away — but not that many. On the other hand, when there are 8 inches of snow, no customers show up. The first covariance is comparably less than the second: –6.875 versus –48.2222. The former number is closer to 0 and tells you that a few inches of snow don't have much effect. The latter number is significantly distanced from 0, and sure enough, when up to 8 inches of snow is considered, customers stay home.

Note that the COVARIANCE.P function is used for the data in rows 5 through 8 because those data points are being considered as a population, not as a sample of a population.

Here's how to use the COVARIANCE.P function:

1. **Enter two lists of numbers.**

    The lists must be the same size.

2. **Position the cursor in the cell where you want covariance to appear.**

3. **Type** =COVARIANCE.P(**to start the function.**

4. **Drag the pointer over the first list or enter the address of the range.**

5. **Type a comma (,).**

6. **Drag the pointer over the second list or enter the address of the range.**

7. **Type a) and press the Enter key.**

CORREL

The CORREL function works in the same manner as COVARIANCE, but the result is always between –1 and 1. The result is, in effect, set to a standard. Then the results of correlations can be compared.

A negative result means that there is an *inverse correlation*. As one set of data goes up, the other goes down. The actual negative value tells you to what degree the inverse correlation is. A value of –1 means the two sets of data move perfectly in opposite directions. A value of –0.5, for example, means that the two sets move in somewhat opposite directions.

The CORREL function returns a value between –1 and 1. A positive value means that the two data sets move in the same direction. A negative value means that the two sets of data move in opposite directions. A value of 0 means that there is no relation between the sets of data.

Figure 9-13 shows three correlation results. The correlations display how customers reacted (as a percentage increase in sales) with regard to three types of advertising. All three advertising campaigns show a positive correlation. As more money is spent on advertising, customer responsiveness increases (or at least doesn't reverse its direction).

		=CORREL(B13:B17,F13:F17)

	A	B	C	D	E	F	G	H	I	J
1										
2		Amount spent on magazine advertising				Customer Responsiveness Percentage				
3										
4		10000				2				
5		20000				4		Correlation:	0.968963	
6		30000				5				
7		40000				7				
8		50000				7				
9										
10										
11		Amount spent on radio advertising								
12										
13		4000				3				
14		5000				6		Correlation:	0.932095	
15		6000				8				
16		7000				8.5				
17		8000				9				
18										
19										
20		Amount spent on direct mail								
21										
22		20000				4				
23		24000				4		Correlation:	0.447214	
24		28000				3.5				
25		32000				4				
26		36000				4.5				
27										

Figure 9-13: Comparing the results of advertising campaigns.

All three returned correlation values fall within the range of 0 to 1 and, therefore, are easy to compare. The evidence is clear: Direct mail is not as efficient as magazine or radio advertising. Both the magazine and radio advertising score high; the returned values are close to 1. However, direct mail returns a correlation of 0.4472. A positive correlation does exist — that is, direct-mail expenditures create an increase in customer responsiveness. But the correlation is not as strong as magazine or radio advertising. The money spent on direct mail would be better spent elsewhere.

Here's how to use the CORREL function:

1. **Enter two lists of numbers.**

   The lists must be the same size.

2. **Position the cursor in the cell where you want correlation to appear.**

3. **Type =CORREL(to start the function.**

4. **Drag the pointer over the first list or enter the address of the range.**

5. **Type a comma (,).**

6. **Drag the pointer over the second list or enter the address of the range.**

7. **Type a) and press the Enter key.**

Analyzing Data with Percentiles and Bins

No, not with trash bins (although you may want to throw your data out at times)! The term *bins* refers to analyzing data by determining how many data points fall into specified ranges, or bins. *Percentiles* is a technique for analyzing data by determining where values relate, percentagewise, to the entire data set.

Imagine this: A pharmaceutical company is testing a new drug to lower cholesterol. The data is 500 cholesterol readings from the people in the sample. Of interest is how the data breaks up with regard to the 25 percent, the 50 percent, and the 75 percent marks. That is, what cholesterol reading is greater than 25 percent of the data (and, therefore, smaller than 75 percent of the data)? What value is at the 50 percent position? These measures are called *quartiles* because they divide the sample into four quarters.

QUARTILE.INC and QUARTILE.EXC

The QUARTILE function is designed specifically for this kind of analysis. The function takes two arguments. One argument is the range of the sample data, and the other indicates which quartile to return. The second argument can be 0, 1, 2, 3, or 4 when you're using QUARTILE.INC; or 1, 2, or 3 when you're using QUARTILE.EXC. QUARTILE.EXC is used when the minimum and maximum values are to be excluded. Therefore, that version of the function does not take 0 or 4 as the second argument:

Formula	*Result*
=QUARTILE.INC(A4:A503,0)	Minimum value in the data
=QUARTILE.INC(A4:A503,1)	Value at the 25th percentile
=QUARTILE.INC(A4:A503,2)	Value at the 50th percentile
=QUARTILE.INC(A4:A503,3)	Value at the 75th percentile
=QUARTILE.INC(A4:A503,4)	Maximum value in the data

QUARTILE.INC (or QUARTILE.EXC) works on ordered data, but you don't have to do the sorting; the function takes care of that. In Figure 9-14, the quartiles have been calculated. The minimum and maximum values have been returned by using 0 and a 4, respectively, as the second argument.

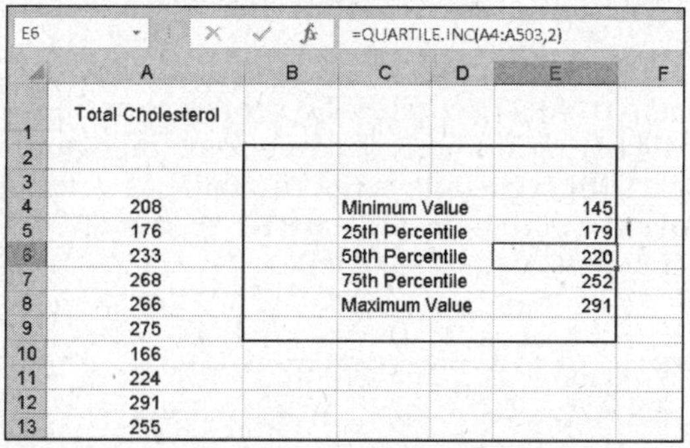

Figure 9-14:
Finding out values at quarter percentiles.

	A	B	C	D	E	F
	Total Cholesterol					
1						
2						
3						
4	208		Minimum Value		145	
5	176		25th Percentile		179	
6	233		50th Percentile		220	
7	268		75th Percentile		252	
8	266		Maximum Value		291	
9	275					
10	166					
11	224					
12	291					
13	255					

E6 · ✗ ✓ *fx* =QUARTILE.INC(A4:A503,2)

Here's how to use the QUARTILE function:

1. **Enter a list of numerical values.**

2. **Position the cursor in the cell where you want a particular quartile to appear.**

3. **Type** =QUARTILE.INC(**to start the function.**

4. **Drag the pointer over the list or enter the address of the range.**

5. **Type a comma (,).**

6. **Enter a value between 0 and 4 for the second argument.**

7. **Type a) and press the Enter key.**

PERCENTILE.INC and PERCENTILE.EXC

The PERCENTILE functions are similar to the QUARTILE functions except that you can specify which percentile to use when returning a value. You aren't locked into fixed percentiles such as 25, 50, or 75.

PERCENTILE.INC (or PERCENTILE.EXC) takes two arguments:

✔ Range of the sample

✔ Value between 0 and 1

The value tells the function which percentile to use. For example, 0.1 is the 10th percentile, 0.2 is the 20th percentile, and so on.

Use the QUARTILE.INC function to analyze data at the fixed 25th, 50th, and 75th percentiles. Use the PERCENTILE.INC function to analyze data at any desired percentile. PERCENTILE.EXC is used when the second argument is exclusive of 0 and 1. In other words, the second argument can be any value between 0 and 1 but not 0 or 1.

Figure 9-15 shows a sample of test scores. Who scored at or above the 90th percentile? The highest-scoring students deserve some recognition. Bear in mind that scoring at the 90th percentile is not the same as getting a score of 90. Values at or above the 90th percentile are those that are in the top 10 percent of whatever scores are in the sample.

			C5		f_x	=IF(B5>=PERCENTILE.INC(B$3:B$27,0.9), "A Winner!", "")		
	A	B	C	D	E	F	G	H
1		Score on the Trivia Test						
2					Score found at the 90th Percentile			
3	Wendy	59						
4	Alex	54				80		
5	Daniel	82	A Winner!					
6	Rob	16						
7	Andrea	53						
8	Matthew	78						
9	Beth	58						
10	Les	58						
11	Michael	62						
12	Louise	80	A Winner!					
13	Mark	37						
14	Steven	25						
15	Lisa	23						
16	Ilse	80	A Winner!					
17	Warren	70						
18	John	38						
19	Lilly	37						
20	Dill	79						
21	Kirk	82	A Winner!					
22	Geoff	72						
23	Nichola	72						
24	Ian	46						
25	Emma	62						

Figure 9-15: Using PER-CENTILE to find high scorers.

It so happens that the score that is positioned at the 90th percentile is 80. Cell F4 has the formula =PERCENTILE.INC(B3:B27,0.9), which uses 0.9 as the second argument.

The cells in C3:C27 all have a formula that tests whether the cell to the left, in column B, is at or greater than the 90th percentile. For example, cell C3 has this formula: =IF(B3>=PERCENTILE.INC(B$3:B$27,0.9),"A Winner!","").

If the value in cell B3 is equal to or greater than the value at the 90th percentile, cell C3 displays the text "A Winner!". The value in cell B3 is 59, which doesn't make for a winner. On the other hand, the value in cell B5 is greater than 80, so cell C5 displays the message.

Here's how to use the PERCENTILE.INC function:

1. **Enter a list of numerical values.**
2. **Position the cursor in the cell where you want the result to appear.**
3. **Type** =PERCENTILE.INC(**to start the function.**
4. **Drag the pointer over the list or enter the address of the range.**
5. **Type a comma (,).**
6. **Enter a value between 0 and 1 for the second argument.**

   This tells the function what percentile to seek.
7. **Type a) and press the Enter key.**

RANK

The RANK.EQ or RANK.AVG function tells you the rank of a particular number — in other words, where the value is positioned — within a distribution. In a sample of ten values, for example, a number could be the smallest (rank = 1), the largest (rank = 10), or somewhere in between. The function takes three arguments:

- **The number being tested for rank:** If this number isn't found in the data, an error is returned.
- **The range to look in:** A reference to a range of cells goes here.
- **A 0 or a 1, telling the function how to sort the distribution:** A 0 (or if the argument is omitted) tells the function to sort the values in descending order. A 1 tells the function to sort in ascending order. The order of the sort makes a difference in how the result is interpreted. Is the value in question being compared to the top value of the data or the bottom value?

The difference between RANK.EQ and RANK.AVG is that if more than one value is at the same rank, RANK.EQ uses the larger value, whereas RANK.AVG uses the average of the values.

Figure 9-16 displays a list of employees and the bonuses they earned. Suppose that you're the employee who earned $4,800. You want to know where you rank in the range of bonus payouts. Cell F4 contains a formula with the RANK.EQ function: =RANK.EQ(C9,C3:C20). The function returns an answer of 4. Note that the function was entered without the third argument. Leaving the third argument out tells the function to sort the distribution in descending order. This makes sense for determining how close to the *top* of the range a value is.

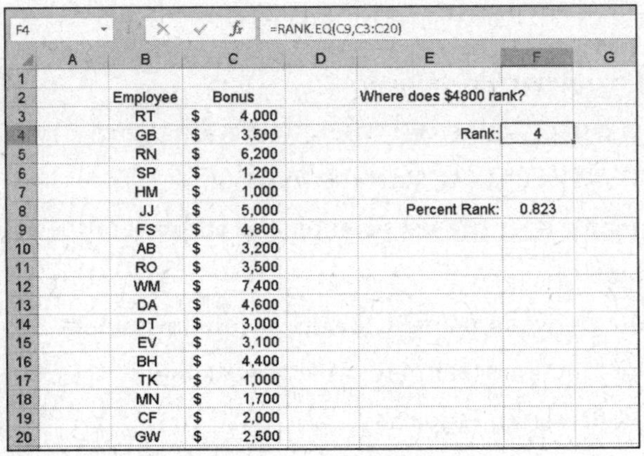

Figure 9-16:
Determining the rank of a value.

	A	B	C	D	E	F	G
F4			fx	=RANK.EQ(C9,C3:C20)			
1							
2		Employee	Bonus		Where does $4800 rank?		
3		RT	$ 4,000				
4		GB	$ 3,500		Rank:	4	
5		RN	$ 6,200				
6		SP	$ 1,200				
7		HM	$ 1,000				
8		JJ	$ 5,000		Percent Rank:	0.823	
9		FS	$ 4,800				
10		AB	$ 3,200				
11		RO	$ 3,500				
12		WM	$ 7,400				
13		DA	$ 4,600				
14		DT	$ 3,000				
15		EV	$ 3,100				
16		BH	$ 4,400				
17		TK	$ 1,000				
18		MN	$ 1,700				
19		CF	$ 2,000				
20		GW	$ 2,500				

Follow these steps to use the RANK function:

1. **Enter a list of numerical values.**

2. **Position the cursor in the cell where you want the result to appear.**

3. **Type =RANK.EQ(to start the function.**

4. **Click the cell that has the value you want to find the rank for or enter its address.**

   You can also just enter the actual value.

5. **Type a comma (,).**

6. **Drag the pointer over the list of values or enter the address of the range.**

7. **If you want to have the number evaluated against the list in *ascending* order, enter a comma (,) and then enter a 1.**

Descending order is the default and doesn't require an argument to be entered.

8. **Type a) and press the Enter key.**

PERCENTRANK

The PERCENTRANK.INC or PERCENTRANK.EXC formula also returns the rank of a value but tells you where the value is as a percentage. In other words, the PERCENTRANK function may tell you that a value is positioned 20 percent into the ordered distribution. PERCENTRANK takes three arguments:

✔ The range of the sample

✔ The number being evaluated against the sample

✔ An indicator of how many decimal places to use in the returned answer (This is an optional argument. If it's left out, three decimal places are used.)

PERCENTRANK.EXC is used when a rank between 0 and 100 percent (between 0 and 1) is to be returned, but not 0 or 1. In Figure 9-16 earlier in this chapter, the percentage rank of the $4,800 value is calculated to be 82.3 percent (0.823). Therefore, $4,800 ranks at the 82.3 percent position in the sample. The formula in cell F8 is =PERCENTRANK.INC(C3:C20,C9).

In the RANK.EQ function, the value being evaluated is the first argument, and the range of the values is the second argument. In the PERCENTRANK.INC function, the order of these arguments is reversed.

Follow these steps to use the PERCENTRANK.INC function:

1. **Enter a list of numerical values.**

2. **Position the cursor in the cell where you want the result to appear.**

3. **Type =PERCENTRANK.INC(to start the function.**

4. **Drag the pointer over the list of values or enter the address of the range.**

5. **Type a comma (,).**

6. **Click the cell that has the value you want to find the rank for or enter its address.**

You can also just enter the actual value.

7. **If you want to have more or less than three decimal places returned in the result, enter a comma (,) and then enter the number of desired decimal places.**

8. **Type a closing) to end the function.**

FREQUENCY

The FREQUENCY function places the count of values in a sample in *bins*. A bin represents a range of values, such as 0–1 or 20–29. Typically, the bins used in an analysis are the same size and cover the entire range of values. For example, if the data values range from 1–100, you might create ten bins each, ten units wide. The first bin would be for values of 1 to 10, the second bin would be for values of 11 to 20, and so on.

Figure 9-17 illustrates this. There are 300 values in the range B3:B302. The values are random, between 1 and 100. Cells D3 through D12 have been set as bins that each cover a range of ten values. Note that for each bin, its number is the top of the range it's used for. For example, the 30 bin is used for holding the count of how many values fall between 21 and 30.

E3		× ✓	f_x	{=FREQUENCY(B3:B302,D3:D12)}		
	A	B	C	D	E	F	G
1		Raw Values		Bins	Count of values, per bin	
2						
3		29		10	24	
4		49		20	12	
5		58		30	6	
6		47		40	28	
7		61		50	101	
8		69		60	1	
9		76		70	45	
10		42		80	6	
11		67		90	34	
12		33		100	43	
13		72				
14		48				
15		64				
16		49				
17		43				
18		46				
19		95				
20		44				
21		83				

Figure 9-17: Setting up bins to use with the FREQUENCY function.

A bin holds the count of values within a numeric range — the number of values that fall into the range. The bin's number is the top of *its* range.

FREQUENCY is an array function and requires specific steps to be used correctly. Here is how it's done:

1. **Enter a list of values.**

   This can be a lengthy list and likely represents some observed data, such as the age of people using the library or the number of miles driven on the job. Obviously, you can use many types of observable data.

2. **Determine the high and low values of the data.**

   You can use the MAX and MIN functions for this.

3. **Determine what your bins should be.**

   This is subjective. For example, if the data has values from 1 to 100, you can use 10 bins that each cover a range of 10 values. Or you can use 20 bins that each cover a range of 5 values. Or you can use 5 bins that each cover a range of 20 values.

4. **Create a list of the bins by entering the high number of each bin's range, as shown in cells D3:D12 in Figure 9-17.**

5. **Click the first cell where you want the output of FREQUENCY to be displayed.**

6. **Drag down to select the rest of the cells.**

   There should now be a range of selected cells. The size of this range should match the number of bins. Figure 9-18 shows what the worksheet should look like at this step.

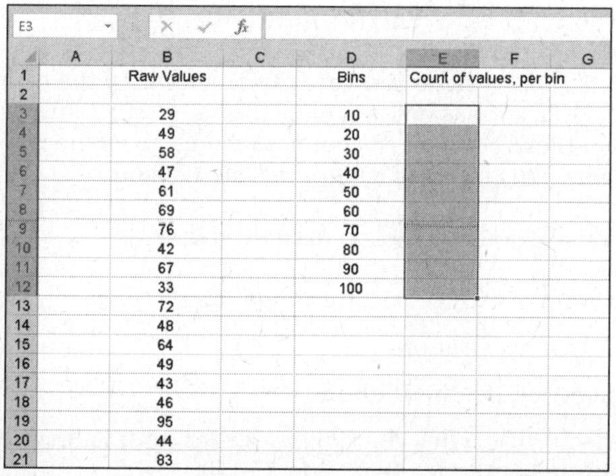

Figure 9-18:
Preparing to enter the FREQUENCY function.

7. Type =FREQUENCY(to start the function.

8. Drag the cursor over the sample data or enter the address of the range.

9. Type a comma (,).

10. Drag the cursor over the list of bins or enter the address of that range.

Figure 9-19 shows what the worksheet should look like at this point.

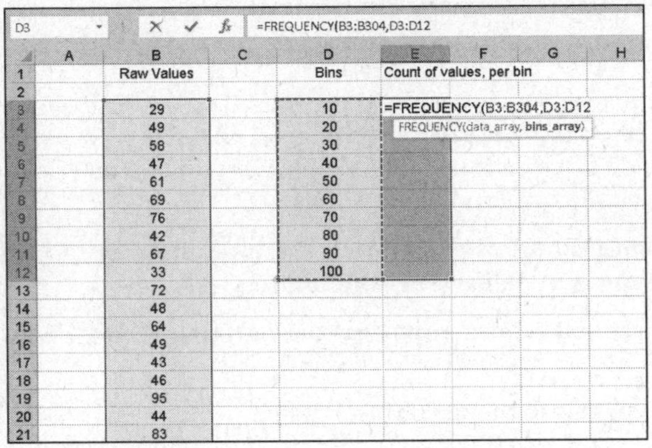

Figure 9-19: Completing the entry of the FREQUENCY function.

11. Type a).

Do *not* press Enter.

12. Press Ctrl+Shift+Enter to end the function entry.

Hurray, you did it! You have entered an array function. All the cells in the range where FREQUENCY was entered have the same exact formula. The returned values in these cells are the count of values from the raw data that falls within the bins. This is called a *frequency distribution*.

Next, take this distribution and plot a curve from it:

1. Select the Count of Values per bin range data.

That's E3:E12 in this example.

2. Click the Insert tab on the Ribbon.

3. In the Charts section, click the Column Chart item to display a selection of column chart styles (see Figure 9-20).

4. Select the desired chart style to create the chart.

Figure 9-21 shows the completed frequency distribution chart.

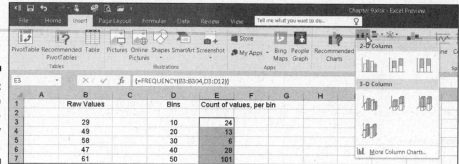

Figure 9-20: Preparing to plot the frequency distribution.

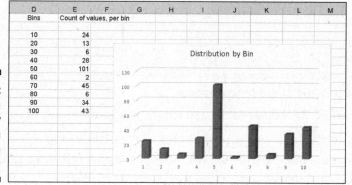

Figure 9-21: Displaying a frequency distribution as a column chart.

A frequency distribution is also known as a *histogram*.

MIN and MAX

Excel has two functions — MIN and MAX — that return the lowest and highest values in a set of data. These functions are simple to use. The functions take up to 255 arguments, which can be cells, ranges, or values.

Figure 9-22 shows a list of home sales. What are the highest and lowest values? Cell F4 displays the lowest price in the list of sales, with this formula: =MIN(C4:C1000). Cell F6 displays the highest price with this formula: =MAX(C4:C1000).

| F18 | ▾ | × ✓ ƒx | =SMALL(C$4:C$1000,5) | | | | |

	A	B	C	D	E	F	G
1		Home Sales					
2							
3		Address	Sale Price				
4		4 McGregor Drive	$ 411,100		Minimum	$ 143,339	
5		10 Mackey Avenue	$ 316,300				
6		8 Bennington Way	$ 418,400		Maximum	$ 568,400	
7		132 Baldwin Avenue	$ 197,600				
8		9 Mason Drive	$ 422,000				
9		44 Miller Road	$ 263,900		Top 5		
10		124 Pennsylvania Blvd	$ 169,300		#1	$ 568,400	
11		105 Groton Way	$ 271,200		#2	$ 497,491	
12		7 Overlook Street	$ 159,000		#3	$ 497,458	
13		8 Oneida Way	$ 393,600		#4	$ 496,523	
14		102 Caswell Avenue	$ 148,500		#5	$ 496,234	
15		7 Caller Street	$ 351,900				
16		166 Adelina Drive	$ 215,000				
17		124 Eastside Drive	$ 218,400		Bottom 5		
18		6 Navarro Way	$ 176,600		#56	$ 144,188	
19		5 Farmer Street	$ 148,300		#57	$ 143,718	
20		22 Ashkurn Blvd	$ 152,100		#58	$ 143,666	
21		15 Paradise Way	$ 327,300		#59	$ 143,418	
22		109 Edison Avenue	$ 260,800		#60	$ 143,339	
23		143 Carleton Street	$ 278,200				
24		6 Teal Street	$ 358,600				

Figure 9-22: Finding high and low values.

Here's how to use the MIN or MAX function:

1. **Enter a list of numerical values.**

2. **Position the cursor in the cell where you want the result to appear.**

3. **Type either =MIN(or =MAX(to start the function.**

4. **Drag the pointer over the list or enter the address of the range.**

5. **Type a) and press the Enter key.**

MIN and MAX return the upper and lower values of the data. What if you need to know the value of the second-highest price? Or the third-highest price?

LARGE and SMALL

The LARGE and SMALL functions let you find out a value that is positioned at a certain point in the data. LARGE is used to find the value at a position that is offset from the highest value. SMALL is used to find the value at a position that is offset from the lowest value.

Figure 9-22 earlier in this chapter displays the top five home sales, as well as the bottom five. Both the LARGE and SMALL functions take two arguments: the range of the data in which to find the value and the position relative to the top or bottom.

The top five home sales are found with LARGE. The highest sale, in cell F10, is returned with this formula: =LARGE(C$4:C$1000,1). Because the function used here is LARGE, and the second argument is 1, the function returns the value at the first position. By no coincidence, this value is also returned by the MAX function.

To find the second-highest home sales, the second argument to LARGE is 2. Cell F11 has this formula: =LARGE(C$4:C$1000,2). The third-, fourth-, and fifth-largest home sales are returned in the same fashion when 3, 4, and 5, respectively, are used as the second argument.

The bottom five sales are returned in the same fashion by the SMALL function. For example, cell F22 has this formula: =SMALL(C$4:C$1000,1). The returned value, $143,339, matches the value returned by the MIN function. The cell just above it, F21, has this formula: =SMALL(C$4:C$1000,2).

Hey, wait! You may have noticed that the functions are looking down to row 1000 for values, but the bottom listing is numbered as 60. An interesting thing to note in this example is that all the functions use row 1000 as the bottom row to look in, but this doesn't mean there are that many listings. This is intentional. There are only 60 listings for now. What happens when new sales are added to the bottom of the list? By giving the functions a considerably larger range than needed, you've built in the ability to handle a growing list.

The labels in cells E10:E14 (#1, #2, and so on) are entered as is. Clearly, any ranking that starts from the top would begin with # 1, proceed to # 2, and so on.

However, the labels in cells E18:E22 (#56, #57, and so on) were created with formulas. The COUNTA function is used to count the total number of listings. Even though the function looks down to row 1000, it finds only 60 listings, so that is the returned count. The #60 label is based on this count. The other labels (#59, #58, #57, and #56) are created by reducing the count by 1, 2, 3, and 4, respectively:

- The formula in cell E22 is ="# " & COUNTA(B$4:B$1000).
- The formula in cell E21 is ="# " & COUNTA(B$4:B$1000)-1.
- The formula in cell E20 is ="# " & COUNTA(B$4:B$1000)-2.
- The formula in cell E19 is ="# " & COUNTA(B$4:B$1000)-3.
- The formula in cell E18 is ="# " & COUNTA(B$4:B$1000)-4.

Here's how to use the LARGE and SMALL functions:

1. **Enter a list of numerical values.**
2. **Position the cursor in the cell where you want the result to appear.**

3. Type =LARGE(or =SMALL(**to start the function.**

4. **Drag the pointer over the list or enter the address of the range.**

5. **Type a comma (,).**

6. **Enter a number indicating the position to return.**

7. **Type a) and press the Enter key.**

Use LARGE to find a value's position relative to the highest value. Use SMALL to find a value's position relative to the smallest value.

Going for the Count

The COUNT and COUNTIF functions return, well, a count. What else could it be with a name like that?

COUNT

COUNT is straightforward. It counts how many items are in a range of values. There is a catch, though: Only numeric values and dates are counted. Text values are not counted; neither are blank cells.

COUNTA works the same way as COUNT, but it counts all cells that are not empty, including text cells.

To use the COUNT function, follow these steps:

1. **Enter a list of numerical values.**

2. **Position the cursor in the cell where you want the result to appear.**

3. **Type =COUNT(to start the function.**

4. **Drag the pointer over the list or enter the address of the range.**

5. **Type a) and press the Enter key.**

Figure 9-23 shows a list of popular movies along with the sales figure and the year for each movie. Cell F5 displays the count of movies, returned with the COUNT function. The formula in cell F5 is =COUNT(C5:C329).

Note that the range entered in the function looks at the sales figures for the movies. This is intentional. Sales figures are numeric. If COUNT used the range of movie titles, in Column B, the count would be 0 because this column contains text data.

COUNTIF

The COUNTIF function is handy when you need to count how many items are in a list that meet a certain condition. In Figure 9-23 earlier in this chapter, cell F7 shows the count of movies made in 2002. The formula in cell F7 is =COUNTIF(D5:D329,2002).

The COUNTIF function takes two arguments:

- The range address of the list to be counted
- The criterion

Table 9-1 presents some examples of criteria for the COUNTIF function.

Table 9-1	Using Criteria with the COUNTIF Function
Example	*Comment*
=COUNTIF(D5:D329,"=2002")	Returns the count of movies made in 2002.
=COUNTIF(D5:D329,2002)	Returns the count of movies made in 2002. Note that this is unique in that the criteria do not need to be in double quotes because the criterion is a simple equality.
=COUNTIF(D5:D329,"<2002")	Returns the count of movies made before 2002.
=COUNTIF(D5:D329,">=2002")	Returns the count of movies made in or after 2002.
=COUNTIF(D5:D329,"<>2002")	Returns the count of movies not made in 2002.

The criteria can also be based on text. For example, COUNTIF can count all occurrences of Detroit in a list of business trips. You can use wildcards with COUNTIF. The asterisk (*) is used to represent any number of characters, and the question mark (?) is used to represent a single character.

As an example, using an asterisk after Batman returns the number of Batman movies listed in Column B in Figure 9-23 earlier in this chapter. The formula that does this looks like this: `=COUNTIF(B5:B329,"Batman*")`. Notice the asterisk after `Batman`. This lets the function count *Batman and Robin*, *Batman Returns*, and *Batman Forever* along with just *Batman*.

Your criterion can be entered in a cell rather than directly in the COUNTIF function. Then just use the cell address in the function. For example, if you enter `"Batman*"` in cell C1, `=COUNTIF(B5:B329,C1)` would have the same result as the previous example. Cell F11 in Figure 9-23 returns the count of movies that have earned more than $200,000,000. The formula is `=COUNTIF(C5:C329,">200000000")`.

What if you need to determine the count of data items that match two conditions? Can do! The formula in cell F15 returns the count of movies that were made in 2004 *and* earned more than $200,000,000. However, COUNTIF is not useful for this type of multiple condition count. Instead, the SUMPRODUCT function is used. The formula in cell F15 follows:

```
=SUMPRODUCT((C5:C329>200000000)*(D5:D329=2004))
```

Believe it or not, this works. Although this formula looks like it's multiplying the number of movies that earned at least $200,000,000 by the number of movies made in 2004, it's really returning the count of movies that meet the two conditions. (Quick trivia: Which two 1998 movies earned at least $200,000,000? The answer [drum roll, please]: *Armageddon* and *Saving Private Ryan*.)

To use the COUNTIF function, follow along:

1. **Enter a list of numerical values.**

2. **Position the cursor in the cell where you want the result to appear.**

3. **Type** `=COUNTIF(` **to start the function.**

4. **Drag the pointer over the list or enter the address of the range.**

5. **Type a comma (,).**

6. **Enter a condition and enclose the condition in double quotes.**

   Use the following as needed:

   - = (equal to)
   - > (greater than)
   - < (less than)
   - * (wildcard)
   - ? (wildcard)
   - <> (not equal to)

7. **Type a) and press the Enter key.**

   The result is a count of cells that match the condition.

There is also a COUNTIFS function. This function allows using multiple ranges and criteria to return a count. COUNTIFS is quite similar to SUMIFS, discussed in Chapter 8.

Chapter 10

Using Significance Tests

*W*hen you have data from a population, you can draw a sample and run your statistical analysis on the sample. You can also run the analysis on the population itself. Is the mean of the sample data the same as the mean of the whole population? You can calculate the mean of both the sample and the population and then know precisely how well the sample represents the population. Are the two means exact? Off a little bit? How much different?

The problem with this, though, is that getting the data of the entire population in the first place isn't always feasible. On average, how many miles per gallon does a Toyota Camry get after five years on the road? You cannot answer this question to an exact degree, because it's impossible to test every Camry out there.

Instead, you infer the answer. Testing a handful, or sample, of Camrys is certainly possible. Then the mean gas mileage of the sample is used to represent the mean gas mileage of all five-year-old Camrys. The mean of the sample group will not necessarily match the mean of the population, but it is the best value that can be attained.

This type of statistical work is known as *estimation,* or *inferential statistics.* In this chapter, I show you the functions that work with the Student's t-test, useful for gaining insight into the unknown population properties. This is the method of choice when you're using a small sample — say, 30 data points or less.

The tests presented in this chapter deal with probabilities. If the result of a test — a t-test, for example — falls within a certain probability range, the result is said to be significant. Outside that range, the result is considered to be nonsignificant. A common rule of thumb is to consider probabilities less than 5 percent, or 0.05, to be significant, but exceptions to this rule exist.

The Student's t-test has nothing to do with students. The originator of the method was not allowed to use his real name due to his employer's rules. Instead, he used the name Student.

Testing to the T

The TTEST function returns the probability that two samples come from populations that have the same mean. For example, a comparison of the salaries of accountants and professors in New York City is under way. Are the salaries, overall (on average), the same for these two groups? Each group is a separate population, but if the means are the same, the average salaries are the same.

Polling all the accountants and professors isn't possible, so a sample of each is taken. Twenty-five random members of each group divulge their salaries in the interest of the comparison. Figure 10-1 shows the salaries of the two groups, as well as the results of the TTEST function.

	A	B	C	D	E	F	G
E8				f_x	=TTEST(A2:A26,B2:B26,2,2)		
1	Accountants	Professors					
2	$ 75,172	$ 86,655			TTEST Arguments		
3	$ 76,761	$ 82,203			2-tailed test		
4	$ 85,329	$ 60,401			Not a paired test		
5	$ 72,421	$ 77,893					
6	$ 54,129	$ 80,727					
7	$ 88,233	$ 77,152			TTEST		
8	$ 73,102	$ 73,092			0.106437		
9	$ 82,714	$ 86,126					
10	$ 76,024	$ 88,745					
11	$ 58,810	$ 84,700					
12	$ 73,072	$ 85,952			Accountants mean:	$ 73,928	
13	$ 65,918	$ 70,997			Professors mean:	$ 78,718	
14	$ 56,465	$ 78,002					
15	$ 73,861	$ 89,023					
16	$ 81,898	$ 77,464					
17	$ 83,360	$ 95,366					
18	$ 68,856	$ 73,093					
19	$ 85,584	$ 91,540					
20	$ 69,243	$ 56,852					
21	$ 58,572	$ 86,642					
22	$ 65,129	$ 81,478					
23	$ 80,350	$ 58,917					
24	$ 87,796	$ 76,012					
25	$ 76,051	$ 89,160					
26	$ 79,354	$ 59,775					

Figure 10-1: Comparing salaries.

The TTEST function returns 10.6 percent (0.106437) based on how the arguments of the function were entered. This percentage says there is a 10.6 percent probability that the mean of the underlying populations are the same.

Said another way, this is the likelihood that the mean of all accountant salaries in New York City matches the mean of all professor salaries in New York City. The formula in cell E8 is =TTEST(A2:A26,B2:B26,2,2).

The arguments of the TTEST function are listed in Table 10-1.

Table 10-1	Arguments of the TTEST Function
Argument	*Comment*
Array 1	The reference to the range of the first array of data.
Array 2	The reference to the range of the second array of data.
Tails	Either 1 or 2. For a one-tailed test, enter 1. For a 2-tailed test, enter 2.
Type	Type of t-test to perform. The choice is 1, 2, or 3. A number 1 indicates a paired test. A number 2 indicates a two-sample test with equal variance. A number 3 indicates a two-sample test with unequal variance.

The third argument of TTEST tells whether to conduct a one-tailed or two-tailed test. A one-tailed test is used when there is a question of whether one set of data is specifically larger or smaller than the other. A two-tailed test is used to tell whether the two sets are just different without specifying larger or smaller.

The first two arguments to TTEST are the ranges of the two sets of values. A pertinent consideration here is how the two sets of data are related. The sets could be comprised of elements that have a corresponding member in each set. For example, there could be a set of "before" data and a set of "after" data.

Seedling	*Height at Week 1*	*Height at Week 2*
#1	4 inches	5 inches
#2	3¾ inches	5 inches
#3	4½ inches	5½ inches
#4	5 inches	5 inches

This type of data is entered in the function as *paired*. In other words, each data value in the first sample is linked to a data value in the second sample. In this case, the link is due to the fact that the data values are "before" and "after" measurements from the same seedlings. Data can be paired in other ways. In the salary survey, for example, each accountant may be paired with a professor of the same age to ensure that length of time on the job does not affect the results. In this case, you would also use a paired t-test.

When you're using TTEST for paired samples, the two ranges entered for the first and second arguments must be the same size. When you're comparing two independent (unpaired) samples, the two samples don't have to be the same size.

Use TTEST to determine the probability that two samples come from the same population.

Here's how to use the TTEST function:

1. **Enter two sets of data.**

2. **Position the cursor in the cell where you want the result to appear.**

3. **Type =TTEST(to start the function.**

4. **Drag the pointer over the first list or enter the address of its range.**

5. **Type a comma (,).**

6. **Drag the pointer over the second list or enter the address of its range.**

7. **Type a comma (,).**

8. **Type 1 for a one-tailed test, or type 2 for a two-tailed test.**

9. **Type a comma (,).**

10. **Enter one of the following:**

    - **1** for a for a paired test

    - **2** for a test of two samples with equal variance

    - **3** for a test of two samples with unequal variance

11. **Type a).**

If you ever took a statistics course, you may recall that a t-test returns a *t-value,* which you then had to look up in a table to determine the associated probability. Excel's TTEST function combines these two steps. It calculates the t-value internally and determines the probability. You never see the actual t-value, just the probability — which is what you're interested in anyway!

The TDIST function returns the probability for a given t-value and degrees of freedom. You would use this function if you had a calculated t-value and wanted to determine the associated probability. Note that the TTEST function doesn't return a t-value but a probability, so you wouldn't use TDIST with the result that is returned by TTEST. Instead, you would use TDIST if you had one or more t-values calculated elsewhere and needed to determine the associated probabilities.

TDIST takes three arguments:

- ✔ The t-value
- ✔ The degrees of freedom
- ✔ The number of tails (1 or 2)

A t-distribution is similar to a normal distribution. The plotted shape is a bell curve. However, a t-distribution differs, particularly in the thickness of the tails. How much so is dependent on the degrees of freedom. The degrees of freedom roughly relate to the number of elements in the sample, less one. All t-distributions are symmetrical around 0, as is the normal distribution. In practice, however, you always work with the right half of the curve — positive t-values.

To use the TDIST function, follow along:

1. Position the cursor in the cell where you want the result to appear.

2. Type =TDIST(to start the function.

3. Enter a value for t or click a cell that has the value.

4. Type a comma (,).

5. Enter the degrees of freedom.

6. Type a comma (,).

7. Enter one of the following:

- • **1** for a one-tailed test
- • **2** for a two-tailed test

8. Type a).

If the t-value is based on a paired test, the degrees of freedom is equal to 1 less than the count of items in either sample. (Remember, the samples are the same size.) When the t-value is based on two independent samples, the degrees of freedom = (count of sample-1 items – 1) + (count of sample-2 items – 1).

The TINV function produces the inverse of TDIST. That is, TINV takes two arguments — the probability and the degrees of freedom — and returns the value of t. To use TINV, follow along:

1. Position the cursor in the cell where you want the result to appear.

2. Type =TINV(to start the function.

3. Enter the probability value (or click a cell that has the value).

4. **Type a comma (,).**
5. **Enter the degrees of freedom.**
6. **Type a).**

Comparing Results with an Estimate

The chi square test is a statistical method for determining whether observed results are within an acceptable range compared with what the results were expected to be. In other words, the chi square is a test of how well a before and after compare. Did the observed results come close enough to the expected results that you can safely assume that there is no real difference? Or were the observed and expected results far enough apart that you must conclude that there is a real difference?

A good example is flipping a coin 100 times. The expected outcome is 50 times heads, 50 times tails. Figure 10-2 shows how a chi square test statistic is calculated in a worksheet without any functions.

F10 =SUM(F5:F6)

	A	B	C	D	E	F	G
1	A Coin Is Tossed 100 Times						
2							
3				Difference	Square of	Square /	
4		Expected Result	Observed	(=Expected - Observed)	the Difference	Expected	
5	Heads	50	44	6	36	0.72	
6	Tails	50	56	-6	36	0.72	
7							
8							
9							
10					Chi Square	1.44	
11							

Figure 10-2: Calculating a chi square.

Cells B5:B6 show the expected results — that heads and tails each show up 50 times. Cells C5:C6 show the observed results. Heads appeared 44 times, and tails appeared 56 times. With this information, here is how the chi square test statistic is calculated:

1. **For each expected and observed pair, calculate the difference as** *(Expected – Observed)*.
2. **Calculate the square of each difference as** $(Expected - Observed)^2$.
3. **Divide the squares from Step 2 by their respective expected values.**
4. **Sum the results of Step 3.**

Of course, a comprehensive equation can be used for the first three steps, such as `=(expected - observed)^2/expected`.

The result in this example is 1.44. This number — the chi square value — is looked up in a table of chi square distribution values. This table is a matrix of degrees of freedom and confidence levels. Seeing where the calculated value is positioned in the table for the appropriate degrees of freedom (one less than the number of data points) shows you the probability that the difference between the expected and observed values is significant. That is, is the difference within a reasonable error of estimation, or is it real (for example, caused by an unbalanced coin)?

You can find the table of degrees of freedom and confidence levels in the appendix of a statistics book or on the Internet.

The CHISQ.TEST function returns the probability value (p) derived from the expected and observed ranges. The function has two arguments: the range of observed (or actual) values and the range of expected values. These ranges must, of course, contain the same number of values, and they must be matched (first item in the *expected* list is associated with the first item in the *observed* list, and so on). Internally, the function takes the degrees of freedom into account, calculates the chi square statistic value, and computes the probability.

Use the CHISQ.TEST function this way:

1. **Enter two ranges of values as expected and observed results.**
2. **Position the cursor in the cell where you want the result to appear.**
3. **Type =CHISQ.TEST(to start the function.**
4. **Drag the cursor over the range of observed (actual) values or enter the address of the range.**
5. **Type a comma (,).**
6. **Drag the cursor over the range of expected values, or enter the address of the range.**
7. **Type a).**

Figure 10-3 shows a data set of expected and actual values. The chi square test statistic is calculated as before, delivering a value of 1.594017, shown in cell F12. The CHISQ.TEST function, in cell D14, returns a value of 0.953006566 — the associated probability. CHISQ.TEST doesn't return the chi square statistic but the associated probability.

D14	▾	× ✓ ƒx	=CHISQ.TEST(C4:C10,B4:B10)			
	A	B	C	D	E	F	G
1		Expected Completed	Actual Completed	Difference	Square of	Square /	
2		Print Runs	Print Runs	(=Expected - Observed)	the Difference	Expected	
3							
4	Monday	15	18	-3	9	0.6	
5	Tuesday	18	20	-2	4	0.222222222	
6	Wednesday	19	19	0	0	0	
7	Thursday	24	20	4	16	0.666666667	
8	Friday	26	25	1	1	0.038461538	
9	Saturday	24	24	0	0	0	
10	Sunday	15	16	-1	1	0.066666667	
11							
12						1.594017094	
13							
14			CHISQ.TEST:	0.953006565			
15							
16			CHISQ.DIST.RT:	0.953006565			
17							
18			CHISQ.INV.RT:	1.594017094			

Figure 10-3: Determining probability.

Now tie in a relationship between the manually calculated chi square and the value returned with CHISQ.TEST. If you looked up your manually calculated chi square value (1.59) in a chi square table for degrees of freedom of 6 (one less than the number of observations), you would find it associated with a probability value of 0.95. Of course, the CHISQ.TEST function does this for you, returning the probability value, which is what you're after. But suppose that you've manually calculated chi square values and want to know the associated probabilities. Do you have to use a table? Nope — the CHISQ.DIST. RT function comes to the rescue. Furthermore, if you have a probability and want to know the associated chi square value, you can use the CHISQ.INV.RT function.

TIP

The RT in the CHISQ.DIST.RT and CHISQ.INV.RT functions is the abbreviation for Right Tail. The functions in the configuration work with the right tail of the distribution.

Figure 10-3 earlier in this chapter demonstrates the CHISQ.DIST.RT and CHI. SQ.INV.RT functions as well. CHISQ.DIST.RT takes two arguments: a value to be evaluated for a distribution (the chi square value, 1.59 in the example) and the degrees of freedom (6 in the example). Cell D16 displays 0.953006566, which is the same probability value returned by the CHISQ.TEST function — just as it should be! The formula in cell D16 is =CHISQ.DIST.RT(F12,6).

CHISQ.TEST and CHISQ.DIST.RT both return the same probability value but calculate the result with different arguments. CHISQ.TEST uses the actual expected and observed values and internally calculates the test statistic to return the probability. This happens behind the scenes; just the probability is returned. CHISQ.DIST.RT needs the test statistic fed in as an argument.

To use the CHISQ.DIST.RT function, follow these steps:

1. **Position the cursor in the cell where you want the result to appear.**

2. **Type** =CHISQ.DIST.RT(**to start the function.**

3. **Click the cell that has the Chi Square test statistic.**

4. **Type a comma (,).**

5. **Enter the degrees of freedom.**

6. **Type a).**

The CHISQ.INV.RT function rounds out the list of chi square functions in Excel. CHISQ.INV.RT is the inverse of CHISQ.DIST.RT. That is, with a given probability and degrees of freedom number, CHISQ.INV.RT returns the chi square test statistic.

Cell D18 in Figure 10-3 earlier in this chapter has the formula `=CHISQ.INV.RT(D14,6)`. This returns the value of the chi square: 1.594017094. CHISQ. INV.RT is useful when you know the probability and degrees of freedom and need to determine the chi square test statistic value.

To use the CHISQ.INV.RT function, follow these steps:

1. **Position the cursor in the cell where you want the result to appear.**

2. **Type** `=CHISQ.INV.RT(` **to start the function.**

3. **Click the cell that has the probability.**

4. **Type a comma (,).**

5. **Enter the degrees of freedom.**

6. **Type a).**

 Working with inferential statistics is difficult! I suggest further reading to help with the functions and statistical examples discussed in this chapter. A great book to read is *Statistics For Dummies,* 2nd Edition, by Deborah J. Rumsey (John Wiley & Sons, Inc.).

Chapter 11

Rolling the Dice on Predictions and Probability

· ·

In This Chapter

▶ Understanding linear and exponential trends

▶ Predicting future data from existing data

▶ Working with normal and Poisson distributions

· ·

*W*hen you're analyzing data, one of the most important steps is usually to determine what model fits the data. No, I'm not talking about a model car or model plane! This is a *mathematical model* or, put another way, a *formula* that describes the data. The question of a model is applicable to all data that comes in X-Y pairs, such as the following:

✔ Comparisons of weight and height measurements

✔ Data on salary versus educational level

✔ Number of fish feeding in a river by time of day

✔ Number of employees calling in sick as related to day of the week

Modeling

Suppose now that you plot all the data points on a chart — a *scatter chart,* in Excel terminology. What does the pattern look like? If the data is linear, the data points fall more or less along a straight line. If they fall along a curve rather than a straight line, they aren't linear and are likely to be exponential. These two models — *linear* and *exponential* — are the two most commonly used models, and Excel provides functions for working with them.

Linear model

In a linear model, the mathematical formula that models the data is
as follows:

$$Y = mX + b$$

This formula tells you that for any X value, you calculate the Y value by multi-plying X by a constant *m* and then adding another constant *b*. The value *m* is called the line's *slope,* and *b* is the *Y intercept* (the value of Y when X = 0). This formula gives a perfectly straight line, and real-world data doesn't fall exactly on such a line. The point is that the line, called the *linear regression line,* is the best fit for the data. The constants *m* and *b* are different for each data set.

Exponential model

In an exponential model, the following formula models the data:

$$Y = bmX$$

The values *b* and *m* are, again, constants. Many natural processes, includ-ing bacterial growth and temperature change, are modeled by exponential curves. Figure 11-1 shows an example of an exponential curve. This curve is the result of the preceding formula when *b* = 2 and *m* = 1.03.

Again, *b* and *m* are constants that are different for each data set.

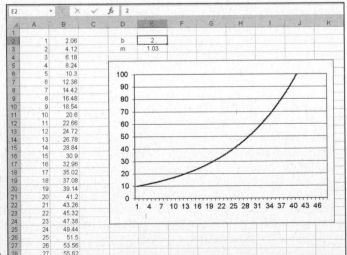

Figure 11-1:
An
exponential
curve.

Getting It Straight: Using SLOPE and INTERCEPT to Describe Linear Data

As I discuss earlier in this chapter, many data sets can be modeled by a straight line. In other words, the data is linear. The line that models the data, known as the linear regression line, is characterized by its slope and its Y intercept. Excel provides the SLOPE and INTERCEPT functions to calculate the slope and Y intercept of the linear regression line for a set of data pairs.

The SLOPE and INTERCEPT functions take the same two arguments:

- ✔ The first argument is a range or array containing the Y values of the data set.
- ✔ The second argument is a range or array containing the X values of the data set.

The two ranges must contain the same number of values; otherwise, an error occurs. Follow these steps to use either of these functions:

1. **In a blank worksheet cell, type** =SLOPE(**or** =INTERCEPT(**to start the function entry**.

2. **Drag the mouse over the range containing the Y data values or enter the range address.**

3. **Type a comma (,).**

4. **Drag the mouse over the range containing the X data values or enter the range address.**

5. **Type a) and press Enter.**

When you know the slope and Y intercept of a linear regression line, you can calculate predicted values of Y for any X by using the formula $Y = mX + b$ where m is the slope and b is the Y intercept. But Excel's FORECAST and TREND functions can do this for you.

Knowing the slope and intercept of a linear regression line is one thing, but what can you do with this information? One very useful thing is to actually draw the linear *regression line* along with the data points. This method of graphical presentation is commonly used; it lets the viewer see how well the data fits the model.

To see how this is done, look at the worksheet in Figure 11-2. Columns A and B contain the X and Y data, and the chart shows a scatter plot of this data. It seems clear that the data is linear and that you can validly use SLOPE and INTERCEPT with them.

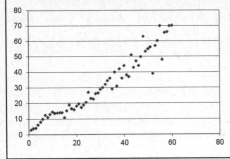

The first step is to put these functions in the worksheet, as follows. (You can use any worksheet that has linear X-Y data in it.)

1. **Type the label** Slope **in an empty cell.**

2. **In the cell to the right, type** =SLOPE(**to start the function entry.**

3. **Drag the mouse over the range containing the Y data values or enter the range address.**

4. **Type a comma (,).**

5. **Drag the mouse over the range containing the X data values or enter the range address.**

6. **Type a).**

7. **Press Enter to complete the formula.**

8. **In the cell below the slope label, type the label** Intercept.

9. **In the cell to the right, type** =Intercept(.

10. **Drag the mouse over the range containing the Y data values or enter the range address.**

11. **Type a comma (,).**

12. **Drag the mouse over the range containing the X data values or enter the range address.**

13. **Type a) and press Enter to complete the formula.**

At this point, the worksheet displays the slope and intercept of the linear regression line for your data. The next task is to display this line on the chart, as follows:

1. **If necessary, add a new empty column to the worksheet to the right of the Y-value column.**

   Do this by clicking any cell in the column immediately to the right of the Y value column, and then, on the Home ribbon, clicking the Insert button and selecting Insert Sheet Columns.

2. **Place the cursor in this column in the same row as the first X value.**

3. **Type an equal sign (=) to start a formula.**

4. **Click the cell where the SLOPE function is located to enter its address in the formula.**

5. **Press F4 to convert the address to an absolute reference.**

   It displays with dollar signs.

6. **Enter the multiplication symbol (*).**

7. **Click the cell containing the X value for that row.**

8. **Enter the addition symbol (+).**

9. **Click the cell containing the INTERCEPT function to enter its address in the formula.**

10. **Press F4 to convert the address to an absolute reference.**

    It displays with dollar signs.

11. **Press Enter to complete the formula.**

12. **Make sure the cursor is in the cell where you just entered the formula.**

13. **Press Ctrl+C to copy the formula to the Clipboard.**

14. **Hold down the Shift key and press the ↓ key until the entire column is highlighted down to the row containing the last X value.**

15. **Press Enter to copy the formula to all selected cells.**

At this point, the column of data you just created contains the Y values for the linear regression line. The final step is to create a chart that displays both the actual data and the computed regression line. Follow these steps:

1. **Highlight all three columns of data: the X values, the actual Y values, and the computed Y values.**

2. **Click the Insert tab on the Ribbon (shown in Figure 11-3).**

3. **Click the Scatter Chart button.**

4. **Select the basic Scatter Chart type.**

5. **Click the Finish button.**

   The chart displays, as shown in Figure 11-4. You can see two sets of points. The scattered points are the actual data, and the straight line is the linear regression line.

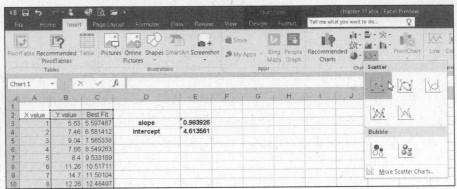

Figure 11-3:
Creating a scatter chart.

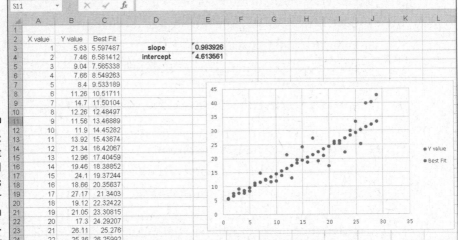

Figure 11-4:
A data set displayed with its linear regression line.

What's in the Future: Using FORECAST, TREND, and GROWTH to Make Predictions

The FORECAST function does just what its name suggests: forecasts an unknown data value based on existing, known data values. The function is based on a single important assumption: that the data is linear. Exactly what does this mean?

FORECAST

The data that FORECAST works with is in pairs; there's an X value and a corresponding Y value in each pair. Perhaps you're investigating the relationship between people's heights and their weight. Each data pair would be one person's height — the X value — and that person's weight — the Y value. Many kinds of data are in this form — sales by month, for example, or income as a function of educational level.

You can use the CORREL function to determine the degree of linear relationship between two sets of data. See Chapter 9 to find out about the CORREL function.

To use the FORECAST function, you must have a set of X-Y data pairs. Then you provide a new X value, and the function returns the Y value that would be associated with that X value based on the known data. The function takes three arguments:

- ✔ The first argument is the X value that you want a forecast for.
- ✔ The second argument is a range containing the known Y values.
- ✔ The third argument is a range containing the known X values.

Note that the X and Y ranges must have the same number of values; otherwise, the function returns an error. The X and Y values in these ranges are assumed to be paired in order.

Don't use FORECAST with data that isn't linear. Doing so produces inaccurate results.

Now you can work through an example of using FORECAST to make a prediction. Imagine that you're the sales manager at a large corporation. You've noticed that the yearly sales results for each of your salespeople is related to the number of years of experience each has. You've hired a new salesman with 16 years of experience. How much in sales can you expect this person to make?

Figure 11-5 shows the existing data for salespeople — their years of experience and annual sales last year. This worksheet also contains a scatter chart of the data to show that it's linear. It's clear that the data points fall fairly well along a straight line. Follow along to create the prediction:

1. **In a blank cell, type** =FORECAST(**to start the function entry.**

    The blank cell is C24 in Figure 11-5.

2. **Type** 16, **the X value that you want a prediction for.**

3. **Type a comma (,).**

4. **Drag the mouse over the Y range or enter the cell range.**

   C3:C17 is the cell range in the example.

5. **Type a comma (,).**

6. **Drag the mouse over the X range or enter the cell range.**

   B3:B17 is the cell range in the example.

7. **Type a) and press Enter to complete the formula.**

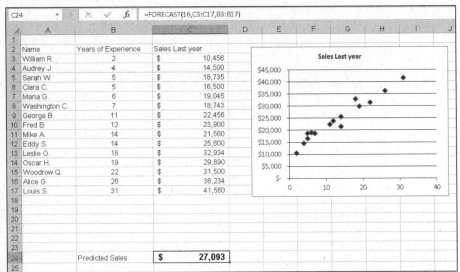

Figure 11-5:
Forecasting
sales.

After you format the cell as Currency, the result shown in Figure 11-5 displays the prediction that your new salesman will make $27,093 in sales his first year. But remember: This is just a prediction, not a guarantee!

TREND

The preceding section shows how the FORECAST function can predict a Y value for a known X based on an existing set of linear X-Y data. What if you have more than one X value to predict? Have no fear; TREND is here! What FORECAST does for a single X value, TREND does for a whole array of X values.

WARNING!

Like FORECAST, the TREND function is intended for working with linear data. If you try to use it with nonlinear data, the results will be incorrect.

The TREND function takes up to four arguments:

✔ The first argument is a range containing the known Y values.

✔ The second argument is a range containing the known X values.

✔ The third argument is a range containing the X values that you want predictions for.

✔ The fourth argument is a logical value. It tells the function whether to force the constant *b* to 0. If the fourth argument is TRUE or omitted, the linear regression line (used to predict Y values) is calculated normally. If this argument is FALSE, the linear regression line is calculated to go through the origin (where both X and Y are 0).

Note that the ranges of known X and Y values must be the same size (contain the same number of values).

TREND returns an array of values, one predicted Y for each X value. In other words, it's an array function and must be treated as such. (See Chapter 3 for help with array functions.) Specifically, this means selecting the range where you want the array formula results, typing the formula, and pressing Ctrl+Shift+Enter rather than pressing Enter alone to complete the formula.

When would you use the TREND function? Here's an example: You've started a part-time business, and your income has grown steadily over the past 12 months. The growth seems to be linear, and you want to predict how much you will earn in the coming six months. The TREND function is ideal for this situation. Here's how to do it:

1. **In a new worksheet, put the numbers 1 through 12, representing the past 12 months, in a column.**

2. **In the adjacent cells, place the income figure for each of these months.**

3. **Label this area** Actual Data.

4. **In another section of the worksheet, enter the numbers 13 through 18 in a column to represent the upcoming six months.**

5. **In the column adjacent to the projected month numbers, select the six adjacent cells (empty at present) by dragging over them.**

6. **Type** =TREND(**to start the function entry.**

7. **Drag the mouse over the range of known Y values or enter the range address.**

   The known Y values are the income figures you entered in Step 2.

8. **Type a comma (,).**

9. **Drag the mouse over the range of known X values or enter the range address.**

   The known X values are the numbers 1 through 12 you entered in Step 1.

10. **Type a comma (,).**

11. **Drag the mouse over the list of month numbers for which you want projections (the numbers 13 through 18).**

    These are the new X values.

12. **Type a).**

13. **Press Ctrl+Shift+Enter to complete the formula.**

When you've completed these steps, you see the projected income figures, calculated by the TREND function, displayed in the worksheet. An example is shown in Figure 11-6. There's no assurance you'll have this income — but it may be even higher! You can always hope for the best.

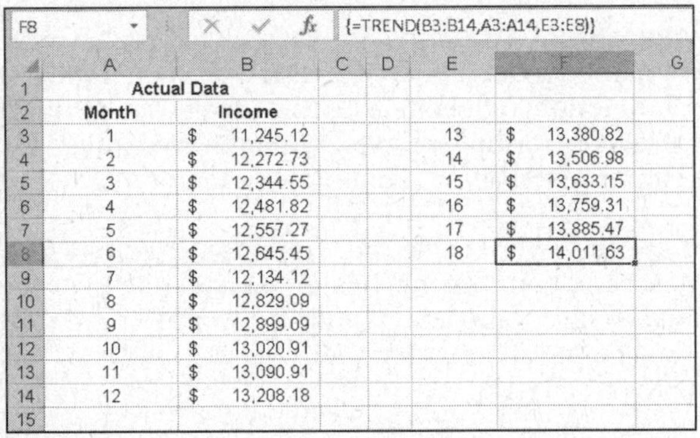

Figure 11-6:
Using the
TREND
function to
calculate
predictions
for an array.

F8		✗ ✓ *fx*	{=TREND(B3:B14,A3:A14,E3:E8)}					
	A	B	C	D	E	F	G	
1		Actual Data						
2	Month	Income						
3	1	$ 11,245.12			13	$ 13,380.82		
4	2	$ 12,272.73			14	$ 13,506.98		
5	3	$ 12,344.55			15	$ 13,633.15		
6	4	$ 12,481.82			16	$ 13,759.31		
7	5	$ 12,557.27			17	$ 13,885.47		
8	6	$ 12,645.45			18	$ 14,011.63		
9	7	$ 12,134.12						
10	8	$ 12,829.09						
11	9	$ 12,899.09						
12	10	$ 13,020.91						
13	11	$ 13,090.91						
14	12	$ 13,208.18						
15								

GROWTH

The GROWTH function is like TREND in that it uses existing data to predict Y values for a set of X values. It's different in that it's designed for use with data that fits an exponential model. The function takes four arguments:

- The first argument is a range or array containing the known Y values.

- The second argument is a range or array containing the known X values.

- The third argument is a range or array containing the X values for which you want to calculate predicted Y values.

✔ The fourth value is omitted or TRUE if you want the constant *b* calculated normally. If this argument is FALSE, *b* is forced to 1. You won't use FALSE except in special situations.

REMEMBER

The number of known X and known Y values must be the same for the GROWTH function; otherwise, an error occurs. As you'd expect, GROWTH is an array formula and must be entered accordingly.

To use the GROWTH function, follow these steps:

(*Note:* These steps assume that you have a worksheet that already contains known X and Y values that fit the exponential model.)

1. **Enter the X values for which you want to predict Y values in a column of the worksheet.**

2. **Select a range of cells in a column that has the same number of rows as the X values you entered in Step 1.**

   Often, this range is in the column next to the X values, but it doesn't have to be.

3. **Type** =Growth(**to start the function entry.**

4. **Drag the mouse over the range containing the known Y values or enter the range address.**

5. **Type a comma (,).**

6. **Drag the mouse over the range containing the known X values or enter the range address.**

7. **Type a comma (,).**

8. **Drag the mouse over the range containing the X values for which you want to predict Y values or enter the range address.**

9. **Type a).**

10. **Press Ctrl+Shift+Enter to complete the formula.**

Figure 11-7 shows an example of using the GROWTH function to forecast exponential data. Columns A and B contain the known data, and the range D10:D19 contains the X values for which predictions are desired. The GROWTH array formula was entered in E10:E19. The chart shows a scatter plot of the actual data, up to X = 40, and the projected data, for X values above 40. You can see how the projected data continues the exponential curves that are fit by the actual data.

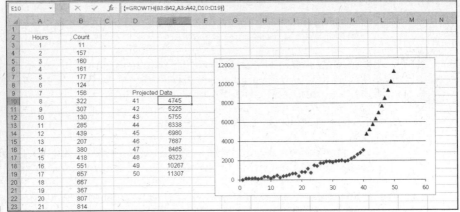

Figure 11-7:
Demonstrating use of the GROWTH function to project exponential data.

Using NORM.DIST and POISSON.DIST to Determine Probabilities

You can get a good introduction to the normal distribution in Chapter 9. To define it briefly, a normal distribution is characterized by its *mean* (the value in the middle of the distribution) and by its *standard deviation* (the extent to which values spread out on either side of the mean). The normal distribution is a continuous distribution, which means that X values can be fractional and aren't restricted to integers. The normal distribution has a lot of uses because so many processes, both natural and human, follow it.

NORM.DIST

The word *normal* in this context doesn't mean "good" or "okay," and a distribution that is not normal is not flawed in some way. Normal is used simply to mean "typical" or "common."

Excel provides the NORM.DIST function for calculating probabilities from a normal distribution. The function takes four arguments:

- ✔ The first argument is the value for which you want to calculate a probability.
- ✔ The second argument is the mean of the normal distribution.
- ✔ The third argument is the standard deviation of the normal distribution.
- ✔ The fourth argument is TRUE if you want the cumulative probability and FALSE if you want the noncumulative probability.

A *cumulative probability* is the chance of getting any value between 0 and the specified value. A *noncumulative probability* is the chance of getting exactly the specified value.

Normal distributions come into play for a wide variety of measurements. Examples include blood pressure, atmospheric carbon-dioxide levels, wave height, leaf size, and oven temperature. If you know the mean and standard deviation of a distribution, you can use NORM.DIST to calculate related probabilities.

Here's an example: Your firm manufactures hardware, and a customer wants to buy a large quantity of 50mm bolts. Due to the manufacturing process, the length of bolts varies slightly. The customer will place the order only if at least 95 percent of the bolts are between 49.9mm and 50.1mm. Measuring each one isn't practical, but previous data show that the distribution of bolt lengths is a normal distribution with a mean of 50 and a standard deviation of 0.05. You can use Excel and the NORM.DIST function to answer the question. Here's the plan:

1. Use the NORM.DIST function to determine the cumulative probability of a bolt's being at least 50.1mm long.

2. Use the NORM.DIST function to determine the cumulative probability of a bolt's being at least 49.9mm long.

3. Subtract the second value from the first to get the probability that a bolt will be between 49.9mm and 50.1mm long.

Here are the steps to follow:

1. **In a new worksheet, enter the values for the mean, standard deviation, upper limit, and lower limit in separate cells.**

   Optionally, add adjoining labels to identify the cells.

2. **In another cell, type** =NORM.DIST(**to start the function entry.**

3. **Click the cell containing the lower limit value (49.9) or enter the cell address.**

4. **Type a comma (,).**

5. **Click the cell containing the mean or enter the cell address.**

6. **Type a comma (,).**

7. **Click the cell containing the standard deviation or enter the cell address.**

8. **Type a comma (,).**

9. **Type** TRUE).

10. Press Enter to complete the function.

This cell displays the probability of a bolt's being less than or equal to the lower limit.

11. In another cell, type =NORMDIST(to start the function entry.

12. Click the cell containing the upper-limit value (50.1) or enter the cell address.

13. Repeat Steps 4 through 10.

This cell displays the probability of a bolt's being less than or equal to the upper limit.

14. In another cell, enter a formula that subtracts the lower-limit probability from the upper-limit probability.

This cell displays the probability that a bolt will be within the specified limits.

Figure 11-8 shows a worksheet that was created to solve this problem. You can see from cell B8 that the answer is 0.9545. In other words, 95.45 percent of your bolts fall in the prescribed limits, and you can accept the customer's order. Note in this worksheet that the formulas in cells B6:B8 are presented in the adjacent cells so you can see what they look like.

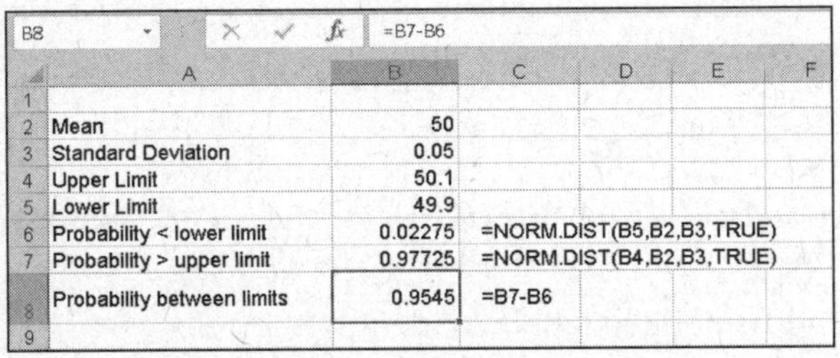

Figure 11-8:
Using the NORM.DIST function to calculate probabilities.

	A	B	C
2	Mean	50	
3	Standard Deviation	0.05	
4	Upper Limit	50.1	
5	Lower Limit	49.9	
6	Probability < lower limit	0.02275	=NORM.DIST(B5,B2,B3,TRUE)
7	Probability > upper limit	0.97725	=NORM.DIST(B4,B2,B3,TRUE)
8	Probability between limits	0.9545	=B7-B6

POISSON.DIST

Poisson is another kind of distribution used in many areas of statistics. Its most common use is to model the number of events taking place in a specified time period. Suppose that you're modeling the number of employees calling in sick each day or the number of defective items produced at your factory each week. In these cases, the Poisson distribution is appropriate.

The *Poisson* distribution is useful for analyzing rare events. What does *rare* mean? People calling in sick at work is hardly a rare event, but a specific number calling in sick is rare, at least statistically speaking. Situations to which Poisson is applicable include numbers of car accidents, counts of customers arriving, and manufacturing defects. One way to express it is that the events are individually rare, but there are many opportunities for them to happen.

The Poisson distribution is a discrete distribution. This means that the X values in the distribution can only take on specified, discrete values such as X = 1, 2, 3, 4, 5 and so on. This is different from the normal distribution, which is a continuous distribution in which X values can take any value (X = 0.034, 1.2365, and so on). The discrete nature of the Poisson distribution is suited to the kinds of data you use it with. For example, with employees calling in sick, you may have 1, 5, or 8 on a given day, but certainly not 1.45, 7.2, or 9.15!

Figure 11-9 shows a Poisson distribution that has a mean of 20. Values on the X axis are number of occurrences (of whatever you're studying), and values on the Y axis are probabilities. You can use this distribution to determine the probability of a specific number of occurrences happening. For example, this chart tells you that the probability of having exactly 15 occurrences is approximately 0.05 (5 percent).

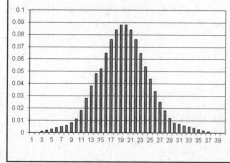

Figure 11-9:
A Poisson distribution with a mean of 20.

The Poisson distribution is a discrete distribution and is used only with data that takes on discrete (integer) values, such as counting items.

A Poisson distribution is not always symmetrical, as is the one shown in Figure 11-9. Negative X values make no sense in a Poisson distribution. After all, you can't have fewer than zero people calling in sick! If the mean is a small value, the distribution will be skewed, as shown in Figure 11-10 for a Poisson distribution with a mean of 4.

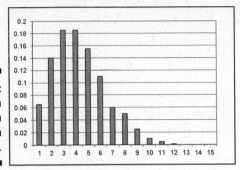

Figure 11-10:
A Poisson distribution with a mean of 4.

Excel's POISSON.DIST function lets you calculate the probability that a specified number of events will occur. All you need to know is the mean of the distribution. This function can calculate the probability two ways:

✔ **Cumulative:** The probability that between 0 and X events will occur

✔ **Noncumulative:** The probability that exactly X events will occur

The two Poisson graphs shown earlier in this chapter are for noncumulative probabilities. Figure 11-11 shows the cumulative Poisson distribution corresponding to Figure 11-9. You can see from this chart that the cumulative probability of 15 events — the probability that 15 or fewer events will occur — is about 0.15.

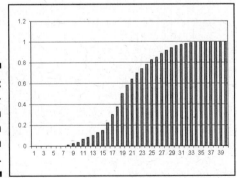

Figure 11-11:
A cumulative Poisson distribution with a mean of 20.

What if you want to calculate the probability that more than X events will occur? Simple! Just calculate the cumulative probability for X and subtract the result from 1.

The POISSON.DIST function takes three arguments:

- ✔ The first argument is the number of events that you want to calculate the probability for. This must be an integer value greater than 0.

- ✔ The second argument is the mean of the Poisson distribution to use. This too must be an integer value greater than 0.

- ✔ The third argument is TRUE if you want the cumulative probability and FALSE if you want the noncumulative probability.

Suppose that you're the manager of a factory that makes brake shoes. Your district manager has announced an incentive: You'll receive a bonus for each day that the number of defective shoes is less than 20. How many days a month will you meet this goal, knowing that the average number of defective brake shoes is 25 per day? Here are the steps to follow:

1. **In a new worksheet, enter the average number of defects per day (25) in a cell.**

   If desired, enter an adjacent label to identify the cell.

2. **In the cell below, type** =POISSON.DIST(**to start the function entry.**

3. **Type the value** 20.

4. **Enter a comma (,).**

5. **Click the cell where you entered the average defects per day or enter its cell address.**

6. **Enter a comma (,).**

7. **Type** TRUE).

8. **Press Enter to complete the formula.**

9. **If desired, enter a label in an adjacent cell to identify this as the probability of 20 or fewer defects.**

10. **In the cell below, enter a formula that multiplies the number of working days per month (22) by the result just calculated with the POISSON.DIST function.**

    In your worksheet, this formula is =22*B3, entered in cell B4.

11. **If desired, enter a label in an adjacent cell to identify this as the number of days per month you can expect to have 20 or fewer defects.**

The finished worksheet is shown in Figure 11-12. In this example, I have formatted cells B3:B4 with two decimal places. You can see that with an average of 25 defects per day, you can expect to earn a bonus 4 days a month.

B3	▾	⟨	× ✓ *fx*	=POISSON.DIST(20,B2,TRUE)	
	A			B	C
1					
2	Average defective shoes per day			25	
3	Probability of 20 or fewer defects			0.19	
4	Days/Months meeting goal			4.08	
5					

Part IV
Dancing with Data

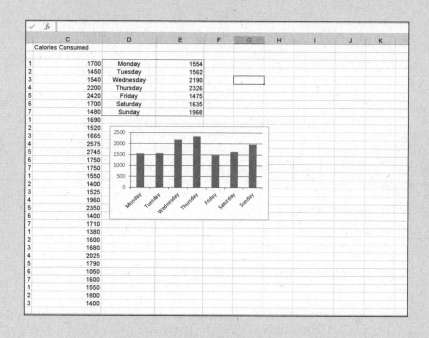

Discover how to parse complex names in the article "Parsing Names the VBA Way" online at www.dummies.com/extras/excelformulasfunctions.

In this part . . .

- ✔ Master dates.
- ✔ Calculate time.
- ✔ Look up data and become logical.
- ✔ Discover information about your data and your computer system.
- ✔ Test-drive the text functions.
- ✔ Dig into data with the database functions.

Chapter 12

Dressing Up for Date Functions

. . . .

. . . .

*O*ften, when working with Excel, you need to manage dates. Perhaps you have a list of dates when you visited a client and need to count how many times you were there in September. On the other hand, maybe you are tracking a project over a few months and want to know how many days are in between the milestones.

Excel has a number of useful Date functions to make your work easier! This chapter explains how Excel handles dates, how to compare and subtract dates, how to work with parts of a date (such as the month or year), and even how to count the number of days between two dates. You can always reference the current data from your computer's clock and use it in a calculation; I show you how.

Understanding How Excel Handles Dates

Imagine that on January 1, 1900, you started counting by ones, each day adding one more to the total. This is just how Excel thinks of dates. January 1, 1900, is one; January 2, 1900, is two; and so on. We'll always remember 25,404 as the day man first walked on the moon, and 36,892 as the start of the new millennium!

The millennium actually started on January 1, 2001. The year 2000 is the last year of the 20th century. Representing dates as a serial number — specifically, the number of days between January 1, 1900, and the date in question — may seem odd, but there are very good reasons for it. Excel can handle dates from January 1, 1900, to December 31, 9999. Using the serial numbering system, that's 1 through 2,958,465!

Because Excel represents dates in this way, it can work with dates in the same manner as numbers. For example, you can subtract one date from another to find out how many days are between them. Likewise, you can add 14 to today's date to get a date two weeks in the future. This trick is very useful, but people are used to seeing dates represented in traditional formats, not as numbers. Fortunately, Excel uses date serial numbers only behind the scenes, and what you see in your workbook are dates in the standard date formats such as Jan 20, 2015, and 12/20/15.

In Excel for the Mac, the serial numbering system begins on January 1, 1904.

The way years are handled requires special mention. When a year is fully displayed in four digits, such as 2015, there is no ambiguity. However, when a date is written in a shorthand style, such as in 3/1/02, it isn't clear what the year is. It could be 2002, or it could be 1902. Suppose that 3/1/02 is a shorthand entry for someone's birthday. On March 1, 2005, he is either 3 years old or 103 years old. In those countries that write dates as dd/mm/yy, this would be January 3, 1902, or January 3, 2002.

Excel and the Windows operating system have a default way of interpreting shorthand years. Windows has a setting in the Customize Regional Options dialog box located in the Control Panel. This setting guides how Excel interprets years. If the setting is 1930 through 2029, 3/1/02 indicates the year 2002, but 3/1/45 indicates the year 1945, not 2045. Figure 12-1 shows this setting.

Here's how to open and set it:

The following instructions may differ depending on which version of Windows you have running on your computer.

1. **Click your computer's Start button (Windows 7 or earlier), or click the Settings button (Windows 8 or later).**

2. **Select Control Panel.**

3. **Select Clock, Language and Region.**

4. **Select Region.**

   The Region dialog box opens.

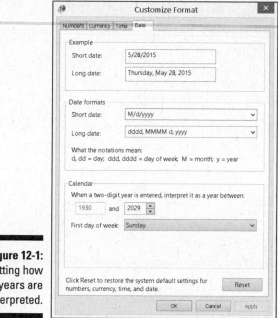

Figure 12-1:
Setting how
years are
interpreted.

5. **Click the Formats tab.**

6. **Click the Additional settings button.**

   The Customize Format dialog box opens.

7. **Click the Date tab.**

8. **In the Calendar section, select a four-digit ending year (such as 2029) to indicate the latest year that will be used when interpreting a two-digit year.**

9. **Click OK to close each dialog box.**

To ensure full accuracy when working with dates, always enter the full four digits for the year.

Formatting Dates

When you work with dates, you probably need to format cells in your worksheet. It's great that Excel tells you that June 1, 2015, is serially represented as 42156, but you probably don't want that in a report. To format dates, you use the Format Cells dialog box, shown in Figure 12-2.

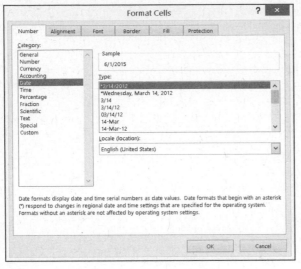

Figure 12-2:
Using the Format Cells dialog box to control how dates are displayed.

To format dates, follow these steps:

1. **If it's not already displayed, click the Home tab at the top of the Excel screen.**

2. **Click the small arrow at the bottom-right corner of the Number section.**

   The Format Cells dialog box appears, revealing the Number tab.

3. **Select Date in the Category List.**

4. **Select an appropriate format from the Type List.**

Now you can turn the useful but pesky serial dates into a user-friendly format.

When you enter a date in a cell using one of the standard date formats, Excel recognizes it as a date and automatically assigns a Date format to the cell. You may want to use the Number Format dialog box to assign a different Date format.

Making a Date with DATE

You can use the DATE function to create a complete date from separate year, month, and day information. The DATE function can be useful because dates don't always appear as, well, dates, in a worksheet. You may have a column of values between 1 and 12 that represents the month and another column of values between 1 and 31 for the day of the month. A third column may hold years — in either two-digit shorthand or the full four digits.

The DATE function combines individual day, month, and year components into a single usable date. This makes using and referencing dates in your worksheet easy. Follow along to use the DATE function:

1. **Select the cell where you want the results displayed.**

2. **Type =DATE(to begin the function entry.**

3. **Click the cell that has the year.**

4. **Type a comma (,).**

5. **Click the cell that has the number (1–12) that represents the month.**

6. **Type a comma (,).**

7. **Click the cell that has the number (1–31) that represents the day of the month.**

8. **Type a) and press Enter.**

Figure 12-3 displays a fourth column of dates that were created by using DATE and the values from the first three columns. The fourth column of dates has been formatted so the dates are displayed in a standard format, not as a raw date serial number.

Figure 12-3: Using the DATE function to assemble a date from separate month, day, and year values.

	MONTH	DAY	YEAR	
1	MONTH	DAY	YEAR	
2				
3	4	19	2015	Sunday, April 19, 2015
4	2	24	2015	Tuesday, February 24, 2015
5	2	23	2013	Saturday, February 23, 2013
6	8	24	2012	Friday, August 24, 2012
7	12	6	2015	Sunday, December 6, 2015
8	7	17	2014	Thursday, July 17, 2014
9	5	14	2013	Tuesday, May 14, 2013
10	1	8	2011	Saturday, January 8, 2011
11	9	28	2013	Saturday, September 28, 2013
12	9	3	2012	Monday, September 3, 2012
13	4	10	2014	Thursday, April 10, 2014
14	3	9	2012	Friday, March 9, 2012
15	10	10	2015	Saturday, October 10, 2015
16	12	6	2013	Friday, December 6, 2013
17	4	30	2013	Tuesday, April 30, 2013
18	8	15	2015	Saturday, August 15, 2015
19	7	31	2015	Friday, July 31, 2015
20	11	14	2012	Wednesday, November 14, 2012

DATE provides some extra flexibility with the month number. Negative month numbers are subtracted from the specified year. For example, the function =DATE(2014, -5, 15) returns the date July 15, 2013, because

July 2013 is 5 months before the first month of 2014. Numbers greater than 12 work the same way. =DATE(2014, 15, 1) returns March 1, 2015, because March 2015 is 15 months after the first month of 2014.

Day numbers work the same way. Negative day numbers are subtracted from the first of the specified month, and numbers that are greater than the last day of the specified month wrap into later months. Thus, =DATE(2013, 2, 30) returns March 2, 2013, because February does not have 30 days. Likewise, =DATE(2013, 2, 40) returns March 12, 2013.

Breaking a Date with DAY, MONTH, and YEAR

That which can be put together can also be taken apart. In the preceding section, I show you how to use the DATE function to create a date from separate year, month, and day data. In this section, you find out how to do the reverse: Split a date into individual year, month, and day components by using the DAY, MONTH, and YEAR functions. In Figure 12-4, the dates in column A are split apart by day, month, and year, respectively, in Columns B, C, and D.

	A	B	C	D
	Date	DAY	MONTH	YEAR
1				
2	1/1/2014	1	1	2014
3	5/22/2015	22	5	2015
4	3/13/2013	13	3	2013
5	9/28/2015	28	9	2015
6	9/3/2012	3	9	2012
7	4/10/2013	10	4	2013
8	3/9/2015	9	3	2015
9	8/15/2012	15	8	2012
10	7/31/2012	31	7	2012
11	11/14/2012	14	11	2012
12	5/8/2013	8	5	2013
13	8/2/2015	2	8	2015
14	2/26/2012	26	2	2012
15	1/20/2013	20	1	2013
16	12/1/2012	1	12	2012
17	4/22/2012	22	4	2012
18	12/12/2013	12	12	2013
19	6/17/2013	17	6	2013
20	5/31/2015	31	5	2015
21	1/31/2013	31	1	2013
22	7/4/2012	4	7	2012

Cell reference B3, formula bar: =DAY(A3)

Figure 12-4: Splitting apart a date with the DAY, MONTH, and YEAR functions.

Isolating the day

Isolating the day part of a date is useful in applications in which just the day, but not the month or year, is relevant. Suppose that you own a store and want to figure out whether more customers come to shop in the first half or the second half of the month. You're interested in this trend over several months. So the task may be to average the number of sales by the day of the month only.

The DAY function is useful for this because you can use it to return just the day for a lengthy list of dates. Then you can examine results by the day only.

Here's how you use the DAY function:

1. **Position the pointer in the cell where you want the results displayed.**

2. **Type** =DAY(**to begin the function entry.**

3. **Click the cell that has the date.**

4. **Type a**) **and then press Enter.**

   Excel returns a number between 1 and 31.

Figure 12-5 shows how the DAY function can be used to analyze customer activity. Column A contains a full year's sequential dates (most of which are not visible in the figure). In Column B, the day part of each date has been isolated. Column C shows the customer traffic for each day.

Figure 12-5:
Using
the DAY
function to
analyze
customer
activity.

E4				*fx*	=SUMIF(B2:B366,"<16",C2:C366)/COUNTIF(B2:B366,"<16")	
	A	B	C	D	E	
1	Date	Day	Customers			
2	1/1/2013	1	8		Average Daily Customers	
3	1/2/2013	2	36		for the 1st through the 15th of the month	
4	1/3/2013	3	48		50.34	
5	1/4/2013	4	41			
6	1/5/2013	5	36			
7	1/6/2013	6	49			
8	1/7/2013	7	34		Average Daily Customers	
9	1/8/2013	8	37		for the 16th through the end of the month	
10	1/9/2013	9	55		54.83	
11	1/10/2013	10	56			
12	1/11/2013	11	34			
13	1/12/2013	12	41			
14	1/13/2013	13	42			
15	1/14/2013	14	33			
16	1/15/2013	15	26			
17	1/16/2013	16	78			
18	1/17/2013	17	64			
19	1/18/2013	18	68			
20	1/19/2013	19	52			
21	1/20/2013	20	65			
22	1/21/2013	21	51			

This is all the information you need to analyze whether there is a difference in the amount of customer traffic between the first half and second half of the month.

Cells E4 and E10 show the average daily customer traffic for the first half and second half of the month, respectively. The value for the first half of the month was obtained by adding all the customer values for day values in the range 1 to 15 and then dividing by the total number of days. The value for the second half of the month was done the same way, using day values in the range 16 to 31.

The day parts of the dates, in Column B, were key to these calculations:

- ✔ In cell E4, the calculation is =SUMIF(B2:B366,"<16",C2:C366)/ COUNTIF(B2:B366"<16").

- ✔ In cell E10, the calculation is =SUMIF(B2:B366,">15",C2:C366)/ COUNTIF(B2:B366,">15").

The SUMIF function is discussed in Chapter 8. The COUNTIF function is discussed in Chapter 9.

The DAY function has been instrumental in showing that more customers visit the fictitious store in the second half of the month. This type of information is great for helping a store owner plan staff assignments, sales specials, and so on.

Isolating the month

Isolating the month part of a date is useful in applications in which just the month, but not the day or year, is relevant. For example, you may have a list of dates on which more than five of your employees call in sick and need to determine whether this event is more common in certain months than others.

You could sort the dates and then count the number for each month. That would be easy enough, but sorting may not be an option based on other requirements. Besides, why manually count when you have, right in front of you, one of the all-time greatest counting software programs ever made?

Figure 12-6 shows a worksheet in which the MONTH function has extracted the numeric month value (1–12) into Column B from the dates in Column A. Cell B2 contains the formula =MONTH(A2) and so on down the column. Columns C and D contain a summary of dates per month. The formula used in cell D3 is =COUNTIF($B$2:$B$260,1).

This counts the number of dates in which the month value is 1 — in other words, January. Cells D4 through D14 contain similar formulas for month values 2 through 12. The figure's data plot makes it clear that calling in sick is more prevalent in December and January. See Chapter 9 for information on the COUNTIF function.

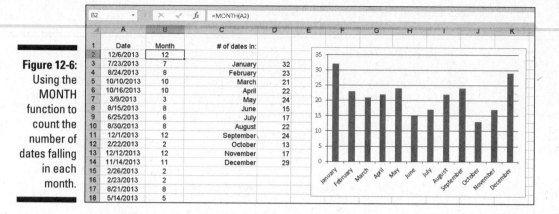

Figure 12-6:
Using the
MONTH
function to
count the
number of
dates falling
in each
month.

Use the MONTH function this way:

1. **Select the cell where you want the results displayed.**

2. **Type** =MONTH(**to begin the function entry.**

3. **Click the cell that has the date.**

4. **Type a) and press Enter.**

   Excel returns a number between 1 and 12.

Isolating the year

Isolating the year part of a date is useful in applications in which only the year, but not the day or month, is relevant. In practice, this is less used than the DAY or MONTH functions because date data is often — though not always — from the same year.

Follow the steps to use the YEAR function:

1. **Select the cell where you want the results displayed.**

2. **Type** =YEAR(**to begin the function entry.**

3. **Click the cell that has the date.**

4. **Type a) and press Enter.**

   Excel returns the four-digit year.

Converting a Date from Text

You may have data in your worksheet that looks like a date but is not represented as an Excel date value. For example, if you enter 01-24-15 in a cell, Excel would have no way of knowing whether this is January 24, 2015, or the code for your combination lock. If it looks like a date, you can use the DATEVALUE function to convert it to an Excel date value.

In practice, any standard date format entered into a cell is recognized by Excel as a date and converted accordingly. However, there may be cases, such as when text dates are imported from an external data source or data is copied and pasted into Excel, for which you need DATEVALUE.

Why not enter dates as text data? Although they may look fine, you can't use them for any of Excel's powerful date calculations without first converting them to date values.

The DATEVALUE function recognizes almost all commonly used ways that dates are written. Here are some ways that you may enter August 5, 2014:

- 8/5/14
- 5-Aug-2014
- 2014/08/14

DATEVALUE can convert these and several other date representations to a date serial number.

After you've converted the dates to a date serial number, you can use the dates in other date formulas or perform calculations with them as described in other parts of this chapter.

To use the DATEVALUE function, follow these steps:

1. **Select the cell where you want the date serial number located.**

2. **Type =DATEVALUE(to begin the function entry.**

3. **Click the cell that has the text format date.**

4. **Type a) and press Enter.**

   The result is a date serial number unless the cell where the result is displayed has already been set to a date format.

Figure 12-7 shows how some nonstandard dates in Column A have been converted to serial numbers with the DATEVALUE function in column B. Then column C displays these serial numbers formatted as dates.

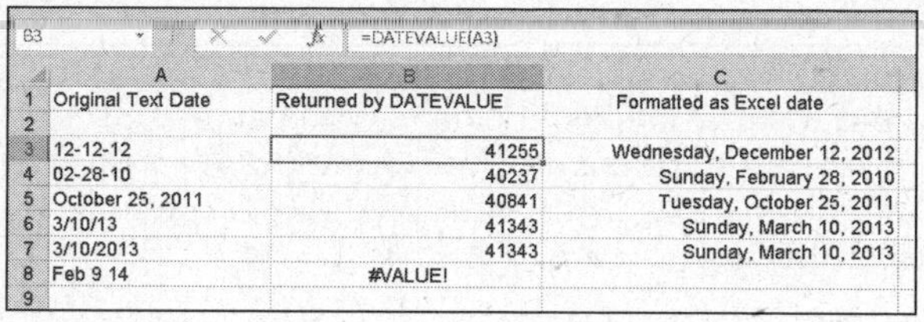

B3 =DATEVALUE(A3)

	A	B	C
1	Original Text Date	Returned by DATEVALUE	Formatted as Excel date
2			
3	12-12-12	41255	Wednesday, December 12, 2012
4	02-28-10	40237	Sunday, February 28, 2010
5	October 25, 2011	40841	Tuesday, October 25, 2011
6	3/10/13	41343	Sunday, March 10, 2013
7	3/10/2013	41343	Sunday, March 10, 2013
8	Feb 9 14	#VALUE!	
9			

Figure 12-7: Converting dates to their serial equivalents with the DATEVALUE function.

Do you notice something funny in Figure 12-7? Normally, you aren't able to enter a value such as the one in cell A4 — 02-28-10 — without losing the leading 0. The cells in Column A had been changed to the Text format. This format tells Excel to leave your entry as is. The Text format is one of the choices in the Category list in the Format Cells dialog box (refer to Figure 12-2 earlier in this chapter).

Note also that the text date in cell A8, `Feb 9 14`, could not be converted by DATEVALUE, so the function returns the error message `#VALUE#`. Excel is great at recognizing dates, but I did not say it is perfect! In cases such as this, you have to format the date another way so DATEVALUE can recognize it.

Finding Out What TODAY Is

When working in Excel, you often need to use the current date. Each time you print a worksheet, for example, you may want the day's date to show. The TODAY function fills the bill perfectly. It simply returns the date from your computer's internal clock. To use the TODAY function, follow these steps:

1. **Position the pointer in the cell where you want the result.**
2. **Type** =TODAY().
3. **Press Enter to end the function.**

That's it! You now have the date from your computer. If your computer's clock is not set correctly, don't blame Excel. As with all dates in Excel, what you really end up with is a serial number, but the Date formatting displays the date in a readable fashion.

As with all functions in Excel, you can embed functions in other functions. For example, if you need to know just the current date's month, you can combine the TODAY function with the MONTH function, like this:

```
=MONTH(TODAY())
```

Counting the days until your birthday

After a certain age, a lot of people wish their birthdays would not come around so often, but if you still like birthdays, you can use Excel to keep track of how many days are left until the next one. Entered in a cell, this formula tells you how many days are left until your birthday (assuming that your next birthday is May 5, 2016):

```
=DATE(2016,5,5) - TODAY()
```

Use the DATE function to enter the day, month, and year of your next birthday. This prevents Excel from interpreting a shorthand entry, such as 5/5/2016, as a mathematical operation on its own.

If the formula were =5/5/2016 - TODAY(), Excel would calculate an incorrect answer because the formula effectively says, "Divide 5 by 5, then divide that result by 2016, then subtract the serial number of today's date." The answer would be incorrect.

Using the DATE function to represent dates in which a mathematical operation is performed is a good idea.

Counting your age in days

When your birthday finally rolls around, someone may ask how old you are. Maybe you'd rather not say. Here's a way to respond, but in a way that leaves some doubt: Answer by saying how old you are in days!

Excel can help you figure this out. All you have to do is count the number of days between your birth date and the current date. A simple formula tells you this:

```
=TODAY() - DATE(birth year, birth month, birth day)
```

Here's an example, assuming that your birthday is March 18, 1976:

```
=TODAY() - DATE(1976, 3, 18).
```

Determining the Day of the Week

The Beatles recorded a song called "Eight Days a Week," but for the rest of us, seven days is the norm. The WEEKDAY function helps you figure out which day of the week a date falls on. Now you can figure out whether your next birthday falls on a Friday. Or you can make sure that a planned business meeting does not fall on a weekend.

Here is how you use the WEEKDAY function:

1. **Select the cell where you want the results displayed.**

2. **Type** =WEEKDAY(**to begin the function entry.**

3. **Select the cell that has the date you want to find out the weekday for.**

4. **Type a) and press Enter.**

   WEEKDAY returns a number between 1 and 7. Table 12-1 shows what the returned number means.

Table 12-1	WEEKDAY Returned Values
Returned Value	*Weekday*
1	Sunday
2	Monday
3	Tuesday
4	Wednesday
5	Thursday
6	Friday
7	Saturday

Don't confuse the returned numbers with actual dates! Just because Table 12-1 shows a value of 4 indicating Wednesday doesn't mean that the fourth day of a month is a Wednesday. The values of the returned numbers are also a bit confusing because most people consider Monday, not Sunday, to be the first day of the week. You can go argue the point with Microsoft, if you like! Better yet, you can include a second, optional, argument that tells WEEKDAY to return 1 for Monday, 2 for Tuesday, and so on:

```
=WEEKDAY(A1, 2)
```

The numbers 1 through 7, returned from the WEEKDAY function, are not the same as the first through seventh of the month.

The WEEKDAY function lets you extract interesting information from date-related data. For example, maybe you're on a diet, and you're keeping a tally of how many calories you consume each day for a month. Then you start wondering "On which days do I eat the most?" Figure 12-8 shows a worksheet that calculates the average calories consumed on each day of the week over a month's time. A glance at the results shows that Saturdays and Sundays are not your high-calorie-consumption days; it's Wednesday and Thursday that you have to watch out for.

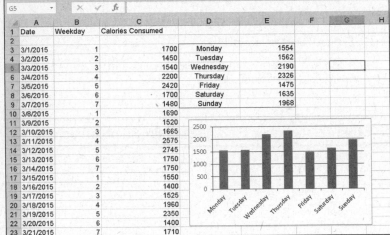

Figure 12-8: Using WEEKDAY tells you which day of the week a date falls on.

Working with Workdays

Most weeks have five workdays — Monday through Friday — and two weekend days. I know; some weeks seem to have 20 workdays, but that's just your imagination! Excel has two functions that let you perform workday-related calculations.

Determining workdays in a range of dates

The NETWORKDAYS function tells you how many working days are in a range of dates. Do you ever sit at your desk and stare at the calendar, trying to count how many working days are left in the year? Excel can answer this vital question for you!

NETWORKDAYS counts the number of days, omitting Saturdays and Sundays, in a range of dates that you supply. You can add a list of dates that should not be counted, if you want. This optional list is where you can put holidays, vacation time, and so on.

Figure 12-9 shows an example using NETWORKDAYS. Cells C3 and C4 show the start and end dates, respectively. In this example, the start date is provided the TODAY function. Therefore, the result always reflects a count that starts from the current date. The end date is the last day of the year. The function in cell C6 is =NETWORKDAYS(C3,C4,C10:C23).

	A	B	C
1			
2			
3		Today's Date	5/28/2015
4		End of Year	12/31/2015
5			
6		**Remaining Work Days:**	148
7			
8			
9			
10		New Year's Day	1/1/2015
11		Martin Luther King Jr. Day	1/19/2015
12		President's Day	2/16/2015
13		Memorial Day	5/25/2015
14		Independence Day	7/4/2015
15		Labor Day	9/7/2015
16		Vacation	9/20/2015
17		Vacation	9/21/2015
18		Vacation	9/22/2015
19		Vacation	9/23/2015
20		Vacation	9/24/2015
21		Columbus Day	10/12/2015
22		Thanksgiving	11/26/2015
23		Christmas	12/25/2015

Figure 12-9: Counting workdays with NET-WORKDAYS.

The function includes the cells that have the start and end dates. Then there is a range of cells: C10 through C23. These cells have dates that should not be counted in the total of workdays: holidays and vacations. You can put anything in these cells, but they do have to be Excel dates. If a date specified in this list falls on a workday, NETWORKDAYS does not count it. If it falls on a weekend, it would not be counted anyway, so it is ignored.

To use NETWORKDAYS, follow these steps:

1. **Select the cell where you want the results displayed.**

2. **Type** =NETWORKDAYS(**to begin the function entry.**

3. **Click the cell that has the start date for the range of dates to be counted.**

4. **Type a comma (,).**

5. **Click the cell that has the number end date for the range of dates to be counted.**

   If you want to add a list of dates to exclude, continue to Steps 6 and 7; otherwise, go to Step 8.

6. **Type a comma (,).**

7. **Click and drag the pointer over the cells that have the dates to exclude.**

8. **Type a) and press Enter.**

   The result is a count of days, between the start and end dates, that do not fall on Saturday or Sunday and are not in an optional list of exclusion dates.

Workdays in the future

Sometimes, you are given a deadline ("Have that back to me in 20 working days"), or you give it to someone else: Fine, but what is the date 20 working days from now? The WORKDAY function comes to the rescue. You specify a start date, the number of working days, and an optional list of holidays that are not to be counted as working days. (This list works just the same as for the NETWORKDAYS function, discussed in the previous section.)

To use WORKDAYS, follow these steps:

1. **Select the cell where you want the results displayed.**

2. **Type =WORKDAY(to begin the function entry.**

3. **Click the cell that has the start date for the calculation.**

4. **Type a comma (,).**

5. **Click the cell that has the number of workdays or enter the number directly in the formula.**

   If you want to add a list of dates to exclude in the count, continue to Steps 6 and 7; otherwise, go to Step 8.

6. **Type a comma (,).**

7. **Click and drag the pointer over the cells that have the dates to be excluded.**

8. **Type a) and press Enter.**

   The result is a date that is the specified number of workdays from the start date, not counting dates in the optional list of exclusion dates.

Calculating Time between Two Dates with the DATEDIF Function

Excel provides the DATEDIF function to calculate the number of days, months, or years between two dates. This is an undocumented function — that is, you won't see it in the Insert Function dialog box, and you cannot find it in the Excel Help system. Why is it undocumented? Beats me — but it sure can be useful! Impress your friends and co-workers. The only thing you have to do is remember how to enter it. Of course, I don't mind if you keep this book around to look it up.

DATEDIF takes three arguments:

✔ Start date

✔ End date

✔ Interval

The interval argument tells the function what type of result to return, summarized in Table 12-2.

Table 12-2		Settings for the Interval Argument of DATEDIF
Value	*What It Means*	*Comment*
"d"	Days	The count of inclusive days from the start date through the end date.
"m"	Months	The count of complete months between the dates. Only those months that fully occur between the dates are counted. For example, if the first date starts after the first of the month, that first month is not included in the count. For the end date, even when it is the last day of the month, that month is not counted. See Figure 12-10 for an example.
"y"	Years	The count of complete years between the dates. Only those years that fully occur between the dates are counted. For example, if the first date starts later than January 1, that first year is not included in the count. For the end date, even when it is December 31, that year is not counted. See Figure 12-10 for an example.

(continued)

Table 12-2 *(continued)*

Value	***What It Means***	***Comment***
`"yd"`	Days excluding years	The count of inclusive days from the start date through the end date, but as if the two dates are in the same year. The year is ignored.
`"ym"`	Months excluding years	The count of complete months between the dates, but as if the two dates are in the same year. The year is ignored.
`"md"`	Days excluding months and years	The count of inclusive days from the start date through the end date, but as if the two dates are in the same month and year. The month and year are ignored.

Figure 12-10 shows some examples of using DATEDIF. Column A has start dates. Column B has end dates. Columns C through H contain formulas with DATEDIF. The DATEDIF function uses the start and end dates on each given row, and the interval is labeled at the top of each column, C through H.

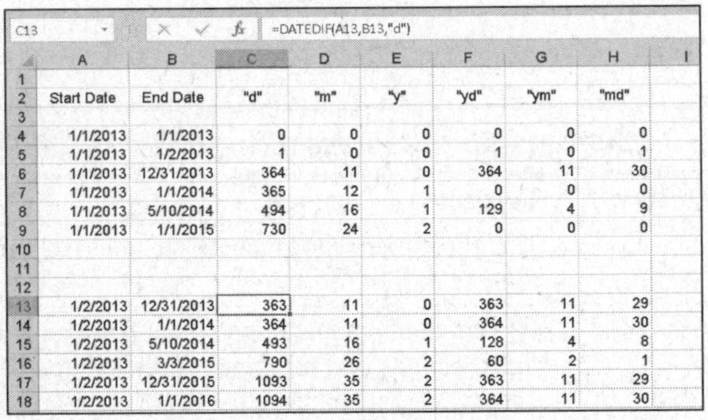

C13 =DATEDIF(A13,B13,"d")

	A	B	C	D	E	F	G	H	I
1									
2	Start Date	End Date	"d"	"m"	"y"	"yd"	"ym"	"md"	
3									
4	1/1/2013	1/1/2013	0	0	0	0	0	0	
5	1/1/2013	1/2/2013	1	0	0	1	0	1	
6	1/1/2013	12/31/2013	364	11	0	364	11	30	
7	1/1/2013	1/1/2014	365	12	1	0	0	0	
8	1/1/2013	5/10/2014	494	16	1	129	4	9	
9	1/1/2013	1/1/2015	730	24	2	0	0	0	
10									
11									
12									
13	1/2/2013	12/31/2013	363	11	0	363	11	29	
14	1/2/2013	1/1/2014	364	11	0	364	11	30	
15	1/2/2013	5/10/2014	493	16	1	128	4	8	
16	1/2/2013	3/3/2015	790	26	2	60	2	1	
17	1/2/2013	12/31/2015	1093	35	2	363	11	29	
18	1/2/2013	1/1/2016	1094	35	2	364	11	30	

Figure 12-10: Counting days, months, and years with DATEDIF.

Here's how to use DATEDIF:

1. **Select the cell where you want the results to appear.**
2. **Type** =DATEDIF(**to begin the function entry.**
3. **Click a cell where you have a date or enter its address.**
4. **Type a comma (,).**

5. Click a cell where you want another date.

This date must be the same or greater than the first date from Step 3; otherwise, you get an error.

6. Type a comma (,).

7. Enter an interval.

Refer to Table 12-2 for the list of intervals that you can use with the function. Make sure that the interval is enclosed in double quotes.

8. Type a) and press Enter.

Chapter 13

Keeping Well-Timed Functions

- -

- -

Excel has a handful of superb functions for working with times and performing calculations on time values. You can analyze data to the hour, minute, or second. And Excel helps you get this done in a New York minute!

Understanding How Excel Handles Time

In Chapter 12, I explain how Excel uses a serial number system to work with dates. Well, guess what? The same system is used to work with time. The key difference is that although dates are represented by the integer portion of a serial number, time is represented by the decimal portion.

What does this mean? Consider this: 41640. That is the serial number representation for January 1, 2014. Notice, though, that there is no indication of the time of day. The assumed time is 12 a.m. (midnight), the start of the day. You can, however, represent specific times if needed.

Excel uses the decimal side of the serial number to represent time as a fraction of the 24-hour day. Thus, 12 p.m. (noon) is 0.5, and 6 p.m. is 0.75. Table 13-1 shows some more examples and reveals how dates and time information are combined in a single serial number.

Table 13-1	How Excel Represents Time
Date and Time	*Serial Format*
January 1, 2014 12:00 a.m.	41640
January 1, 2014 12:01 a.m.	416409.00069
January 1, 2014 10:00 a.m.	41640.41667
January 1, 2014 12:00 p.m.	41640.5
January 1, 2014 4:30 p.m.	41640.6875
January 1, 2014 10:00 p.m.	41640.91667
January 1, 2014 11:59 p.m.	41640.99931

Time is represented in a decimal value — up to five digits to the right of
the decimal point. A value of 0 is the equivalent of 12 a.m. A value of .5 is the
equivalent of 12 p.m. — the midpoint of the day. The value of .99931 is
the same as the 23rd hour and *start* of the 59th minute. A value of .99999
is the same as the 23rd hour, the 59th minute, and the 59th second — in
other words, 1 second before the start of the next day.

Can you represent time without a date? You bet! Use a value less than 1 for
this purpose. For example, the serial number 0.75 represents 6 p.m. with no
date specified.

Representing time as a serial number provides the same advantages as it
does for dates: the ability to add and subtract times. For example, given a
date/time serial number, you can create the serial number for the date/time
one and a half days later by adding 1.5 to it.

Formatting Time

When you work with time values, you probably need to format cells in your
worksheet so the times display in a standard format that people will understand. The decimal numbers don't make sense to us human folk. To format
time, you use the Format Cells dialog box, shown in Figure 13-1.

To format time, follow these steps:

1. **If it's not already displayed, click the Home tab at the top of the Excel
   screen.**

2. **Click the small arrow in the bottom-right corner of the Number section.**

   The Format Cells dialog box appears.

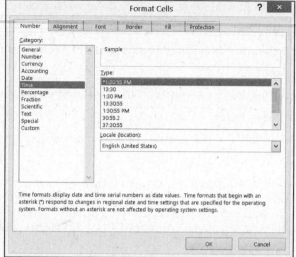

Figure 13-1:
Using the
Format Cells
dialog box
to specify
how time
values are
displayed.

3. **Select Time in the Category List.**

4. **Select an appropriate format in the Type List.**

You can display time in several ways. Excel can format time so that hours in a day range from 1 a.m. to 12 a.m. and then 1 p.m. to 12 p.m. Alternatively, the hour can be between 0 and 23, with values 13 through 23 representing 1 p.m. through 11 p.m. The latter system, known to some as *military time or 24-hour time,* is commonly used in computer systems.

Note that Excel stores a date and time together in a single serial number. Therefore, some of the formatting options in the time and date categories display a complete date and time.

Keeping TIME

You can use the TIME function to combine hours, minutes, and seconds into a single usable value. Figuring out the serial number representation of a particular moment in time isn't easy. Luckily, the TIME function does this for you. You provide an hour, minute, and second, and TIME tells you the serial value. To do this, follow these steps:

1. **Select the cell where you want the result displayed.**

2. **Type** =TIME(**to begin the function entry.**

3. **Click the cell that has the hour (0–23) or enter such a value.**

4. **Type a comma (,).**

5. **Click the cell that has the minute (0–59) or enter such a value.**

6. **Type a comma (,).**

7. **Click the cell that has the second (0–59) or enter such a value.**

8. **Type a) and press Enter.**

   The result is a decimal serial number, or a readable time if the cell is formatted properly.

You should be aware that the minute and second values "wrap." A value of 60 or greater for seconds wraps to the next minute. For example, 75 seconds is interpreted as 1 minute 15 seconds. Likewise, a minute value of 90 is interpreted as 1 hour 30 minutes. Hours wrap, too. An hour value of 26 is interpreted as 2 a.m.

Converting Text to Time with TIMEVALUE

If you enter a time in a standard format in a cell, Excel recognizes it as a time. It is converted to a serial number, and the cell is assigned the default time format. If you are pasting or importing data from another application, you may encounter times in text format, such as "2:28 PM". You can convert these to a time serial number by using the TIMEVALUE function. Here's how:

1. **Select the cell where you want the result displayed.**

2. **Type =TIMEVALUE(to begin the function entry.**

3. **Click the cell that contains the time in text format.**

4. **Type a) and press Enter.**

TIMEVALUE works just with text. If the TIMEVALUE function returns the error code #VALUE#, it probably means one of two things:

✔ The time is in a text format that Excel does not recognize, such as "2:28PM" (no space before PM) instead of "2:28 PM".

✔ The time is not actually in text format but is an Excel time serial number formatted to look that way. Change the cell format to General to check.

Deconstructing Time with HOUR, MINUTE, and SECOND

Any moment in time really is a combination of an hour, a minute, and a second. In the preceding section, I show you how the TIME function puts these three components together. In this section, I show you how to break them apart by using the HOUR, MINUTE, and SECOND functions. The worksheet in Figure 13-2 shows a date and time in several rows going down Column A. The same dates and times are shown in Column B, with a different format. Columns C, D, and E show the hour, minute, and second, respectively, from the values in Column A.

Note that if the date/time serial number contains a date part, HOUR, MINUTE, and SECOND ignore it; all they care about is the time part.

Figure 13-2:
Splitting
time with
the HOUR,
MINUTE,
and
SECOND
functions.

	C5	▾	× ✓ *fx*	=HOUR(A5)		
	A		B	C	D	E
1	Date and Time		Date and Time	Hour	Minute	Second
2	in General Format		in Date and Time Format			
3						
4						
5	40375.89935		7/16/2010 9:35:04 PM	21	35	4
6	40328.55234		5/30/2010 1:15:22 PM	13	15	22
7	40435.2303		9/14/2010 5:31:38 AM	5	31	38
8	40185.3452		1/7/2010 8:17:05 AM	8	17	5
9	40186.33802		1/8/2010 8:06:45 AM	8	6	45
10	40282.6486		4/14/2010 3:33:59 PM	15	33	59
11	40496.36667		11/14/2010 8:48:00 AM	8	48	0
12	40407.839		8/17/2010 8:08:10 PM	20	8	10
13	40359.13837		6/30/2010 3:19:15 AM	3	19	15
14	39168.04307		3/27/2007 1:02:01 AM	1	2	1
15						

Isolating the hour

Extracting the hour from a time is useful in applications that tally hourly events. A common use of this occurs in call centers. If you've ever responded to an infomercial or a pledge drive, you may realize that a group of workers wait for incoming phone calls such as the one you made. (I hope you got a good bargain.) A common metric in this type of business is the number of calls per hour.

Figure 13-3 shows a worksheet that summarizes calls per hour. Calls have been tracked for October 2015. The incoming call dates and times are listed in Column A. In Column B, the hour of each call has been isolated with the HOUR function. Column D is a summary of calls per hour over the course of the month.

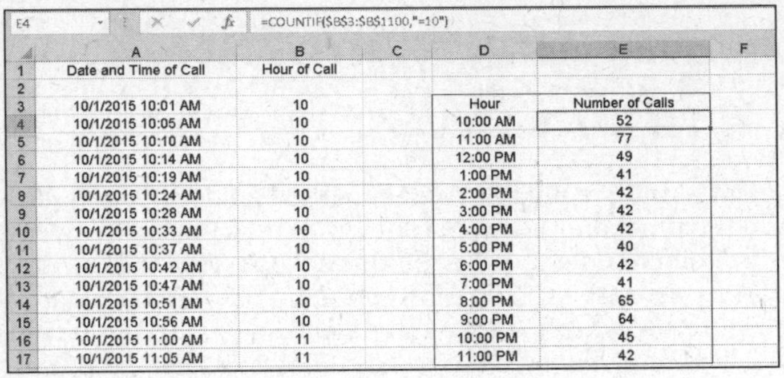

E4 =COUNTIF($B$3:$B$1100,"=10")

	A	B	C	D	E	F
1	Date and Time of Call	Hour of Call				
2						
3	10/1/2015 10:01 AM	10		Hour	Number of Calls	
4	10/1/2015 10:05 AM	10		10:00 AM	52	
5	10/1/2015 10:10 AM	10		11:00 AM	77	
6	10/1/2015 10:14 AM	10		12:00 PM	49	
7	10/1/2015 10:19 AM	10		1:00 PM	41	
8	10/1/2015 10:24 AM	10		2:00 PM	42	
9	10/1/2015 10:28 AM	10		3:00 PM	42	
10	10/1/2015 10:33 AM	10		4:00 PM	42	
11	10/1/2015 10:37 AM	10		5:00 PM	40	
12	10/1/2015 10:42 AM	10		6:00 PM	42	
13	10/1/2015 10:47 AM	10		7:00 PM	41	
14	10/1/2015 10:51 AM	10		8:00 PM	65	
15	10/1/2015 10:56 AM	10		9:00 PM	64	
16	10/1/2015 11:00 AM	11		10:00 PM	45	
17	10/1/2015 11:05 AM	11		11:00 PM	42	

Figure 13-3: Using the HOUR function to summarize results.

In Figure 13-3, the values in Column D are calculated by the COUNTIF function. There is a COUNTIF for each hour from 10 a.m. through 11 p.m. Each COUNTIF looks at the range of numbers in Column B (the hours) and counts the values that match the criteria. Each COUNTIF uses a different hour value for its criteria. Following is an example:

```
=COUNTIF($B$3:$B$1100,"=16")
```

Here is how to use the HOUR function:

1. **Select the cell where you want the result displayed.**
2. **Type** =HOUR(**to begin the function entry.**
3. **Click the cell that has the full-time (or date/time) entry.**
4. **Type a) and press Enter.**

   Excel returns a number between 0 and 23.

Isolating the minute

Isolating the minute part of a time is necessary in applications that track activity down to the minute. A timed test is a perfect example. Remember when the teacher would yell, "Pencils down"?

Excel can easily calculate how long something takes by subtracting one time from another. In the case of a test, the MINUTE function helps with the calculation because how long something took in minutes is being figured out. Figure 13-4 shows a list of times it took for students to take a test. All students started the test at 10 a.m. Then, when each student finished, the time was noted. The test *should* have taken a student no more than 15 minutes.

D3			✕ ✓ *fx*	=IF(MINUTE(C3)-MINUTE(B3)<=15,"Yes","No")	

	A	B	C	D	E
1	Student ID	Start Time	End Time	Finished on Time	
2					
3	S2223	10:00 AM	10:18 AM	No	
4	G7854	10:00 AM	10:12 AM	Yes	
5	A4973	10:00 AM	10:14 AM	Yes	
6	M4211	10:00 AM	10:20 AM	No	
7	H7840	10:00 AM	10:22 AM	No	
8	G4381	10:00 AM	10:10 AM	Yes	
9	J4009	10:00 AM	10:11 AM	Yes	
10	T5545	10:00 AM	10:15 AM	Yes	
11	W9329	10:00 AM	10:13 AM	Yes	
12	M8050	10:00 AM	10:16 AM	No	
13	S2377	10:00 AM	10:23 AM	No	
14	R1967	10:00 AM	10:14 AM	Yes	
15					

Figure 13-4: Calculating minutes elapsed with the MINUTE function.

For each data row, Column D contains a formula that subtracts the minute in the end time, in Column C, from the start time, in Column B. This math operation is embedded in an IF statement. If the result is 15 or less, Yes appears in column D; otherwise, No appears.

```
=IF(MINUTE(C3)-MINUTE(B3)<=15,"Yes","No")
```

Like the HOUR function, the MINUTE function takes a single time or date/time reference as its argument.

Isolating the second

Isolating the second from a date value is useful in situations in which highly accurate time calculations are needed. In practice, this isn't a common requirement in Excel applications.

Follow these steps to use the SECOND function:

1. **Position the pointer in the cell where you want the results displayed.**

2. **Type =SECOND(to begin the function entry.**

3. **Click the cell that has the time value or enter a time value.**

4. **Type a) to end the function, and press Enter.**

Finding the Time NOW

Sometimes when you're working in Excel, you need to access the current time. For example, you may be working on a client project and need to know how much time you've spent on it. Use the NOW function when you first open the workbook, and use it again when you're finished. Subtracting one value from the other provides the elapsed time.

Here's how to use the NOW function:

1. **Select the cell where you want the result.**
2. **Type** =NOW().
3. **Press Enter to end the function.**

You must take one additional step to make the preceding NOW time calculation work. When you get the current time at the start, copy the value and then use Paste Special to paste it back as a value. This strategy prevents the time from constantly updating. You can also do this by selecting the cell, clicking the Formula Bar, and then pressing F9.

NOW provides not just the current time, but also the current date. This is similar to the TODAY function. TODAY returns the current date — without the current time. NOW returns the full current date and time. See Chapter 12 for more information on the TODAY function.

Calculating Elapsed Time over Days

Each day has 24 hours. Multiplying 24 by 7 tells you that there are 168 hours in a week. How many hours are in a month? This is not as easy to tell. A month may have 28, 29, 30, or 31 days.

Counting elapsed time, in hours, could require a complex algorithm. Although Excel has no single function for this task, you can combine a couple of functions in a formula to get the answer. This is another benefit of the fact that Excel represents date/time values as serial numbers. This makes it easy to calculate the number of hours that have passed between two date/time values.

Figure 13-5 shows a worksheet with start and end date/time values in two columns. A third column shows the calculated number of elapsed hours for each start/end pair.

In Column A and Column B are dates and times. These dates and times are really just serial numbers with a decimal portion. Using the INT function, Excel counts the difference in days, even if the span pops over to a new year. Then it uses the HOUR function to calculate the difference of the decimal portion. The formula for the first row is

```
=(INT(B3)-INT(A3))*24 + HOUR(B3) - HOUR(A3)
```

	C9	▾	✕ ✓ ƒx	=(INT(B9)-INT(A9))*24+HOUR(B9)-HOUR(A9)

	A	B	C
1	Start Date and Time	End Date and Time	Count of Elapsed Hours
2			
3	11/15/2012 9:00	11/15/2012 9:30	0
4	11/15/2012 9:00	11/15/2012 21:00	12
5	11/15/2012 9:00	11/15/2012 23:59	14
6	11/15/2012 9:00	11/16/2012 0:00	15
7	11/15/2012 9:00	11/16/2012 2:00	17
8	11/15/2012 9:00	11/16/2012 9:00	24
9	11/15/2012 9:00	11/23/2012 11:30	194
10	11/15/2012 9:00	12/2/2012 15:30	414
11	11/15/2012 9:00	12/30/2012 1:45	1072
12	11/15/2012 9:00	1/15/2013 16:00	1471
13	11/15/2012 9:00	1/18/2013 10:00	1537
14	11/15/2012 9:00	3/15/2013 9:00	2880
15	11/15/2012 9:00	11/15/2013 8:58	8759
16	11/15/2012 9:00	11/15/2013 9:00	8760
17			

Figure 13-5:
Calculating
elapsed
time.

Each successive row has the same formula in Column C, but with the cell references pointed to the values on the row. The first part of the formula calculates the difference in days and multiplies this by 24 for the total number of hours in the number of days.

The trick is to correctly calculate the time between the start and end values. The hour portion of both the start and end values is determined with the HOUR function; then one value is subtracted from the other. The result of this subtraction is added to the precalculated number of hours from the count of days. Note that minutes are ignored. Perhaps you can figure out how to modify the formula to take seconds into account!

Chapter 14

Using Lookup, Logical, and Reference Functions

Decision, decisions! If one of your students gets an 88 on the test, is that a B+ or is it an A? If your company's new product earns at least $15 million in revenue, how much of a bonus should you give to the team? Or do you have to get to $20,000,000 before you do that? How does this affect the financial statements?

Excel cannot make decisions for you, but it can help you make better decisions. Using functions, such as IF and CHOOSE, you can set up your worksheet to chart a course through the possibilities. Hey, things could be worse! Were it not for Excel, you might have to try the old Ouija-board technique.

Excel also can help you find what you're looking for. Looking for something in a large, complex worksheet can seem like the old needle-in-a-haystack routine. It's okay to admit it. After all, it happens to the best of us! I'm here to help. In this chapter, I show you a slew of functions that make it easy to look up information that's spread around the rows and columns.

Testing on One Condition

The IF function is like the Swiss Army knife of Excel functions. Really, it is used in many situations. Often, you can use it with other functions, which I do often in this chapter. IF, structurally, is easy to understand. The function takes three arguments:

- A test that gives a true or false answer. For example, the test `"is the value in cell A5 equal to the value in cell A8"` can have only one of two possible answers, yes or no. In computer talk, that's true or false. This is not a calculation, mind you, but a comparison.
- The data to be returned by the IF function if the test is true.
- The data to be returned by the IF function if the test is false.

Sounds easy enough. Here are some examples:

Function	Comment
`=IF(D10>D20, D10, D20)`	If the value in D10 is greater than the value in D20, the value in D10 is returned because the test is true. If the value in D10 is not greater than — that is, smaller or equal to — the value in D20, the value in D20 is returned. If the values in D10 and D20 are equal, the test returns false, and the value in D20 is returned.
`=IF(D10>D20, "Good news!", "Bad news!")`	If the value in D10 is greater than the value in D20, the text `"Good News!"` is returned. Otherwise, `"Bad News!"` is returned.
`=IF(D10>D20, "", "Bad news!")`	If the value in D10 is greater than the value in D20, *nothing* is returned. Otherwise, `"Bad News!"` is returned. Note that the second argument is a pair of empty quotes.
`=IF(D10>D20, "Good news!", "")`	If the value in D10 is greater than the value in D20, `"Good News!"` is returned. Otherwise, *nothing* is returned. Note that the third argument is empty quotes.

TIP

An important aspect to note about using IF: letting the second or third argument return nothing. An empty string is returned, and the best way to do this is to place two double quote marks together with nothing in the middle. The result is that the cell containing the IF function remains blank.

IF, therefore, lets you set up two results to return: one for when the test is true and another for when the test is false. Each result can be a number, some text, a function or formula, or even blank.

As you see in the preceding example, a common use of IF is to see how two values compare and return either one value or the other, depending on how you set up the test in the first argument.

IF is often used as a validation check to prevent errors. Suppose that you have a financial worksheet that uses a variable percentage in its calculations. The user must enter this percentage each day, but it must never be greater than 10 percent. To prevent the chance of errors, you could use the IF function to display an error message in the adjacent cell if you mistakenly enter a value outside the permitted range. Assuming that the percentage is entered in cell A3, here's the required IF function:

```
=IF(A3>.1, "ERROR: the % in A3 IS TOO LARGE", "")
```

Figure 14-1 shows how IF can be put to good use in a business application. A fictitious store shop — Ken's Guitars (kinda snappy, don't you think?) — keeps tabs on inventory in an Excel worksheet.

	A	B	C	D	E	F	G
1	Ken's Guitars						
3	Inventory Report		Monday, June 1, 2015				
6	Vendor	Product	Last Date Product Sold	Current Inventory	Reorder Level	Status	
8	Great Guitars	Stratoblaster 9000	5/29/2015	3	2		
9	Great Guitars	Flying X	5/4/2015	2	2	ORDER	
10	Great Guitars	Guitarist's Super Road Kit	3/12/2015	7	10	ORDER	
11	Great Guitars	All-in-one Effects Box	2/25/2015	12	10		
12	Sound Accessories	Glow in the Dark Guitar Strap	4/16/2015	3	12	ORDER	
13	Sound Accessories	Wireless Gig Kit	5/19/2015	7	8	ORDER	
14	Sound Accessories	Classic Amp Imitator	11/14/2014	9	6		
15	Sound Accessories	1 Foot Cables	4/4/2015	33	25		
16	Sound Accessories	6 Foot Cables	5/30/2015	21	25	ORDER	
17	Sound Accessories	10 Foot Cables	5/30/2015	16	20	ORDER	
18	Sound Accessories	18 Foot Cables	4/25/2015	16	12		
19	Sound Accessories	Mini Road Recorder	2/6/2015	3	2		
20	Sound Accessories	Sustainer Sound Box	3/15/2015	4	6	ORDER	
21	Sound Accessories	Rocker Pedal	1/7/2015	1	6	ORDER	
22	Sound Accessories	Rocker Pedal Deluxe	5/9/2015	5	6	ORDER	
23	Traditional Instruments	Beginner Banjo	12/15/2014	3	2		
24	Traditional Instruments	Intermediate Banjo	4/17/2015	4	2		
25	Traditional Instruments	Beginner Mandolin	5/10/2015	1	2	ORDER	
26	Traditional Instruments	Intermediate Mandolin	5/14/2015	3	2		
27	Traditional Instruments	Beginner Guitar	5/30/2015	0	5	ORDER	
28	Traditional Instruments	Intermediate Guitar	5/7/2015	1	5	ORDER	

F8 · × ✓ fx =IF(D8<=E8, "ORDER", "")

Figure 14-1:
Keeping an eye on inventory at the guitar shop.

Column D shows the inventory levels, and Column E shows the reorder levels. It works this way: When a product's inventory level is the same or less than the reorder level, it is time to order more of the product. (I don't know about you, but I love the thought of being surrounded by a bunch of guitars!) The cells in column F contain a formula.

The formula in cell F8 is =IF(D8<=E8,"ORDER",""). It says that if the number of Stratoblaster 9000 guitars in stock is the same or less than the reorder level, return Order. If the number in stock is greater than the reorder level, return nothing. Nothing is returned because three are in stock and the reorder level is two. In the next row, the number of Flying Xs is equal to the reorder level; therefore, cell F9 displays Order.

Using IF is easy. Follow these steps:

1. **Enter two values in a worksheet.**

   These values should have some meaning to you, such as the inventory levels example in Figure 14-1.

2. **Click the cell where you want the result to appear.**

3. **Type** =IF(**to start the function.**

4. **Decide what test you want to perform.**

   You can see whether the two values are equal; whether one is larger than the other; whether subtracting one from the other is greater than, equal to, or less than 0; and so on. For example, to determine whether the first value equals the second value, click the first cell (or enter its address), enter an equal sign (=), and then click the second cell (or enter its address).

5. **Type a comma (,).**

6. **Enter the result that should appear if the test is *true*.**

   For example, enter "**The values are equal**". Text must be enclosed in quotes.

7. **Type a comma (,).**

8. **Enter the result that should appear if the test is *false*.**

   For example, enter "**The values are not equal**".

9. **Type a), and press Enter.**

The IF function can do a whole lot more. Nested IF functions give you a lot more flexibility in performing tests on your worksheet data. A bit of perseverance is necessary to get through this. *Nested* means that you can place an IF function inside another IF function. That is, the inner IF is placed where the true or false argument in the outer IF goes (or even use internal IFs for both of the arguments). Why would you do this?

The other night, we were deciding where to go for dinner. We were considering Italian and decided that if we went to an Italian place and it served manicotti, we would have manicotti. Otherwise, we decided to eat pizza.

Logically, this decision looks like this:

```
If the restaurant is Italian, then
If the restaurant serves manicotti, then
we will have manicotti
else
we will have pizza
```

This looks a lot like programming code. I have left out the `End If` statements on purpose to prevent confusion because the IF function has no equivalent value.

That's it! Make note that the inner IF statement has a result for both the true and false possibilities. The outer IF does not. Here is the structure as nested Excel IF statements:

```
=IF(Restaurant=Italian, IF(Restaurant serves manicotti, "manicotti",
           "pizza"), "")
```

If the restaurant were not Italian, it wouldn't matter what we ate (as indicated by the third argument of the outer IF being empty).

You can nest up to 64 IF statements, although things are likely to get very complicated once you go beyond 4 or 5.

You can apply a nested IF statement to increase the sophistication of the inventory worksheet from Figure 14-1. Figure 14-2 has an additional column: Hot Item. A Hot Item can take three forms:

- If the inventory level is half or less of the reorder level and the last sale date is within the last 30 days, this is a *Hot Item*. The point of view is that in 30 days or less the stock sold down to half or less than the reorder level. This means that the inventory is turning over at a fast pace.

- If the inventory level is half or less of the reorder level and the last sale date is within the last 31–60 days, this is a *Warm Item*. The point of view is that in 31–60 days the stock sold down to half or less than the reorder level. This means that the inventory is turning over at a medium pace.

- If neither of the preceding two conditions is met, the item is not assigned any special status.

G8 =IF(D8<=(E8*0.5),IF(NOW()-C8<=30,"HOT!",IF(NOW()-C8<=60,"Warm!","")),"")

	A	B	C	D	E	F	G
1	Ken's Guitars						
3	Inventory Report	Monday, June 1, 2015					
5			Last Date	Current	Reorder		
6	Vendor	Item	Item Sold	Inventory	Level	Status	Hot Item
8	Great Guitars	Stratoblaster 9000	5/29/2015	3	2		
9	Great Guitars	Flying X	5/4/2015	2	2	ORDER	
10	Great Guitars	Guitarist's Super Road Kit	3/12/2015	7	10	ORDER	
11	Great Guitars	All-in-one Effects Box	2/25/2015	12	10		
12	Sound Accessories	Glow in the Dark Guitar Strap	4/16/2015	3	12	ORDER	Warm!
13	Sound Accessories	Wireless Gig Kit	5/19/2015	4	8	ORDER	HOT!
14	Sound Accessories	Classic Amp Imitator	11/14/2014	9	6		
15	Sound Accessories	1 Foot Cables	4/4/2015	33	25		
16	Sound Accessories	6 Foot Cables	5/30/2015	21	25	ORDER	
17	Sound Accessories	10 Foot Cables	5/30/2015	16	20	ORDER	
18	Sound Accessories	18 Foot Cables	4/25/2015	16	12		
19	Sound Accessories	Mini Road Recorder	2/8/2015	3	2		
20	Sound Accessories	Sustainer Sound Box	3/15/2015	4	6	ORDER	
21	Sound Accessories	Rocker Pedal	1/7/2015	1	6	ORDER	
22	Sound Accessories	Rocker Pedal Deluxe	5/9/2015	5	6	ORDER	
23	Traditional Instruments	Beginner Banjo	12/15/2014	3	2		
24	Traditional Instruments	Intermediate Banjo	4/17/2015	4	2		
25	Traditional Instruments	Beginner Mandolin	5/10/2015	1	2	ORDER	HOT!
26	Traditional Instruments	Intermediate Mandolin	5/14/2015	3	2		
27	Traditional Instruments	Beginner Guitar	5/30/2015	0	5	ORDER	HOT!
28	Traditional Instruments	Intermediate Guitar	5/7/2015	1	5	ORDER	HOT!

Figure 14-2: Looking for hot inventory items.

There are Hot Items, and there are Warm Items. Both must meet the common criterion that the inventory is 50 percent or less of the reorder level. Only after this first condition is met does the second criterion — the number of days since the last order — come into play. Sounds like a nested IF to me! Here is the formula in cell G8:

```
=IF(D8<=(E8×0.5),IF(NOW()-C8<=30,"HOT!",IF(NOW()-C8<=60,"Warm!","")),"").
```

Okay, take a breath. I leave no Excel user behind!

The outer IF tests whether the inventory in column D is equal to or less than half (50 percent) of the reorder level. The piece of the formula that does that is `=IF(D8<=(E8×0.5)`. This test, of course, produces a true or false answer. If it is false, the false part of the outer IF is taken (which is just an empty string found at the end of the formula: `,""))`.

That leaves the whole middle part to wade through. Stay with it!

If the first test is true, the true part of the outer IF is taken. It just so happens that this true part is another IF function:

```
IF(NOW()-C8<=30,"HOT!",IF(NOW()-C8<=60,"Warm!",""))
```

The first argument of the inner IF tests whether the number of days since the last order date (in column C) is less than or equal to 30. You do this by subtracting the last order date from `today`, as obtained from the NOW function.

If the test is true, and the last order date is within the last 30 days, HOT! is returned. A hot seller indeed! If the test is false. . . wait, what's this? Another IF function! Yes: an IF inside an IF inside an IF. If the number of days since the last order date is greater than 30, the next nested IF tests whether the number of days is within the last 60 days:

```
IF(NOW()-C8<=60
```

If this test is true, Warm! is returned. If the test is false, nothing is returned.

A few key points about this triple-level IF statement:

- The IF that tests whether the number of elapsed days is 30 or fewer has a value to return if true (HOT!) and a value to return for false (whatever is returned by the next nested IF).
- The outer IF and the innermost IF return nothing when their test is false.
- On the surface, the test for 60 or fewer days *also would catch a date that is 30 days or fewer since the last order date!* This is not really what is meant to be. The test should be whether the number of elapsed days is 60 or fewer *but more than 30!* You do not have to actually spell it out this way, because the formula got to the point of testing for the 60-day threshold only because the 30-day threshold already failed. Gotta watch out for these things!

Choosing the Right Value

The CHOOSE function is ideal for converting a value to a *literal*. In plain-speak, this means turning a number, such as 4, into a word, such as April. CHOOSE takes up to 30 arguments. The first argument acts as key to the rest of the arguments. In fact, the other arguments do not get processed per se by the function. Instead, the function looks at the value of the first argument and, based on that value, returns one of its other arguments.

The first argument must be, or evaluate to, a number. This number in turn indicates which of the following arguments to return. For example, the following returns Two:

```
=CHOOSE(2, "One", "Two", "Three")
```

The first argument is the number 2. This means that the function will return the second argument in the list of arguments *following* the first argument. But watch out — this is not the same as returning the second argument of the function! It means to return the second argument, counting from the second argument.

Figure 14-3 shows a useful example of CHOOSE. Suppose that you have a column of months that are in the numerical form (1 through 12). You need to have these displayed as the month names (January through December). CHOOSE to the rescue!

C4	▾	×	✓	fx	=CHOOSE(B4,"January", "February", "March", "April", "May", "June", "July", "August",

	A	B	C	D	E	F	G	H
1								
2		Month Number	Month Name					
3								
4		1	January					
5		2	February					
6		3	March					
7		4	April					
8		5	May					
9		6	June					
10		7	July					
11		8	August					
12		9	September					
13		10	October					
14		11	November					
15		12	December					
16								

Figure 14-3:
Choosing
what to see.

Cells C4:C15 contain formulas with the CHOOSE function. The formula in cell C4 follows:

```
=CHOOSE(B4,"January", "February", "March", "April", "May", "June", "July",
        "August", "September", "October", "November", "December")
```

Cell B4 contains the value 1, so the first argument starting in the list of possible returned strings (that is, "January") is returned.

CHOOSE is most often used to return meaningful text that relates to a number, such as returning the name of a month from its numeric value. But CHOOSE is not restricted to returning text strings. You can use it to return numbers.

Try it yourself! Here's how:

1. **Enter a list of numeric values in a worksheet column.**

   These values should all be small, such as 1, 2, 3, and so on.

2. **Click the cell to the right of the first value.**

3. **Type** =CHOOSE(**to start the function.**

4. **Click the cell to the left (the one that has the first value) or enter its address.**

5. **Type a comma (,).**

6. **Enter a list of text strings that each have an association with the numbers you entered in Step 1.**

   Each text string should be in double quotes and separated with commas (for example, **"January", "February", "March"**).

7. Type a) and press Enter.

The cell to the right of the first item displays the returned text.

8. Use the fill handle from the first cell with the formula, and drag the formula down to all the other cells adjacent to list entries.

Let's Be Logical

I once worked on a grammar problem that provided a paragraph with no punctuation and asked that the punctuation be added:

That that is is not that that is not is not that it it is

The answer follows:

That that is, is not that that is not. Is not that it? It is.

So true! That that is, such as an apple, is not that that is not, such as an orange. (Is your head spinning yet?)

NOT

NOT is a logical operator. It is used to reverse a logical value, turning true to false or false to true.

Type this formula in a cell:

```
= 5 + 5 = 10
```

The result is the word TRUE. Makes sense. The math checks out. Now try this:

```
=NOT(5 + 5 = 10)
```

What happens? The word FALSE is returned.

The NOT function provides greater flexibility when you're designing the test portion of a SUMIF function (which you read about in Chapter 8). Sometimes, it is easier to define what you want omitted from the sum than to define what you want included. Figure 14-4 shows an example of how this works. The task is to sum up all orders except those in June. Column A lists the months, and column C lists the amounts.

	A	B	C	D	E	F	G
C24		fx	{=SUM(IF(NOT(A2:A20="June"),C2:C20,""))}				
1	Month	Company	Amount				
2	August	Best	$ 18				
3	June	Best	$ 28				
4	August	Super Supply	$ 47				
5	July	Super Supply	$ 75				
6	June	Acme	$ 93				
7	August	Acme	$ 94				
8	June	Winners	$ 104				
9	July	Acme	$ 134				
10	June	Best	$ 157				
11	June	Acme	$ 171				
12	July	Best	$ 178				
13	June	Winners	$ 179				
14	August	Super Supply	$ 282				
15	August	Acme	$ 209				
16	July	Best	$ 212				
17	July	Winners	$ 260				
18	August	Winners	$ 265				
19	June	Acme	$ 284				
20	July	Acme	$ 332				
21							
22			$ 3,122	TOTAL OF ALL ORDERS			
23							
24			$ 2,106	TOTAL OF ORDERS EXCLUDING JUNE			

Figure 14-4:
Being
selective
with
summing.

Cell C22 calculates the full sum with this formula:

```
=SUM(C2:C20)
```

The total is $3,122.

On the other hand, the formula in cell C24 is

```
{=SUM(IF(NOT(A2:A20="June"),C2:C20,""))}
```

This says to sum values in the range C2:C20 only when the associated month in column A is not June.

Note that this formula is an array formula. When entered, the entry was completed by pressing Ctrl+Shift+Enter instead of just plain Enter. See Chapter 3 for more information on array formulas.

AND and OR

Next are the AND and OR functions. AND and OR both return a single logical answer, true or false, based on the values of two or more logical tests (such as the way IF works):

- ✔ The AND function returns true if *all* the tests are true. Otherwise, false is returned.

- ✔ The OR function returns true if *any* one or more of the tests is true. Otherwise, false is returned.

The syntax of both AND and OR is to place the tests inside the function's parentheses; the tests themselves are separated by commas. Here is an example that returns true if the value in cell D10 equals 20 *or* 30 *or* 40:

```
=OR(D10=20,D10=30,D10=40)
```

Check out how this works. In Figure 14-3 earlier in this chapter, you see how you can use the CHOOSE function to return the name of a month derived from the number of the month. That works okay, but what if you type a wrong number or even a non-numerical value as the first argument in CHOOSE?

As is, the CHOOSE function shown in Figure 14-3 returns the #VALUE! error if the first argument is a number greater or less than the number of arguments (not counting the first argument). So as is, the function only works when the first argument evaluates to a number between 1 and 12. If only life were that perfect!

The next-best thing, then, is to include a little validation in the function. Think this through. Both statements must be true:

- ✔ The first argument must be greater than 0.
- ✔ The first argument must be less than 13.

The formula that uses CHOOSE needs an overhaul, and here it is, courtesy of the AND function:

```
=IF(AND(B4>0,B4<13),CHOOSE(B4,"January", "February", "March", "April", "May",
        "June", "July", "August", "September", "October", "November",
        "December"),"That is not a month!")
```

Wow, that's a mouthful (or a cellfull). The CHOOSE function is still there, but it is nested inside an IF. The IF has a test (which I explain shortly). If the test returns true, the CHOOSE function returns the name of the month. If the IF test returns false, a simple That is not a month! message is returned. Figure 14-5 shows this in action.

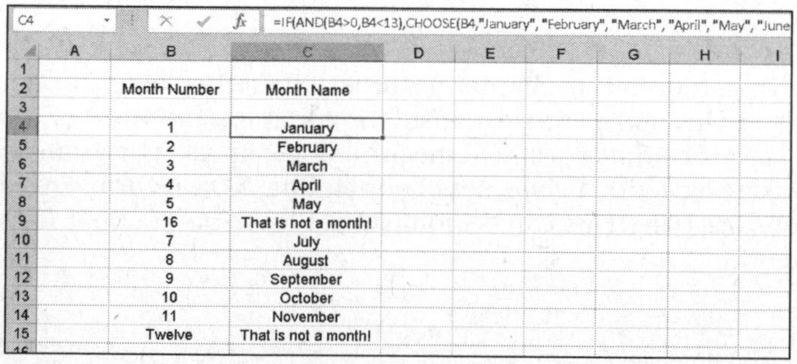

Figure 14-5:
Being
logical
about what
to choose.

The test part of the IF function is this:

```
AND(B4>0,B4<13)
```

The AND returns true if the value in Cell B4 is both greater than 0 *and* less than 13. When that happens, the true part of the IF statement is taken, which uses the CHOOSE statement to return a month name. Otherwise, the `"That is not a month!"` statement is displayed. In Figure 14-5, this is just what happens in cells C9 and C15, which look at the data values in cells B9 and B15, respectively.

Can you figure out how to accomplish the same thing by using OR instead of AND? Think for a moment and then look at the answer:

```
=IF(OR(B4<1,B4>12),"That is not a month!", CHOOSE(B4,"January", "February",
            "March", "April", "May", "June", "July", "August", "September",
            "October", "November", "December"))
```

AND returns true when every condition is true. OR returns true when any condition is true.

Here's how to use AND or OR:

1. **Click a cell where you want the result to appear.**

2. **Type either** =AND(**or** =OR(**to start the function.**

3. **Enter one or more logical tests.**

   A test typically is a comparison of values in two cells or an equation, such as A1 = B1 or A1 + B1 = C1. Separate the tests with commas.

4. **Type a), and press Enter.**

   If you enter the AND function, the result is true if all the tests are true. If you enter the OR function, the result is true if at least one of the tests is true.

XOR

OR, shown earlier in this chapter, returns TRUE when at least one condition is true. This makes sense, considering that it's the word *or* — as in "this or that." So what does XOR mean? In logic speak XOR is an acronym for Exclusive Or. With a given set of conditions, XOR returns FALSE if all the conditions are true. This can be confusing! Please don't shoot me; I'm just the messenger!

Seriously, you really must wonder what is going on here. I have always found that the best way to think of XOR is that it does the opposite of OR. In other words, if only one condition needs to be true in an OR test to have it return TRUE, and if only one condition in an XOR test is true, it returns FALSE. Believe it or not, there are useful applications for this.

Figure 14-6 shows a worksheet that compares the percentage of change in revenue month to month over a three-year span. For example, Feb 2011 had an increase of 9 percent from the same period in the previous year. Feb 2012 has an increase of 11 percent from the same period in 2011, and Feb 2013 had an increase of 16 percent from Feb 2012. In a nutshell, revenue has been increasing each February compared with the previous February. This is the type of news that makes business manager types all tingly and ready to go out dancing.

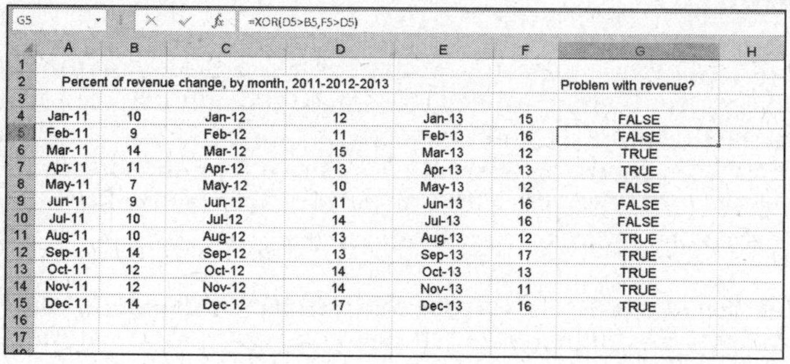

Figure 14-6:
Using XOR
to find
where data
is not
what was
expected.

	A	B	C	D	E	F	G	H
	G5				fx	=XOR(D5>B5,F5>D5)		
1								
2	Percent of revenue change, by month, 2011-2012-2013						Problem with revenue?	
3								
4	Jan-11	10	Jan-12	12	Jan-13	15	FALSE	
5	Feb-11	9	Feb-12	11	Feb-13	16	FALSE	
6	Mar-11	14	Mar-12	15	Mar-13	12	TRUE	
7	Apr-11	11	Apr-12	13	Apr-13	13	TRUE	
8	May-11	7	May-12	10	May-13	12	FALSE	
9	Jun-11	9	Jun-12	11	Jun-13	16	FALSE	
10	Jul-11	10	Jul-12	14	Jul-13	16	FALSE	
11	Aug-11	10	Aug-12	13	Aug-13	12	TRUE	
12	Sep-11	14	Sep-12	13	Sep-13	17	TRUE	
13	Oct-11	13	Oct-12	14	Oct-13	13	TRUE	
14	Nov-11	12	Nov-12	14	Nov-13	11	TRUE	
15	Dec-11	14	Dec-12	17	Dec-13	16	TRUE	
16								
17								

The revenue percentage change is shown for all 12 months over the three-year span. The XOR is put in column G and is used with the two conditions in the same row. In other words, cell G5 contains an XOR that has two conditions — a test to see whether the percentage change from Feb 2011 to Feb 2012 is an increase and a test to see whether the percentage change of Feb 2012 to Feb 2013 is also an increase. The revenue percentage change has been increasing — good news — and the XOR returns the word FALSE. When a manager looks over this report, he can scan column G, and if he sees the word FALSE, that's a signal to ignore. The question is, did revenue dip somewhere along the three years, in February? The answer is no — that is, the answer is FALSE. The manager skips looking any further at that line. The formula in cell G5 looks like this:

```
=XOR(D5>B5, F5>D5)
```

To the manager's eye, other lines in the worksheet are worthy of attention. For example, cell G15 contains an XOR that looks at the revenue change for December over the three-year period. Sure enough, the revenue percentage change went up and then down — not good news. The XOR function returns TRUE.

Finding Where It Is

You can find a plethora of things with the ADDRESS, ROW, ROWS, COLUMN, COLUMNS, and OFFSET functions.

ADDRESS

The ADDRESS function takes a row number and a column number as arguments and returns a standard cell reference (cell address). For example, if you pass the row number 4 and the column number 3, the function returns C4. ADDRESS can return an absolute or relative reference in either of Excel's two reference formats. Before I get to the details, I review the differences between absolute and relative cell references:

- ✔ A *relative reference* is expressed as just the column letter and row number (for example, M290). When you copy a formula that contains a relative cell reference, the reference — the row number and the column letter — is adjusted to reflect the location to which you copied the formula.

- ✔ An *absolute reference* has a dollar sign in front of the column letter and the row number (for example, $M$290). When you copy a formula that contains an absolute cell reference, the reference does not change.

- ✔ A *partial absolute reference* has a dollar sign in front of the column letter or the row number (for example, $M290 or M$290). When you copy a formula that contains a partial absolute cell reference, the part of the reference with the dollar sign does not change, but the other part does.

Figure 14-7 shows a worksheet in which entering a formula with a completely relative cell reference causes a problem. Totals are the result of adding the tax to the amount. The tax is a percentage (0.075) for a 7.5 percent tax rate. This percentage is in cell C1 and is referenced by the formulas. The first formula that was entered is in cell C7 and looks like this: =B7*(1 + C1).

C7	·	⁝	×	✓	f_x	=B7*(1+C1)		

	A	B	C	D	E	F
1		Sales Tax Rate	0.075			
2						
3						
4						
5						
6		Amount	Total (includes tax)			
7		$ 17.95	$ 19.30	=B7*(1+C1)		
8		$ 10.95	$ 10.95	=B8*(1+C2)		
9		$ 21.95	$ 21.95	=B9*(1+C3)		
10						
11						
12						
13						
14						
15						
16		Amount	Total (includes tax)			
17		$ 17.95	$ 19.30	=B17*(1+C$1)		
18		$ 10.95	$ 11.77	=B18*(1+C$1)		
19		$ 21.95	$ 23.60	=B19*(1+C$1)		
20						
21						
22						

Figure 14-7: Changing a reference from relative to absolute.

The formula in cell C7 works correctly. It references cell C1 to calculate the total. But if you use the fill handle to copy the formula from cell C7 to cells C8 and C9, there's a problem. The reference to cell C1 changed to cell C2 and C3. Because these cells are empty, the results in cells C8 and C9 are incorrect; they are the same as the amounts to the left. (No tax is added.)

To better understand, column D displays the formulas that are in column C. When the formula in cell C7 was dragged down, the C1 reference changed to C2 in cell C8, and to C3 in cell C9. Often, this is what you want — for Excel to automatically change cell references when a formula is copied. But sometimes, as in this situation, it is *not* what you want. You need an absolute cell reference.

The formula in cell C17 is almost identical to the one in cell C7 except that the reference to cell C1 has been made row absolute by placing a dollar sign in front of the row number. The formula in cell C17 looks like this: =B17* (1 + C$1). When this formula was dragged down into C18 and C19, the reference was not adjusted but stayed pointing at cell C1. Note that in this example, only the row part of the reference is made absolute. That's all that is necessary. You could have made the reference completely absolute by doing this: =B17*(1 + $C$1). The result would be the same, but it's not required in this example.

Put a dollar sign in front of the column letter of a cell reference to create an absolute column reference. Put a dollar sign in front of the row number to create an absolute row reference.

Excel supports two cell reference styles: the good old A1 style and the R1C1 style. You see the A1 style — a column letter followed by a row number — throughout this book (D4 or B2:B10, for example). The R1C1 style uses a numerical system for both the row and the column, such as this: R4C10. In this example, R4C10 means Row 4 Column 10.

To change the cell reference style, choose File➪Options, and check the R1C1 reference style on the Formulas tab. Using the R1C1 format also forces the columns on the worksheet to display as numbers instead of the lettering system. This is useful when you're working with a large number of columns. For example, column CV positionally is the 100th column. Remembering 100 is easier than remembering CV.

To get back to the ADDRESS function, it takes up to five arguments:

- The row number of the reference.
- The column number of the reference.
- A number that tells the function how to return the reference. The default is 1, but it can be
  - 1 for full absolute
  - 2 for absolute row and relative column
  - 3 for relative row and absolute column
  - 4 for full relative
- A value of 0 or 1 to tell the function which reference style to use:
  - 0 uses the R1C1 style.
  - 1 (the default if omitted) uses the A1 style.
- A worksheet or external workbook and worksheet reference.

Only the first two arguments are required: the row number and column number being addressed. The function returns the specified reference as text. Table 14-1 shows a few examples of using the ADDRESS function.

Table 14-1	Using the ADDRESS Function	
Syntax	Result	Comment
=ADDRESS(5,2)	$B$5	Only the column and row are provided as arguments. The function returns a full absolute address.
=ADDRESS(5,2,1)	$B$5	When a 1 is used for the third argument, a full absolute address is returned. This is the same as leaving out the third argument.

Syntax	Result	Comment
=ADDRESS(5,2,2)	B$5	When a 2 is used for the third argument, a mixed reference is returned, with the column relative and the row absolute.
=ADDRESS(5,2,3)	$B5	When a 3 is used for the third argument, a mixed reference is returned, with the column absolute and the row relative.
=ADDRESS(5,2,4)	B5	When a 4 is used for the third argument, a full relative reference is returned.
=ADDRESS(5,2,1,0)	R5C2	When the fourth argument is false, an R1C1-style reference is returned.
=ADDRESS(5,2,3,0)	R[5]C2	This example tells the function to return a mixed reference in the R1C1 style.
=ADDRESS(5,2,1,,"Sheet4")	Sheet4!$B$5	The fifth argument returns a reference to a worksheet or external workbook. This returns an A1-style reference to cell B5 on Sheet 4.
=ADDRESS(5,2,1,0,"Sheet4")	Sheet4!R5C2	This returns an R1C1-style reference to B5 on Sheet 4.

Use ADDRESS this way:

1. **Click a cell where you want the result to appear.**

2. **Type** =ADDRESS(**to start the function.**

3. **Enter a row number, a comma (,), and a column number.**

   You can also enter references to cells where those values are located.

4. **If you want the result to be returned in a mixed or full reference, enter a comma (,) and the appropriate number:** 2, 3, or 4.

5. **If you want the result to be returned in R1C1 style, enter a comma (,) and enter** 0.

6. **If you want the result to be a reference to another worksheet, enter a comma and put the name of the worksheet in double quote marks.**

   If you want the result to be a reference to an external workbook, enter a comma and enter the workbook name and worksheet name together. The workbook name goes in brackets, and the entire reference goes in double quote marks, such as this: "[Book1]Sheet2".

7. **Type a) and press Enter.**

TIP

Instead of entering a row number and column number directly in ADDRESS, you can enter cell references. However, the values you find in those cells must evaluate to numbers that can be used as a row number and column number.

ROW, ROWS, COLUMN, and COLUMNS

The ADDRESS function is rarely used on its own. Most often, it is used as part of a more complex formula. A useful example of ADDRESS follows the discussion of ROW, ROWS, COLUMN, and COLUMNS.

ROW and COLUMN are passed a reference to a cell or range and return the row number or the column number, respectively. Sounds simple enough. These functions take a single optional argument. The argument is a reference to a cell or range. The function returns the associated row number or column number. When the reference is a range, it is the first cell of the range (the upper left) that is used by the function.

ROW and COLUMN are particularly useful when the argument is a name (for a named area). When you use ROW or COLUMN without an argument, it returns the row number or column number of the cell the function is in. What the point of that is, I don't know. Here are examples of ROW and COLUMN:

Formula	Result
=ROW(D3)	3
=ROW(D3:G15)	3
=COLUMN(D3)	4
=COLUMN(D3:G15)	4
=ROW(Team_Scores)	The first row of the Team_Scores range
=COLUMN(Team_Scores)	The first column of the Team_Scores range

The ROWS and COLUMNS functions (notice that these are now plural), respectively, return the number of rows or the number of columns in a reference:

Formula	Result
=ROWS(Team_Scores)	Number of rows in the Team_Scores range
=COLUMNS(Team_Scores)	Number of columns in the Team_Scores range

Now you are getting somewhere. You can use these functions with ADDRESS to do something useful. Here's the scenario: You have a named range in which the bottom row has summary information, such as averages. You need to get at the bottom row but don't know the actual row number. Figure 14-8 shows this situation. The Team_Scores range is B3:C9. Row 9 contains the average score. You need that value in a calculation, even if another team is added to the list and the row number changes.

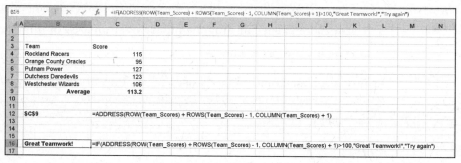

Figure 14-8:
Using reference functions to find a value.

Cell B12 uses a combination of ADDRESS, ROW, ROWS, and COLUMN to determine the cell address where the average score is calculated. That formula follows:

```
=ADDRESS(ROW(Team_Scores) + ROWS(Team_Scores) - 1, COLUMN(Team_Scores) + 1)
```

- ✔ ROW returns the row number of the first cell of Team_Scores. That row number is 3.

- ✔ ROWS returns the number of rows in the named range. That count is 7.

Adding these two numbers is not quite right. A 1 is subtracted from that total to give the last row (9). In this example, you need only COLUMN to get the column number because it understood that the range's second column is the column of scores. In other words, you have no idea how many rows the range has, so ROW and ROWS are both used, but you do know the scores are in the range's second column. This tells you that cell C9 contains the average score. Now what?

Cell B16 contains an IF that uses the address to perform its calculation:

```
=IF(ADDRESS(ROW(Team_Scores) + ROWS(Team_Scores) - 1, COLUMN(Team_Scores) +
        1)>100,"Great Teamwork!","Try again")
```

The IF function tests whether the average score is greater than 100. If it is, the `"Great Teamwork!"` message is displayed. This test is possible because the ADDRESS, ROW, ROWS, and COLUMN functions all help give the IF function the address of the cell where the average score is calculated.

Using ROW, ROWS, COLUMN, or COLUMNS is easy. Here's how:

1. **Click the cell where you want the results to appear.**

2. **Type** =ROW(, =ROWS(,=COLUMN(, **or** =COLUMNS(**to start the function.**

3. **Enter a reference or drag the mouse over an area of the worksheet.**

4. **Type a) and press Enter.**

Again, these functions are rarely used alone; they are almost always used in a more complex formula, as in the preceding example.

OFFSET

The OFFSET function lets you get the address of the cell that is offset from another cell by a certain number of rows and/or columns. For example, cell E4 is offset from cell B4 by three columns because it is three columns to the right. OFFSET takes up to five arguments. The first three are required:

- **A cell address or a range address:** Named ranges are not allowed.
- **The number of rows to offset:** This can be a positive or negative number. Use 0 for no row offset.
- **The number of columns to offset:** This can be a positive or negative number. Use 0 for no column offset.
- **The number of rows in the returned range:** The default is the number of rows in the reference range (the first argument).
- **The number of columns to return:** The default is the number of columns in the reference range.

If you omit the last two arguments, OFFSET returns a reference to a single cell. If you include a value greater than 1 for either or both, the function's return references a range of the specified size with the top-left cell at the specified offset.

Figure 14-9 shows some examples of using OFFSET. Columns A through C contain a ranking of the states in the United States by size in square miles. Column E shows how OFFSET has returned different values from cells that are offset from cell A3.

E10	▾	✕ ✓ *fx*	=SUM(OFFSET(A3,1,2,50,1))					

	A	B	C	D	E	F	G	H
1	**A1**	**B1**	**01**					
2								
3	State	Area Rank	Square Miles					
4	Alaska	1	656,425		State	=OFFSET(A3,0,0)		
5	Texas	2	268,601		656425	=OFFSET(A3,1,2)		
6	California	3	163,707		New Mexico	=OFFSET(A3,5,0)		
7	Montana	4	147,046		A1	=OFFSET(A3,-2,0)		
8	New Mexico	5	121,593		#REF!	=OFFSET(A3,0,-2)		
9	Arizona	6	114,006					
10	Nevada	7	110,567		3,786,816	=SUM(OFFSET(A3,1,2,50,1))		
11	Colorado	8	104,100					
12	Oregon	9	98,386					
13	Wyoming	10	97,818					
14	Michigan	11	96,810					
15	Minnesota	12	86,943					
16	Utah	13	84,904					
17	Idaho	14	83,574					
18	Kansas	15	82,282					
19	Nebraska	16	77,358					
20	South Dakota	17	77,121					
21	Washington	18	71,303					
22	North Dakota	19	70,704					
23	Oklahoma	20	69,903					

Figure 14-9:
Finding
values by
using the
OFFSET
function.

Some highlights follow:

✔ Cell E4 returns the value of cell A3 because both the row and column offset is set to 0: =OFFSET(A3,0,0).

✔ Cell E7 returns the value you find in cell A1 (the value also is A1). This is because the row offset is –2. From the perspective of A3, minus two rows is row number 1: =OFFSET(A3,-2,0).

✔ Cell E8 displays an error because OFFSET is attempting to reference a column that is less than the first column: =OFFSET(A3,0,-2).

✔ Cell E10 makes use of the two optional OFFSET arguments to tell the SUM function to calculate the sum of the range C4:C53: =SUM(OFFSET (A3,1,2,50,1)).

Here's how to use the OFFSET function:

1. **Click a cell where you want the result to appear.**

2. **Type** =OFFSET(**to start the function.**

3. **Enter a cell address or click a cell to get its address.**

4. **Type a comma (,).**

5. **Enter the number of rows you want to offset where the function looks for a value.**

   This number can be a positive number, a negative number, or 0 for no offset.

6. **Type a comma (,).**

7. **Enter the number of columns you want to offset where the function looks for a value.**

   This can be a positive number, a negative number, or 0 for no offset.

8. **Type a) and press Enter.**

OFFSET is another of those functions that can be used alone but is usually used as part of a more complex formula.

Looking It Up

Excel has a neat group of functions that let you extract data from lists and tables. What is a table? A *table* is a dedicated matrix of rows and columns that collectively form a cohesive group of data. Tables usually have labels in the top row or the left column that identify the columns and rows of data. The remainder of the table contains the data itself.

HLOOKUP and VLOOKUP

The HLOOKUP and VLOOKUP functions extract the data from a particular cell in a table. HLOOKUP starts by searching across the first row of the table to find a value that you specify. When it finds that value, it goes down the column a specified number of rows and returns the value in the target cell. VLOOKUP works the same way except that it searches down the first column of the table and then moves across a specified number of columns.

HLOOKUP takes four arguments, and the first three are required:

- ✔ **The value to find in the top row of the table:** This can be text or a number.
- ✔ **The address of the table itself:** This is either a range address or a named range.
- ✔ **The row offset from the top row:** This is not a fixed row number but rather the number of rows relative from the top row.
- ✔ **A true or false value:** If true (or omitted), a partial match is acceptable for Step 1. If false, only an exact match is allowed.

Figure 14-10 shows how HLOOKUP pulls values from a table and displays them elsewhere in the worksheet. This function is quite useful if you need to print a report with a dedicated print area and must include some, but not all, of the data in the table. This example uses the HLOOKUP function to extract the desired data and display it for printing.

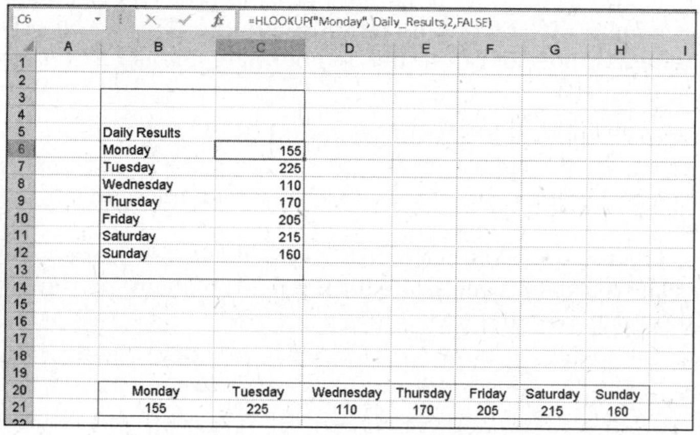

Figure 14-10:
Using
HLOOKUP to
locate data
in a table.

Why not just use a cell reference to the table cell that contains the desired data? A cell reference will not return the correct data if the table is moved or if one or more columns are added. With HLOOKUP and VLOOKUP, you know you'll always get data from the correct column or row.

In Figure 14-10, the table is the range B20:H21, which has been assigned the name Daily_Results. Each cell in the range C6:C12 uses HLOOKUP to locate a specific value in the table. For example, cell C6 has this formula:

```
HLOOKUP("Monday",Daily_Results,2,FALSE)
```

✔ **The first argument:** Tells the function to search for Monday in the first row of the table.

✔ **The second argument:** Specifies the table itself by its assigned name.

✔ **The third argument:** Tells the function to return the data in the second row of the specified column. This table has just two rows, but there is no effective size limit to the table you use with HLOOKUP.

✔ **The fourth argument:** Specifies that an exact match for Monday must be found. If you set this argument to true or omit it, HLOOKUP finds an approximate match. For approximate matching to work properly, the values in the row must be sorted, left to right, in ascending order.

VLOOKUP works in the same way, except that it finds a value in the first column of the table and then moves over a specified number of columns. The arguments follow:

- ✔ **The value to find in the leftmost column of the table.**

- ✔ **The address of the table itself:** This is either a range or a named area.

- ✔ **The column offset from the leftmost column:** This is not a fixed column number but rather the number of columns relative from the leftmost column.

- ✔ **A true or false value:** If true (or omitted), VLOOKUP finds an approximate match. If false, an exact match is required. For an approximate match, the column must be sorted in ascending order.

Figure 14-11 shows an example of using VLOOKUP. The worksheet displays products and annual revenue data for the fictitious guitar shop. The range A6:D27 has been named `Sales`.

	A	B	C	D
B4		=VLOOKUP("Wireless Gig Kit",OFFSET(Sales,0,1),3,FALSE)		
1				
2				
3				
4	Total for the Wireless Gig Kit	$ 75,000		
5				
6	Vendor	Product	Category	Amount
7	Great Guitars	All-in-one Effects Box	Accessory	$ 6,750
8	Great Guitars	Guitarist's Super Road Kit	Accessory	$ 32,000
9	Great Guitars	Flying X	Instrument	$ 87,000
10	Great Guitars	Stratoblaster 9000	Instrument	$ 129,000
11	Sound Accessories	18 Foot Cables	Accessory	$ 2,250
12	Sound Accessories	1 Foot Cables	Accessory	$ 4,000
13	Sound Accessories	Glow in the Dark Guitar Strap	Accessory	$ 4,350
14	Sound Accessories	Rocker Pedal Deluxe	Accessory	$ 5,250
15	Sound Accessories	10 Foot Cables	Accessory	$ 6,250
16	Sound Accessories	Sustainer Sound Box	Accessory	$ 7,000
17	Sound Accessories	Rocker Pedal	Accessory	$ 7,250
18	Sound Accessories	6 Foot Cables	Accessory	$ 8,500
19	Sound Accessories	Classic Amp Imitator	Accessory	$ 16,700
20	Sound Accessories	Mini Road Recorder	Accessory	$ 40,000
21	Sound Accessories	Wireless Gig Kit	Accessory	$ 75,000
22	Traditional Instruments	Beginner Mandolin	Instrument	$ 1,450
23	Traditional Instruments	Intermediate Guitar	Instrument	$ 3,500
24	Traditional Instruments	Intermediate Mandolin	Instrument	$ 6,500
25	Traditional Instruments	Beginner Guitar	Instrument	$ 7,500

Figure 14-11: Using VLOOKUP to locate data in a table.

The goal is to use VLOOKUP to extract the sales amount for the Wireless Gig Kit. However, the product names are in the second column of the Sales range, and VLOOKUP normally searches in the first column. You can use OFFSET to force VLOOKUP to search for Wireless Gig Kit in the second column of the range. This is the formula in cell B3:

```
=VLOOKUP("Wireless Gig Kit",OFFSET(Sales,0,1),3, FALSE)
```

Note that the offset specified as the third argument to VLOOKUP is 3. That's because the sales figures are in the third column relative to the Products column, where VLOOKUP is performing its search.

Here's how to use either HLOOKUP or VLOOKUP:

1. **Click a cell where you want the result to appear.**

2. **Type either** =HLOOKUP(**or** =VLOOKUP(**to start the function.**

3. **If using**

    - HLOOKUP: Enter the value that you want to find in the top row of the table.

    - VLOOKUP: Enter the value that you want to find in the first column of the table.

4. **Type a comma (,).**

5. **Enter the range address that defines the table of data, or enter its name, if it has been assigned one.**

6. **Type a comma (,).**

7. **If using**

    - HLOOKUP: Enter a number to indicate the row of the value to return.

    - VLOOKUP: Enter a number to indicate the column of the value to return.

    The number you enter here is relative to the range or area defined in the second argument.

8. **(Optional) Type a comma (,) and** FALSE.

    This forces the function to find an exact match for the value entered in the first argument.

9. **Type a) and press Enter.**

Excel also provides the LOOKUP function, which is specialized for returning values from single-column or single-row ranges. See Excel Help for more information on this function.

MATCH and INDEX

The MATCH function returns the relative row number or column number of a value in a table. The key point here is that MATCH returns the relative value but does not return the value itself.

This function is useful when you need an item's position. You are not often interested in this information by itself but may use it in a more complex formula. I show you how shortly.

MATCH takes three arguments:

- ✔ **The value to search for:** This can be a number, text, or a logical value.

- ✔ **Where to look:** This is a range spanning a single row or column, or a named area that comprises a single row or column.

- ✔ **How the match is to be applied:** This argument is optional.

The third argument can be one of three values. They work as follows:

- ✔ 1 tells MATCH to find the largest value that is less than or equal to the lookup value. The array must be sorted in ascending order. This is the default value if the argument is omitted.

- ✔ -1 tells MATCH to find the smallest value that is greater than or equal to the lookup value. The array must be sorted in descending order.

- ✔ 0 tells MATCH to find the first value that is an exact match. The array need not be sorted.

Figure 14-12 shows the products and revenue for the guitar shop. Note that the information has been sorted in ascending order according to the Amount column. The goal is to get a count of how many products have sales less than $10,000. MATCH makes this easy, as shown in Figure 14-12. This formula is in cell B4:

```
=MATCH(10000,OFFSET(Sales,0,3,ROWS(Sales),1))-1
```

Take this formula apart from the inside out. First, you know that MATCH needs a reference to the column where it is to search — in this case, the Amount column in the Sales range. Sounds like a job for OFFSET! Type the following:

```
OFFSET(Sales,0,3,ROWS(Sales),1)
```

This returns a range that has the following characteristics:

- ✔ Offset by no rows and three columns from the Sales range
- ✔ Has a height equal to the number of rows in Sales
- ✔ Has a width of one column

B4		× ✓ fx	=MATCH(10000,OFFSET(Sales,0,3,ROWS(Sales),1))-1		

	A	B	C	D
1				
2				
3				
4	Products with sales < 10,000	13		
5				
6	Vendor	Product	Category	Amount
7	Traditional Instruments	Beginner Mandolin	Instrument	$ 1,450
8	Sound Accessories	18 Foot Cables	Accessory	$ 2,250
9	Traditional Instruments	Intermediate Guitar	Instrument	$ 3,500
10	Sound Accessories	1 Foot Cables	Accessory	$ 4,000
11	Sound Accessories	Glow in the Dark Guitar Strap	Accessory	$ 4,350
12	Sound Accessories	Rocker Pedal Deluxe	Accessory	$ 5,250
13	Sound Accessories	10 Foot Cables	Accessory	$ 6,250
14	Traditional Instruments	Intermediate Mandolin	Instrument	$ 6,500
15	Great Guitars	All-in-one Effects Box	Accessory	$ 6,750
16	Sound Accessories	Sustainer Sound Box	Accessory	$ 7,000
17	Sound Accessories	Rocker Pedal	Accessory	$ 7,250
18	Traditional Instruments	Beginner Guitar	Instrument	$ 7,500
19	Sound Accessories	6 Foot Cables	Accessory	$ 8,500
20	Traditional Instruments	Intermediate Banjo	Instrument	$ 14,750
21	Sound Accessories	Classic Amp Imitator	Accessory	$ 16,700
22	Traditional Instruments	Beginner Banjo	Instrument	$ 27,000
23	Great Guitars	Guitarist's Super Road Kit	Accessory	$ 32,000
24	Sound Accessories	Mini Road Recorder	Accessory	$ 40,000
25	Sound Accessories	Wireless Gig Kit	Accessory	$ 75,000

Figure 14-12: Making a match.

Now that you have this range, you can tell MATCH to look for the largest value that is less than or equal to 10000. Because the data is sorted, the relative position of this value in the range is one more than the number of products with sales less than $10,000. Why one more? The heading row at the top of the range is counted too — so you subtract 1 to get the final answer.

Here's how to use the MATCH function:

1. **Click a cell where you want the result to appear.**

2. **Type** =MATCH(**to start the function.**

3. **Enter a value to match.**

   This can be a numeric, text, or logic value. You can enter a cell address provided that the referenced cell has a usable value.

4. **Type a comma (,).**

5. **Enter the range in which to look for a match.**

   This can be a range reference or a named area.

6. **(Optional) Enter a comma (,) and enter a –1, 0, or 1 to tell the function how to make a match.**

   The default is 1. A 0 forces an exact match.

7. **Type a) and press Enter.**

The information returned by MATCH can be helpful when you use it with the INDEX function. INDEX returns the value found at a specified row-and-column intersection within a table. You can use MATCH to find the row and find the column and then use INDEX to get the actual data.

INDEX takes three arguments:

- ✔ The table to look in as a range address or range name
- ✔ The row number relative to the table's first row
- ✔ The column number relative to the table's leftmost column

The return value is the value of the cell where the row and column intersect.

Figure 14-13 shows an example in which INDEX retrieves a value from a table that summarizes some guitar-shop sales by product and quarter. The table range in this example has been named Sales_by_qtr.

C3		fx	=INDEX(Sales_by_qtr, MATCH("6 Foot Cables",OFFSET(Sales_by_qtr,0,0,RO

	A	B	C	D	E	F	G
1							
2							
3		6 Foot Cables, Qtr 2	$ 195				
4							
5							
6							
7		Product	Qtr 1	Qtr 2	Qtr 3	Qtr 4	
8		Beginner Mandolin	$ 320	$ 264	$ 290	$ 325	
9		1 Foot Cables	$ 232	$ 355	$ 310	$ 316	
10		6 Foot Cables	$ 177	$ 195	$ 170	$ 173	
11		Acoustic Guitar Strings, Heavy	$ 432	$ 475	$ 415	$ 423	
12		Acoustic Guitar Strings, Medium	$ 380	$ 395	$ 345	$ 405	
13		Acoustic Guitar Strings, Light	$ 400	$ 440	$ 385	$ 390	
14		Electric Guitar Strings, Heavy	$ 143	$ 152	$ 158	$ 170	
15		Electric Guitar Strings, Medium	$ 350	$ 388	$ 465	$ 422	
16		Electric Guitar Strings, Light	$ 435	$ 515	$ 500	$ 520	
17		Glow in the Dark Guitar Strap	$ 226	$ 265	$ 265	$ 300	
18		Rocker Pedal Deluxe	$ 280	$ 290	$ 272	$ 308	

Figure 14-13: Using INDEX to extract data from a table.

The following formula, in cell C2, extracts the sales for 6 Foot Cables for Qtr 2:

```
=INDEX(Sales_by_qtr, MATCH("6 Foot Cables",
        OFFSET(Sales_by_qtr,0,0,ROWS(Sales_by_qtr),1),0), MATCH("Qtr 2",
        OFFSET(Sales_by_qtr, 0,0,1,COLUMNS(Sales_by_qtr))))
```

Wow, that's quite a cell full of formula! But you already know everything you need to understand it. The first argument of INDEX is no mystery; it is simply the name assigned to the table. The second and third arguments, which tell INDEX what cell to look in, are complicated. Look at the first one, for the row argument:

```
MATCH("6 Foot Cables", OFFSET(Sales_by_qtr, 0,0,ROWS(Sales_by_qtr),1),0)
```

You want to look down the table's first column, where the product names are listed, and find the row that contains 6 Foot Cables. You also know that the MATCH function is just right for this job and that the function needs to know where to look. In other words, you must tell it the address of the table's first column. Here is where OFFSET comes into play:

```
OFFSET(Sales_by_qtr, 0, 0, ROWS(Sales_by_qtr), 1)
```

This call to OFFSET returns a range address that has the following characteristics:

- ✔ Is located with reference to the range Sales_by_qtr
- ✔ Is offset from Sales_by_qtr by zero rows and zero columns (in other words, starts at cell B7)
- ✔ Contains the same number of rows as Sales_by_qtr
- ✔ Contains one column

The result is that this call to OFFSET returns the range B7:B18. The MATCH function becomes this, in effect:

```
MATCH("6 Foot Cables", B7:B18, 0)
```

Because an exact match is requested, the data does not have to be sorted. MATCH finds the search text in the fourth row relative to the top of the table. This is the value that INDEX uses for its row argument. The column argument to INDEX is handled in the same way.

Here's how to use the INDEX function:

1. **Click a cell where you want the result to appear.**

2. **Type =INDEX(to start the function.**

3. **Enter a reference to the table.**

   You can drag the mouse over the range or enter its address. If the table has been named, you can enter the name.

4. **Type a comma (,).**

5. **Enter the row number relative to the table's first row.**

   This number can be the result of a calculation or the value returned from a function.

6. **Type a comma (,).**

7. **Enter the column number relative to the table's leftmost column.**

This number can be the result of a calculation or the value returned from a function.

8. **Type a) and press Enter.**

FORMULATEXT

FORMULATEXT displays the syntax of a formula. It's simple and yet serves a great feature. Think about it. You might have a workbook full of formulas; however, all you see is the result of the calculations. What if you need to see the formulas themselves? It's great to have the answer given by a calculation, but often, you need to know how the calculation works!

FORMULATEXT to the rescue! This function references a cell that has a formula and displays the formula without having it calculate the answer. Figure 14-14 shows how this works. Columns A and B contain numbers. Column C contains formulas that return calculated values using the numbers in Columns A and B. Column D uses FORMULATEXT to display the formulas in Column C.

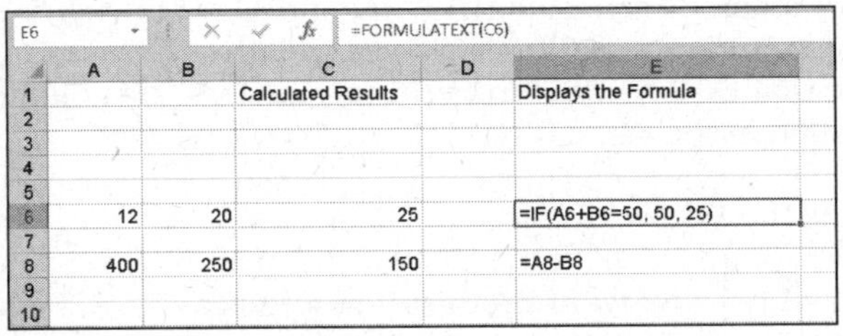

Figure 14-14: Using FORMULATEXT to see the syntax of formulas.

	A	B	C	D	E
			Calculated Results		Displays the Formula
1					
2					
3					
4					
5					
6	12	20	25		=IF(A6+B6=50, 50, 25)
7					
8	400	250	150		=A8-B8
9					
10					

E6 · ✕ ✓ *fx* =FORMULATEXT(C6)

Here's how to use the FORMULATEXT function:

1. **Click a cell where you want the result to appear.**

2. **Type** =FORMULATEXT(**to start the function.**

3. **Click a cell that has a formula.**

4. **Type a) and press Enter.**

There is a setting in Excel's options to always display formulas as syntax instead of showing the calculated results. Look in the Display options for this worksheet on the Advanced tab in Excel Options to see where this option is set. This setting converts all formulas to text, and you can see them all. The caveat in using this approach is no calculations occur! If you need to see all the calculations' inner workings, this is a good option. However, if you want to still have the formulas calculate answers and want to see how they are written, use FORMULATEXT.

NUMBERVALUE

NUMBERVALUE is used to format numbers that appear as text back to appearing as actual numbers. For example, your worksheet might display a value such as "14.25%". Excel will treat this correctly as a number if used in a formula, function, or calculation, but the percent sign is not part of the number.

A percentage is usually a decimal-based number.

The 14.25 percent, when not formatted, is .1425.

Perhaps you need to display such a nice-looking number for the raw value it really is. This is where NUMBERVALUE comes to the rescue.

Figure 14-15 shows a worksheet with two numbers in column A that, in one way or another, appear to be a bit non-numeric. Besides 14.25 percent, there is "1 2 3 4" (spaces between each digit).

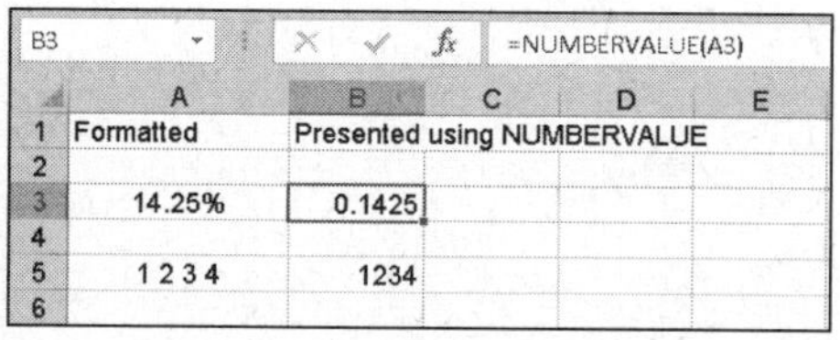

Figure 14-15: Using NUM- BERVALUE to return the numeric presentation of a number.

B3	▾	✕ ✓ ƒx	=NUMBERVALUE(A3)		
	A	B	C	D	E
1	Formatted	Presented using NUMBERVALUE			
2					
3	14.25%	0.1425			
4					
5	1 2 3 4	1234			
6					

Column B shows how the numbers look when you use NUMBERVALUE. For example, cell B3 contains this:

```
=NUMBERVALUE(A3)
```

Chapter 15

Digging Up the Facts

. . . .

In This Chapter

▶ Getting information about a cell or range

▶ Finding out about Excel or your computer system

▶ Testing for numbers, text, and errors

. . . .

*I*n this chapter, I show you how to use Excel's information functions, which you use to obtain information about cells, ranges, and the workbook you're working in. You can even get information about the computer you're using. What will they think of next?

The information functions are great for getting formulas to focus on just the data that matter. Some functions even help shield you from Excel's confusing error messages. The first time I saw the #NAME? error, I thought Excel was asking me to enter a name (just another of the more exciting Excel moments). Now at least I know to use the ISERROR or ERROR.TYPE functions to make error messages more meaningful. And after reading this chapter, so will you!

Getting Informed with the CELL Function

The CELL function provides feedback about cells and ranges in a worksheet. You can find out what row and column a cell is in, what type of formatting it has, whether it's protected, and so on.

CELL takes two arguments:

✔ The first argument, which is enclosed in double quotes, tells the function what kind of information to return.

✔ The second argument tells the function which cell or range to evaluate. If you specify a range that contains more than one cell, the function returns information about the top-left cell in the range. The second argument is optional; when it isn't provided, Excel reports back on the most recently changed cell.

Table 15-1 shows the list of possible entries for the first argument of the CELL function.

Table 15-1   Selecting the First Argument for the CELL Function

Argument	*Example*	*Comment*
address	=CELL("address")	Returns the address of the last changed cell.
col	=CELL("col",Sales)	Returns the column number of the first cell in the Sales range.
color	=CELL("color",B3)	Tells whether a particular cell (in this case, cell B3) is formatted in such a way that negative numbers are represented in color. The number, currency, and custom formats have selections for displaying negative numbers in red. If the cell is formatted for color-negative numbers, a 1 is returned; otherwise, a 0 is returned.
contents	=CELL("contents",B3)	Returns the contents of a particular cell (in this case, cell B3). If the cell contains a formula, returns the result of the formula and not the formula itself.
filename	=CELL("filename")	Returns the path, filename, and worksheet name of the workbook and worksheet that has the CELL function in it (for example, C:\Customers\ [Acme Company]Sheet1). The function results in a blank answer in a new workbook that has not yet been saved.

Argument	Example	Comment
format	=CELL("format",D12)	Returns a cell's number format (in this case, cell D12). See Table 15-2 for a list of possible returned values.
parentheses	=CELL("parentheses", D12)	Returns 1 if a cell (in this case, D12) is formatted to have either positive values or all values displayed with parentheses. Otherwise, 0 is returned. A custom format is needed to make parentheses appear with positive values in the first place.
prefix	=CELL("prefix",R25)	Returns the type of text alignment in a cell (in this case, cell R25). There are a few possibilities: a single quotation mark (') if the cell is left-aligned; a double quotation mark (") if the cell is right-aligned; a caret (^) if the cell is set to centered; or a backslash(\) if the cell is fill-aligned. If the cell being evaluated is blank or has a number, the function returns nothing.
protect	=CELL("protect",D12)	Returns 1 if a cell's protection (in this case, cell D12) is set to locked; otherwise, a 0 is returned. The returned value is not affected by whether the worksheet is currently protected.
row	=CELL("row",Sales)	Returns the row number of the first cell in the Sales range.

(continued)

Table 15-1 *(continued)*

Argument	Example	Comment
type	=CELL("type",D12)	Returns a value corresponding to the type of information in a cell (in this case, cell D12). There are three possible values: b if the cell is blank; 1 if the cell has alphanumeric data; and v for all other possible values, including numbers and errors.
width	=CELL("width")	Returns the width of the last changed cell, rounded to an integer. For example, a width of 18.3 is returned as 18.

The second argument, whether it's there or not, plays a key role in how the CELL function works. When it's included, the second argument is a cell address, such as B12, or a range name, such as Sales. Of course, you could have a range that is only one cell, but I won't confuse the issue!

If you enter a nonexistent range name for the second argument, Excel returns the #NAME? error. Excel can't return information about something that doesn't exist!

An interesting way to use CELL is to keep track of the last entry on a worksheet. Say you're updating a list of values. The phone rings, and you're tied up for a while on the call. When you get back to your list, you've forgotten where you left off. Yikes! What a time to think "If only I had used the CELL function!"

Figure 15-1 shows such a worksheet. Cell B18 displays the address of the last cell that was changed.

Using CELL with the filename argument is great for displaying the workbook's path. This technique is common for printed worksheet reports. Being able to find the workbook file that a report was printed from six months ago is a real time-saver. Don't you just love it when the boss gives you an hour to create a report, doesn't look at it for six months, and *then* wants to make a change? Here's how you enter the CELL function to return the filename:

```
=CELL("filename")
```

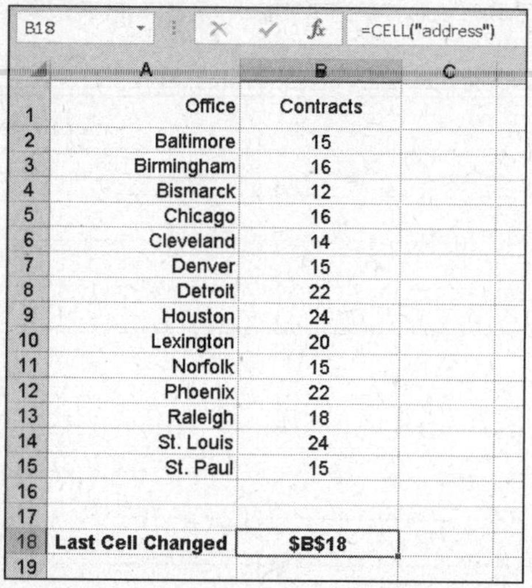

Figure 15-1:
Keeping track of which cell had the latest entry.

You can format cells in many ways. When the first argument of CELL is `format`, a code is returned that corresponds to the formatting. The possible formats are those listed in the Format Cells dialog box. Table 15-2 shows the formats and the code that CELL returns.

Table 15-2	Returned Values for the `format` Argument
Format	**Returned Value from CELL Function**
General	G
0	F0
#,##0	,0
0.00	F2
#,##0.00	,2
$#,##0_);($#,##0)	C0
$#,##0_);[Red]($#,##0)	C0-
$#,##0.00_);($#,##0.00)	C2
$#,##0.00_);[Red]($#,##0.00)	C2-
0%	P0
0.00%	P2
0.00E+00	S2
# ?/? or ??/??	G

(continued)

Table 15-2 *(continued)*

Format	Returned Value from CELL Function
`m/d/yy` or `m/d/yy h:mm` or `mm/dd/yy`	D4
`d-mmm-yy` or `dd-mmmm-yy`	D1
`d-mmm` or `dd-mmm`	D2
`mmm-yy`	D3
`mm/dd`	D5
`h:mm AM/PM`	D7
`h:mm:ss AM/PM`	D6
`h:mm`	D9
`h:mm:ss`	D8

Using CELL with the `format` argument lets you add a bit of smarts to your worksheet. Figure 15-2 shows an example of CELL making sure information is correctly understood. The dates in Column A are of the `d-mmm` format. The downside of this format is that the year is not known. So cell A1 has been given a formula that uses CELL to test the dates' format. If the `d-mmm` format is found in the first date (in cell A4), cell A1 displays a message that includes the year from cell A4. After all, cell A4 *has* a year; it's just formatted not to show it. This way, the year is always present — either in the dates themselves or at the top of the worksheet.

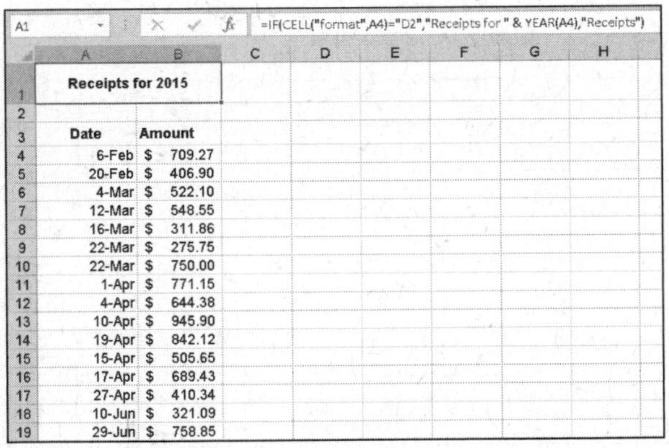

Figure 15-2:
Using CELL and the `format` argument to display a useful message.

The formula in cell A1 — `=IF(CELL("format",A4)="D2","Receipts for "&YEAR(A4),"Receipts")` — says that if the formatting in A4 is d-mmm (according to the values in Table 15-2), display the message with the year; otherwise, just display Receipts.

Here's how to use the CELL function:

1. **Position the cursor in the cell where you want the results to appear.**

2. **Type** =CELL(**to begin the function entry.**

3. **Enter one of the first argument choices listed in Table 15-1.**

   Make sure to surround it with double quotes (" ").

4. **If you want to tell the function which cell or range to use, type a comma (,).**

5. **If you want, enter a cell address or the name of a range.**

6. **Type a) and press Enter.**

Getting Information about Excel and Your Computer System

Excel provides the INFO function to get information about your computer and about the program itself. INFO takes a single argument that tells the function what type of information to return. Table 15-3 shows how to use the INFO function.

Table 15-3	Using INFO to Find Out about Your Computer or Excel	
Argument	*Example*	*Comment*
directory	=INFO("directory")	Returns the path of the current directory. Note that this is not necessarily the same path of the open workbook.
Numfile	=INFO("numfile")	Returns the number of worksheets in all open workbooks. The function includes worksheets of add-ins, so the number could be misleading.
origin	=INFO("origin")	Returns the address of the cell at the top and to the left of the scrollable area. An A$ prefix in front of the cell address is for compatibility with Lotus 1-2-3.

(continued)

Table 15-3 *(continued)*

Argument	Example	Comment
osversion	=INFO("osversion")	Returns the name of the current operating system.
recalc	=INFO("recalc")	Returns the status of the recalculation mode: Automatic or Manual.
release	=INFO("release")	Returns the version number of Excel being run.
system	=INFO("system")	Returns the name of the operating environment: mac or pcdos.

One useful application of the INFO function is to use the returned Excel version number to determine whether the workbook can use a newer feature. For example, the ability to work with XML data has been available only in Excel 2002 and later. By testing the version number, you can be notified whether you can work with XML data. This formula uses the release choice as the argument:

```
=IF(INFO("release")>9,"This version can import XML", "This version cannot
       import XML")
```

Figure 15-3 shows values returned with the INFO function.

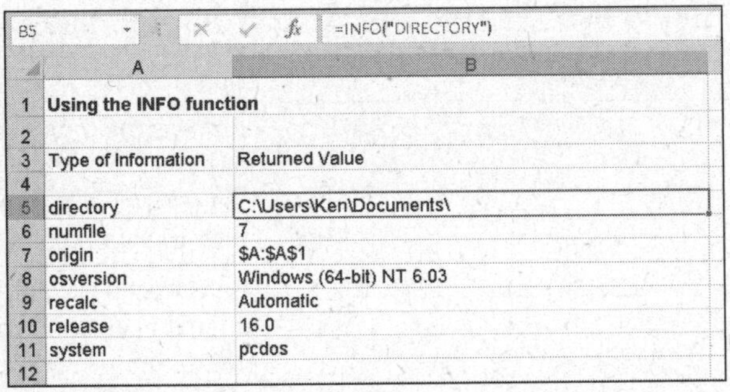

Figure 15-3: Getting facts about the computer with the INFO function.

Here's how to use the INFO function:

1. **Position the cursor in the cell where you want the results to appear.**

2. **Type** =INFO(**to begin the function entry.**

3. Enter one of the argument choices listed in Table 15-3.

Make sure to surround it with double quotes (" ").

4. Type a) and press Enter.

Finding What IS and What IS Not

A handful of IS functions report back a true or false answer about certain cell characteristics. For example, is a cell blank, or does it contain text? These functions are often used in combination with other functions — typically, the IF function — to handle errors or other unexpected or undesirable results.

The errors Excel reports are not very friendly. What on earth does #N/A really tell you? The functions I describe in this section don't make the error any clearer, but they give you a way to instead display a friendly message like "Something is wrong, but I don't know what it is."

Table 15-4 shows the IS functions and how they're used. They all return either True or False, so the table just lists them.

Table 15-4	Using the IS Functions to See What Really Is
Function	**Comment**
=ISBLANK(value)	Tells whether a cell is blank.
=ISERR(value)	Tells whether a cell contains any error other than #N/A.
=ISERROR(value)	Tells whether a cell contains any error.
=ISEVEN(value)	Tells whether a number is even.
=ISFORMULA	Tells whether the cell contains a formula.
=ISLOGICAL(value)	Tells whether the value is logical.
=ISNA(value)	Tells whether a cell contains the #N/A error.
=ISNONTEXT(value)	Tells whether a cell contains a number or error.
=ISNUMBER(value)	Tells whether a cell contains a number.
=ISODD(value)	Tells whether a number is odd.
=ISOWEEKNUM	Tells the ISO week number for the entered date. (ISO is the International Organization for Standardization, a standards-setting consortium.)
=ISREF(value)	Tells whether the value is a reference.
=ISTEXT(value)	Tells whether a cell contains text.

ISERR, ISERROR, and ISNA

Three of the IS functions — ISERR, ISERROR, and ISNA — tell you about an error.

Error Function	***Comments***
ISERR	Returns true if the error is anything except the `#N/A` error. For example, the `#DIV/0!` error returns true.
ISNA	The opposite of ISERR. It returns true only if the error is `#N/A`.
ISERROR	Returns true for any type of error, including `#N/A`, `#VALUE!`, `#REF!`, `DIV/0!`, `#NUM!`, `#NAME?`, and `#NULL!`.

Why is `#N/A` treated separately? It is excluded from being handled with ISERR and has its own ISNA function. Actually, you can use `#N/A` to your advantage to avoid errors. How so? Figure 15-4 shows an example that calculates the percentage of surveys returned for some of Florida's larger cities. The calculation is simple: Just divide the returned number by the number sent.

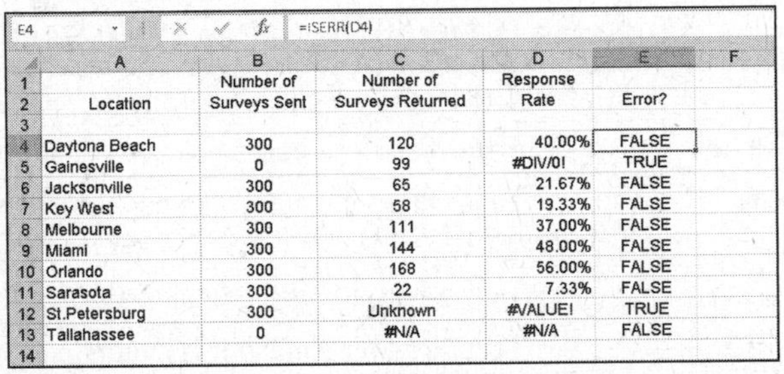

E4 =ISERR(D4)

	A	B	C	D	E	F
1		Number of	Number of	Response		
2	Location	Surveys Sent	Surveys Returned	Rate	Error?	
3						
4	Daytona Beach	300	120	40.00%	FALSE	
5	Gainesville	0	99	#DIV/0!	TRUE	
6	Jacksonville	300	65	21.67%	FALSE	
7	Key West	300	58	19.33%	FALSE	
8	Melbourne	300	111	37.00%	FALSE	
9	Miami	300	144	48.00%	FALSE	
10	Orlando	300	168	56.00%	FALSE	
11	Sarasota	300	22	7.33%	FALSE	
12	St.Petersburg	300	Unknown	#VALUE!	TRUE	
13	Tallahassee	0	#N/A	#N/A	FALSE	
14						

Figure 15-4: Using an error to your advantage.

However, errors do creep in. (Creepy errors, yuck!) For example, no surveys were sent to Gainesville, yet 99 came back. Interesting! The calculation becomes a division by zero error, which makes sense. On the other hand, Tallahassee had no surveys sent, but here, the returned value is the `#N/A` error, purposely entered. Next, look at Column E. In this column, `True` or `False` is returned to indicate whether the calculation, per city, should be considered an error: Gainesville true, Tallahassee false.

The result `true` or `false` appears in Column E because all the cells in Column E use the ISERR function. The formula in cell E13, which tests the calculation for Tallahassee, is =ISERR(D13).

Simply put, D13 displays the #N/A error because its calculation (=C13/B13) uses a cell with an entered #N/A. The ISERR does not consider #N/A to be an error; therefore, E13 returns `False`. The upshot is that eyeballing Column E makes it easy to distinguish entry and math errors from purposeful flagging of certain rows as having incomplete data.

ISBLANK, ISNONTEXT, ISTEXT, and ISNUMBER

The ISBLANK, ISNONTEXT, ISTEXT, and ISNUMBER functions tell you what type of data is in a cell.

Error Function	Comments
ISBLANK	Returns true if the cell is empty; otherwise, returns false.
ISNONTEXT	Returns true if the cell contains anything that is not text: a number, a date/time, or an error. The function returns true if the cell is blank or false if the cell contains text or a formula whose result is text.
ISTEXT	The opposite of ISNONTEXT: Returns true if the cell contains text or a formula whose result is text; otherwise, returns false.
ISNUMBER	Returns true if the cell contains a number or a formula whose result is a number; otherwise, returns false.

ISBLANK returns true when nothing is in a cell. Using ISBLANK is useful for counting how many cells in a range are blank. Perhaps you're responsible for making sure that 200 employees get their time sheets in every week. You can use a formula that lets you know how many employees have not yet handed in their hours.

Such a formula uses ISBLANK along with the IF and SUM functions, like this:

```
{=SUM(IF(ISBLANK(B5:B26),1,0))}
```

This formula makes use of an array. See Chapter 3 for more information on using array formulas. Figure 15-5 shows how this formula works. In columns A and B are lists of employees and their hours. The formula in cell A1 reports how many employees are missing their hours.

A1				f_x	{=SUM(IF(ISBLANK(B5:B26),1,0))}	
	A	B	C	D	E	F
1	6	Employees have not entered hours				
2						
3						
4	Employee ID	Hours				
5	63375	18				
6	81673					
7	36361	40				
8	29102	40				
9	22894					
10	60026	26				
11	61325					
12	34215	28				
13	82594	24				
14	38281	35				
15	62154					
16	25190	38				
17	69382	27				
18	27418	46				
19	33452	42				
20	34563					
21	70292	38				
22	51187					
23	70823	25				
24	68803	40				
25	28709	42				
26	70740	34				
27						

Figure 15-5:
Calculating how many employees are missing an entry.

ISTEXT returns `True` when a cell contains any type of text. ISNONTEXT returns `True` when a cell contains anything that is not text, including numbers, dates, and times. The ISNONTEXT function also returns `True` if the cell contains an error.

The ISNUMBER function returns `True` when a cell contains a number, which can be an actual number or a number resulting from evaluation of a formula in the cell. You can use ISNUMBER as an aid to help data entry. Say you designed a worksheet that people fill out. One of the questions is age. Most people would enter a numeric value such as 18, 25, 70, and so on. But someone could type the age as text, such as eighteen, thirty-two, or "none of your business." An adjacent cell could use ISNUMBER to return a message about entering the numeric age. The formula would look something like this:

```
=IF(ISNUMBER(B3),"","Please enter your age as a number")
```

Here's how to use any of the IS functions:

1. **Position the cursor in the cell where you want the results to appear.**

2. **Enter one of the IS functions.**

   For example, type **=ISTEXT(** to begin the function entry.

3. **Enter a cell address.**

4. **Type a) and press Enter.**

   The result is always True or False.

Getting to Know Your Type

The TYPE function tells you what the type of the information is. Possible types follow:

- ✔ Number
- ✔ Text
- ✔ A logical value
- ✔ An error
- ✔ An array

In all cases TYPE returns a number:

- ✔ 1 is returned for numbers.
- ✔ 2 is returned for text.
- ✔ 4 is returned for logical values.
- ✔ 16 is returned for errors.
- ✔ 64 is returned for arrays.

Figure 15-6 shows each of these values returned by the TYPE function. Cells B3:B7 contain the TYPE function, with each row looking at the adjacent cell in Column A. The returned value of 64 in cell B7 is a little different. This indicates an array as the type. The formula in cell B7 is =TYPE(A7:A9). This is an array of values from cells A7:A9.

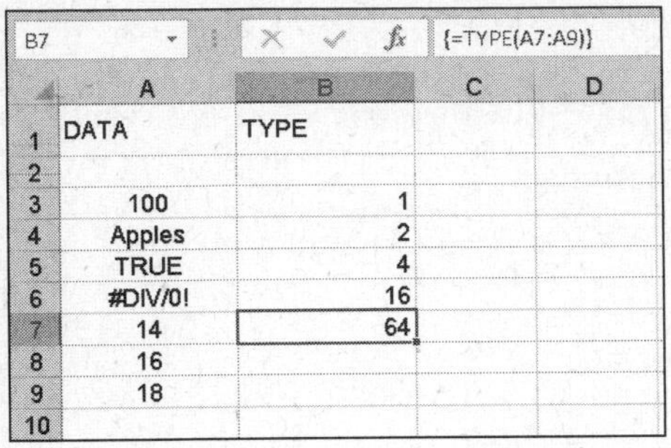

Figure 15-6:
Getting the
type of the
data.

Here's how to use the TYPE function:

1. **Position the cursor in the cell where you want the results to appear.**

2. **Enter =TYPE(to begin the function entry.**

3. **Enter a cell address or click a cell.**

4. **Type a) and press Enter.**

The ERROR.TYPE function returns a number that corresponds to the particular error in a cell. Table 15-5 shows the error types and the returned numbers.

Table 15-5   **Getting a Number of an Error**

Error Type	Returned Number
#NULL!	1
#DIV/0!	2
#VALUE!	3
#REF!	4
#NAME?	5
#NUM!	6
#N/A	7

The best thing about the ERROR.TYPE function is that you can use it to change those pesky errors to something readable! To do this, use the CHOOSE function along with ERROR.TYPE, like this:

```
=CHOOSE(ERROR.TYPE(H14),"Nothing here!","You can't divide by 0","A bad number
    has been entered", "The formula is referencing a bad cell or
    range","There is a problem with the entry","There is a problem
    with the entered value","Something is seriously wrong!")
```

See Chapter 14 for assistance on using the CHOOSE function. This is how you use the ERROR.TYPE function:

1. **Position the cursor in the cell where you want the results to appear.**
2. **Enter** =ERROR.TYPE(**to begin the function entry.**
3. **Enter a cell address or click a cell.**
4. **Type a) and press Enter.**

Chapter 16

Writing Home about Text Functions

In This Chapter

▶ Assembling, altering, and formatting text

▶ Figuring out the length of text

▶ Comparing text

▶ Searching for text

A rose is still a rose by any other name. Or maybe not, when you use Excel's sophisticated text-manipulation functions to change it into something else. Case in point: You can use the REPLACE function to change a rose into a tulip or a daisy, literally!

Did you ever have to work on a list in which people's full names are in one column, but you need to use only their last names? You could extract the last names to another column manually, but that strategy gets pretty tedious for more than a few names. What if the list contains hundreds of names? This is just one example of text manipulations that you can do easily and quickly with Excel's text functions.

Breaking Apart Text

Excel has three functions that are used to extract part of a text value (often referred to as a *string*). The LEFT, RIGHT, and MID functions let you get to the parts of a text value that their name implies, extracting part of a text value from the left, the right, or the middle. Mastering these functions gives you the power to literally break text apart.

How about this? You have a list of codes of inventory items. The first three characters are the vendor ID, and the other characters are the part ID. You need just the vendor IDs. How do you do this? Or how do you get the part numbers not including the vendor IDs? Excel functions to the rescue!

Bearing to the LEFT

The LEFT function lets you grab a specified number of characters from the left side of a larger string. All you do is tell the function what or where the string is and how many characters you need to extract.

Figure 16-1 demonstrates how the LEFT function isolates the vendor ID in a hypothetical product code list (Column A). The vendor ID is the first three characters in each product code. You want to extract the first three characters of each product code and put them in column B. You put the LEFT function in Column B with the first argument, specifying where the larger string is (Column A) and the second argument specifying how many characters to extract (three). See Figure 16-1 for an illustration of this worksheet with the LEFT formula visible in the Formula Bar. (What's Column C in this worksheet? I'll get to that in the next section.)

Figure 16-1:
Getting the three left characters from a larger string.

	A	B	C
	B4	*fx* =LEFT(A4,3)	
1	INVENTORY CONTROL		
2			
3	Product Code	Vendor	Internal Tracking Number
4	WES7164	WES	7164
5	NER6578	NER	6578
6	NER8400	NER	8400
7	APP5333	APP	5333
8	POW9655	POW	9655
9	WES2141	WES	2141
10	APP7496	APP	7496
11	POW1500	POW	1500
12	POW1600	POW	1600
13	WES8224	WES	8224
14	NER2112	NER	2112
15	NER4228	NER	4228
16	APP6077	APP	6077
17	TRE4444	TRE	4444
18	WES9055	WES	9055
19	BOT1255	BOT	1255
20	TRE6942	TRE	6942
21	WES4221	WES	4221
22	BOT7876	BOT	7876
23	TRE5042	TRE	5042
24	WES8315	WES	8315
25			

What if you ask LEFT to return more characters than the entire original string contains? No problem. In this case, LEFT simply returns the entire original string. The same is true for the RIGHT function, explained in the next section.

The LEFT function is really handy and so easy to use. Try it yourself:

1. **Position the cursor in the cell where you want the extracted string displayed.**

2. **Type** =LEFT(**to start the function.**

3. **Click the cell containing the original string or enter its address.**

4. **Type a comma (,).**

5. **Enter a number.**

   This number tells the function how many characters to extract from the left of the larger string. If you enter a number that is equal to or larger than the number of characters in the string, the whole string is returned.

6. **Type a) and press Enter.**

Swinging to the RIGHT

Excel does not favor sides. Because there is a LEFT function, there also is a RIGHT function. RIGHT extracts a certain number of characters from the right of a larger string. It works pretty much the same way as the LEFT function.

Column C in Figure 16-1 earlier in this chapter uses the RIGHT function to extract the rightmost four characters from the product codes. Cell C4, for example, has this formula: =RIGHT(A4,4).

Here's how to use the RIGHT function:

1. **Position the cursor in the cell where you want the extracted string displayed.**

2. **Type** =RIGHT(**to start the function.**

3. **Click the cell containing the original string or enter its address.**

4. **Type a comma (,).**

5. **Enter a number.**

   This number tells the function how many characters to extract from the right of the larger string. If you enter a number that is equal to or larger than the number of characters in the string, the whole string is returned.

6. **Type a) and press Enter.**

TIP

Use LEFT and RIGHT to extract characters from the start or end of a text string. Use MID to extract characters from the middle.

Staying in the MIDdle

MID is a powerful text-extraction function. It lets you pull out a portion of a larger string — from anywhere within the larger string. The LEFT and RIGHT functions allow you to extract from the start or end of a string, but not the middle. MID gives you essentially complete flexibility.

MID takes three arguments: the larger string (or a reference to one), the character position to start at, and how many characters to extract. Here's how to use MID:

1. **Position the cursor in the cell where you want the extracted string displayed.**

2. **Type** =MID(**to start the function.**

3. **Click the cell that has the full text entry or enter its address.**

4. **Type a comma (,).**

5. **Enter a number to tell the function which character to start the extraction from.**

   This number can be anything from 1 to the full count of characters of the string. Typically, the starting character position used with MID is greater than 1. Why? If you need to start at the first position, you may as well use the simpler LEFT function. If you enter a number for the starting character position that is greater than the length of the string, nothing is returned.

6. **Type a comma (,).**

7. **Enter a number to tell the function how many characters to extract.**

   If you enter a number that is greater than the remaining length of the string, the full remainder of the string is returned. For example, if you tell MID to extract characters 2 through 8 of a 6-character string, MID returns characters 2 through 6.

8. **Type a) and press Enter.**

Here are some examples of how MID works:

Example	Result
=MID("APPLE",4,2)	LE
=MID("APPLE",4,1)	L
=MID("APPLE",2,3)	PPL
=MID("APPLE",5,1)	E

Figure 16-2 shows how the MID function helps isolate the fourth and fifth characters in the hypothetical inventory shown in Figure 16-1. These characters could represent a storage-bin number for the inventory item. The MID function makes it easy to extract this piece of information from the larger product code.

Figure 16-2:
Using MID
to pull
characters
from any
position in
a string.

	A	B	C	D	E
	D4	fx	=MID(A4,4,2)		
1	INVENTORY CONTROL				
2					
3	Product Code	Vendor	Internal Tracking Number	Bin Number	
4	WES7164	WES	7164	71	
5	NER6578	NER	6578	65	
6	NER8400	NER	8400	84	
7	APP5333	APP	5333	53	
8	POW9655	POW	9655	96	
9	WES2141	WES	2141	21	
10	APP7496	APP	7496	74	
11	POW1500	POW	1500	15	
12	POW1600	POW	1600	16	
13	WES8224	WES	8224	82	
14	NER2112	NER	2112	21	
15	NER4228	NER	4228	42	
16	APP6077	APP	6077	60	
17	TRE4444	TRE	4444	44	
18	WES9055	WES	9055	90	
19	BOT1255	BOT	1255	12	
20	TRE6942	TRE	6942	69	
21	WES4221	WES	4221	42	
22	BOT7876	BOT	7876	78	
23	TRE5042	TRE	5042	50	
24	WES8315	WES	8315	83	
25					

Finding the long of it with LEN

The LEN function returns a string's length. It takes a single argument: the string being evaluated. LEN is often used with other functions, such as LEFT or RIGHT.

Manipulating text sometimes requires a little math. For example, you may need to calculate how many characters to isolate with the RIGHT function. A common configuration of functions to do this is RIGHT, SEARCH, and LEN, like this:

```
=RIGHT(A1,LEN(A1) - SEARCH(" ",A1))
```

This calculates the number of characters to return as the full count of characters less the position where the space is. Used with the RIGHT function, this returns the characters to the right of the space.

The LEN function is often used with other functions, notably LEFT, RIGHT, and MID. In this manner, LEN helps determine the value of an argument to the other function.

Here's how to use LEN:

1. **Position the cursor in the cell where you want the results to appear.**

2. **Type =LEN(to begin the function.**

3. **Perform one of these steps:**

   • Click a cell that contains text.

   • Enter the cell's address.

   • Enter a string enclosed in double quotation marks.

4. **Type a) and press Enter.**

Putting Text Together with CONCATENATE

The CONCATENATE function pulls multiple strings together into one larger string. A good use of this is when you have a column of first names and a column of last names and need to put the two together to use as full names.

CONCATENATE takes up to 255 arguments. Each argument is a string or a cell reference, and the arguments are separated by commas. The function does not insert anything, such as a space, between the strings. If you need to separate the substrings, as you would with the first name and last name example, you must explicitly insert the separator. Figure 16-3 makes this clear. You can see that the second argument to the CONCATENATE function is a space.

Figure 16-3: Putting strings together with CON-CATENATE.

	A	B	C
	First Name	Last Name	Full Name
1	First Name	Last Name	Full Name
2			
3	Mary	Lipani	Mary Lipani
4	Bob	Nobleson	Bob Nobleson
5	Sue	Farina	Sue Farina
6	Muriel	Clarke	Muriel Clarke
7	Evan R.	Nataller	Evan R. Nataller
8	Sarah	Ronnenberg	Sarah Ronnenberg
9	Cheryl	Hart	Cheryl Hart
10	Jeffrey	Keating	Jeffrey Keating
11	Billy	Akford	Billy Akford
12	Judi	Turchen	Judi Turchen
13	Norm	Godieski	Norm Godieski
14	Lucy Z.	Tisch	Lucy Z. Tisch
15	Ginny	Bergin	Ginny Bergin
16	Karen	Comeau	Karen Comeau
17	Angie	Mountler	Angie Mountler
18	Mel	Linden	Mel Linden
19	Wilfred	Fairbanks	Wilfred Fairbanks
20	Bruce	Clandton	Bruce Clandton
21			

C3 =CONCATENATE(A3," ",B3)

In Figure 16-3, the full names displayed in Column C are concatenated from the first and last names in Columns A and B, respectively. In the function's arguments, enter a space between the references to cells in columns A and B. You enter a space by enclosing a space between double quotation marks, like this: " ".

There is another way to concatenate strings. You can use the ampersand (&) character instead and skip using CONCATENATE. Another way to create the full names shown in Figure 16-3 is to enter the following formula in the target cell: =A3 & " " & B3. Either method gets the job done. There really is no compelling reason to use one over the other; it's up to you, empowered user!

You can give this a whirl on your own. Surely, you must have a list of names somewhere in an Excel workbook. Open that workbook, or at least enter first names and last names on your own, and then follow these steps:

1. **Position the cursor in an empty column, in the same row as the first text entry, and type** =CONCATENATE(**to start the function.**

2. **Click the cell that has the *first* name, or enter its address.**

3. **Type a comma (,).**

4. **Enter a space inside double quotation marks.**

   It should look like this: " ".

5. **Type a comma (,).**

6. **Click the cell that has the *last* name or enter its address.**

7. **Type a) and press Enter.**

8. **Use the fill handle to drag the function into the rows below, as many rows as there are text entries in the first column.**

You can combine text strings in two ways: Use the CONCATENATE function or use the ampersand (&) operator.

Changing Text

There must be a whole lot of issues about text. I say that because a whole lot of functions let you work with text. There are functions that format text, replace text with other text, and clean text. (Yes, text needs a good scrubbing at times.) There are functions for just making lowercase letters into uppercase and uppercase letters into lowercase.

Making money

Formatting numbers as currency is a common need in Excel. The Format Cells dialog box or the Currency Style button in the Number Formatting options of the Home tab of the Ribbon are the usual places to go to format cells as currency. Excel also has the DOLLAR function. On the surface, DOLLAR seems to do the same thing as the similar currency formatting options but has some key differences:

- ✔ **DOLLAR converts a number to text.** Therefore, you cannot perform math on a DOLLAR value. For example, a series of DOLLAR amounts cannot be summed into a total.

- ✔ **DOLLAR displays a value from another cell.** As its first argument, DOLLAR takes a cell address or a number entered directly in the function. DOLLAR is handy when you want to preserve the original cell's formatting. In other words, you may need to present a value as currency in one location but also let the number display in its original format in another location. DOLLAR lets you take the original number and present it as currency in another cell — the one you place the DOLLAR function in.

- ✔ **DOLLAR includes a rounding feature.** DOLLAR has a bit more muscle than the currency style. DOLLAR takes a second argument that specifies how many decimal places to display. When negative values are entered for the second argument, this serves to apply rounding to the digits on the left side of the decimal.

Figure 16-4 shows how the DOLLAR function can display various numeric values just the way you want. At the bottom of the worksheet is an area of detailed revenues. At the top is a summary that uses DOLLAR.

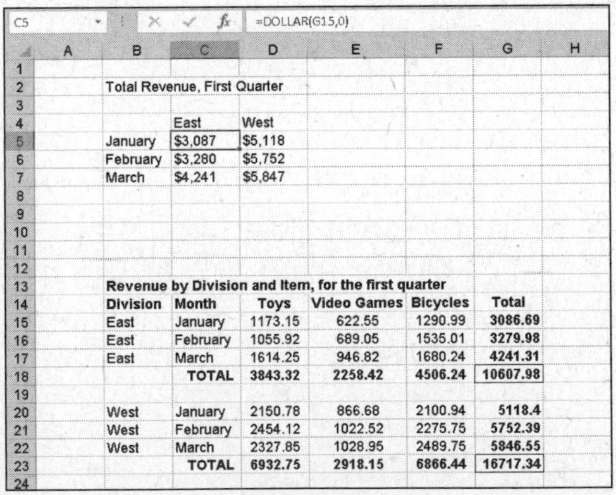

Figure 16-4: Using DOLLAR to round numbers and format them as currency.

Unless a cell has been formatted otherwise, you can tell the type of entry by alignment. Text aligns to the left; numbers, to the right.

Specifically, the cells in the range C5:D7 use the DOLLAR function to present values from the detail area and also round them down to no decimals. For example, cell C5 contains =DOLLAR(G15,0). Here are examples of how the rounding feature works:

Example	*Result*
=DOLLAR(1234.56,2)	$1,234.56
=DOLLAR(1234.56,1)	$1,234.6
=DOLLAR(1234.56,0)	$1,235
=DOLLAR(1234.56,-1)	$1,230
=DOLLAR(1234.56,-2)	$1,200
=DOLLAR(1234.56,-3)	$1,000

Using DOLLAR is easy. Follow these steps:

1. **Position the cursor in the cell where you want the results to appear.**

2. **Type =DOLLAR(to begin the function entry.**

3. **Click a cell that contains a number or enter a number.**

4. **Type a comma (,).**

5. **Enter a number to indicate the number of decimal points to display.**

   If the number is 0, no decimal points are displayed. Numbers less than 0 force rounding to occur to the left of the decimal point.

6. **Type a) and press Enter.**

The DOLLAR function is named DOLLAR in countries that use dollars, such as the United States and Canada. In versions of Excel designed for countries that use a different currency, the name of the function should match the name of the currency.

Turning numbers into text

The TEXT function is a bit like the DOLLAR function in that it converts a number value to text data, but it gives you more formatting options for your results. TEXT can format numbers as currency, like DOLLAR, but is not limited to this.

The first TEXT argument is a number or reference to a cell that contains a number. The second argument is a formatting pattern that tells the function how to format the number. You can see some formatting patterns in the Custom category on the Number tab of the Format Cells dialog box (shown in Figure 16-5).

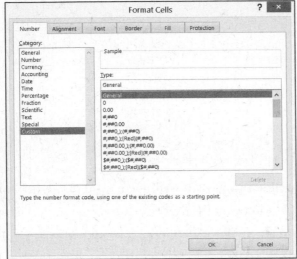

Figure 16-5:
Formatting options in the Format Cells dialog box.

Excel lets you create custom formatting patterns so you can present your data just the way you need to. For example, you can specify whether numbers use a thousands separator, whether decimal values are always displayed to the third decimal point, and so on.

These patterns are created with the use of a few key symbols. A pound sign (#) is a placeholder for a number — that is, a single digit. Interspersing pound signs with fixed literal characters (such as a dollar sign, a percent sign, a comma, or a period) establishes a pattern. For example, this pattern — $#,###.# — says to display a dollar sign in front of the number, to use a comma for a thousands separator, and to display one digit to the right of the decimal point. Some formatting options used with the TEXT function are shown in Table 16-1. Look up custom number formatting in Excel Help for more information on custom format patterns, or go to www.microsoft.com and search for guidelines for custom number formats.

Table 16-1	Formatting Options for the TEXT Function
Format	*Displays*
=TEXT(1234.56,"#.##")	1234.56
=TEXT(1234.56,"#.#")	1234.6
=TEXT(1234.56,"#")	1235
=TEXT(1234.56,"$#")	$1235
=TEXT(1234.56,"$#,#")	$1,235
=TEXT(1234.56,"$#,#.##")	$1,234.56
=TEXT(0.4,"#%")	40%
=TEXT("3/15/2005","mm/dd/yy")	03/15/05
=TEXT("3/15/2005","mm/dd/yyyy")	03/15/2005
=TEXT("3/15/2005","mmm-dd")	Mar-15

Figure 16-6 shows how the TEXT function is used to format values that are incorporated into sentences. Column C contains the formulas that use TEXT. For example, C4 has this formula: ="We spent " & TEXT(B4,"$#,#.#0") & " on " & A4. Cell C8 has this formula: ="We opened the office on " & TEXT(B8,"mmm d, yyyy").

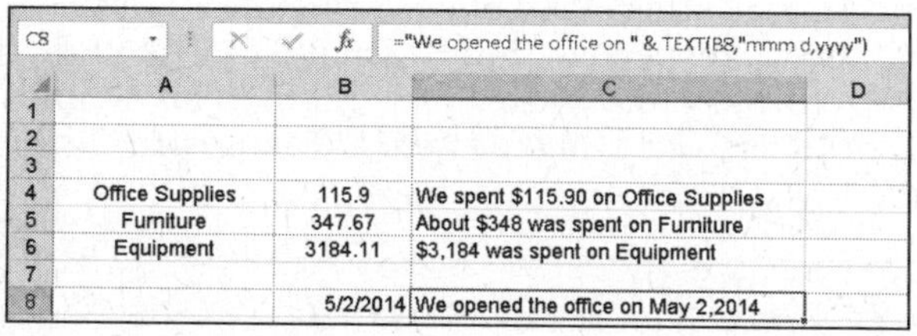

Figure 16-6:
Using TEXT
to report in
a well-
formatted
manner.

Here's how to use TEXT:

1. **Position the cursor in the cell where you want the results to appear.**

2. **Type** =TEXT(**to begin the function entry.**

3. **Click a cell that contains a number or a date or enter its address.**

4. **Enter a comma (,).**

5. **Enter a " and then enter a formatting pattern.**

   See the Format Cells dialog box (the Custom category of the Number tab) for guidance.

6. **Enter a " after the pattern is entered.**

7. **Type a) and press Enter.**

The VALUE function does the opposite of TEXT; it converts strings to numbers (this is not to say text such as `twenty`, but numbers that have been formatted as text). Excel does this by default anyway, so I don't cover the VALUE function here. You can look it up in Excel's Help system if you're curious about it.

Repeating text

REPT is a nifty function that does nothing other than repeat a string of text. REPT has two arguments:

- ✔ The string or a reference to a cell that contains text
- ✔ The number of times to repeat the text

REPT makes it a breeze to enter a large number of repeating characters. Figure 16-7 shows how this works. Cells B14 and B15 contain important summary information. To make this stand out, a string of asterisks (*) has been placed above and below, respectively, in B13 and B16. The REPT function was used here, with this formula: `=REPT("*",120)`. This simple function has removed the drudgery of having to enter 120 asterisks.

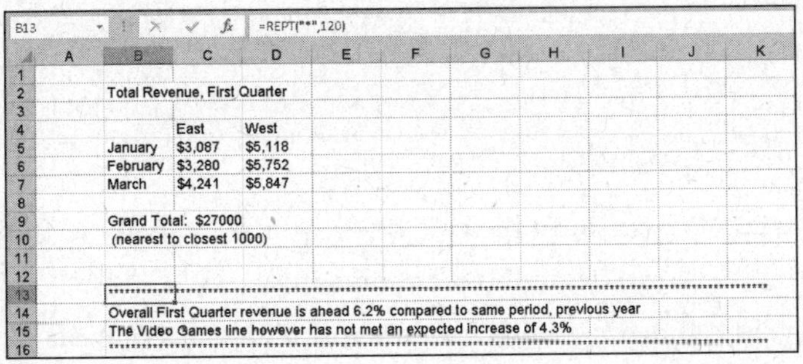

Figure 16-7: Repeating text with the REPT function.

Try it out:

1. **Position the cursor in the cell where you want the results to appear.**

2. **Type =REPT(to begin the function entry.**

3. **Click a cell that contains text or enter text enclosed in double quotation marks.**

   Typically, you would enter a character (such as a period or an asterisk), but any text will work.

4. **Type a comma (,).**

5. **Enter a number to tell the function how many times to repeat the text.**

6. **Type a) and press Enter.**

Swapping text

Two functions — REPLACE and SUBSTITUTE — replace a portion of a string with other text. The functions are nearly identical in concept but are used in different situations.

Both REPLACE and SUBSTITUTE replace text within other text. Use REPLACE when you know the position of the text you want to replace. Use SUBSTITUTE when you don't know the position of the text you want to replace.

REPLACE

REPLACE takes four arguments:

- The target string as a cell reference
- The character position in the target string at which to start replacing
- The number of characters to replace
- The string to replace with (does not have to be the same length as the text being replaced)

For example, if cell A1 contains the string `Our Chicago office has closed.`, the formula `=REPLACE(A1,5,7,"Dallas")` returns the string `Our Dallas office has closed`.

Figure 16-8 shows how to use REPLACE with the Inventory Control data first shown in the "Breaking Apart Text" section. A new task is at hand. For compatibility with a new computer system, you have to modify the product codes in the inventory data with two dashes between the vendor ID and the internal tracking number. The original codes are in Column A. Use a combination of REPLACE and LEFT functions to get the job done: `=REPLACE(A4, 1, 3, LEFT(A4,3) & "--")`.

	A	B	C	D	E
	D4	▾ : ✕ ✓ fx	=REPLACE(A4,1,3,LEFT(A4,3) & "--")		
1	INVENTORY CONTROL				
2					
3	Product Code	Vendor	Internal Tracking Number	New Product Code	
4	WES7164	WES	7164	WES--7164	
5	NER6578	NER	6578	NER--6578	
6	NER8400	NER	8400	NER--8400	
7	APP5333	APP	5333	APP--5333	
8	POW9655	POW	9655	POW--9655	
9	WES2141	WES	2141	WES--2141	
10	APP7496	APP	7496	APP--7496	
11	POW1500	POW	1500	POW--1500	
12	POW1600	POW	1600	POW--1600	
13	WES8224	WES	8224	WES--8224	
14	NER2112	NER	2112	NER--2112	
15	NER4228	NER	4228	NER--4228	
16	APP6077	APP	6077	APP--6077	
17	TRE4444	TRE	4444	TRE--4444	
18	WES9055	WES	9055	WES--9055	
19	BOT1255	BOT	1255	BOT--1255	
20	TRE6942	TRE	6942	TRE--6942	
21	WES4221	WES	4221	WES--4221	
22	BOT7876	BOT	7876	BOT--7876	
23	TRE5042	TRE	5042	TRE--5042	
24	WES8315	WES	8315	WES--8315	

Figure 16-8:
Using REPLACE to change text.

These arguments replace the original three characters in each product code with the same three characters followed by two dashes. Figure 16-8 shows how REPLACE alters the product codes. In the figure, the first three product code characters are replaced with themselves and the dashes. The LEFT function and the dashes serve as the fourth argument of REPLACE.

Keep in mind a couple of points about REPLACE:

✓ **You need to know where the text being replaced is in the larger text.** Specifically, you have to tell the function at what position the text starts and how many positions it occupies.

✓ **The text being replaced and the new text taking its place don't have to be the same size.**

Here's how to use the REPLACE function:

1. **Position the cursor in the cell where you want the result to appear.**

2. **Type** =REPLACE(**to begin the function entry.**

3. **Click a cell that contains the full string of which a portion is to be replaced.**

4. **Type a comma (,).**

5. **Enter a number to tell the function the starting position of the text to be replaced.**

6. **Type a comma (,).**

7. **Enter a number to tell the function how many characters are to be replaced.**

8. **Type a comma (,).**

9. **Click a cell that contains text or enter text enclosed in double quotation marks.**

   This is the replacement text.

10. **Type a) and press Enter.**

You can also use REPLACE to delete text from a string. Simply specify an empty string (" ") as the replacement text.

SUBSTITUTE

Use the SUBSTITUTE function when you don't know the position in the target string of the text to be replaced. Instead of telling the function the starting position and number of characters (as you do with REPLACE), you just tell it what string to look for and replace.

SUBSTITUTE takes three required arguments and a fourth optional argument:

- ✔ A reference to the cell that contains the target text string
- ✔ The string within the target string that is to be replaced
- ✔ The replacement text
- ✔ An optional number to tell the function which occurrence of the string to replace

The fourth argument tells SUBSTITUTE which occurrence of the text to be changed (the second argument) and actually replaced with the new text (the third argument). The text to be replaced may appear more than once in the target string. If you omit the fourth argument, all occurrences are replaced. This is the case in the first example in Table 16-2; all spaces are replaced with commas. In the last example in Table 16-2, only the second occurrence of the word two is changed to the word three.

Table 16-2   **Applying the SUBSTITUTE Function**

Example	Returned String	Comment
=SUBSTITUTE("apple banana cherry fig", " ",",")	apple,banana, cherry,fig	All spaces are replaced with commas.
=SUBSTITUTE("apple banana cherry fig", " ",",",1)	apple,banana cherry fig	The first space is replaced with a comma. The other spaces remain as they are.
=SUBSTITUTE("apple banana cherry fig", " ",",",3)	apple banana cherry,fig	The third space is replaced with a comma. The other spaces remain as they are.
=SUBSTITUTE("There are two cats and two birds.","two","three")	There are three cats and three birds.	Both occurrences of two are replaced with three.
=SUBSTITUTE("There are two cats and two birds.","two","three",2)	There are two cats and three birds.	Only the second occurrence of two is replaced with three.

Try it yourself! Here is what you do:

1. **Position the cursor in the cell where you want the result to appear.**

2. **Type** =SUBSTITUTE(**to begin the function entry.**

3. **Click a cell that contains text or enter its address.**

   This is the full string of which a portion is to be replaced.

4. **Type a comma (,).**

5. **Click a cell that contains text or enter text enclosed in double quotation marks.**

   This is the portion of text that is to be replaced.

6. **Type a comma (,).**

7. **Click a cell that contains text or enter text enclosed in double quotation marks.**

This is the replacement text. If you want to specify which occurrence of text to change, continue to Steps 8 and 9; otherwise, go to Step 10.

8. **Type a comma (,).**

9. **Enter a number that tells the function which occurrence to apply the substitution to.**

10. **Type a) and press Enter.**

You can use SUBSTITUTE to remove spaces from text. In the second argument (what to replace), enter a space enclosed in double-quote marks. In the third argument, enter two double-quote marks *with nothing between them*. This is known as an *empty string*.

Giving text a trim

Spaces have a way of sneaking in and ruining your work. The worst thing is that you often can't even see them! When the space you need to remove is at the beginning or end of a string, use the TRIM function to remove them. The function simply clips any leading or trailing spaces from a string. It also removes extra spaces from within a string; a sequence of two or more spaces is replaced by a single space.

Figure 16-9 shows how this works. In Column A is a list of names. Looking closely, you can see that some unwanted spaces precede the names in cells A5 and A10. Column B shows the correction using TRIM. Here is the formula in cell B5: =TRIM(A5).

	A	B	C
B5		f_x =TRIM(A5)	
1			
2			
3	Kevin C. Zamore	Kevin C. Zamore	
4	Wayne Danna	Wayne Danna	
5	Arthur Gasco	Arthur Gasco	
6	Jose Campbell	Jose Campbell	
7	Connor G. Douglas	Connor G. Douglas	
8	Herbie Lampert	Herbie Lampert	
9	Joyce Lord	Joyce Lord	
10	Laura Irwin	Laura Irwin	
11	Tamara Macdonald	Tamara Macdonald	
12	Danielle W. Ellis	Danielle W. Ellis	
13	Fred C. Russel	Fred C. Russel	
14	Gary Heacox	Gary Heacox	
15	Doris Avakian	Doris Avakian	
16	Nina O. Bereal	Nina O. Bereal	
17	Patricia Escala	Patricia Escala	

Figure 16-9: Removing spaces with the TRIM function.

TRIM takes just one argument: the text to be cleaned of leading and trailing spaces. Here's how it works:

1. **Position the cursor in the cell where you want the result to appear.**

2. **Type** =TRIM(**to begin the function entry.**

3. **Click a cell that contains the text that has leading or trailing spaces, or enter the cell address.**

4. **Type a) and press Enter.**

Be on the lookout: Although you generally use it to remove leading and trailing spaces, TRIM removes extra spaces in the middle of a string. If two or more spaces are next to each other, TRIM removes the extra spaces and leaves one space in place.

This is usually a good thing. Most times, you don't want extra spaces in the middle of your text. But what if you do? Here are a couple of alternatives to remove a leading space, if it is there, without affecting the middle of the string:

Formula to Remove Leading Space	Comment
=IF(LEFT(E10,1)=" ",SUBSTITUTE(E10," ","",1), E10)	If a space is found in the first position, substitute it an empty string; otherwise, just return the original string.
=IF(LEFT(E10,1)=" ",RIGHT(E10,LEN(E10)-1), E10)	If a space is found in the first position, return the right side of the string, less the first position. (See the section on LEN, earlier in this chapter.)

Making a case

In school, you were taught to use an uppercase letter at the start of a sentence as well as for proper nouns. But that was a while ago, and now the brain cells are a bit fuzzy. Lucky thing Excel has a way to help fix case, er Case, um CASE — well, you know what I mean.

Three functions alter the case of text: UPPER, LOWER, and PROPER. All three functions take a single argument — the text that will have its case altered. Here are a few examples:

Formula	Result
=LOWER("The Cow Jumped Over The Moon")	the cow jumped over the moon
=UPPER("the cow jumped over the moon")	THE COW JUMPED OVER THE MOON
=PROPER("the cow jumped over the moon")	The Cow Jumped Over The Moon

Try this:

1. **Enter a sentence in a cell.**

   Any old sentence will do, but don't make any letters uppercase. For example, type **excel is great** or **computers give me a headache**.

2. **Position the cursor in an empty cell.**

3. **Type** =UPPER(**to start the function.**

4. **Click the cell that has the sentence or enter its address.**

5. **Type a), and press Enter.**

6. **In another empty cell, type** =PROPER(**to start the function.**

7. **Click the cell that has the sentence or enter its address.**

8. **Type a) and press Enter.**

   You should now have two cells that show the sentence with a case change. One cell has the sentence in uppercase; the other cell, in proper case.

Perhaps you noticed another possibility that needs to be addressed. What about when just the first word needs to start with an uppercase letter and the rest of the string is all lowercase? Some people refer to this as *sentence case*. You can create sentence case by using the UPPER, LEFT, RIGHT, and LEN functions. (LEN is explained earlier in this chapter.) With the assumption that the text is in cell B10, here is how the formula looks:

```
=UPPER(LEFT(B10,1)) & RIGHT(B10,LEN(B10)-1)
```

In a nutshell, the UPPER function is applied to the first letter, which is isolated with the help of the LEFT function. This result is concatenated with the remainder of the string. You know how much is left by using LEN to get the length of the string and using the RIGHT function to get all the characters from the right, less one. This type of multiuse function work takes a bit of getting used to.

Comparing, Finding, and Measuring Text

Excel has many functions that manipulate text, but sometimes you just need to find out about the text before you do anything else! A handful of functions determine whether text matches other text, let you find text inside other text, and tell you how long a string is. These functions are *passive* — that is, they do not alter text.

Going for perfection with EXACT

The EXACT function lets you compare two strings of text to see whether they're the same. The function takes two arguments — the two strings of text — and returns a true or false value. EXACT is case sensitive, so two strings that contain the same letters but with differing case produce a result of false. For example, `Apple` and `APPLE` are not identical.

EXACT is great for finding changes in data. Figure 16-10 shows two lists of employees, one for each year, in Columns A and B. Are they identical? You could spend a number of minutes staring at the two lists. (That would give you a headache!) Or you can use EXACT. The cells in Column C contain the EXACT function, used to check Column A against Column B. The returned values are true for the most part. This means there is no change.

Figure 16-10: Comparing strings with the EXACT function.

	A	B	C	D
			=EXACT(A4,B4)	
	A	**B**	**C**	**D**
1				
2	Employees 2014	Employees 2015	Exact?	
3				
4	Steve Moulin	Steve Moulin	TRUE	
5	Victor Cushman	Victor Cushman	TRUE	
6	Anthony H. Elmore	Anthony H. Elmore	TRUE	
7	Nancy Aguilera	Nancy Aguilera	TRUE	
8	Raymond Majolin	Ray Majolin	FALSE	
9	Kristie Graber	Kristie Graber	TRUE	
10	Sal Rizzo	Sal Rizzo	TRUE	
11	Ed Woodworth	Ed Woodworth	TRUE	
12	Pat Carter	Pat Wilson	FALSE	
13	Kimberly K. Layman	Kimberly K. Layman	TRUE	
14	Ernest DeGraw	Ernest DeGraw	TRUE	
15	Lynn Alandale	Lynn Alandale	TRUE	
16	Corrina Harran	Corrina Harran	TRUE	
17	Mark Branson	Mark Bransonn	FALSE	
18	Nina Garonznik	Nina Garonznik	TRUE	
19	Steve Hallerman	Steve Hallerman	TRUE	
20	Mary Astor	Mary Astor	TRUE	

A few names are different in the second year. Marriage, divorce, misspellings — the mismatched data could be any of these. EXACT returns false for these names, which means they aren't identical in the two lists and should be checked manually.

Here's how you use EXACT:

1. **Position the cursor in the cell where you want the results to appear.**
2. **Type** =EXACT(**to begin the function entry.**
3. **Click a cell that contains text or enter its address.**
4. **Type a comma (,).**
5. **Click another cell that has text or enter its address.**
6. **Type a) and press Enter.**

If you get a true result with EXACT, the strings are identical. A false result means they're different.

What if you want to compare strings without regard to case? In other words, APPLE and apple would be considered the same. Excel does not have a function for this, but the result is easily obtained with EXACT and UPPER. The idea is to convert both strings to uppercase and compare the results:

```
=EXACT(UPPER("APPLE"), UPPER("apple"))
```

You could just as well use LOWER here.

Finding and searching

Two functions, FIND and SEARCH, work in a quite similar fashion. A couple of differences are key to figuring out which to use. Both FIND and SEARCH find one string inside a larger string and tell you the position at which it was found (or produce #VALUE if it is not found). The differences follow:

FIND	*SEARCH*
Case-sensitive. It will not, for example, find At inside heat.	Not case-sensitive.
You cannot use the wildcards * and ?.	You can use the wildcards * and ?.

FIND

FIND takes three arguments:

- ✔ The string to find.
- ✔ The larger string to search in.
- ✔ The position in the larger string to start looking at; this argument is optional.

If the third argument is left out, the function starts looking at the beginning of the larger string. Here are some examples:

Value in Cell A1	Function	Result
Happy birthday to you	=FIND("Birthday",A1)	#VALUE!
Happy birthday to you	=FIND("birthday",A1)	7
Happy birthday to you	=FIND("y",A1)	5
Happy birthday to you	=FIND("y",A1,10)	14

In the first example using FIND, an error is returned. The #VALUE! error is returned if the text cannot be found. Birthday is not the same as birthday, at least to the case-sensitive FIND function.

SEARCH

The SEARCH function takes the same arguments as FIND. The two common wildcards you can use are the asterisk (*) and the question mark (?). An asterisk tells the function to accept any number of characters (including zero characters). A question mark tells the function to accept any single character. It is not uncommon to see more than one question mark together as a wildcard pattern. Table 16-3 shows several examples.

Table 16-3	Using the SEARCH Function		
Value in Cell A1	**Function**	**Result**	**Comment**
Happy birthday to you	=SEARCH ("Birthday",A1)	7	*birthday* starts in position 7.
Happy birthday to you	=SEARCH ("y??",A1)	5	The first place where a *y* is followed by any two characters is at position 5. This is the last letter in *Happy*, a space, and the first letter in *birthday*.

Value in Cell A1	Function	Result	Comment
Happy birthday to you	=SEARCH ("yo?",A1)	19	The first place where *yo* is followed by any single character is the word *you*.
Happy birthday to you	=SEARCH ("b*d",A1)	7	The search pattern is the letter *b*, followed by any number of characters, followed by the letter *d*. This starts in position 7.
Happy birthday to you	=SEARCH ("*b",A1)	1	The asterisk says search for any number of characters before the letter *b*. The start of characters before the letter *b* is at position *1*. Using an asterisk at the start is not useful. It will either return a *1* or an error if the fixed character(s) (the letter *b* in this example) is not in the larger text.
Happy birthday to you	=SEARCH ("t*",A1)	10	The asterisk says search for any number of characters after the letter *t*. Because the search starts with a fixed character, its position is the result. The asterisk serves no purpose here.
Happy birthday to you	=SEARCH ("t",A1,12)	16	Finds the position of the first letter *t*, starting after position 12. The result is the position of the first letter in the word *to*. The letter *t* in birthday is ignored.

Back in Figure 16-3, I show you how to concatenate first and last names. What if you have full names to separate into first names and last names? SEARCH to the rescue! (Does that make this a search-and-rescue mission?) Figure 16-11 shows how the SEARCH, LEFT, RIGHT, and ISERROR functions work together to turn names into individual first and last names.

Isolating the first name from a full name is straightforward. You just use LEFT to get characters up to the first space. The position of the first space is returned from the SEARCH function. Here is how this looks:

```
=LEFT(A3,SEARCH(" ",A3)-1)
```

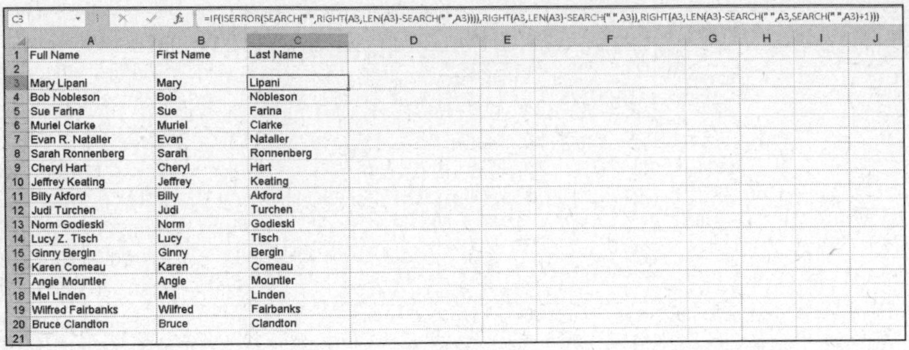
C3 =IF(ISERROR(SEARCH(" ",RIGHT(A3,LEN(A3)-SEARCH(" ",A3)))),RIGHT(A3,LEN(A3)-SEARCH(" ",A3)),RIGHT(A3,LEN(A3)-SEARCH(" ",A3,SEARCH(" ",A3)+1)))

	A	B	C
1	Full Name	First Name	Last Name
2			
3	Mary Lipani	Mary	Lipani
4	Bob Nobleson	Bob	Nobleson
5	Sue Farina	Sue	Farina
6	Muriel Clarke	Muriel	Clarke
7	Evan R. Nataller	Evan	Nataller
8	Sarah Ronnenberg	Sarah	Ronnenberg
9	Cheryl Hart	Cheryl	Hart
10	Jeffrey Keating	Jeffrey	Keating
11	Billy Akford	Billy	Akford
12	Judi Turchen	Judi	Turchen
13	Norm Godieski	Norm	Godieski
14	Lucy Z. Tisch	Lucy	Tisch
15	Ginny Bergin	Ginny	Bergin
16	Karen Comeau	Karen	Comeau
17	Angie Mountler	Angie	Mountler
18	Mel Linden	Mel	Linden
19	Wilfred Fairbanks	Wilfred	Fairbanks
20	Bruce Clandton	Bruce	Clandton
21			

Figure 16-11: Splitting names apart.

Getting the last names is just as simple — *not!* When the full name has only first and last names (no middle name or initials), you need SEARCH, RIGHT, and LEN, like this:

```
=RIGHT(A3,LEN(A3)-SEARCH(" ",A3))
```

However, this does not work for middle names or initials. What about Franklin D. Roosevelt? If you rely on the last name's being after the first space, the last name becomes D. Roosevelt. An honest mistake, but you can do better. What you need is a way to test for the second space and then return everything to the right of that space. There are likely a number of ways to do this.

Here is what you see in Column C, in Figure 16-11:

```
=IF(ISERROR(SEARCH(" ",RIGHT(A3,LEN(A3)-SEARCH(" ",A3)))),RIGHT(A3,LEN(A3)-
           SEARCH(" ",A3)),RIGHT(A3,LEN(A3)-SEARCH(" ",A3,SEARCH(" ",A3)+1)))
```

Admittedly, it's a doozy. But it gets the job done. Here is an overview of what this formula does:

- It's an IF function and therefore tests for either true or false.
- The test is if an error is returned from SEARCH for trying to find a space to the right of the first space:

  ```
  ISERROR(SEARCH(" ",RIGHT(A3,LEN(A3)-SEARCH(" ",A3))))
  ```

- If the test is true, there is no other space. This means there is no middle initial, so just return the portion of the name after the first space:

  ```
  RIGHT(A3,LEN(A3)-SEARCH(" ",A3))
  ```

✓ If the test is false, there is a second space, and the task is to return the portion of the string after the second space. SEARCH tells both the position of the first space and the second space. This is done by nesting one SEARCH inside the other. The inner SEARCH provides the third argument — where to start looking from. A 1 is added so the outer SEARCH starts looking for a space one position after the first space:

```
RIGHT(A3,LEN(A3)-SEARCH(" ",A3,SEARCH(" ",A3)+1))
```

Your eyes have probably glazed over, but that's it!

The monster formula isolates last names from full names that include a middle initial. A task for you to try, if you have any working brain cells left, is to write a formula that isolates the middle initial, if there is one. Here's how to use FIND or SEARCH:

1. **Position the cursor in the cell where you want the results to appear.**

2. **Type** =FIND(**or** =SEARCH(**to begin the function entry.**

3. **Enter a string of text that you want in a larger string, enclosed with double quotation marks, or click a cell that contains the text.**

4. **Type a comma (,).**

5. **Click a cell that contains the larger text or enter its address.**

   If you want the function to begin searching at the start of the larger string, go to Step 7. If you want to have the function begin the search in the larger string at a position other than 1, go to Step 6.

6. **Type a comma (,) and the position number.**

7. **Type a), and press Enter.**

Chapter 17

Playing Records with Database Functions

*B*elieve it or not, an Excel worksheet has the same structure as a database table. A database table has fields and records; an Excel worksheet has columns and rows. Same thing. Given this fact, why not ask questions of, or *query,* your information in much the same way as you do with a database?

In this chapter, I tell you how to use Excel's database functions to get quick answers from big lists. Say you have a client list on a worksheet — name, address, that sort of thing. You want to know how many clients are in New York. You may think about sorting your list by state and then counting the number of rows. Forget it. That's the old way! In this chapter, I show you how to do this sort of thing with a single function.

Putting Your Data into a Database Structure

To use the database functions, you need to put your data into a structured format. Excel is very flexible. Usually, you put data wherever you want. But to make the best of the database functions, you need to get your data into a contiguous area of rows and columns. Each row is a record, and each column is a field. The top row contains labels that identify the fields.

Figure 17-1 shows a database in a worksheet. This example is a list of students (by ID number) and their classes, teachers, and grades. Each student occupies a row — in other words, a record — in the database. Each of the four fields — Student ID, Class, Teacher, and Final Grade — is in one column and is identified by a label in the top row.

	A	B	C	D	E
1	Student ID	Class	Teacher	Final Grade	
2	VM4128	Calculus 101	Mr. Crasdale	77	
3	CH8965	Ancient Greece	Mr. Young	81	
4	SG9555	Accounting 101	Ms. Morley	76	
5	AB5235	Calculus 101	Mr. Crasdale	86	
6	KD0656	Accounting 101	Mr. Harris	98	
7	JG1183	Accounting 101	Mr. Harris	98	
8	HE7976	Masters of Philosophy	Mr. Crasdale	78	
9	NR5090	Calculus 101	Mr. Porter	79	
10	AJ3549	Accounting 101	Mr. Harris	85	
11	CW8495	English Literature	Mr. Johnson	66	
12	NR5090	Calculus 101	Mr. Porter	88	
13	QT6233	Accounting 101	Ms. Morley	73	
14	MP9632	English Literature	Ms. Rendson	84	
15	DK7492	Accounting 101	Mr. Richards	71	
16	RE3968	Ancient Greece	Mr. Young	75	
17	AP8356	Accounting 101	Mr. Richards	88	
18	FL1423	Masters of Philosophy	Ms. Untermeyer	93	
19	BW2559	Calculus 101	Mr. Porter	86	
20	QL9026	Calculus 101	Mr. Crasdale	77	
21	FE4903	English Literature	Ms. Appleson	74	
22	TY3987	Calculus 101	Mr. Porter	74	
23	EE4688	English Literature	Mr. Johnson	73	
24	WD0448	Ancient Greece	Mr. Young	76	
25	GY7754	English Literature	Mr. Johnson	66	

Figure 17-1: Using a database to store student information.

The data in the worksheet in Figure 17-1 is really just normal data. There is nothing special about it. However, the data sits in organized rows and columns, making it ready for working with Excel's database functions:

✔ Each column is a field that holds one particular item of data, such as Student ID or Class. It must contain no other data.

✔ Each row contains one record. In this example, a record is the data for one student.

✔ The top row of the database contains labels that identify the fields.

This sample data is used in this chapter to demonstrate the database functions. Of course, you can have a database in Excel and never use the database functions, but you have a lot more power at your fingertips if you do use them.

Working with Database Functions

The database functions all work in basically the same way. They perform some calculation on a specified field for those records that meet specified criteria. For example, you can use a database function to calculate the average final grade for all students in Accounting 101.

All database functions use the following three arguments:

- ✓ **The database range:** This argument tells the function where the database is. You enter it by using cell addresses (for example, A1:D200) or a named range (for example, Students). The range must include all records, including the top row of field names.

- ✓ **The field:** You must tell a database function which field to operate on. You can't expect it to figure this out by itself! You can enter either the column number or the field name. A column number, if used, is the number of the column offset from the first column of the database area. In other words, if a database starts in Column C, and the field is in Column E, the column number is 3, not 5. If a heading is used, put it inside a set of double quotation marks. Database functions calculate a result based on the values in this field. Just how many values are used depends on the third argument: the criteria.

- ✓ **The criteria:** This tells the function where the criteria are located; it is not the criteria per se. The criteria tell the function which records to use in its calculation. You set up the criteria in a separate part of the worksheet, apart from the database area. This area's address is passed to the database function. Criteria are explained in detail throughout the chapter.

Establishing your database

All database functions take a database reference as the first argument. The database area must include *headers* (field names) in the first row. In Figure 17-1 earlier in this chapter, the first row uses Student ID, Class, Teacher, and Final Grade as headers to the information in each respective column.

A great way to work with the database functions is to name the database area and then enter the name, instead of the range address, in the function.

To set up a name, follow these steps:

1. **Select the entire database area.**

   Make sure the top row has headers and is included in the selection.

2. **Click the Formulas tab (at the top of the Excel window).**

3. **Click Define Name in the Defined Names area.**

   The New Name dialog box appears, with the range address set in the Refers To box.

4. **Type a name in the Name Box (or use the suggested name).**

5. **Click OK to close the dialog box.**

Later, if records are added to the bottom of the database, you have to redefine the named area's range to include the new rows. You can do this as follows:

1. **Click the Name Manager button on the Excel Formulas tab.**

   The Name Manager dialog box appears.

2. **Click the name in the list you want to redefine.**

3. **Click the Edit button in the dialog box.**

   Excel opens the Edit Name dialog box, shown in Figure 17-2, with information about the selected range.

Figure 17-2:
Updating
the
reference
to a named
area.

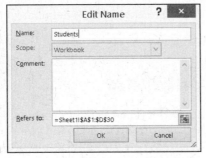

4. **Change the reference in the Refers To box.**

   You can use the small square button to the right of the Refers To box to define the new reference by dragging the mouse pointer over it. Clicking the small square button reduces the size of the Edit Name dialog box and allows you access to the worksheet. When you are done dragging the mouse over the new worksheet area, press Enter to get back to the Edit Name dialog box.

5. **Click the OK button to save the reference change and close the dialog box.**

6. **Click Close.**

TIP

If you add records to your database range by inserting new rows somewhere in the middle, rather than adding them on at the end, Excel automatically adjusts the reference to the named range.

Establishing the criteria area

As I mention earlier, the criteria are not part of the database function arguments but are somewhere in the worksheet and then referenced by the function. The criteria area can contain a single criterion, or it can contain two or more criteria. Each individual criterion is structured as follows:

- ✔ In one cell, enter the field name (header) of the database column that the criterion will apply to.

- ✔ In the cell below, enter the value that the field data must meet.

Figure 17-3 shows the student database with a criteria area to the right of the database. There are places to put criteria for the Class, Teacher, and Final Grade. In the example, a criterion has been set for the Class field. This criterion forces the database function to process only records (rows) where the Class is Accounting 101. Note, though, that a criterion can be set for more than one field. In this example, the Teacher and Final Grade criteria have been left blank so they don't affect the results.

Figure 17-3:
Selecting criteria to use with a database function.

FS			fx	=DAVERAGE(Students, "Final Grade", F2:H3)			
	A	B	C	D	E	F	G	H	I
1	Student ID	Class	Teacher	Final Grade			Criteria Area		
2	VM4128	Calculus 101	Mr. Crasdale	77		Class	Teacher	Final Grade	
3	CH8965	Ancient Greece	Mr. Young	81		Accounting 101			
4	SG9555	Accounting 101	Ms. Morley	76					
5	AB5235	Calculus 101	Mr. Crasdale	86					
6	KD0656	Accounting 101	Mr. Harris	98					
7	JG1183	Accounting 101	Mr. Harris	98					
8	HE7976	Masters of Philosophy	Mr. Crasdale	78		84			
9	NR5090	Calculus 101	Mr. Porter	79		Average Grade of all students enrolled in Accounting 101			
10	AJ3549	Accounting 101	Mr. Harris	85					

The DAVERAGE function has been entered into cell F8 and uses this criteria range. The three arguments are in place. The name Students tells the function where the database is, the Final Grade field (column) is where the function finds values to calculate the average, and the criteria are set to the worksheet range that has criteria that tell the function to use only records where the Class is Accounting 101 — in other words, F2:H3. The entry in cell F8 looks like this:

```
=DAVERAGE(Students,"Final Grade",F2:H3)
```

Why does this function refer to F2:H3 as the criteria range when the only defined criterion is located in the range F2:F3? It's a matter of convenience. Because cells G3 and H3 in the criteria range are blank, the Teacher and Final Grade fields are ignored by a database function that uses this criteria range. However, if you want to enter a criterion for one of those fields, just enter it in the appropriate cell; there is no need to edit the database function arguments. What about assigning a name to the criteria area and then using the name as the third argument to the database function? That works perfectly well, too.

Whether you use a named area for your criteria or simply type the range address, you must be careful to specify an area that includes all the criteria but does *not* include any blank rows or columns. If you do, the database function's results will be incorrect.

Here's how you enter any of the database functions. This example uses the DSUM function, but the instructions are the same for all the database functions; just use the one that performs the desired calculation. Follow these steps:

1. **Import or create a database of information in a worksheet.**

   The information should be in contiguous rows and columns. Be sure to use field headers.

2. **Optionally, use the New Name dialog box to give the database a name.**

   To name your database, see the section "Establishing your database" earlier in this chapter.

3. **Select a portion of the worksheet to be the criteria area and then add headers to this area that match the database headers.**

   You have to provide criteria headers only for database fields that criteria are applied to. For example, your database area may have ten fields, but you need to define criteria to three fields. Therefore, the criteria area can be three columns wide.

4. **Position the cursor in the cell where you want the results to appear.**

   This cell must not be in the database area or the criteria area.

5. **Type =DSUM(to begin the function entry.**

6. **Enter the database range or a name, if one is set.**

7. **Type a comma (,).**

8. **Enter either of the following:**

   - The header name, In quotation marks, of the database field that the function should process

   - The column number

9. **Type a comma (,).**

10. **Enter the range of the criteria area.**

11. **Type a) and press Enter.**

Fine-Tuning Criteria with AND and OR

Excel's database functions would not be of much use if you could not create fairly sophisticated queries. A few common types of queries follow:

✔ Records that match two or more individual criteria

✔ Records that match any one of several criteria

✔ Values that fall within a specified range

To find records that match two or more criteria, place the criteria in adjacent columns in the criteria area. Continuing with the student-grade database, the criteria area shown in Figure 17-4 matches records where the Class field contains Accounting 101 and the Teacher field contains Mr. Harris. This is called an AND criterion.

Figure 17-4:
Finding records that match two criteria.

Class	Criteria Area	
Class	Teacher	Final Grade
Accounting 101	Mr. Harris	

To match records that meet any one of several criteria, place the individual criteria in two or more rows below the field name. Figure 17-5 shows a criteria range that matches all records where the Class field contains either Accounting 101 or English Literature. This is called an OR criterion.

To combine AND with OR in a criteria range, use two or more columns and two or more rows. Figure 17-6 shows a criteria range that finds all records where Class is Accounting 101 and Teacher is either Mr. Harris or Mr. Richards.

Figure 17-5:
Finding
records that
match any
one of two
or more
criteria.

	Criteria Area	
Class	**Teacher**	**Final Grade**
Accounting 101		
English Literature		

Figure 17-6:
Combining
AND and OR
criteria.

	Criteria Area	
Class	**Teacher**	**Final Grade**
Accounting 101	Mr. Harris	
Accounting 101	Mr. Richards	

To define a criterion that uses ranges, use these numerical comparison operators:

✔ < for less than

✔ > for greater than

✔ <= for less than or equal to

✔ >= for greater than or equal to

Of course, you can apply these to fields with numerical values. Figure 17-7 shows two criteria areas. The upper one matches all records in which Final Grade is 90 or higher. The lower one matches all records in which Final Grade is equal to or greater than 80 and less than 90.

Final Grade
>=90

Figure 17-7:
Defining
numerical
range
criteria.

Final Grade
<90
>=80

Adding Only What Matters with DSUM

The DSUM function lets you sum numbers in a database column for just those rows that match the criteria you specify. For example, take a database that contains data on individual sale amounts for sales people. The database range is named Sales. You want to calculate total sales for each of the three sales representatives. Figure 17-8 shows how this is done. Three criteria areas are defined in D2:D3, E2:E3, and F2:F3. The DSUM function is entered in cells E8:E10. The formula in cell E8 is

```
=DSUM(SALES, "Sale Amount", D2:D3)
```

The functions entered in E9 and E10 are identical except for referencing a different criteria range. The results show clearly that Amy is the sales leader.

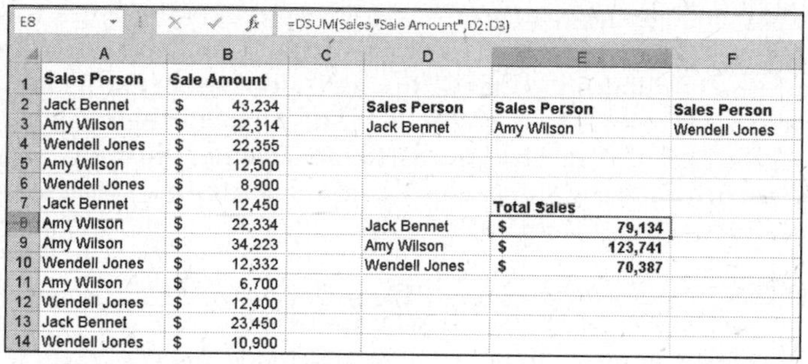

E8 =DSUM(Sales,"Sale Amount",D2:D3)

	A	B	C	D	E	F
1	Sales Person	Sale Amount				
2	Jack Bennet	$ 43,234		Sales Person	Sales Person	Sales Person
3	Amy Wilson	$ 22,314		Jack Bennet	Amy Wilson	Wendell Jones
4	Wendell Jones	$ 22,355				
5	Amy Wilson	$ 12,500				
6	Wendell Jones	$ 8,900				
7	Jack Bennet	$ 12,450			Total Sales	
8	Amy Wilson	$ 22,334		Jack Bennet	$ 79,134	
9	Amy Wilson	$ 34,223		Amy Wilson	$ 123,741	
10	Wendell Jones	$ 12,332		Wendell Jones	$ 70,387	
11	Amy Wilson	$ 6,700				
12	Wendell Jones	$ 12,400				
13	Jack Bennet	$ 23,450				
14	Wendell Jones	$ 10,900				

Figure 17-8: Calculating the sum of sales with the DSUM function.

Going for the Middle with DAVERAGE

The DAVERAGE function lets you find the average, or *mean,* of a field for just the rows that match the criteria. For this example, you return to the student database.

Figure 17-9 shows a worksheet in which the average grade for each course has been calculated by DAVERAGE. For example, cell G22 shows the average grade for Masters of Philosophy. Here is the formula:

```
=DAVERAGE(Students,"Final Grade",F14:G15)
```

Each calculated average uses a different criteria area. Each area filters the result by a particular course. In all cases, the criteria area for the Teacher is left blank and, therefore, has no effect on the results.

For the sake of comparison, DAVERAGE is also used in cell G24 to show the overall average for all courses. Because a criterion is a required function argument, the calculation in cell G24 is set to look at an empty cell. None of the Class criteria cells is free, so the function looks to the Teacher criterion in cell G3. Because this cell has no particular teacher entered as a criterion, all of the records in the database are used to create this average — just what you want. Here is the formula in cell G24:

```
=DAVERAGE(Students,"Final Grade",G2:G3)
```

It doesn't matter which field header you use in the criterion when you're getting a result based on all records in a database. What *does* matter is that there is no actual criterion below the header.

Counting Only What Matters with DCOUNT

The DCOUNT function lets you determine how many records in the database match the criteria.

Figure 17-10 shows how DCOUNT can determine how many students took each course. Cells G18:G22 contain formulas that count records based on the criterion (the Class) in the associated criteria sections. Here is the formula used in cell G20, which counts the number of students in Calculus 101:

```
=DCOUNT(Students,"Final Grade",F8:G9)
```

Figure 17-10:
Calculating the number of students in each course.

Note that DCOUNT requires a column of numbers to count. Therefore, the Final Grade heading is put in the function. Counting on Class or Teacher would result in zero. Using a column that specifically has numbers may seem a little odd. The function is not summing the numbers; it just counts the number of records. But what the heck? It works.

Now take this a step further. How about counting the number of students who got a grade of 90 or better in any class? How can this be done? This calculation requires a different criterion — one that selects all records where Final Grade is 90 or greater. Figure 17-11 shows a worksheet with this criterion and the calculated result shown.

Figure 17-11:
Calculating the number of students who earned a grade of 90 or better.

The result in cell F6 *concatenates* — that is, combines but does not add — the answer from the DCOUNT function with some text. The formula looks like this:

```
=DCOUNT(Students,"Final Grade",F2:F3) & " students received a 90 or better."
```

The criterion specifically states to use all records where the Final Grade is greater than `89` (>89). You can specify >=90 with the exact same result.

Finding Highest and Lowest with DMIN and DMAX

The DMIN and DMAX functions find the minimum or maximum value, respectively, in a database column, for just the rows that match the criteria. Figure 17-12 shows how these two functions can find the highest and lowest grades for English Literature.

F8 =“The highest grade in ” & $F$3 & ” is ” & DMAX(Students, “Final Grade”, $F$2:$F$3)

	A	B	C	D	E	F
1	Student ID	Class	Teacher	Final Grade		
2	VM4128	Calculus 101	Mr. Crasdale	77		Class
3	CH8965	Ancient Greece	Mr. Young	81		English Literature
4	SG9555	Accounting 101	Ms. Morley	76		
5	AB5235	Calculus 101	Mr. Crasdale	86		
6	KD0656	Accounting 101	Mr. Harris	98		
7	JG1183	Accounting 101	Mr. Harris	98		
8	HE7976	Masters of Philosophy	Mr. Crasdale	78		The highest grade in English Literature is 90
9	NR5090	Calculus 101	Mr. Porter	79		
10	AJ3549	Accounting 101	Mr. Harris	85		The lowest grade in English Literature is 66
11	CW8495	English Literature	Mr. Johnson	66		
12	NR5090	Calculus 101	Mr. Porter	88		
13	QT6233	Accounting 101	Ms. Morley	73		
14	MP9632	English Literature	Ms. Rendson	84		
15	DK7492	Accounting 101	Mr. Richards	71		
16	RE3968	Ancient Greece	Mr. Young	75		

Figure 17-12: Calculating the highest and lowest grades for a specified class.

The formulas in cells F8 and F10 are practically identical. Here is the formula in cell F8:

```
="The highest grade in " & $F$3 & " is " & DMAX(Students,"Final Grade",$F$2:$F$3)
```

Finding Duplicate Values with DGET

DGET is a unique database function. It does not perform a calculation but checks for duplicate entries. The function returns one of three values:

- If one record matches the criterion, DGET returns the criterion.
- If no records match the criterion, DGET returns the `#VALUE!` error.
- If more than one record matches the criterion, DGET returns the `#NUM!` error.

By testing to see whether DGET returns an error, you can discover problems with your data. Perhaps you suspect that a student has registered twice for a specific class. If this is true, two records will have the same Student ID and Class.

Figure 17-13 shows how to check whether student NR5090 is entered more than once for Calculus 101. If there is more than one record, DGET returns an error. Cell F5 contains a formula that nests the DGET function inside the ISERROR function; all that is inside the IF function. If DGET returns an error, return one message; if DGET does not return an error, return a different message. Here is the formula:

```
=IF(ISERROR(DGET(Students,"Student ID",F2:G3)),F3 & " has duplicate records",
              F3 & " has one record")
```

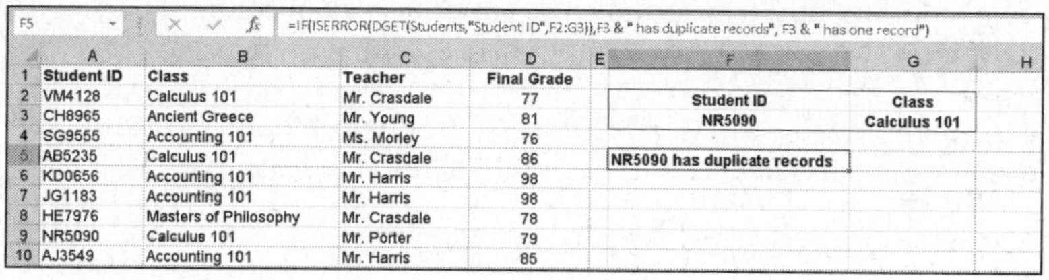

Figure 17-13:
Using DGET
to test for
duplicate
records in a
database.

Being Productive with DPRODUCT

DPRODUCT multiplies values that match the criterion in a database. This is powerful but also able to produce results that are not the intention. In other words, it's one to thing to add and derive a sum. That is a common operation on a set of data. Looking back at Figure 17-8, you can see that the total sales for Jack Bennet, $79,134, are the sum of three amounts: $43,234, $12,450, and $23,450. If multiplication were applied to the three amounts, the answer (the product) would be $12,622,274,385,000. Oops! That's over 12 *trillion* dollars!

DPRODUCT multiplies and, therefore, is not likely to be used as often as a function like DSUM, but when you need to multiply items in a database, DPRODUCT is a tool of choice.

Figure 17-14 shows a situation in which DPRODUCT is productive. The database area contains shirts. For each shirt size, there are two rows: the price per shirt and the number of shirts that are packed in a carton. The cost for a carton of shirts is, therefore, the product of the price per shirt times the number of shirts. There are four shirt sizes, each with its own price and carton count.

To be sure, you work with just one size per use of DPRODUCT, four criteria areas are set up — one for each size. Any single criteria area has the Shirt Size heading and the actual shirt size, such as Medium. For example, D8:D9 contains the criteria for medium-size shirts.

Four cells each contain DPRODUCT, and within each cell, the particular criteria area is used. For example, cell E18 has this formula:

```
=DPRODUCT(A1:C9, "Value", D8:D9)
```

The database range is A1:C9. Value is the field the function looks in for values to multiply, and the multiplication occurs on values for which the shirt size matches the criteria.

A worksheet set up like the one shown in Figure 17-14 is especially useful when new data are occasionally pasted into the database area. The set of DPRODUCT functions will always provide the products based on whatever data are placed in the database area. This particular example of DPRODUCT shows how to work with data in which more than one row pertains to an item. In this case, each shirt size has a row showing the price per shirt and a second row showing the number of shirts that fit in a carton.

Part V
The Part of Tens

See a bunch of useful real-life formulas in the online article "More Than Ten Useful Calculations to Use in Excel" at www.dummies.com/extras/excel formulasfunctions.

In this part . . .

- Discover ten top tips for working with formulas.
- See ten functions you really should know.
- Use some really cool functions.

Chapter 18

Ten Tips for Working with Formulas

Several elements can help you be as productive as possible when writing and correcting formulas. You can view all your formulas at once and correct errors one by one. You can use add-in wizards to help write functions. You can even create functions all on your own!

Master Operator Precedence

One of the most important factors in writing formulas is getting the operators correct, and I do not mean telephone-company operators. This has to do with mathematical operators — you know, little details such as plus signs, and multiplication signs, and where the parentheses go. *Operator precedence* — the order in which operations are performed — can make a big difference in the result. You have an easy way to keep your operator precedence in order. All you have to remember is "Please excuse my dear Aunt Sally."

No, I have not lost my mind! This phrase is a mnemonic for the following:

Parentheses

Exponents

Multiplication

Division

Addition

Subtraction

Thus, parentheses have the first (highest) precedence, and subtraction has the last precedence. Well, to be honest, multiplication has the same precedence as division and addition has the same precedence as subtraction, but you get the idea!

For example, the formula =1 + 2 × 15 equals 31. If you think it should equal 45, you'd better go visit your aunt! The answer equals 45 if you include parentheses, such as this: =(1 + 2) × 15.

Getting the order of the operators correct is critical to the well-being of your worksheet. Excel generates an error when the numbers of open and closed parentheses do not match, but if you mean to add two numbers before the multiplication, Excel does not know that you simply left the parentheses out!

A few minutes of refreshing your memory on operator order can save you a lot of headaches down the road.

Display Formulas

In case you haven't noticed, it's kind of hard to view your formulas without accidentally editing them. That's because any time you are in "edit" mode and the active cell has a formula, the formula may incorporate the address of any other cell you click. This totally messes things up.

Wouldn't it be easy if you could just *look* at all your formulas? There is a way! It's simple. Click File at the top left of the Excel workspace, click Options, click the Advanced tab, and scroll down to the Display options for this worksheet section (see Figure 18-1).

Notice the Show formulas in cells instead of their calculated results check box. This box tells Excel that for any cells that have formulas to display the formula itself instead of the calculated result. Figure 18-2 shows a worksheet that displays the formulas. To return to normal view, repeat these steps and deselect the option. This option makes it easy to see what all the formulas are!

You can accidentally edit functions even when you have selected the View Formulas option. Be careful clicking around the worksheet.

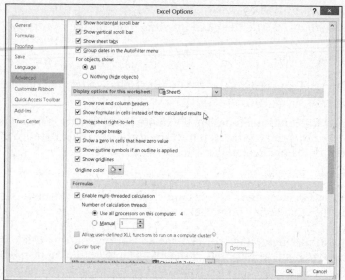

Figure 18-1:
Setting
options.

Figure 18-2:
Viewing for-
mulas the
easy way.

Month	Toys	Video Games	Bicycles	Total
January	1173.15	622.55	1290.99	=SUM(D4:F4)
February	1055.92	689.05	1535.01	=SUM(D5:F5)
March	1614.25	946.82	1680.24	=SUM(G4:G5)
TOTAL	=SUM(D4:D6)	=SUM(E4:E6)	=SUM(F4:F6)	=SUM(G4:G6)

Fix Formulas

Suppose that your worksheet has some errors. Don't panic! It happens to
even the savviest users, and Excel can help you figure out what's going
wrong. On the Formulas tab in the Formula Auditing section is the Error
Checking button. Clicking the button displays the Error Checking dialog box,
shown in Figure 18-3. That is, the dialog box appears if your worksheet has
any errors. Otherwise, it just pops up a message that the error check is complete. It's that smart!

Error Checking ? ✕

Error in cell C11
=4/0

Divide by Zero Error
The formula or function used is dividing by zero or empty
cells.

Help on this error

Show Calculation Steps...

Ignore Error

Edit in Formula Bar

Options...   Previous   Next

Figure 18-3:
Checking for
errors.

When there *are* errors, the dialog box appears and sticks around while you work on each error. The Next and Previous buttons let you cycle through all the errors before the dialog box closes. For each error it finds, you choose what action to take:

- ✔ **Help on This Error:** This leads to the Help system and displays the topic for the particular type of error.

- ✔ **Show Calculation Steps:** The Evaluate Formula dialog box opens, and you can watch step by step how the formula is calculated. This lets you identify the particular step that caused the error.

- ✔ **Ignore Error:** Maybe Excel is wrong. Ignore the error.

- ✔ **Edit in Formula Bar:** This is a quick way to fix the formula yourself if you don't need any other help.

The Error Checking dialog box also has an Options button. Clicking the button opens the Formulas tab of the Excel Options dialog box. On the Formulas tab, you can select settings and rules for how errors are recognized and triggered.

Use Absolute References

If you are going to use the same formula for a bunch of cells, such as those going down a column, the best method is to write the formula once and then drag it down to the other cells by using the fill handle. The problem is that when you drag the formula to new locations, any relative references change.

Often, this *is* the intention. When there is one column of data and an adjacent column of formulas, typically, each cell in the formula column refers to its neighbor in the data column. But if the formulas all reference a cell that is not adjacent, the intention usually is for all the formula cells to reference an unchanging cell reference. Get this to work correctly by using an absolute reference to the cell.

To use an absolute reference to a cell, use the dollar sign ($) before the row number, before the column letter, or before both. Do this when you write the first formula, before dragging it to other cells, or you will have to update all the formulas.

For example, don't write this:

```
=A4 × (B4 + A2)
```

Write it this way instead:

```
=A4 × (B4 + $A$2)
```

This way, all the formulas reference A2 no matter where you copy them, instead of that reference's turning into A3, and A4, and so on.

Turn Calc On/Turn Calc Off

The Excel default is to calculate your formulas automatically as they are entered or when you change the worksheet. In some situations, you may want to set the calculation to manual. Leaving the setting on automatic is usually not an issue, but if you are working on a hefty workbook with lots of calculations, you may need to rethink this one.

Imagine this: You have a cell that innocently does nothing but display the date. But dozens of calculations throughout the workbook reference that cell. Then dozens more calculations reference the first batch of cells that reference the cell with the data. Get the picture? In a complex workbook, there could be a lot of calculating going on, and the time it takes can be noticeable.

Turning the calculation setting to manual lets you decide when to calculate. Do this in the Excel Options dialog box; click the File tab on the Ribbon and then click Options. In the dialog box, click the Formulas tab, in which calculation options are selected, as shown in Figure 18-4. You can select one of the automatic calculation settings or manual calculation.

Figure 18-4: Setting the calculation method.

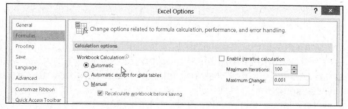

Pressing F9 calculates the workbook. Use it when the calculation is set to Manual. Here are some further options:

What You Press	What You Get
F9	Calculates formulas that have changed since the last calculation, in all open workbooks
Shift+F9	Calculates formulas that have changed since the last calculation, just in the active worksheet
Ctrl+Alt+F9	Calculates all formulas in all open workbooks, regardless of when they were last calculated

Use Named Areas

Heck, maybe it's just me, but I think it is easier to remember a word such as *Customers* or *Inventory* or *December* than it is to remember B14:E26 or AF220:AR680. So I create names for the ranges that I know I'll reference in my formulas and functions.

Naming areas is easy to do, and in fact, you can do it a few ways. The first is to use the New Name dialog box. You can get to this by clicking the Define Name button on the Formulas tab of the Ribbon. In the dialog box, you set a range, give it a name, and click the OK button (see Figure 18-5).

Figure 18-5:
Defining a named area.

The Name Manager is another dialog box that you can display by clicking its button on the Formulas tab. This dialog box lets you add, update, and delete named areas. A really quick way to just add them (but not update or delete) is to follow these steps:

1. **Select an area on the worksheet.**

2. **Click the Name Box and enter the name.**

   The Name Box is part of the Formula Bar and sits to the left of where formulas are entered.

3. **Press Enter.**

Done! Now you can use the name as you please. Figure 18-6 shows a name being entered in the Name Box. Of course, you can use a particular name only once in a workbook. After the defined name is entered, you can find it in the Name Box by clicking the down arrow in the right of the box.

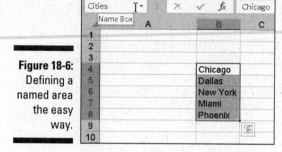

Figure 18-6: Defining a named area the easy way.

Use Formula Auditing

There are precedents and dependents. There are external references. There is interaction everywhere. How can you track where the formula references are coming from and going to?

Use the formula auditing tools, that's how! On the Formulas tab is the Formula Auditing section. In the section are various buttons that control the visibility of auditing trace arrows (see Figure 18-7).

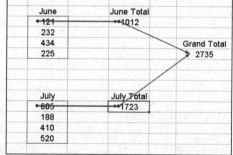

Figure 18-7: Auditing formulas.

The formula auditing toolbar has several features that let you wade through your formulas. Besides showing tracing arrows, the toolbar also lets you check errors, evaluate formulas, check for invalid data, and add comments to worksheets.

Use Conditional Formatting

Just as the IF function returns a certain value when the first argument condition is true and another value when it's false, conditional formatting lets you apply a certain format to a cell when a condition is true. On the Home tab in the Styles section is a drop-down menu with many conditional formatting options. Figure 18-8 shows some values that have been treated with conditional formatting. Conditional formatting lets you set the condition and select the format that is applied when the condition is met. For example, you could specify that the cell be displayed in bold italic when the value it contains is greater than 100.

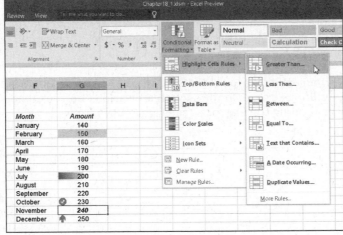

Figure 18-8:
Applying a
format when
a condition
is met.

Conditions are set as rules. The Rule Types are

- ✔ Format all cells based on their values.
- ✔ Format only cells that contain. . . .
- ✔ Format only top or bottom ranked values.
- ✔ Format only values that are above or below average.
- ✔ Format only unique or duplicate values.
- ✔ Use a formula to determine which cells to format.

When the condition is true, formatting can control the following:

- ✔ Borders
- ✔ Font settings (style, color, bold, italic, and so on)
- ✔ Fill (a cell's background color or pattern)

Cells can also be formatted with color schemes or icon images placed in the cell.

Use Data Validation

On the Data tab, in the Data Tools section, is Data Validation. Data Validation lets you apply a rule to a cell (or cells) such that entry must adhere to the rule. For example, a cell can be set to accept only an integer entry between 50 and 100 (see Figure 18-9).

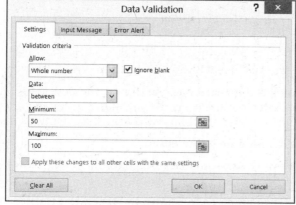

Figure 18-9: Setting data validation.

When entry does not pass the rule, a message is shown (see Figure 18-10).

The error message can be customized. For example, if someone enters the wrong number, the displayed error message can say `Noodlehead — learn how to count!` Just don't let the boss see that.

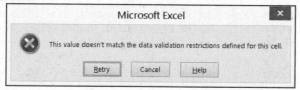

Figure 18-10: Caught making a bad entry.

Create Your Own Functions

Despite all the functions provided by Excel, you may need one that you just don't see offered. Excel lets you create your own functions by using VBA programming code; your functions show up in the Insert Function dialog box.

Okay, I know what you're thinking: Me, write VBA code? No way! It's true — this is not for everyone. But nonetheless, here is a short-and-sweet example. If you can conquer this, you may want to find out more about programming VBA. Who knows — maybe one day you'll be churning out sophisticated functions of your own! Make sure you are working in a macro-enabled workbook (one of the Excel file types).

Follow along to create custom functions:

1. **Press Alt + F11.**

    This gets you to the Visual Basic Editor, where VBA is written.

    You can also click the Visual Basic button on the Developer tab of the Ribbon. The Developer tab is visible only if the Developer checkbox is checked on the Customize Ribbon tab of the Excel Options dialog box.

2. **Choose Insert ⇨ Module in the editor.**

    You have an empty code module sitting in front of you. Now it's time to create your very own function!

3. **Type this programming code, shown in Figure 18-11:**

    ```
    Public Function Add(number1 As Double, number2 As Double)
      Add = number1 + number2
    End Function
    ```

4. **Save the function.**

    Macros and VBA programming can be saved only in a macro-enabled workbook.

    After you type the first line and press Enter, the last one appears automatically. This example function adds two numbers, and the word `Public` lists the function in the Insert Function dialog box. You may have to find the Excel workbook on the Windows taskbar because the Visual Basic Editor runs as a separate program. Or press Alt+ F11 to toggle back to the Workbook.

5. **Return to Excel.**

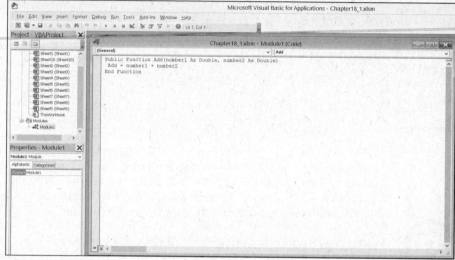

Figure 18-11:
Writing your
own
function.

6. **Click the Insert Function button on the Formulas tab to display the Insert Function dialog box (see Figure 18-12).**

Figure 18-12:
Finding the
function in
the User
Defined
category.

7. **Click OK.**

The Function Arguments dialog box opens, ready to receive the arguments (see Figure 18-13). Isn't this incredible? It's as though you are creating an extension to Excel, and in essence, you are.

Figure 18-13:
Using the
custom Add
function.

This is a very basic example of what you can do by writing your own func-tion. The possibilities are endless, but of course, you need to know how to program VBA. I suggest reading *Excel VBA Programming For Dummies,* 4th Edition, by John Walkenbach (John Wiley & Sons, Inc.).

Macro-enabled workbooks have the file extension .xlsm.

Chapter 19

Ten Functions You Really Should Know

This chapter lists the top ten Excel functions. Actually, it lists the top 15, but in some cases, two related functions are treated as a single item. To be fair, there is no absolute top ten list of functions, but over the years (don't ask how many!), I have worked on hundreds of worksheets and have seen some of the same functions being used all the time.

The functions in this list are of the type that apply to a wide array of needs. You won't see a financial function or any advanced statistical function — just the basics — but knowing the functions in this chapter is essential to good Excel work. You can always refer here for a quick brush-up on how to use these important functions.

SUM

Adding numbers is one of the most basic mathematical operations, and so there is the SUM function, dedicated to doing just that. SUM takes up to 255 arguments.

Each argument can be a single number or a range containing multiple numbers. That means SUM can add up a whole bunch of numbers! The syntax follows:

```
=SUM(number 1, number 2, ...)
```

You can also use SUM with a range, as shown here:

```
=SUM(A1:A12)
```

You can also use SUM with more than one range, such as this:

```
=SUM(A1:A12, B1:B12)
```

AVERAGE

Although technically a statistical function, AVERAGE is used so often that it deserves a place in the top ten functions. Everyone is interested in averages. What's the average score? What's the average salary? What's the average height? What's the average number of hours we watch TV? (That's a sore spot in my home!)

AVERAGE can take up to 255 arguments. Each argument can be a number or a range that contains numbers. The syntax follows:

```
=AVERAGE(number 1 ,number 2 ,...)
```

You can also use AVERAGE with a range, as shown here:

```
=AVERAGE(A1:A12)
```

You can also use AVERAGE with more than one range, such as this:

```
=AVERAGE(A1:A12, B1:B12)
```

COUNT

COUNT counts the number of cells in a range that contain numbers. It does not provide any sum — just the count. For a list with ten numbers, for example, COUNT returns 10, regardless of what the numbers are.

COUNT takes up to 255 arguments, which can be cell references, range references, or numbers themselves. COUNT ignores non-numeric values. If an argument to COUNT is A1:A10 but only two cells contain a number, COUNT returns 2. The syntax follows:

```
=COUNT(cell reference 1, cell reference 2,...)
```

You can also use COUNT with a range, as shown here:

```
=COUNT(A1:A12)
```

You can also use COUNT with more than one range, such as this:

```
=COUNT(A1:A12, B1:B12)
```

INT and ROUND

The INT and ROUND functions both work by removing or reducing a number's decimal portion. They differ in exactly *how* they remove it.

INT

INT simply drops the decimal portion without rounding — that is, without regard to whether the number is closer to the next higher integer or the next lower integer. Be aware that INT always truncates to the next lower integer. For example, INT changes 12.05 to 12, but it also changes 12.95 to 12. Also, INT changes both –5.1 and –5.9 to –6, not to –5, because –6 is the next lower integer. INT takes a single number argument (as an actual number or a cell reference). The syntax follows:

```
=INT(number or cell reference)
```

ROUND

On the other hand, the ROUND function lets you control how the decimal portion is handled. ROUND takes two arguments: the number to be manipulated and the number of decimal places to round to. This gives you more control. A number such as 5.6284 can become 5.628, 5.63, 5.6, or just 6. ROUND always rounds up or down to the nearest number of the next significant digit, so 5.628 becomes 5.63, not 5.62.

ROUND turns 12.95 into either 12.9 or 13, depending on the setting of the second argument. Note that two functions — ROUNDUP and ROUNDDOWN — round in one direction only. The syntax for ROUND follows:

```
=ROUND(number, number of decimal places to round to)
```

The syntax for ROUNDUP and ROUNDDOWN is the same as ROUND:

```
=ROUNDUP(number, number of decimal places to round to)
=ROUNDDOWN(number, number of decimal places to round to)
```

IF

IF is a very handy function. It tests a condition and returns one of two results, depending on the outcome of the test. The test must return a true or false answer. For example, a test may be B25 > C30. If true, IF returns its second argument. If false, IF returns its third argument.

IF is often used as a validation step to prevent unwanted errors. The most common use of this is to test whether a denominator is 0 before doing a division operation. By testing for 0 first, you can avoid the #DIV/0! error.

One of the great things about IF is that the result can be a blank. This function is great when you want to return a result if the test comes out one way but not if the result is otherwise. The syntax follows:

```
=IF(logical test, value if true, value if false)
```

NOW and TODAY

The NOW function returns the current date and time according to your computer's internal clock. TODAY returns just the date. If the date or time is wrong, it can't help you with that.

A common use of NOW is to return the date and time for a printed report. You know, so a message such as Printed on 12/20/2015 10:15 can be put on the printed paper.

A common use for TODAY is to calculate the elapsed time between a past date and today. For example, you may be tracking a project's duration. A cell on the worksheet has the start date. Another cell has a formula that subtracts that date from TODAY. The answer is the number of days that have gone by.

NOW and TODAY take no arguments. The syntax for each follows:

```
=NOW()
=TODAY()
```

HLOOKUP and VLOOKUP

HLOOKUP and VLOOKUP both find a value in a table. A *table* is an area of rows and columns that you define. Both of these functions work by using a search value for the first argument that, when found in the table, helps return a different value.

In particular, you use HLOOKUP to return a value in a row that is in the same column as the search value. You use VLOOKUP to return a value in a column that is in the same row as the search value. The syntax for these functions follows:

```
=HLOOKUP(lookup value, table area, row, match type)
=VLOOKUP(lookup value, table area, column, match type)
```

ISNUMBER

A rose is a rose and by any other name would smell as sweet, but numbers don't get off that easy. For example, 15 is a digit, but *fifteen* is a word. The ISNUMBER function tells you, flat-out true or false, if a value in a cell is a number (including the results of formulas). The syntax follows:

```
=ISNUMBER(value)
```

MIN and MAX

MIN and MAX find the respective lowest or highest numeric value in a range of values. These functions take up to 255 arguments, and an argument can be a range. Therefore, you can test a large list of numbers simply by entering the list as a range. The syntax for these functions follows:

```
=MAX(number1,number2,...)
=MIN(number1,number2,...)
```

You can also use MIN and MAX with a range, as shown here:

```
=MAX(A1:A12)
```

or with more than one range, such as this:

```
=MAX(A1:A12, B1:B12)
```

SUMIF and COUNTIF

SUMIF and COUNTIF sum or count values, respectively, if a supplied criterion is met. This makes for some robust calculations. With these functions, it's easy to return answers for a question such as "How many shipments went out in October?" or "How many times did the Dow Jones Industrial Average close over 18,000 last year?"

SUMIF takes three arguments:

- A range in which to apply the criteria
- The actual criteria
- The range from which to sum values

A key point here is that the first argument may or may not be the same range from which values are summed. Therefore, you can use SUMIF to answer a question such as "How many shipments went out in October?" but also one such as "What is the sum of the numbers over 100 in this list?" The syntax of SUMIF follows:

```
=SUMIF(range,criteria,sum_range)
```

Note, too, that the third argument in SUMIF can be left out. When this happens, SUMIF uses the first argument as the range in which to apply the criteria and also as the range from which to sum.

COUNTIF counts the number of items in a range that match criteria. This is just a count. The value of the items that match the criteria doesn't matter past the fact that it matches the criteria. But after a cell's value matches the criteria, the count of that cell is 1. COUNTIF takes just two arguments:

- The range from which to count the number of values
- The criteria to apply

The syntax for COUNTIF follows:

```
COUNTIF(range,criteria)
```

Chapter 20

Some Really Cool Functions

- -

In This Chapter

▶ Converting numbers among base systems

▶ Converting values from one unit of measure to another

▶ Finding a common divisor and common multiple

▶ Generating random numbers with a twist

▶ Converting to Roman numerals

▶ Getting a fast factorial

▶ Finding out the percentage of a year

▶ Testing the data type

- -

The hits just keep on coming! Just when you thought you had all the Excel functions down pat, here I go rocking the boat. Add this mix of useful functions to your plate of Excel goodies, and you will be that much more of an Excel master. Be the envy of all the kids on the block!

Work with Hexadecimal, Octal, Decimal, and Binary Numbers

In certain lines of work, it is desirable or even necessary to work in another base system. Designing computer systems is a good example. The computer chips that run our PCs work with a binary system. Circuits are either on or off. This means that there are just two possible states — and they are often expressed as 0 and 1.

In base 2, or binary, all numbers are expressed with the digit 0 or 1. The number 20 as we know it in decimal is 10100 in binary. The number 99 is 1100011. The binary system is based on powers of 2.

In other words, in base 10 you count up through ten digits in one position before moving one position to the left for the next significant digit. And then the first position cycles back to the beginning digit. To make it simple, you count 0 to 9, add a 1 to the next significant digit, and start the first position over at 0. Therefore, 10 comes after 9.

Binary, octal, and hexadecimal each count up to a different digit before incrementing the next significant digit. That's why when any larger base number, such as a base 10 number, is converted to binary, there are more actual digit places. Look at what happens to the number 20. In base 10, 20 is represented in 2 digits. In binary, 20 is represented in 5 digits.

Octal, based on powers of 8, counts up to 8 digits — 0 through 7. The digits 8 and 9 are never used in octal. Hexadecimal, based on powers of 16, counts up to 16 digits, but how? What is left after 9? The letters of the alphabet, that's what!

Hexadecimal uses these digits: 0, 1, 2, 3, 4, 5, 6, 7, 8, 9, A, B, C, D, E, and F. The letters A through F represent the decimal values 10 through 15, respectively. If you have ever worked on the colors for a website, you may know that FFFFFF is all white. The web server recognizes colors represented in hexadecimal notation and responds appropriately.

The number 200 in decimal notation becomes C8 in hexadecimal notation. The number 99 in decimal notation becomes 63 in hexadecimal notation.

The point of all this is that there is a group of functions to do all these conversions. These functions take into account all combinations of conversion among binary, octal, decimal, and hexadecimal. These functions are shown in the following table.

Function	*What It Does*
BIN2DEC	Converts binary to decimal
BIN2HEX	Converts binary to hexadecimal
BIN2OCT	Converts binary to octal
DEC2BIN	Converts decimal to binary
DEC2HEX	Converts decimal to hexadecimal
DEC2OCT	Converts decimal to octal
HEX2BIN	Converts hexadecimal to binary
HEX2DEC	Converts hexadecimal to decimal
HEX2OCT	Converts hexadecimal to octal
OCT2BIN	Converts octal to binary
OCT2DEC	Converts octal to decimal
OCT2HEX	Converts octal to hexadecimal

You can find these functions in the Engineering section of the Insert Function dialog box. Click the Insert Function button on the Formulas tab on the Ribbon.

Convert Units of Measurement

CONVERT is a really great function that Excel provides. Not surprisingly, it converts things. More specifically, it converts measurements. The number of measurements it converts is truly impressive. The function converts feet to inches, meters to feet, Fahrenheit to Celsius, pints to liters, horsepower to watts, and much more. In fact, more than a dozen categories contain dozens of units of measure to convert from and to. The major categories follow:

- Weight and mass
- Distance
- Time
- Pressure
- Energy
- Power
- Temperature
- Liquid measure

The function takes three arguments: the value, the "from" unit of measure, and the "to" unit of measure. As an example, here is the function syntax for converting 10 gallons to liters: =CONVERT(10,"gal", "l"). By the way, the answer is 37.85.

Consult the Excel Help system for a full list of available conversions.

Find the Greatest Common Divisor and the Least Common Multiple

A *greatest common divisor* is the largest integer that divides evenly into each number in a set of numbers. In other words, it divides with no remainder. Take the numbers 5, 10, and 100. The greatest common divisor is 5 because each of the numbers divided by 5 returns another integer (no decimal portion).

The GCD function takes up to 255 values as its arguments. Noninteger values are truncated. By its nature, any returned greatest common divisor must equal or be smaller than the lowest argument value. Often, there is no greatest common divisor other than 1 — which all integers share. The syntax of the GCD function follows:

```
GCD(number1,number2, ...)
```

The least common multiple is an integer that is the lowest multiple common among a group of integers. For example, the least common multiple of 2, 4, and 6 is 12. The least common multiple of 9, 15, and 48 is 720.

The LCM function takes up to 255 values as its arguments. Noninteger values are truncated. The syntax of the LCM multiple function follows:

```
LCM(number1,number2, ...)
```

Easily Generate a Random Number

The Excel RAND function returns a number between 0 and 1. And that's it. Usually, you have to massage the returned number into something useful. The typical thing to do is multiply it by some number to get it within a range of values, add the lower limit to that, and finally use INT to turn the whole thing into an integer. The days of drudgery are over!

The RANDBETWEEN function returns a random integer between two values. Two arguments are used: the low end of the range and the high end of the range. Just what you need! For example, =RANDBETWEEN(5, 10) returns a whole number between 5 and 10. Always.

Convert to Roman Numerals

C, V, L, I; I get these mixed up. Is C for 100 or 1000? What is L for? Whew — I don't have to memorize these anymore.

The ROMAN function takes care of it all. Just throw a number in the normal format you are familiar with, and out comes the equivalent Roman numeral. Easy! The syntax is

```
=ROMAN(number to convert, optional style)
```

Factor in a Factorial

If you like multiplication, you will love the FACT function. A *factorial,* simply put, is the product of multiplying sequential integers. In math notation, 6! (notice the exclamation point) is 1 x 2 x 3 x 4 x 5 x6, which equals 720. Try it on your calculator or use an Excel sheet, of course.

The FACT function makes the tedious entry go away, which I think you will like. FACT just takes a number — the number of integers to use for the grand product.

Determine Part of a Year with YEARFRAC

If you need to know what percentage of a year a range of dates is, Excel has the perfect function for you! YEARFRAC returns a percentage of a year. You feed the function a start and end date, and an optional basis for how to count dates (such as a 360-day year, a 365-day year, and so on). The number given back from the function is a percentage — a number less than 1, assuming that the range of dates is less than a full year. An exact one-year range returns 1, and a range longer than a year returns a number larger than 1.

Find the Data TYPE

The content in a cell may be text, a number, a logical value, an error, or an array. The TYPE function tells you which type the content is. When you're looking at a cell, it's obvious what the type is. However, if your formulas are using cell references then you may wish to put the TYPE function into the formula before attempting a mathematical operation. This ensures you can have a valid result returned instead of an error. For example, A4 has 25 and A5 has "Apple". An attempt to add these results in an error. Instead put the TYPE function into the formula to determine if the calculation should take place. The formula would look like this:

```
=IF(TYPE(A4)=1&TYPE(A5)=1,A4+A5,"Unable to calculate")
```

The result in this case is Unable to calculate because you cannot add a number with text.

The TYPE function returns five possible values: 1=number; 2=text; 4= a logical value (And, Or, and so on); 16= an error; 64=an array.

Index

• *F* •

About the Author

Ken Bluttman has been working as a software and web developer for more than two decades. Ken specializes in Excel/VBA- and database-centric web applications. He has written several articles and books on various computer topics, including Office/VBA development, XML, SQL Server, JavaScript, HTML5, and PHP. On the creative side, he has written about Photoshop, and has penned a book on photography. Ken lives in North Carolina with his wife, son, two cats, a rather large white tree frog, and a couple of geckos.

Dedication

In memory of Howard Bluttman, 1929–1951.

Author's Acknowledgments

Much activity goes on behind the scenes in bringing a book from idea to reality. Many people are involved. I wish to thank the great Wiley staff — Charlotte Kughen, Katie Mohr, and everyone else on the Wiley team — for all their hard work. Thanks to Mike Talley for tech editing. Thanks to Stacey Czarnowski and the great staff at StudioB.

Special thanks to my family for understanding that, at times, sitting in front of a computer is a priority, even when it means I have to miss something special. But, darn, I did miss watching some fun movies and shows (sigh).

Publisher's Acknowledgments

Senior Acquisitions Editor: Katie Mohr

Project Editor: Charlotte Kughen

Copy Editor: Kathy Simpson

Technical Editor: Mike Talley

Sr. Editorial Assistant: Cherie Case

Production Editor: Kinson Raja

Cover Image: © Getty Images/Adam Gault

Apple & Mac

iPad For Dummies,
6th Edition
978-1-118-72306-7

iPhone For Dummies,
7th Edition
978-1-118-69083-3

Macs All-in-One
For Dummies, 4th Edition
978-1-118-82210-4

OS X Mavericks
For Dummies
978-1-118-69188-5

Blogging & Social Media

Facebook For Dummies,
5th Edition
978-1-118-63312-0

Social Media Engagement
For Dummies
978-1-118-53019-1

WordPress For Dummies,
6th Edition
978-1-118-79161-5

Business

Stock Investing
For Dummies, 4th Edition
978-1-118-37678-2

Investing For Dummies,
6th Edition
978-0-470-90545-6

Personal Finance
For Dummies, 7th Edition
978-1-118-11785-9

QuickBooks 2014
For Dummies
978-1-118-72005-9

Small Business Marketing
Kit For Dummies,
3rd Edition
978-1-118-31183-7

Careers

Job Interviews
For Dummies, 4th Edition
978-1-118-11290-8

Job Searching with Social
Media For Dummies,
2nd Edition
978-1-118-67856-5

Personal Branding
For Dummies
978-1-118-11792-7

Resumes For Dummies,
6th Edition
978-0-470-87361-8

Starting an Etsy Business
For Dummies, 2nd Edition
978-1-118-59024-9

Diet & Nutrition

Belly Fat Diet For Dummies
978-1-118-34585-6

Mediterranean Diet
For Dummies
978-1-118-71525-3

Nutrition For Dummies,
5th Edition
978-0-470-93231-5

Digital Photography

Digital SLR Photography
All-in-One For Dummies,
2nd Edition
978-1-118-59082-9

Digital SLR Video &
Filmmaking For Dummies
978-1-118-36598-4

Photoshop Elements 12
For Dummies
978-1-118-72714-0

Gardening

Herb Gardening
For Dummies, 2nd Edition
978-0-470-61778-6

Gardening with Free-Range
Chickens For Dummies
978-1-118-54754-0

Health

Boosting Your Immunity
For Dummies
978-1-118-40200-9

Diabetes For Dummies,
4th Edition
978-1-118-29447-5

Living Paleo For Dummies
978-1-118-29405-5

Big Data

Big Data For Dummies
978-1-118-50422-2

Data Visualization
For Dummies
978-1-118-50289-1

Hadoop For Dummies
978-1-118-60755-8

Language &
Foreign Language

500 Spanish Verbs
For Dummies
978-1-118-02382-2

English Grammar
For Dummies, 2nd Edition
978-0-470-54664-2

French All-in-One
For Dummies
978-1-118-22815-9

German Essentials
For Dummies
978-1-118-18422-6

Italian For Dummies,
2nd Edition
978-1-118-00465-4

Available in print and e-book formats.

Available wherever books are sold. **For more information or to order direct visit www.dummies.com**

Math & Science

Algebra I For Dummies,
2nd Edition
978-0-470-55964-2

Anatomy and Physiology
For Dummies, 2nd Edition
978-0-470-92326-9

Astronomy For Dummies,
3rd Edition
978-1-118-37697-3

Biology For Dummies,
2nd Edition
978-0-470-59875-7

Chemistry For Dummies,
2nd Edition
978-1-118-00730-3

1001 Algebra II Practice
Problems For Dummies
978-1-118-44662-1

Microsoft Office

Excel 2013 For Dummies
978-1-118-51012-4

Office 2013 All-in-One
For Dummies
978-1-118-51636-2

PowerPoint 2013
For Dummies
978-1-118-50253-2

Word 2013 For Dummies
978-1-118-49123-2

Music

Blues Harmonica
For Dummies
978-1-118-25269-7

Guitar For Dummies,
3rd Edition
978-1-118-11554-1

iPod & iTunes
For Dummies, 10th Edition
978-1-118-50864-0

Programming

Beginning Programming
with C For Dummies
978-1-118-73763-7

Excel VBA Programming
For Dummies, 3rd Edition
978-1-118-49037-2

Java For Dummies,
6th Edition
978-1-118-40780-6

Religion & Inspiration

The Bible For Dummies
978-0-7645-5296-0

Buddhism For Dummies,
2nd Edition
978-1-118-02379-2

Catholicism For Dummies,
2nd Edition
978-1-118-07778-8

Self-Help & Relationships

Beating Sugar Addiction
For Dummies
978-1-118-54645-1

Meditation For Dummies,
3rd Edition
978-1-118-29144-3

Seniors

Laptops For Seniors
For Dummies, 3rd Edition
978-1-118-71105-7

Computers For Seniors
For Dummies, 3rd Edition
978-1-118-11553-4

iPad For Seniors
For Dummies, 6th Edition
978-1-118-72826-0

Social Security
For Dummies
978-1-118-20573-0

Smartphones & Tablets

Android Phones
For Dummies, 2nd Edition
978-1-118-72030-1

Nexus Tablets
For Dummies
978-1-118-77243-0

Samsung Galaxy S 4
For Dummies
978-1-118-64222-1

Samsung Galaxy Tabs
For Dummies
978-1-118-77294-2

Test Prep

ACT For Dummies,
5th Edition
978-1-118-01259-8

ASVAB For Dummies,
3rd Edition
978-0-470-63760-9

GRE For Dummies,
7th Edition
978-0-470-88921-3

Officer Candidate Tests
For Dummies
978-0-470-59876-4

Physician's Assistant Exam
For Dummies
978-1-118-11556-5

Series 7 Exam For Dummies
978-0-470-09932-2

Windows 8

Windows 8.1 All-in-One
For Dummies
978-1-118-82087-2

Windows 8.1 For Dummies
978-1-118-82121-3

Windows 8.1 For Dummies,
Book + DVD Bundle
978-1-118-82107-7

e Available in print and e-book formats.

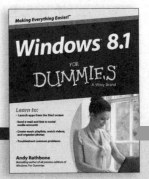

Take Dummies with you everywhere you go!

Whether you are excited about e-books, want more from the web, must have your mobile apps, or are swept up in social media, Dummies makes everything easier.

Leverage the Power

For Dummies is the global leader in the reference category and one of the most trusted and highly regarded brands in the world. No longer just focused on books, customers now have access to the For Dummies content they need in the format they want. Let us help you develop a solution that will fit your brand and help you connect with your customers.

Advertising & Sponsorships

Connect with an engaged audience on a powerful multimedia site, and position your message alongside expert how-to content.

Targeted ads • Video • Email marketing • Microsites • Sweepstakes sponsorship

21 Million Monthly Page Views & 13 Million Unique Visitors